five
Rebuild your desktop

Choose Restart from the Special menu and hold down the ⌘ and Option keys all during the startup process, until you see a dialog box asking you if you are sure you want to rebuild. Click OK in the dialog box. Do it more often if you open and close things often or move lots of things around on the desktop. You lose all comments in the Info boxes for your applications and documents when you rebuild.

six
Defragment your hard disk once a month or so.

Use a utility like the Norton Utilities Speed Disk to rearrange all your documents and applications on your hard disk so the hard disk can work at optimum efficiency. Make sure you back up all your work before you defragment. See Chapter 6 for details.

seven
Keep only ONE copy of the system software in the Mac at a time.

You can have only one System Folder on your hard disk, with one System file in it, and you should not normally put any floppy disks into your Mac that have system software on them. See the "Extra Connections" section of Chapter 1 for details.

eight
Keep your System file small and keep your System Folder tidy.

Keep only the fonts and sounds you really need in your System file, and keep only the most important utilities and extensions in your System Folder.

nine
If you have an external hard drive, make sure it is on whenever the Mac is on.

Start the external drive before you start your Mac and turn the external drive off after you shut down and turn off the Mac. See Chapter 6 for details.

ten
If you have more than one external hard drive, make sure they have different ID numbers.

Set the SCSI ID numbers to be something other than 0 (zero) or 7, and make sure they are different from each other. See "Connect and Initialize the Hard Drive Properly" in Chapter 6 for details.

• •
Books that Work Just Like Your Mac

As a Macintosh user, you enjoy unique advantages. You enjoy a dynamic user environment. You enjoy the successful integration of graphics, sound, and text. Above all, you enjoy a computer that's fun and easy to use.

When your computer gives you all this, why accept less in your computer books?

At SYBEX, we don't believe you should. That's why we've committed ourselves to publishing the highest quality computer books for Macintosh users. Externally, our books emulate the Mac "look and feel," with powerful, appealing illustrations and easy-to-read pages. Internally, our books stress "why" over "how," so you'll learn concepts, not sequences of steps. Philosophically, our books are designed to help you get work done, not to teach you about computers.

In short, our books are fun and easy to use—just like the Mac. We hope you find them just as enjoyable.

For a complete catalog of our publications:
SYBEX Inc.
2021 Challenger Drive, Alameda, CA 94501
Tel: (510) 523-8233/(800) 227-2346 Telex: 336311
Fax: (510) 523-2373

SYBEX is committed to using natural resources wisely to preserve and improve our environment. As a leader in the computer book publishing industry, we are aware that over 40% of America's solid waste is paper. This is why we have been printing the text of books like this one on recycled paper since 1982.

This year our use of recycled paper will result in the saving of more than 15,300 trees. We will lower air pollution effluents by 54,000 pounds, save 6,300,000 gallons of water, and reduce landfill by 2,700 cubic yards.

In choosing a SYBEX book you are not only making a choice for the best in skills and information, you are also choosing to enhance the quality of life for all of us.

Your First Mac

Your First Mac®

◆ ◆

Tom Cuthbertson

SYBEX® • San Francisco • Paris • Düsseldorf • Soest

Acquisitions Editors: Dianne King and Dave Clark
Developmental Editor: Kenyon Brown
Editor: Brendan Fletcher
Project Editor: Valerie Potter
Technical Editors: Erik Ingenito, Celia Stevenson, and Dan Tauber
Production Editor: Carolina Montilla
Book Designer: Alissa Feinberg
Production Artist: Suzanne Albertson
Screen Graphics and Technical Illustrations: John Corrigan
Typesetter: Deborah Maizels
Indexer: Nancy Guenther
Cover Designer: Ingalls + Associates
Cover Photographer: Harumi Kubo

SYBEX is a registered trademark of SYBEX Inc.

TRADEMARKS: SYBEX has attempted throughout this book to distinguish proprietary trademarks from descriptive terms by following the capitalization style used by the manufacturer.

SYBEX is not affiliated with any manufacturer.

Every effort has been made to supply complete and accurate information. However, SYBEX assumes no responsibility for its use, nor for any infringement of the intellectual property rights of third parties which would result from such use.

An earlier version of this book was published under the title *Anybody's Mac Book* copyright © 1992 SYBEX Inc.

Copyright © 1993 SYBEX Inc., 2021 Challenger Drive, Alameda, CA 94501. World rights reserved. No part of this publication may be stored in a retrieval system, transmitted, or reproduced in any way, including but not limited to photocopy, photograph, magnetic or other record, without the prior agreement and written permission of the publisher.

Library of Congress Card Number: 93-85349
ISBN: 0-7821-1316-8

Manufactured in the United States of America
10 9 8 7 6 5 4 3 2 1

♦ **For Colleen!**

Acknowledgments

◆ ◆

More than thanks to Colleen for supporting me through the maelstrom. Also, many thanks to those among the friends and computer cohorts who helped me, answered my endless questions, and gave me their support so I could put my heart and mind into this book.

First, the great editors at SYBEX: developmental editor Ken Brown; project editor Val Potter; editor Brendan Fletcher; and technical editors Dan Tauber, Celia Stevenson, and Erik Ingenito.

The editorial and production team at SYBEX: Deborah Maizels, typesetter; Carolina Montilla, production editor; John Corrigan, screen graphics and technical illustrations; Alissa Feinberg, designer; and Suzanne Albertson, production artist. Thanks to Ken, Brendan, Dan, Celia, Deliah Brown, and Suzanne for their help on this book in its first incarnation, too.

My hardworking procedure drafters: Isaiah Carew (FileMaker Pro and Excel), Tracey Smith (PageMaker), and Nancy Dannenberg (Quicken).

The Computerware Santa Cruz team of Isaiah Carew, Eric Kopf, Kevin Quigley, Max Fischer, Steve Nakagawa, Dave Watson, Vaino Kees, Cathy and Mike Boucher, and Timothy Marshall; and Rose Meagher of the Computerware Training Center.

Bill McDermott, the wonderful chief leprechaun of the MaCruzers user's group, and Scott Sandow, the former chairman of that group.

Keri Walker, Bob Olliver, Doedy Hunter, and Kate Paisley at Apple Computer; and Erica Sandstedt, Chris Wesselman, Lisa Dronzek, Kelly Anne Marshall, and Dianne Jackson of Apple Support.

J.H. Alexander at Preferred Publishers, Freda Cook of Aldus, Karen Umholt of Broderbund, Jan Jacobs of Fifth Generation, David Schargel of Aladdin Systems, Nancy Stevenson of Symantec, David Brannon of La Cie, Dave Miller of Intuit, Beth Regardz of Cabrillo College, Kevin Verboort (and a lot of other helpful people whose names I didn't get) of Microsoft Word Support, Jeffrey Hing of SCO, Howard Schneider of Canyon Consultants, David Mays of Dave's Computer Services in Santa Cruz, and Jim Rolens and Debra Spencer.

Clair, Sam, Cory, Ian, Tosh, Dylan, and Chancy (Kid Pix Consultants), and Jim Jones.

Contents at a Glance

Introduction — xxi

Part One   Introducing the Macintosh
1. Meet the Mac — 3
2. Meet the Mouse and the Desktop — 29
3. Printing — 53

Part Two   Exploring the Mac
4. Working with Applications and Documents — 87
5. Using Folders to Organize Your Files — 109
6. Storage: Hard and Floppy Disks — 123
7. Memory: Checking and Adjusting Your RAM Use — 153
8. Customizing Your Mac — 165

Part Three   Applications for the Mac
9. Word Processors — 187
10. Graphics Applications — 215
11. Page Layout Applications — 237
12. Spreadsheets — 269
13. Databases — 291
14. Managing Personal Finances — 317
15. Integrating Your Work — 339

APPENDICES
A. Graphic File Formats — 363
B. Installing the System Software on a Customized Mac — 365

Index — 369

Table of Contents

Introduction — xxi

Part One
Introducing the Macintosh

One
Meet the Mac

What's inside Your Mac?	6
The Keyboard and the Mouse	6
The CPU and Memory	6
Floppy Disks and Hard Disks	7
The System Software	8
Which Mac for You?	8
Compact Macs	9
Modular Macs	10
PowerBook Macs	11
Setting Up Your Mac	13
Basic Setup Steps	14
Special Setup Steps for Mac Models	14
Extra Connections	15
Getting the First Smile from Your Mac	17
Shutting Down Your Macintosh	18

Setting Up Your Hard Disk for Future Startups	19
Troubleshooting Hardware and Installation Problems	21

Two
Meet the Mouse and the Desktop

Introducing the Desktop	32
Using the Mouse	34
Selecting, Dragging, and Opening Icons	35
Choosing Commands from Menus	36
Using the Keyboard and Mouse to Work with Text	37
Showing and Hiding Help Balloons	39
Doing Things to Windows	40
Dragging Things to the Trash	42
Using Dialog and Alert Boxes	43
Dialog Boxes	43
Alert Boxes	45
Troubleshooting Problems with the Mouse and Desktop	46

Three
Printing

Which Printer for You?	56
Ink-Jet Printers	56
Laser Printers	58
Dot-Matrix Printers	58
Setting Up Printing in the Chooser	59
Taking Care of Your Printer	61
Care and Feeding of a StyleWriter II	61
Care and Feeding of a DeskWriter	62
Care and Feeding of a LaserWriter	63
Care and Feeding of an ImageWriter	65
Printing Documents	66
Using the PrintMonitor	68
Using Page Setup for Special Printing Needs	69
Printing a Window in the Finder	70
Printing a Snapshot of the Screen	70
Using the Right Fonts for Your Printer	71
Kinds of Fonts	72
Installing Fonts	75
Removing Fonts	75

Using Key Caps to Compare Fonts	76
Using Accented Characters	77
Troubleshooting Printing	78

Part Two
Exploring the Mac

Four
Working with Applications and Documents

Introducing Applications and Documents	90
Installing an Application	91
Opening an Installed Application or an Alias	93
Opening a Document	94
Saving Your Work on a Document	96
Saving a Document for the First Time	96
Saving As You Edit	97
Special Saving Techniques	98
Managing Your Applications	98
Opening Applications from the Apple Menu	99
Switching between Applications	100
Managing Your Documents	100
Finding Misplaced Documents	101
Switching between Documents	101
Changing Your Desktop View of Documents and Folders	102
Using List Views	103
Troubleshooting Problems with Applications and Documents	106

Five
Using Folders to Organize Your Files

Creating Folders	113
Naming and Nesting Folders to Make a Hierarchy	113
Using List Views to Work with Folders	117
Troubleshooting Problems with Files and Folders	119

xiii

Six
Storage: Hard and Floppy Disks

Introducing Hard Disks	126
Introducing Floppy Disks	127
Bytes, Kilobytes, Megabytes	128
Which Disk for You?	129
Care and Feeding of a Hard Disk	131
Connect and Initialize the Hard Drive Properly	131
Turn the External Drive On First, and Turn It Off Last	132
Be Kind to Your Hard Disk	132
Save and Back Up	134
Defragment the Hard Disk Before It Fills Up	135
Care and Feeding of Floppy Disks	137
Floppy Disk Precautions	139
Preparing a Floppy Disk for Use	139
Floppy Disks for Different Uses	140
The Startup Disk	140
System Disks and Application Disks	140
Data Disks	141
Backing Up Files on System and Application Disks	141
Copying an Entire Floppy Disk	142
Locking and Unlocking a Floppy Disk	144
Erasing a Floppy Disk	145
Checking Disk Capacity	145
Troubleshooting Problems with Hard and Floppy Disks	146

Seven
Memory: Checking and Adjusting Your RAM Use

What RAM Is	156
Monitoring Your Memory Use	157
Adjusting Application Allocations	158
Adjusting the Disk Cache (RAM Cache)	159
Troubleshooting Problems with Memory	162

Eight
Customizing Your Mac

Looking Around Your System Folder	168
Specifying Startup Applications and Documents	170
Using Special Customizing Files	171
Using Control Panels	172
General Controls Settings	173
Brightness Control Settings	174
Color Control Settings	174
Keyboard Control Settings	177
Mouse Control Settings	178
Sound Control Settings	178
Views Control Settings	178
Memory Control Settings	180
Closing Control Panels	180
Customizing Icons	180
Troubleshooting Customization Problems	182

Part Three
Applications for the Mac

Nine
Word Processors

Which Word Processor for You?	190
Word Processors for Big Writing Jobs	191
A Word Processor for Everyday Jobs	192
Bargain Word Processors	193
Using Microsoft Word	193
Opening a New Document	193
Entering Text	195
Editing Text	196
Moving, Copying, and Replacing Text via the Clipboard	198
Using the Ruler to Format Text	198
Changing Text Style	202
Saving and Printing a Document	203
Shortcuts, Shortcuts	203

Using MacWrite Pro	204
Opening a Document	204
Entering Text	205
Editing Text	206
Using the Ruler to Format Text	207
Changing Text Style	210
Saving and Printing a Document	210
Troubleshooting Problems with Your Word Processor	212

Ten
Graphics Applications

Which Graphics Application for You?	218
A Great Beginner's Graphics Application	218
Workhorse Applications That Paint and Draw	219
High-Power Drawing Applications	220
Using Kid Pix	221
Opening a Document	222
Drawing Lines	223
Undoing and Erasing Mistakes	223
Placing Stamps	224
Painting with the Wacky Brush	225
Painting an Area with the Paint Can	225
Saving and Printing a Kid Pix Document	226
Using MacDraw Pro	226
Opening a Document	227
Creating a Shape	228
Creating a Fill	230
Adding Text to a Graphic	230
Placing a Frame around a Graphic	231
Saving and Printing a MacDraw Pro Document	232
Troubleshooting Problems with Graphics Applications	234

Eleven
Page Layout Applications

Which Page Layout Application for You?	241
An Inexpensive Page Layout Tool for Small Jobs	241
Page Layout Applications for Big Jobs	241

Using PageMaker   243
    Making a Rough Sketch and Collecting Files   243
    Opening a Document   245
    Making Preliminary Page Settings   246
    The PageMaker Document Window   247
    Creating Master Pages   249
    Placing Text   251
    Placing a Graphic   252
    Changing Your View of the Page   254
    Adjusting Text Blocks   254
    Adjusting the Layout of a Document   256
    Changing Text Style for Headings   260
    Adding a Graphic and Wrapping Text around It   261
    Saving and Printing a PageMaker Document   263
Troubleshooting Problems in PageMaker   265

Twelve
Spreadsheets

Which Spreadsheet for You?   272
    High-Power Spreadsheet Applications   272
    Budget Spreadsheet Applications   273
Using Excel   274
    Starting a New Document   274
    Entering Some Data   276
    Changing Type Style and Format   277
    Using Insert   279
    Using the Font Dialog Box   279
    Range Selection and Changing the Number Format   279
    Using Formulas   280
    Using the Fill Function   282
    Absolute Cell Referencing   282
    Completing the Spreadsheet   283
    Using Charts   283
    Saving and Printing an Excel Document   285
Troubleshooting Problems with Spreadsheet Applications   287

Thirteen
Databases

Which Database Application for You?	295
Relational Databases	295
Flat-File Databases	297
Budget Databases	298
Using FileMaker Pro	299
Designing a Database	299
Opening a Document	300
Setting Up the Fields	301
Entering Records	302
Using the Toolbar	303
Sorting Records	304
Finding Records	305
Changing Your Layout	306
Adding to the Database	308
Creating a Mailing	309
Saving and Printing a FileMaker Pro Document	313
Troubleshooting Problems with FileMaker Pro	314

Fourteen
Managing Personal Finances

Which Money Managing Application for You?	320
Bargain Budgeting Tools	320
High-Cost Financial Management Applications	321
Using Quicken	322
Creating a File for Your Quicken Accounts	322
Opening a New Account	324
Using the Check Register	325
Recording a Check in the Register	326
Entering Deposits in the Register	327
Correcting Mistakes in the Register	328
Using Categories	328
Choosing a Category or Transfer Account	329
Setting Up a Category and Adding It to the List	330
Writing Checks	330
Memorizing Transactions	332
Printing	333
Troubleshooting Problems with Quicken	336

Fifteen
Integrating Your Work

Cutting, Copying, and Pasting	342
Introducing the Clipboard	342
Cutting and Pasting to Move Parts of Documents	343
Copying and Pasting	345
Copying Parts of Documents between Applications	345
Using the Scrapbook	348
Undoing Clipboard Mistakes	350
Dynamic Updating with Links	350
Linking a Text Document to a Spreadsheet	350
Special Considerations for Linked Documents	352
Publishing and Subscribing to Parts of Documents	352
Using Integrated Applications	355
Opening a Claris Works Document	357
Using Claris Works Frames	357
Troubleshooting Problems with Data Integration	360

Appendix A
Graphic File Formats   363

Appendix B
Installing the System Software on a Customized Mac   365

Index   369

Introduction

I would like to introduce you to a computer with a heart.

Meet the Macintosh, the computer that was made for your enjoyment. The whole intent of the Mac is to encourage you to do your best work, and to make working on a computer so easy that anybody can enjoy it.

Why is the Mac so nice to use? Because it was designed by people who cared. Of course, most computers are designed by folks who care about their product. But the Mac designers went beyond that; they didn't just care about the bits, bytes, bells and whistles. They cared about the people who would *use* the thing. As Mac software whiz Andy Hertzfeld said, "It's the product I want my best friends to have."

This attitude has continued to guide the development of the Mac to this day. With each improvement in the Mac's design— whether the change was to the hardware or to the system software that runs the Mac—Apple engineers have made ease of use their top priority. Now, with the introduction of System 7, the Mac is more powerful and friendlier than ever.

If you have been hesitating about buying a first computer, now is an excellent time to take the initiative and buy a Mac. The Mac is not only more powerful and easier to use than ever, it is also less expensive. In response to falling prices of all other computers, Apple is lowering the prices of its Macintosh line. You can buy your first Mac at a bargain price and be the envy of all those Mac hot-shots who bought their computers several years ago. You'll soon be able to do more things than they can on their old Macs, and do them faster, without spending all the money it used to cost to get into the Mac world.

How This Book Can Help You

This book is an introductory guide to buying and using the Mac. It is designed to help you choose the best Mac and the best computing tools or applications for your work. Once you've purchased your first Mac, it will help you make the most of the Macintosh desktop interface and all the things you can do with it. You can do *so much* with a Mac! Anybody can! No matter who you are or what you do, you can use a Mac to be more productive, more creative, and more self-sufficient. You don't have to be a nerd. You don't have memorize obscure commands. You just point that mouse and click what you want! And almost anything you want is available on the Mac, from a kid's sketching pad to full-color magazine layout tools, from a button calculator to financial planning tools that can handle a corporation's budget.

A Mac Book for New Users

My goal in this book is to help you do the best you can with your Mac. I want to help you get over that queasy feeling of being intimidated by new things on the computer. In a way, the job is easy; the Mac itself is the best encouragement you could have. It rewards you with positive feedback when you try something new and it works, and it gives you gentle warnings and reminders if you ever try something new that could lead to problems. All I have done in this book is give you helpful advice, so you can make a good start with the friendly Mac.

Help with Buying Your Mac

If you are looking at computers for the first time, I offer you lots of tips and advice as to which Mac you should get for the particular kind of work you do, and I give you information about the applications that will be the best tools for your work. There are brief descriptions of the key Mac models, printers, and application software. Each of these Product at a Glance summaries tells you who makes the product, what requirements or specifications it has, and what it can do for you, in simple, clear terms. You can make good choices when you shop, without being intimidated by all the options or the sales talk of the vendors.

Help with Using Your Mac

Once you have your first Mac, you can turn to the chapters that tell how to set up and use it effectively, and how to make the best use of the applications you have chosen to do your work. If you take things one step at a time you'll soon feel right at home working on your Mac, without going through a period of being intimidated by every new procedure you learn.

Now, you don't have to be doing any earth-shaking type of work to get that intimidated feeling. I remember my first day with the Mac; I was intimidated every time I pulled down a menu. I was scared I'd blow the thing up or corrupt all the data on it if I released the mouse button when the wrong command was highlighted. I wrote this book to help you overcome that scary feeling.

If you are new to the Mac and computers in general, the first chapters and the simple exercises for each application can help you get past being intimidated by the Mac itself. I encourage you to feel your way into the use of the mouse, the keyboard, and the desktop, and then I show you easy things to do that give you confidence and a sense of how much fun it is to do work on the Mac. After writing a little memo or two and painting a few simple pictures, you'll forget you were ever afraid of menus.

After you have used your Mac some, you still might not be able to get much out of it because you feel intimidated by applications that seem hard to learn. Or the techniques of using the desktop may seem too complex. This book will give you a quick, easy way to get into the powerful features of the Mac and its applications. You can use this book as a springboard, a way to make the leap from just plugging along to really making the most of your Mac.

How the Parts of This Book Work Together

This book has three parts, and they cover things in order, from picking out a Mac to doing your best with applications. But you don't have to plow through the book from start to finish. I wrote each chapter in such a way that you can find and learn just the information you need for whatever you want to do at a particular time. You can look up things quickly, as if you were using an encyclopedia. If you have a question or problem, you can find an answer easily, because each chapter in each part is designed to help you find out what you need to know in order to get on with your work.

At the beginning of each chapter there is a description or explanation of the hardware or software the chapter focuses on. I tell you what this item can do for you and what to look for if you are shopping for the item. Then I give clear example procedures that give you hands-on experience learning how to use the item. Finally, I provide a troubleshooting section, to resolve the most common problems you may have in using the item.

Part One: Introducing the Macintosh

This part of the book gives you a clear, relaxed first view of the Mac: how to choose one, how to start and stop one, and how to use the basic parts of the computer comfortably. There are plenty of simple exercises you can do along the way, so you develop a feeling of confidence as you learn about your Mac.

- Chapter 1 gives you a thorough introduction to the Mac, helps you decide which Mac is best for your needs, and tells you how to set up and turn on your Mac.
- Chapter 2 shows you how to use the mouse, the keyboard, and the desktop. It takes you through the basic techniques one step at a time and helps you master the fundamentals so that all your other work on the Mac will come more easily.

- Chapter 3 tells you how to print things you create on your Mac. It also helps you choose, set up, and maintain the printer that's right for you.

Part Two: Exploring the Mac

This part of the book describes the System 7 software, the almost magical program that runs the Mac interface and helps you do your work and store it. No matter what you do on the Mac, your efforts will depend on the workings of the system software described in Part Two. You may not want to learn every detail in this part of the book right at first, but you can keep referring to the section to increase your power as a user.

- Chapter 4 covers the basic techniques for using applications and documents. Applications are the tools for your Mac work and documents are the products of your work on the Mac. You learn how to install and start applications, how to find and open documents, and how to switch between application and document windows as you work.

- Chapter 5 tells you how to organize your work on the Mac desktop. You learn to put all your documents in well-organized folders, so you can find things easily and move quickly from one item to another.

- Chapter 6 explains how to use hard and floppy disks to save your work. You also learn how to take care of your disks so that you'll never lose any important files.

- Chapter 7 shows you how to manage your Mac's memory. Each Mac has only so much, and you learn how to make the most of what you have.

- Chapter 8 is about customizing your Mac so it looks, sounds, and works just the way you want it to.

Part Three: Applications for the Mac

The third part describes the tools you can use to do the special kind of work you choose on the Mac. Once you have the Mac basics down, you can branch out to work in whatever applications suit you, and you can take advantage of the application that will help you most. Just read the chapters that apply to your needs, and forge ahead. The sky is the limit.

- Chapters 9 through 15 cover all of the basic types of applications you can use on the Mac. Each chapter tells you how to pick the application that will work best for you and how to start doing your work with it. There are chapters on word processing, page layout applications, painting and drawing applications, spreadsheets, databases, and money management applications. There is also a chapter that explains how to combine different kinds of work from different applications in a single, integrated document.

Some Special Help along the Way

As you learn about the basics and then develop your own special field of Mac expertise, you may have some problems. The Mac is wonderful, but it is not perfect. Both the Mac and the software that runs on it were made by humans like you and me, and we all make mistakes. To take care of the problems you may encounter, there are troubleshooting sections at the ends of all the chapters. Whenever you have a problem, look at the end of the chapter that deals with what you are doing and see if your problem is covered. If it isn't covered in that chapter, look in the index; it might be covered under a different heading. With a little patience and effort, you can usually get the Mac running smoothly again in a matter of minutes.

The illustrations in this book are intended to be supportive of the text, but they are not meant to limit what you do at all. Many were made by taking pictures of what was on my Mac's screen. They may look a bit different from what you see on your Mac. My Mac shows shades of gray, so lots of things look three-dimensional on it; if your Mac shows only black and white, you won't see all those little shadows and shapes to the objects on the screen. The examples of data are my own inventions, too. You should come up with examples that work best for you and are fun for you. If your screen looks a bit different from mine for one reason or another, don't let the different scenery throw you; the basic workings of the Mac behind the scenery are the same.

In fact, the key to using this book and your Mac is to keep trying things, even if they seem a little new and different. The Mac will reward your efforts. That's why I say it is a computer with a heart: It encourages you to do your best. And my greatest hope is that this book can give you the same sort of encouragement.

Part One

Introducing the Macintosh

• •

The first part of this book is an introduction to the Macintosh for new users. You'll start by learning about the Macintosh hardware (the pieces of machinery you set down on your desk) and software (the programs that go in the machinery and make it do what you want). You'll also learn how to set up your Mac and get it running.

Then you'll explore the basic techniques for using the Mac: how to use the mouse and the keyboard, how to maneuver around on the desktop that appears on the screen, and how to tell the Mac to do things. Finally, you'll learn how to print documents you produce on the Mac.

One

Meet the Mac

• •

Featuring

- What's inside your Mac and how it works
- Which Mac is best for your needs: compact, modular, or PowerBook
- How to set up your Mac so it's well-connected and ready to use
- Starting, shutting down, and turning off the Mac
- Setting up the Mac's hard disk if it isn't set up already
- Troubleshooting problems with setup and starting your Mac

First Steps

To decide which Mac you should buy: 8

You should learn the basics of how a computer works and what it does. Then you can think about what your real and immediate needs are. Decide what jobs you need to do with the computer, and how much you can spend. Then compare the different models, keeping in mind that the faster the CPU (the processor chip) is, the more RAM (memory) a computer has, and the more space it has on its hard disk, the more you will be able to do with it.

To set up your Mac: 13

First you need to unpack all the components (if they are still in the boxes) and make sure the components are all there and in good condition. Then make sure the power switch on the Mac is set to Off. Once everything is prepared, plug the power cord into a grounded, surge-protected outlet. Connect the keyboard, mouse, and (if necessary) monitor to the computer, and connect anything else you need to, such as a printer or an external hard drive.

To turn on your Mac: 17

Turn on any external devices such as a printer or hard drive, then turn on the Mac's power switch and (if necessary) the monitor. If you don't turn the external devices on first, the Mac can't recognize them when it is starting up, so they don't become available to you.

CHAPTER 1

To shut down and turn off your Mac: 18

Remember to save your work in any applications you are using before you shut down or turn off your Mac. When you have saved your work, quit the applications. Then choose Shut Down from the Special menu. When you see the dialog box that says it's safe to do so, you can turn off the Mac's power switch and (if necessary) the monitor. Finally, turn off any external devices you have been using, such as a printer or hard drive.

To set up your hard disk so the Mac runs off it instead of off floppy disks: 20

First turn your Mac off, then insert the Install 1 floppy disk and turn the Mac on. A welcome window appears, and you click the OK button in it after reading the message. Soon a large dialog box appears, with choices for installation. After you make sure the hard disk you want is selected (you click the Switch Disk button to select a different disk), you can click the Install button in this dialog box. The installation program takes over. You just insert the floppy disks that the installer requests. At the end of the installation process a dialog box should appear, telling you that installation was successful.

The Macintosh is a simple machine, designed and built so you can use it with ease. But just because the Mac is easy and pleasant to use doesn't mean it is a frivolous toy without power for serious computing. You can select a Macintosh that can handle whatever kind of computing you want to do, from writing short letters to desktop publishing, from keeping a small business inventory to planning the national budget, from cartoon sketching to three-dimensional full-color computer-aided design.

This chapter will help you find and set up the Mac that's right for you. It introduces the different basic types of Macintosh models and describes the features that make each type good for a particular use. If you have bought a Mac and it is set up already, you can skip the hints for choosing a Mac and setting up in this chapter. But if you are new to computers, read the "What's inside Your Mac?" section that follows, so you'll know what things are when I refer to them later on.

What's inside Your Mac?

> **Note**
> The messages you send to the computer from the keyboard and mouse are called the **input**. The results of your keyboard and mouse input are shown on the screen, or display, and are known as **output**. The output can be anything from text or numbers to three-dimensional views of space stations. All the types of output are referred to as **data**.

A Macintosh computer isn't all that complicated, really. It sounds complicated if you describe every little part in great technical detail, but you don't need to understand all those details in order to do your work. So here are the parts of your Macintosh, described in nontechnical terms.

The Keyboard and the Mouse

First let's look at the outer, more obvious units. There are the parts of the computer that you interact with: the keyboard (with letter keys, numbers, symbols, and some special control keys), and the mouse, which you move around to make a little pointer or cursor scurry around on the screen. Anything you want to tell the computer to do, you can tell it to by using these simple tools.

The CPU and Memory

The internal parts of the computer do the processing and storing of the data. There is a part of the computer that is somewhat like your brain. It doesn't really think, it just processes data. Computer people call it the *CPU* (Central Processing Unit). The faster this little chip of silicon can process your data, the more it costs, and the more your Mac costs. Exception: Newer Macs tend to have quicker CPUs, even the cheaper models. People use all kinds of complex jargon and empirical details to describe how fast the CPU works, but the concept is simple: Cheap old Macs are slow, new Macs are quick, and pricey new Macs go like blazes.

The *memory* is the part of the computer that remembers things. There are several types of memory, but for your purposes Random Access Memory (RAM) is the key. Your Mac's CPU needs memory it can use any time it wants, and that's what RAM is.

The more RAM your Mac has inside it, the more it can remember as it works on things. If your Mac doesn't have enough RAM, it works slowly, just as you write slowly if you keep forgetting the meanings of words you want to use. If you don't have much memory in your Mac, you may not be able to open more than one program at a time. There is a vital difference between your memory and your Mac's, though. You can go to sleep and wake up in the morning and still remember *most* of what you had in your memory the day before. When you shut down your Mac for the night, everything in the RAM disappears.

Floppy Disks and Hard Disks

Since your Mac forgets everything in the RAM when it's off, there has to be a place where your Mac can store things permanently. This is called disk storage. If you want to keep something from disappearing when you turn your Mac off, you save it on a disk.

There are two basic types of disks. *Floppy disks* go in a floppy disk drive slot at the front of your Mac, or in an external floppy disk drive that plugs into the back. A floppy disk drive is sort of a cross between a record player and a cassette player/recorder; it can write things onto the floppy disk and read things off it. It works much faster than a record player, though. A floppy disk can hold a fair amount of stuff, like a book's worth of text.

There are also *hard disks* (sometimes called hard drives; the disk and the drive mechanism are usually all in one unit). Hard drives can be internal, inside the Mac, or external, sitting next to the Mac or under it. A hard disk can hold much more than a floppy disk, like a personal library's worth of text, or more. Hard drives read and write data faster than floppy disk drives, too. Needless to say, the bigger a hard disk you have, the less you'll have to shuttle those

What's inside Your Mac? **7**

slow little floppy disks in and out of your floppy drive. If your Mac is an older model without a hard disk inside it, you should get an external hard disk drive.

The System Software

> **Note**
> For more information on the interface, see Chapter 2. For more information on memory and storage, see Chapters 6 and 7.

The parts of the Mac that I've described so far are all *hardware*. The last and most important part of the Mac is the *system software*, the coded instructions that make the whole system work. The combination of hardware and software that you interact with is called the *interface*. It is my humble opinion that the Macintosh interface is far and away the best one in the computer world.

Which Mac for You?

If you have not bought a Macintosh yet, first make sure you understand the basic concepts of what makes a Mac run, as described in the previous section. Then look at the descriptions of the different models and decide which one will work best for your needs. Of course, you must remember that Apple is always introducing new models, and a model may be sold with two names, such as the Classic II and Performa 200. The prices for all models tend to drop at varying rates, too, as new models are introduced. It can get quite confusing. But no matter which model you buy, remember this general rule; you want the fastest CPU, the most memory (RAM), and the greatest amount of storage you can afford. The last two items are measured in *megabytes*, or MBs. For example, an LC III (at the time of this writing) can come with 4MB of RAM and a 120MB hard drive. This configuration is sometimes shortened to 4/120.

Keep in mind the fact that you might need to expand your computer's features as you expand your work. For instance, if you are a graphic designer or artist, sooner or later you will want to take on work in color or grayscale formats. Some Macs can handle color and grayscale, others can be upgraded to handle them, and some cannot handle either color or grayscale, no matter what you do to them. If you can't afford a Mac that can handle color or grayscale, you should at least buy one that can be expanded to do so, so you can move on up when you're ready.

Compact Macs

These models are the basic, no-frills Macs. They can (and for most uses should) have a 40MB or 80MB hard disk inside them (internal), or connected outside. The older compact models have no fans in them. This means they run warm (hence the nickname "toasters"), but they are wonderfully quiet. Figure 1.1 shows a compact Macintosh.

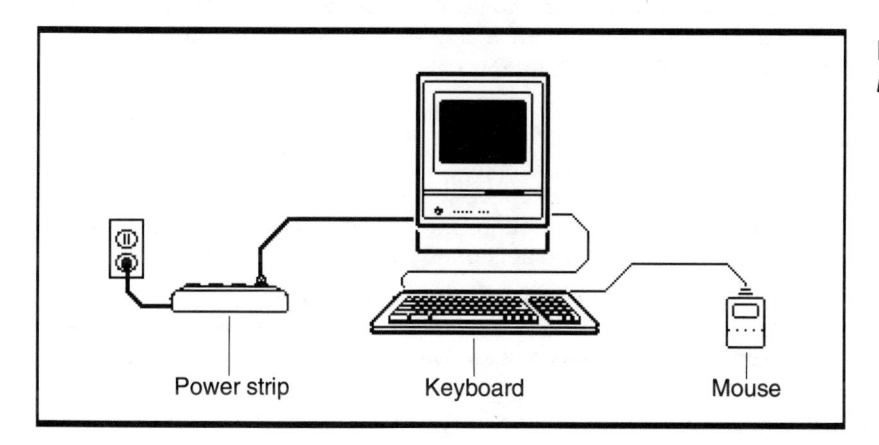

Figure 1.1
A compact Macintosh

Most of the older compact Macs can't carry much memory. Few can take more than 4MB of RAM, and that's barely enough to run System 7 with one or two applications. They have good, clear screens, but the screens are small, and they cannot show true grayscale or color, so they are better for working with numbers and text than for doing professional graphics. They do not have any slot for expansion cards, so it is hard to adapt them for use with other monitors or things like Ethernet networks.

One good thing about the compact models is that they combine the computer and the monitor or display screen in one box. All you have do to prepare the Mac is plug in the power cord, mouse, and keyboard. The simplicity of the compacts make them good for basic work such as word processing or database and spreadsheet applications, as long as you don't have to see large portions of a document at one time. Although they weigh too much to be considered truly portable, you can get them around quite easily as long as you don't have to carry them far. Compact Macs, especially the older ones, are not good for color or grayscale graphics work, nor are they designed for heavy-duty number crunching.

Which Mac for You?

> **Product at a Glance**
>
> ### The Color Classic
>
> **Manufacturer:**
> Apple Computer, Inc.
>
> **System Specifications (Basic Model):**
> CPU: 16MHz 68030
> RAM: 4MB
> Hard Disk: 80MB
>
> *Description:*
> Although it is a descendent of the original Macintosh, and is about the same size and shape, the Color Classic is different in many ways. It has (at the time of this writing) a 16MHz 68030 CPU, and the basic model comes with 4MB of RAM and an 80MB hard drive. It has an expansion slot for instant upgrades or accelerators, and most important, it has color.
>
> The design is new, too. It uses up a space on your desk that is about 10 inches by 12½ inches, and it is 14½ inches tall, so it is just a bit bigger than the old compact Macs. It has a larger bezel around the color screen, so the flat front of the Mac looks bigger, too; the rest of it has a rounder look, though, and there are those cute little round feet. The whole effect is like a squatting basset hound with a very flat face.
>
> The Color Classic is much faster than the original Mac, but not as fast as most other current Macintosh models. The Color Classic is best suited to word processing, simple paint applications, and educational games that are fun to play in color. It costs about a third again as much as the least expensive compact Macintosh.

Modular Macs

These Macs are made up of several components, or modules, as opposed to the all-in-one-box compact models. You can use either a color or a monochrome monitor with any of the modular models. They all have one or more slots for expansion cards, which can be used to extend the Mac's power or to allow the use of Apple IIe software. The expansion slot can also be used to attach another monitor or to attach your Mac to an Ethernet network. Figure 1.2 shows a modular Mac.

There are some modular Macs with relatively slow CPUs, and others that are about as fast as desktop computers can get. Most models come with RAM that is only adequate for basic use, but all allow for easy addition of RAM. The main differences between the models are the speed of the CPU, the degree of expandability, and the power of the color video support. Some models are well suited for desktop publishing, others are good for number-crunching, and still others are perfect for high-resolution, large-scale color graphics editing.

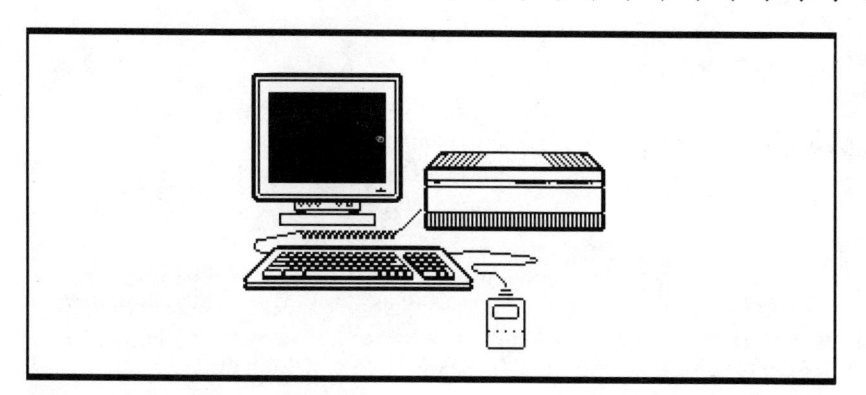

Figure 1.2
A modular Mac

The most expensive modular Macs are powerful enough to use as network servers on big Ethernet/AppleTalk networks, or they can be used as workstations for scientists, engineers, and high-tech designers who use three-dimensional applications or multicolored formats. The CPU of a high-end Mac can be more than ten times as fast as some of the older compact models.

The options for the top Macs are staggering. For example, some can carry more than 200 times as much RAM as the old Mac plus came with, and they can have more than a gigabyte of data stored on a hard disk inside; SCSI ports allow for almost unlimited external storage. They support all kinds of different monitors, including many made by companies other than Apple.

PowerBook Macs

PowerBook Macs, like the one in Figure 1.3, are at a different extreme from the high-end modular models. They are masterpieces of miniaturization. They pack a surprising amount of power for their size, but they definitely have limits.

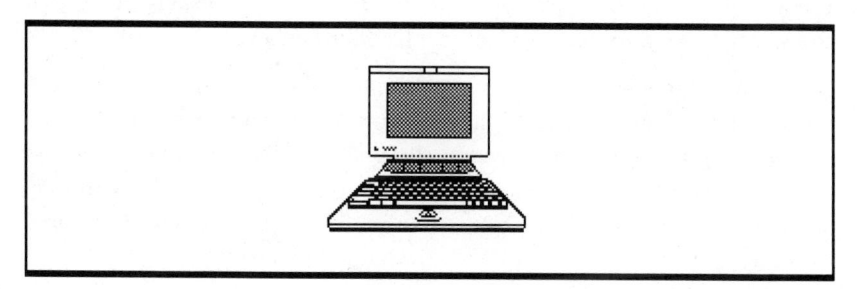

Figure 1.3
A PowerBook Mac

Which Mac for You?

Product at a Glance

The LC III

Manufacturer:
Apple Computer, Inc.

System Specifications (Basic Model):
CPU: 25MHz 68030 CPU
RAM: 4MB
Hard Disk: 80MB

Description:
This is the Mac for all seasons. It is relatively powerful and relatively inexpensive. It has (at the time of this writing) a 25MHz 68030 CPU, and the basic model comes with 4MB of RAM and an 80 MB hard drive. It has built-in support for 256 colors on 13-inch, 14-inch, and 16-inch monitors, or a whopping 32,768 colors on a 12-inch monitor.

The LC III is fast enough to handle all business and desktop publishing applications, and it can churn through some of the more demanding graphics and number-crunching applications if you put an appropriate accelerator or coprocessor in the expansion slot. By the way, you can put all kinds of expansion cards in that slot, for everything from running Apple IIe software to running the LC III at a blistering 50Mz. But it isn't a big, cumbersome machine. It takes up a space on your desk that is about 12 inches by 14½ inches, and the total height is about 15 to 16 inches, depending on which monitor you use.

The LC III is suited to almost all kinds of computer work, other than very demanding graphics and math applications. It is so popular that it will be around for years, and it is so easy to upgrade that you can count on it to grow with your needs and the growth of computer technology. Such a deal.

The lowest priced PowerBooks are slowish, have only a small hard drive (20MB–40MB) and smaller, less readable screens than some other portables.

The more expensive PowerBooks are faster, have higher capacity hard drives, and clearer, larger displays. However, most cannot be expanded easily, nor can you add RAM easily. Many cannot display color or grayscale graphics. Also, they have a slightly undersized keyboard, which takes a while to get used to if you are a touch-typist, and the touch is unusual—somewhat squishy compared to the crisp feel of most Mac keyboards.

Instead of the mouse, the portable and PowerBooks have a built-in trackball. It is a ball in a socket in front of the keyboard. You use it to move the pointer, and you use the buttons next to it to click. The trackball is used as a way to keep the whole unit simple, and to save the space it takes to use a mouse. Some users don't like the trackball as much as a mouse, but others find it easy to adapt to.

Overall, PowerBook Macs are best used to fill special needs, like recording changes in financial data or writing text while you are on an extensive trip with many stopovers. Jet-set executives love them. So do globe-trotting journalists.

Product at a Glance

The PowerBook 180

Manufacturer:
Apple Computer, Inc.

System Specifications (Basic Model):
CPU: 25MHz 68030
RAM: 4MB
Hard Disk: 80MB

Description:
This Mac is for those who fly first class. And who fly a lot. I get around on a bicycle, for the most part, so the PowerBook 180 reaches beyond my needs and has a price tag beyond my means. But I admire it. It zips through work with its 25MHz 68030 CPU. The standard model comes with 4MB of RAM and an 80MB hard drive, but if I were getting one, I'd go for the 8/120 option. There aren't any expansion slots in PowerBooks, but the 180 can do all of the word-processing, spreadsheet, and presentation work that business people do, with agile grace and ease. Your work appears in gorgeous, clear, grayscale images on the 180's active matrix screen, and if you want to do a color presentation for a group, you can plug a color monitor into it and get on with the show. The 180 has built-in support for 256 colors on a 16-inch monitor. You can install a fax modem right in your PowerBook for communication with the home office or makeshift printing.

The 180 is the same size as the other PowerBooks, 11.25 inches by 9.3 inches by 2.25 inches, and it weighs less than 7 pounds. Wow. It really is a wonderful, powerful little computer. The one drawback is that all its power uses up batteries quickly. Get the best batteries you can find, always carry at least one extra, and make sure your battery charger is top-quality. You can do various tricks to extend battery life, but the best rule is to plug in the PowerBook whenever possible. There are some airlines that provide outlets for you to plug your PowerBook into. Of course, that's only on first class.

Setting Up Your Mac

The first thing you'll notice as you unpack any Mac is that it looks simple; there aren't hundreds of indescribable little parts and connectors that you have to put together. And there are very simple instructions for hooking things together, in the setup booklet. Follow those instructions and within about ten or fifteen minutes you'll have your Mac all connected and ready to go. If anything is unclear in the booklet, or if you have lost it, or bought your Mac secondhand, just read the basic setup steps that follow, and any special steps that apply to your model of Mac.

Basic Setup Steps

Warning

Before turning the power switch on, make sure the Mac is placed where you want to use it. Don't move the Mac after it's on, especially if there is an internal hard disk in it. You can ruin a hard disk by joggling it while it is spinning.

To hook up any Mac (except the Plus), you need to plug the power cord into a grounded, surge-protected outlet first, then plug in the mouse and the keyboard (the Plus has separate cables for the mouse and keyboard). All of the mouse and keyboard sockets have the little Apple Desktop Bus (ADB) icon, which looks like some kind of odd plumbing contraption.

The ADB plugs go in flat side up. You can plug the mouse into either the right or left end of the keyboard, depending on which hand you want to use on the mouse; just plug the keyboard cord into the other end. That's all there is to setting up, for the basic Mac. There are special steps for some models of the Mac, however; see the following paragraphs and read the notes that apply to your model.

Special Setup Steps for Mac Models

If you have a modular Macintosh, it requires a display or monitor. Set the computer on a flat, secure surface, like the top of a table or desk. Put the monitor on top of the computer or near it. Plug in the power cords for both units. Then plug one end of the video cable into the monitor (if it isn't already attached), and plug the other end into the video port (socket) on the computer. This port has an icon under it that looks like a TV screen. If the connector at either end of the video cable has thumbscrews, screw them in tight.

If you have a Mac model that has expansion slots and you have an expansion card, unplug the power cord for the computer, then press the expansion card into place, as explained in the instructions included with the card. If those instructions are unclear, just have the people who sold you the card and the Mac put the card in for you; they should do this without charge.

If you have a model of Mac that accepts sound input and you want to add sounds to it, or if you use sound in your work on it, connect the microphone to the socket with the microphone icon above it, or connect your audio output plugs to the phono-plug adapter, as shown in the Apple setup booklet.

Chapter 1: Meet the Mac

If you have PowerBook Mac, you may wonder how to turn the thing on. In most cases, you can just press any key to power up. If that doesn't work, see the owner's guide.

No matter which model of Mac you have, if you have any other extra things to connect to it, such as an external disk drive, a printer, or a network cable, see the "Extra Connections" section below.

Extra Connections

By itself, a Mac is a somewhat limited machine. But you can hook all kinds of things up to it. Many are self-explanatory, such as trackballs and stylus pointers that replace the mouse, or modems that plug into the modem port (the socket with an icon that looks like a telephone), or printers that plug directly into the printer port. Just do your plugging in *before* you turn the Mac on, follow the instructions for the item you are connecting, and make sure you have the software to make use of the hardware you are connecting up.

There are some extra connections that take a little extra know-how, however. If you are connecting your Mac to a network or an external hard drive, use the following tips to make sure you set up the connection correctly.

Connecting to a Network

To connect your Mac to a network, or to connect a laser printer via network cabling, you have to have the right kind of connector and cables. For some networks, you also need to install an expansion card in your Mac. The simplest kind of network, an AppleTalk network, doesn't require any hardware or software changes to your Mac at all. Just get a connector that will attach the network cable to your printer port (the socket with the little printer icon above it) on the back of your Mac. Apple sells connectors and cabling for AppleTalk networks (they call the hardware LocalTalk), but there are much cheaper cabling and connector options, such as the Farallon PhoneNET stuff, and the many clones of PhoneNET. These cheaper alternatives use standard phone cabling and connectors, which actually stay plugged in more reliably than the LocalTalk connectors.

A good, inexpensive network lets your Mac do much more; it can reach out to printers, other users, shared information sources, and large storage devices or servers, where you can keep big files so you don't fill up your Mac's hard drive. If you are connecting a LaserWriter or any other laser printer that

Setting Up Your Mac **15**

works via AppleTalk to your Mac, all you need is two connectors, one for the Mac and one for the printer, and a piece of cable.

Connecting an External Hard Drive

If you are connecting an external SCSI (pronounced "scuzzy;" it stands for Small Computer System Interface) hard drive to your Macintosh, you need to check a few things. First make sure the software that runs the drive (called the "driver," of all things) is compatible with your Mac's version of the system software. For example, if you have version 7.0 of the system software, make sure the external drive's driver works with version 7.0.

Then make sure your external hard drive is "terminated." This doesn't mean dead; it means that the hard drive is at the end of a series of two or more SCSI devices. The signals running along the series will stop there, instead of bouncing back and forth among the devices.

Your SCSI drive needs to be terminated even if it is the only thing you've added to your Mac. Some external SCSI drives have a terminator built into them, like internal hard drives do. Other external hard drives require that you push a terminator, a thing that looks like a cordless SCSI plug (available at all Mac stores), into the second SCSI port on your hard drive. Look in the owner's manual that came with your hard drive to see if you have to terminate it or not. For a clear picture of when you need to terminate things connected to your Mac, see the table in the "Expanding Your Macintosh System" chapter of the Macintosh Reference.

When you have assured yourself that your external drive is properly terminated, check its ID number. There's usually a little dial or a window with a number showing, somewhere on the back of the SCSI drive case. If the ID number of your external SCSI drive is set to 0 (zero) and you have an internal hard drive in your Mac, there can be problems; the internal drive is normally set to 0 too. The same type of problem can occur if the SCSI drive ID number is 7, which is the ID number of the Mac itself. To avoid confusing the poor Mac, you must change the external SCSI drive to some ID number other than 0 or 7; you just push a little button or turn the dial to change the number.

Finally, if you are using more than one hard drive and each hard disk has a System Folder on it, make sure you designate one of the disks as the startup one, preferably your internal hard disk. If there are different versions of the system software on different disks in your system and the Mac can't figure out which one to run off of, it can lead to all kinds of trouble, including applications that don't work, data that disappears, and frequent, data-destroying system crashes. The easiest way to make sure you only have one System Folder, and system software that works right, is to use the official Installation floppy disks as described in "Setting Up Your Hard Disk for Future Startups" later in this chapter.

Getting the First Smile from Your Mac

OK, so you have your Mac all set up where you want it and all the cables and cords are connected. Now it's time to turn the thing on and watch it smile at you. To get your Mac's first smile, just switch the power on, and it beeps or strikes a nice musical chord, and then it whirrs quietly, and the screen gets bright, and you'll see the Happy Mac icon shown in Figure 1.4. In some cases, you may see the question mark icon shown in Figure 1.4 instead of a smile—just insert a startup disk if this happens, and you'll see the smile. (If you need help inserting the startup disk, see "The Happy Mac Does Not Appear" in the Troubleshooting section later in this chapter.)

Figure 1.4
Icons you may see when you start your Mac

After the smiling Mac goes away, you see a little sign on the screen that says "Welcome to Macintosh." Now, I know that smiley faces and welcome mats can get trite. You can get sick of hearing "Have a nice day" from every clerk you deal with all day, especially if you're having an awful day. But the Mac doesn't force its smile on you repeatedly. In fact, once you've turned on the Mac a few times, you'll probably ignore the Happy Mac icon and the welcome screen. That's OK. But I think they are a good sign. They remind me that at the very beginning, at the heart, if you will, the Mac is a positive machine, made to encourage us, the people who use it. Some other computers are not so nice.

Shutting Down Your Macintosh

When you are through working on the Mac, you need to shut down the system software before you turn the computer off. If you are looking at the desktop, pull down the Special menu as shown in Figure 1.5, and choose Shut Down.

Figure 1.5
Shutting down your Mac

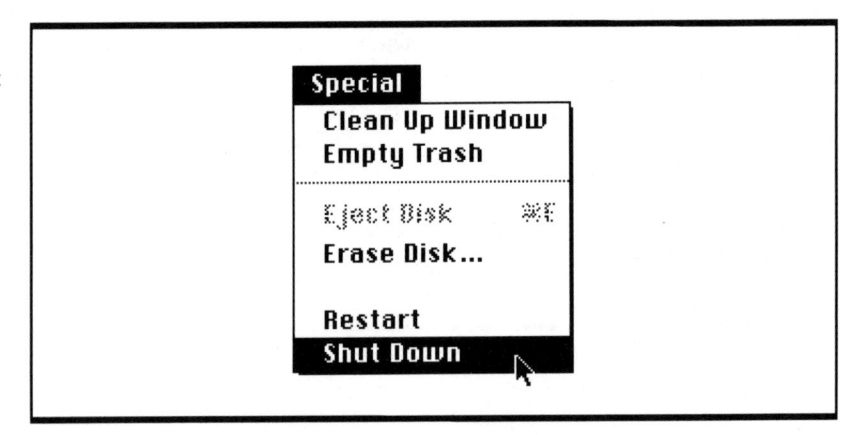

```
Special
Clean Up Window
Empty Trash
┄┄┄┄┄┄┄┄┄┄┄┄┄
Eject Disk      ⌘E
Erase Disk...
┄┄┄┄┄┄┄┄┄┄┄┄┄
Restart
Shut Down
```

Warning
NEVER turn off the Mac without saving the work you are doing and shutting down! If you don't save your work first, it is lost when you turn the Mac's power off. For information on saving, see Chapter 4.

If you need more information about the desktop and how to use menus, see Chapter 2, "Meet the Mouse and the Desktop." After you choose Shut Down, the screen goes black. Some modular and PowerBook models turn themselves off automatically. Lower priced modular Macs and compact models show you an alert box, telling you that it is now safe to switch off your Macintosh. Press the on/off switch on the back of the computer to turn the power off. If you have an external hard disk drive or printer, you can turn it off after turning off the Mac. If you have a portable Mac, all you have to do is choose Shut Down from the Special menu, and the computer turns itself off. If you want to put your PowerBook in the half-off state that you get when you use Shut Down on other Macs, choose Sleep from the Special menu.

If you ever want to restart your Mac without turning it all the way off, you can either choose Restart from the Special menu, or you can click the Restart button in the alert box that appears after you choose Shut Down.

Setting Up Your Hard Disk for Future Startups

This section applies to you only if you have an internal or external hard disk drive for your Mac, and you saw a blinking question mark icon instead of a Happy Mac when you switched the power on, so you had to put a startup floppy disk into your Mac to make it run. If you have a hard disk, you should put the system software on your hard disk. If you have a hard disk and you saw the Happy Mac, then your hard disk is set up right already and you can skip this section.

If you don't have a hard drive, you have to insert the System Startup disk in your floppy drive every time you start your Mac. That is a pain; if you can possibly afford it, buy an internal or external hard drive for your Mac, and put the system software on the hard disk.

The system software you need to install is on a series of floppy disks, beginning with Before You Install System 7, then Install 1, and so on. These disks are contained in a software package you received with your Mac. You may need to run an install floppy disk for your hard disk if it is a non-Apple hard disk. Do this before you install the system software. The following procedure explains how to copy the system software onto your hard disk, assuming that this is a first-time install.

The procedure takes some time, but don't try to take any shortcuts. It is *absolutely critical* that you get everything installed in the right place inside your System Folder on your hard disk; that means installing a whole set of system software that works together, and chucking out anything that won't work with the stuff you install. So do it once, and do it right, as described below. It'll save you an enormous amount of grief, believe me.

If you are new to the Mac and to computing in general, work through Chapter 2, "Meet the Mouse and the Desktop," or at least take the Macintosh Basics tour before you do the following installation procedure. You need to be familiar with the mouse and how to use things on the desktop to complete this procedure.

Tip
If you are an old hand at the Mac, or if you are working on a Mac that an old hand has been fiddling around with, your setup may be customized. See Appendix B, "Installing the System Software on a Customized Mac."

1. Start with your Mac turned off. Insert the Install 1 disk into the floppy drive in your Mac and turn it on. Click the OK button in the welcome screen to get the installer started.
2. Check the target hard disk named on the Easy Install screen, then click the Install button. If you want to install the system software on a hard disk other than the one named, click the Switch Disk button.
3. Insert the disks that the screen messages tell you to. When you see a message that installation was successful, click the Quit button. If you see a message that says installation was not successful, start the procedure over. If it fails again, get help from your dealer. When installation is successful and complete, a dialog box appears; click the Restart button in this dialog box. Your Mac restarts, running the system software you installed on your hard disk.

Congratulations. You now have the system software on your hard disk, and you can start up the Mac and use it without ever having to worry about what's running the show behind the scenes. One word of caution, though; make sure there is only one System Folder on that hard disk. The only time you should ever have two sets of system software available to your Mac is when the system software in your hard drive is broken, and you have to use a floppy startup disk (such as Install 1) just to get the Mac going again and reinstall the system software on your hard drive.

Troubleshooting Hardware and Installation Problems

The following sections discuss the problems you can have in installing and starting up your Mac.

Mac Doesn't Start Up

The screen stays dark and you don't hear any startup beep or whirring of the hard drive. Like, you turn the switch on, and NUTHIN' happens. The Mac is not getting power. Check that the power cord is plugged in firmly. You'd be amazed how many people call Apple Support every day in a cold sweat, ranting about how their Mac has died, only to discover that it isn't plugged in right. Test the outlet by plugging a lamp or something into it to make sure you are getting power there. Try turning the computer's power switch off and then on again.

If none of these things help, you either have a bad connection or a broken power supply in your Mac. If you can get another power cord for the Mac and swap it with yours, try that. No luck? Then it's time to take the Mac to a repair shop.

If you have an early Mac Plus, you may have lots of power supply failures unless you make sure the voltage is set to exactly 5 volts. Tell the shop to adjust the potentiometer to *precisely* 5 volts after they have replaced the power supply and warmed up the Mac for the first time to test it. You can also put a fan in your old Mac Plus to keep the power supply unit cool, but that means it will no longer be silent.

Screen Stays Dark

The Mac beeps after you turn it on, and you hear the disk drive whirring, but nothing shows up on the screen. Something is wrong with your display. If you have a modular Mac with a separate monitor, check that the monitor is plugged in and turned on. Most monitors have a little light that goes on when you turn them on.

If the monitor is on, or if you have a compact Mac with the screen in the same box with the computer, check the brightness control. On many Macs and monitors, there is a dial somewhere around the screen (usually on the side or under the front of the screen).

On some compacts, such as the Classic, you have to adjust the brightness with menus and dialog boxes. This is a bit tough when you can hardly see the screen. Pull down the Apple menu at the far left end of your menu bar and choose Control Panels. When the window opens, double-click the brightness panel icon (the one with the sun in it). The control bar shown in Figure 1.6 appears. Drag the slide bar to the right to turn up the brightness until you can see the desktop bright and clear.

Figure 1.6
The Brightness control slide bar

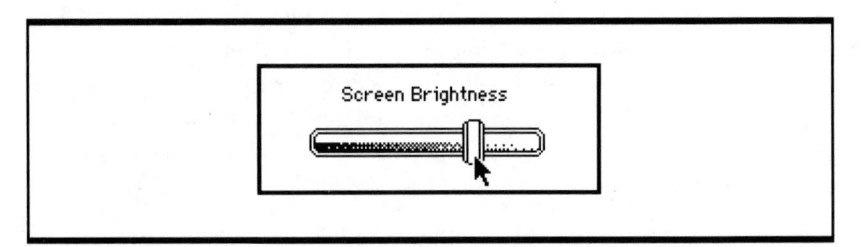

If your Mac has been on a while and the screen goes dark, you may have a screen saver installed that is turning the screen black to preserve it. Just move or click the mouse or hit any key on the keyboard, and the screen saver will turn the screen on again.

If you try all the above fixes for a black screen and none of them work, it's time to take the monitor or the whole Mac to a good Mac shop for repairs.

Glare on Screen

The Mac starts up OK, but when the desktop appears, you see a lot of glare from lights or things that are reflecting light in the room behind you. This can be hard on your eyes.

The only fool-proof solution is to put the Mac in a place where there aren't any bright lights or reflections that will cause glare. Don't put it in front of a bright light or a window, though, because the contrast of the dark screen frame and the glare behind it is hard on your eyes too. Does this mean you have to sit in a cave to work on your Mac? No. I work in a room with a nice big window, but it is to the side of me and the Mac. I can look out at the sunlight filtering through the trees, but the sun can't shine directly on the screen or in my eyes. It is easiest to avoid glare if you work in a room with a north-facing or east-facing window.

Gray Waves Fluttering across Screen

You looked at your Mac from across the room and saw strange gray shadows fluttering in waves up and down the screen. Not to worry. You are not seeing ghosts. You are just seeing harmonic patterns of light and dark as they play tricks on your eyes' nerve endings. If you ever see these fluttering forms when you are sitting right in front of the Mac, you should either see your qualified Mac technician and get the display fixed, or see your eye doctor.

The Happy Mac Does Not Appear

Your Mac is having trouble getting going on the system software that is available to it. You can tell more or less what the problem is by what icon you see instead of the Happy Mac.

If You See an X Icon: If you see a disk icon with an X on it (like the one in Figure 1.7) and the floppy disk you put into the disk drive spits out, it just means that the floppy disk didn't have a System Folder with the system software in it. If you wait a moment, you should see the question mark disk icon. Then, if there is a System Folder with the system software on your hard disk, you'll soon see the Happy Mac.

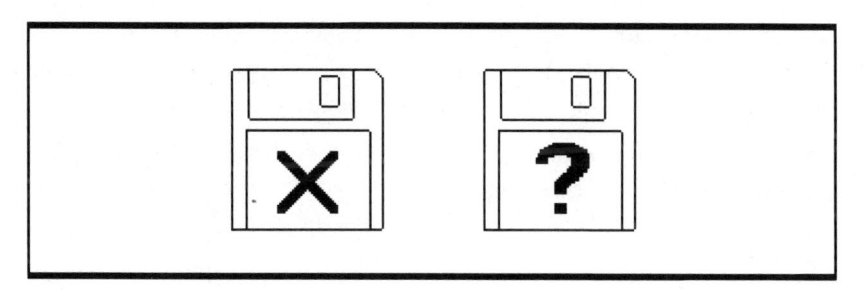

Figure 1.7
The X and ? disk icons

If You See a ? Icon: If the disk icon with a flashing question mark on it (see Figure 1.7) stays on-screen, your Mac has looked around for the system software, and it is saying "Huh? I can't figure out what to do!" A few things could be wrong. The Mac didn't recognize your startup hard disk, or there are two hard disks with the same ID number and it can't figure out which one to go to for system software. Or maybe there isn't any system software available, because either you haven't got it on your hard disk, or you don't *have* a hard disk and you haven't inserted a floppy disk with the system software on it.

The simple answer to the question mark is to insert a startup floppy disk, such as Disk Tools, from your system software kit. Your Mac looks first in its floppy drive for the system software; when it finds it there, it displays the Happy Mac and starts up.

If you use a floppy as a startup disk and your hard disk icon doesn't show up on the desktop, see "Hard Disk Icon Doesn't Appear," later in this chapter. If you have a hard disk and its icon appears, you should set it up for future startups, as described earlier in this chapter. If you have two or more hard disks, including an internal one, you should make the internal one your startup disk, and change the numbers of the external drive or drives to numbers other than 0 (zero) or 7. Also, make sure only one System Folder, with one set of the system software, is available on your whole system. For more information on this, see the end of the "Extra Connections" section earlier in this chapter.

If you have only one hard drive, and the system software is on it, and you still get the question mark disk flashing at startup, or if the X disk and the question mark disk alternate back and forth, there is something wrong with the system software you installed. Reinstall it, as described in the "Setting Up Your Hard Disk for Future Startups" section earlier in this chapter. If you have two versions of the system software and you are using a utility such as Blesser or System Switcher to switch between versions, just switch to another version of the software and then reinstall the faulty system software.

If You See a Sad Mac Icon: If you see the Sad Mac icon (it looks more like a peevish drunk Mac to me; see Figure 1.8) you've got serious problems. Either the system software is damaged, or there is something wrong with the Macintosh hardware.

Where the Mac Looks for System Software at Startup

If you don't see the Happy Mac at startup, your Mac is having some problems finding the system software it needs to run. The problems may depend on just where the Mac is looking for the system software. The following list tells the particular order of the places where the Mac looks. You should check things out in this order, too.

1. Its own floppy drive (the internal floppy drive).
2. Its own second floppy drive if it has two internal floppy drives.
3. The external floppy drive if you have connected one to your Mac.
4. The hard disk you specify in the Startup Disk control panel; you can only change this if you have more than one hard disk connected to your Mac.
5. The external serial (as opposed to SCSI) hard drive. It is very unlikely that you'll have one of these; they are so slow they are almost extinct.
6. The internal hard disk, or, if you have no internal hard disk, the external SCSI drive with ID number 0.
7. Other external SCSI drives with ID numbers 6 through 1, in that order.

If the Mac finds no system software after trying all those devices, it waits 15 seconds and goes back to its own internal floppy drive for a second try.

Figure 1.8
The Sad Mac icon

If you inserted a floppy disk, turn off the computer, then hold down the mouse button while you turn the Mac on again. This ejects the disk; try starting up again with a different startup disk. If the Sad Mac appears again, you may have a problem with the part of the Mac's memory (PRAM) that is supposed to recognize startup disks. To solve this problem, you have to zap the PRAM. If you have an older Mac, like a Plus or anything earlier, you have to turn off the Mac, take the battery out, and wait for about twenty minutes or so. Then put the battery back in, turn the Mac on, and reset the time and date in the General Controls control panel. If you have a Mac of any other kind, it's time to take the Mac to a qualified repair shop.

Startup Sound Is Weird

Some models of Mac, including all modular ones and PowerBooks, make a C major chord sound instead of a beep when they start up. If the chord sounds disharmonious, or if one note does not sound at the same time as the others, or if there is an arpeggio (running up a scale, instead of all notes at once), then there is probably something wrong with the memory of your Mac. It may just be that one of the memory chips is loose in its socket, or it may mean that a chip has failed. Take your Mac to a qualified technician for a checkup and repair.

If the memory chips are OK, there are two other rare problems you may have. If you have a Mac II, there may be a problem with one of your NuBus expansion cards. Take your Mac to a qualified technician for help. If you have an external SCSI hard drive, there may be a problem with the driver software that controls the hard drive. Reinstall your driver software. If that doesn't help, take the Mac and the hard drive to a qualified technician.

Hard Disk Icon Doesn't Appear

You have a hard disk, either an internal or an external one, and when your Mac starts up, the desktop appears as in Figure 1.9, but there is no hard disk icon in sight.

The hard disk is not communicating with the CPU (the main computing chip) of your Mac. The Mac doesn't even know it's there. The solution to the problem depends on what kind of drive it is and how you are using it. If it's an internal hard drive, turn off your Mac and leave it off for a minute or so.

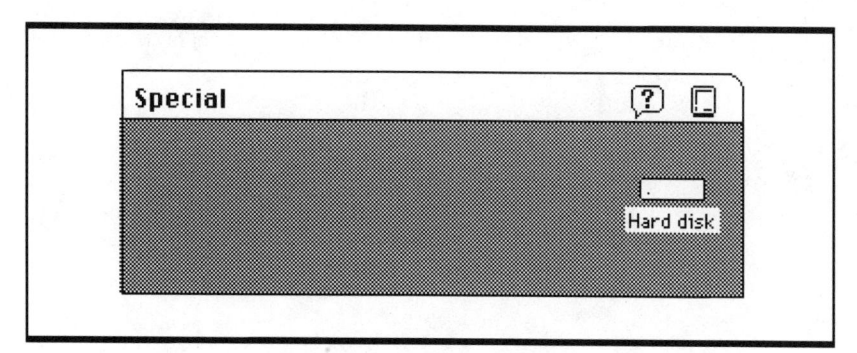

Figure 1.9
The upper right corner of desktop with hard disk icon

Then turn it back on. If it's an external hard drive, make sure it is plugged in, turned on, and connected to the Mac correctly. Then choose Restart from the Special menu. If the hard disk is your startup disk, turn off the Mac and wait a minute. Then insert a startup floppy disk, and start the Mac again. If the hard disk icon appears, reinstall the system software on the hard disk.

If you have more than one hard disk, check the ID number of any external hard disk to make sure it is not the same as the internal hard disk or the computer. For more information on this identity crisis, see the end of the "Extra Connections" section earlier in this chapter.

Two

Meet the Mouse and the Desktop

• •

Featuring

- ◆ An introduction to the mouse and the Mac desktop
- ◆ Using the mouse to point at, click, open, and drag things
- ◆ Choosing menu commands with the mouse and keyboard
- ◆ How to work with text; entering, selecting, deleting, editing
- ◆ How to show and hide help balloons
- ◆ How to work with windows; selecting, moving, sizing, zooming, scrolling
- ◆ How to select, move, and open icons in windows
- ◆ How to use the Trash; dragging things to it, opening it, emptying it
- ◆ Using dialog and alert boxes
- ◆ Troubleshooting problems with the mouse and desktop

First Steps

To select or open an icon: 35

Grasp the mouse between your thumb and fingers, letting your index finger float above the mouse button. When you move the mouse, the pointer moves in the same direction, as long as you keep the mouse's cable pointing away from you. To select an icon, you place the tip of the pointer on it and click the mouse button. You do the same thing but click the button twice quickly to open the icon.

To move an icon: 36

Place the pointer on the item, press the mouse button down and hold it down, then move the mouse the way you want the icon to move.

To choose a menu command: 36

Place the tip of the pointer on a menu title and drag downwards, releasing the mouse button on the command you want. Once you are familiar with the commands, you can use the ⌘ key and other keys on the keyboard as shortcuts for them.

CHAPTER 2

To enter and edit text with the mouse and keyboard: 37

Place the insertion point where you want the text to appear. Then type the appropriate letters to make the text appear. If you want to change or delete text you have already written, you drag across the text. Then you can use the backspace or delete key to delete the text, or you can type in new text to replace the old text.

To scroll through a window: 41

You can click on the scroll arrows to scroll slowly in a window, or click in the gray part of the scroll bar to move more quickly. You can drag the scroll box to scroll by leaps and bounds. You can also scroll in a window by slowly dragging an icon in it until it nudges the edge of the window. This only works if the window can be scrolled in that direction.

To delete things by using the Trash: 42

You need to be in the Finder to use the Trash. From any Finder window, you can drag an icon to the Trash can on the desktop, and it will be kept there. To save an item from the Trash before emptying the Trash, open the Trash by double-clicking it and drag the item back to whatever window you want. To empty the Trash and delete the items you have dragged there, choose Empty Trash from the Special menu.

The mouse is the little box you push around to make the arrow move on the screen. The desktop is everything you see on the screen. These are the fundamental parts of the Macintosh *interface*, which is simply the means by which you talk to the computer. You can also use the keyboard, but if you have done any typing at all, it is pretty self-explanatory.

It is the mouse and the desktop that separate the Mac from most other computers. Other computers began by depending on the keyboard and clumsy, hard-to-remember commands. Some have made interfaces that imitate the Mac, but even these are relatively clumsy. The Mac mouse and desktop were designed to work beautifully together, from the start. They make it easy to give commands and make choices that tell the machine what to do.

This chapter tells you how to get good at using the fundamental tools of the Mac interface. It's worth the trouble to really get the basics right, because you use the same tools all the time on the Macintosh, no matter what application you work with.

If you are new to Macs and have the Macintosh Basics icon on your hard disk or on a separate floppy disk, double-click (click the mouse button twice, quickly) on the icon to start up the program, or get a Mac user to start up the program for you. You will be treated to a leisurely, clear introduction to the mouse, the desktop, and the basic techniques for using them. If you don't have the Basics program, or if you lost it and want a quick reminder of the fundamental Mac tools and techniques, here they are.

Introducing the Desktop

The *desktop* is what you see when you turn the Mac on and it is ready to use. It is what the Finder (that magical piece of wizardry in the system software) shows you. It is called a desktop because you do things with it that you would normally do on a desk. Figure 2.1 shows a sample desktop and its basic elements. Although your desktop may look somewhat different from this one (if you start up from a hard disk, for instance, you won't see a floppy disk icon

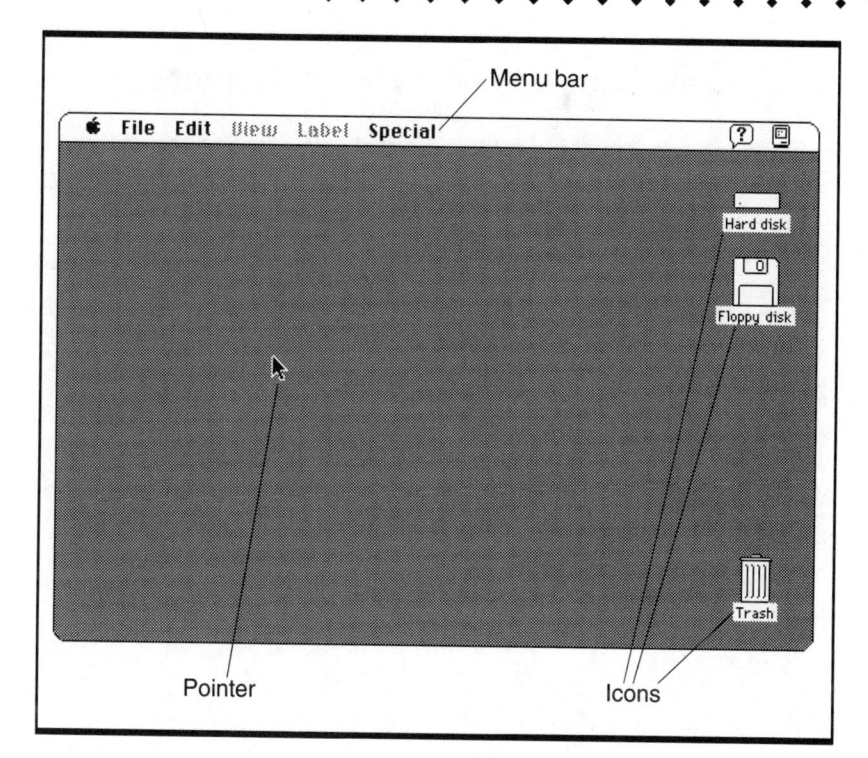

Figure 2.1
Key elements of the Macintosh desktop

until you insert a floppy disk), the menu bar, icons, and the pointer are always there. These elements of the desktop have clear, practical purposes and uses:

- The *menu bar* contains the titles of the menus you can choose from.
- *Icons* tell you what places are available to you for storing things, what tools are available for you to work with, and what things your work has produced.
- The *pointer* points at things so you can choose them, move them, look inside them, start using them, or close them up and put them away. It's a very powerful little gadget.

The desktop is created by the Finder, which is the part of the Macintosh system software that helps you find whatever you need to do your work. Whenever you are looking at the desktop, you are "in" the Finder. If this book or some Mac guru tells you to go to the Finder, they don't mean anything deep or cosmic. They're really just telling you to change your view to the desktop. For more information on going to the Finder, see "Desktop Views" in Chapter 4.

Does Your Desktop Look Different?

You may see something a little different from the desktop in Figure 2.1. This may mean that you are using a simplified version of the desktop, or an older version of the system software. You can tell by looking for some specific clues.

If you can see only three menu titles, File, Edit, and Special, and there are two big manila folder type windows on the screen, one for Applications and one for Documents, then your Mac has At Ease, a simplified desktop. At Ease lets you start applications and open documents by simply clicking on them. But it makes it hard to do anything other than what the manager of the system wants you to do. At Ease is usually on Macs that are connected to a network, or used by many people, under the control of a manager or administrator. See this person to find out which applications and documents you can use, then just click away, and you can go right to work.

If your desktop looks more or less like the one in Figure 2.1, but there is no balloon with a question mark near the right end of the menu bar, then your Mac is running on a version of the system software prior to System 7. Some of the procedures you use will be different from those described in this book. You will also notice minor differences in icons and titles for screen objects in the text of the book. Most procedures are similar, however, so you can still use our text and illustrations as guidelines.

Using the Mouse

The mouse is the primary tool you use to control the Mac. Fortunately, it's easy to use. Just hold the mouse with the cable pointing away from you. Grasp it gently with your thumb on one side and your other fingers on the other side, but leave your index finger hovering over the button, ready to click at any time.

Now move the mouse, and notice how the on-screen pointer moves that direction, too. You can move the mouse from side to side and up and down, but don't twist it; keep the cable pointing directly away from you at all times. Twisting the mouse makes the pointer move in strange and unpredictable ways. As you move the mouse, slide the heel of your hand along the surface of the desk or mouse pad. If you don't have a mouse pad, get one with a firm, clean, textured surface. It improves the responsiveness of the mouse, and keeps it clean and smooth-running.

Tip
The mouse pointer has a hot spot that you have to place on or over any screen object you want to take an action on. Usually the hot spot is at the tip of the pointer arrow.

Selecting, Dragging, and Opening Icons

To take an action on the Mac desktop, you often begin by selecting an icon. To select an icon, move the pointer tip over the icon, then hold the mouse still and press and quickly release the mouse button. The mouse button clicks and the icon becomes highlighted (the dark areas become light, and the light areas dark). For example, if you select the Trash icon in the lower right corner of the desktop, it turns dark, as in the left panel of Figure 2.2. In Macintosh manuals, selecting is often referred to as *clicking* or *highlighting*.

Figure 2.2
Clicking, dragging, and double-clicking the Trash icon

To move or *drag* an icon, put the pointer tip over it, press the mouse button, and hold it down while you move the mouse. A *ghost* outline of the icon moves with the pointer as you move the mouse, as shown in the middle panel of Figure 2.2. When the icon is where you want it, release the mouse button.

To open an icon, move the pointer tip over it, then click the mouse button twice, quickly, without moving the mouse. This is called *double-clicking*. In many cases, double-clicking an icon opens a *window*. The window shows what is inside the icon. For example, double-clicking on the Trash icon opens a window similar to the one shown in the right panel of Figure 2.2. The window you see for your Trash may be a different size and shape, but they all work the same. To close the icon's window, you click in the close box, the small blank square in the upper left corner of the window.

Choosing Commands from Menus

To tell your Mac what to do, you choose a command from a pull-down menu. Put the tip of the pointer over one of the menu titles in the menu bar and press the mouse button to see the menu. Then hold the mouse button down and move the mouse toward yourself. You'll see a dark bar, a highlight, moving down through the commands in the menu. When the highlight is on the command you want, release the mouse button.

To see a simple example of how a menu command works, choose the New Folder command from the File menu (move the pointer to the word *File*, then pull the highlight down to the words *New Folder*). A new folder appears, with the name "untitled folder." You can drag the empty folder to the Trash if you don't want to leave it lying around. (See "Dragging Things to the Trash" later in this chapter for more information.)

In some menus you'll find that some of the commands are *dimmed* or *grayed*. This means that these commands cannot be used in your current situation. If you pull down a menu and find that the command you want to use is dimmed, just keep the mouse button pressed down and pull the mouse toward you until the highlight goes off the bottom of the menu.

⌘-Key Shortcuts

If you use a command often, you can memorize the keyboard shortcut for the command. Each keyboard shortcut consists of the ⌘ key (the Command key) and a letter; each command's shortcut is displayed to its right on the pull-down menu. To use a keyboard shortcut, you just hold down the ⌘ key and press the letter key on the keyboard. For instance, to give the Open command, hold down the ⌘ key and press O. You don't have to reach over and grab the mouse, pull down the File menu, and select Open.

Using the Keyboard and Mouse to Work with Text

Although you'll be using the mouse to perform most actions on your Mac, you still need to use the keyboard to create text. But before you can, you have to place a beginning point, or *insertion point*, so your computer knows where to display the text on the screen.

When you start word processing applications, the insertion point appears immediately, but you can place an insertion point on the desktop, too. For example, you can use the insertion point to change a folder name. Just follow these steps:

1. Click on the name of the untitled folder you just created, so it is highlighted as in the left panel of Figure 2.3. (If you threw the untitled folder into the Trash, create another by choosing New Folder from the File menu.)
2. Notice that when the text becomes highlighted, the pointer soon changes into a vertical line with sprouts at the ends. This is known as the *I-beam*, and it is the pointer you see whenever you can create text.

3. Click the mouse button; the I-beam becomes an insertion point. Then move the I-beam out of the way, as shown in Figure 2.3.

Figure 2.3
Placing an insertion point and typing text

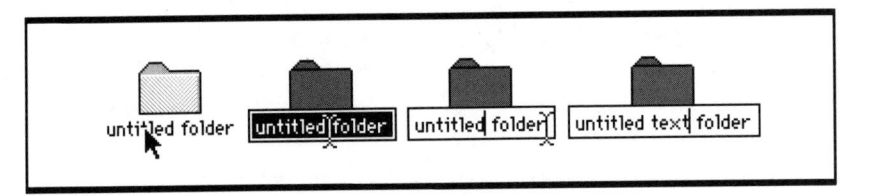

4. Type in the word **text**. It appears at the insertion point, and if there are any words to the right of the insertion point, they move over to make room for the new text. Whenever you are typing, the I-beam disappears. Do not type in too much text; icon labels can only be 31 characters long.

Now you've added to your icon title, but what if you want to replace it? You just delete what you don't want. To delete some text, you need to select it first. This is the most basic rule in text processing: *Select first, then operate.*

For example, to delete the word *untitled*, first double-click on the word, then press the Delete key to delete it. The word disappears, as in Figure 2.4. If you highlight some text, then decide you want to deselect it, just click somewhere else with the insertion point. The highlighting disappears.

To replace some text, first select it, then type in the new text. For example, to replace the word *folder* with the word *samples*, as in Figure 2.4, double-click on *folder*, then type **samples**.

If you want to select more than one word of text for deletion or replacement, drag the highlight over all the words.

Figure 2.4
Deleting and replacing text

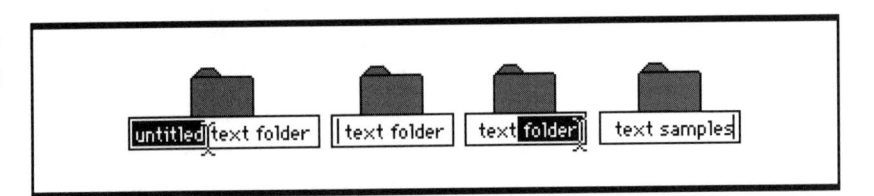

Chapter 2: Meet the Mouse and the Desktop

Showing and Hiding Help Balloons

To see helpful information about items on the desktop and in windows, choose Show Balloons from the Help menu, which is under the cartoon balloon icon with a question mark in it (see Figure 2.5).

When balloon help is active, you can put the tip of the pointer on any object you need information about, and read the text that appears in a balloon.

If you are an experienced Mac user, many balloon help messages may seem a bit boring to you, but for an interesting example, choose the About This Macintosh command from the Apple menu at the left end of the menu bar, then put the pointer on the two-tone horizontal bars that show how much memory each application is using. A precise reading of the number of kilobytes of memory for each application appears in the balloon.

To turn the balloons off and go back to work, choose Hide Balloons from the Help menu. Notice how the Show Balloons command becomes Hide Balloons when the help balloons are showing. After you hide the balloons, you can pull down the menu and see the Show Balloons command again. This switching back and forth of a command depending on the situation is called *toggling*.

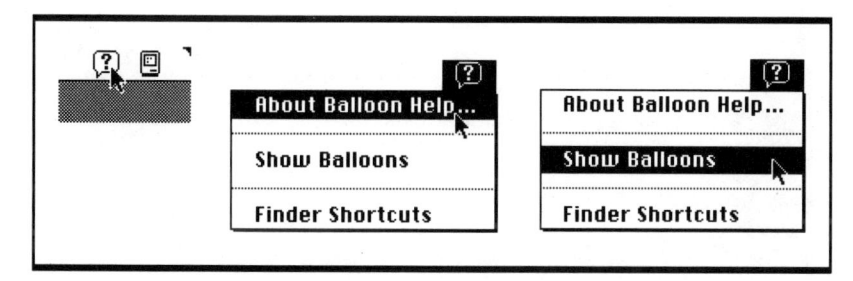

Figure 2.5
Choosing Show Balloons from the Help menu

Doing Things to Windows

Windows give you a view of what's in your Mac, or what's on your floppy and hard disks. If there are no windows open on the desktop, as in Figure 2.1, just double-click on your hard disk or floppy disk icon to see its window. If you open a window or do something in it, it becomes the *active window*. The window titled "Hard disk" in Figure 2.6 is the active one. There are a bunch of horizontal lines running across the *title bar* of the active window. By contrast, the title bar, the side bar, and bottom bar of inactive windows are all blank. If windows overlap, as in Figure 2.6, the active window appears in front.

Figure 2.6
An active window and an inactive window

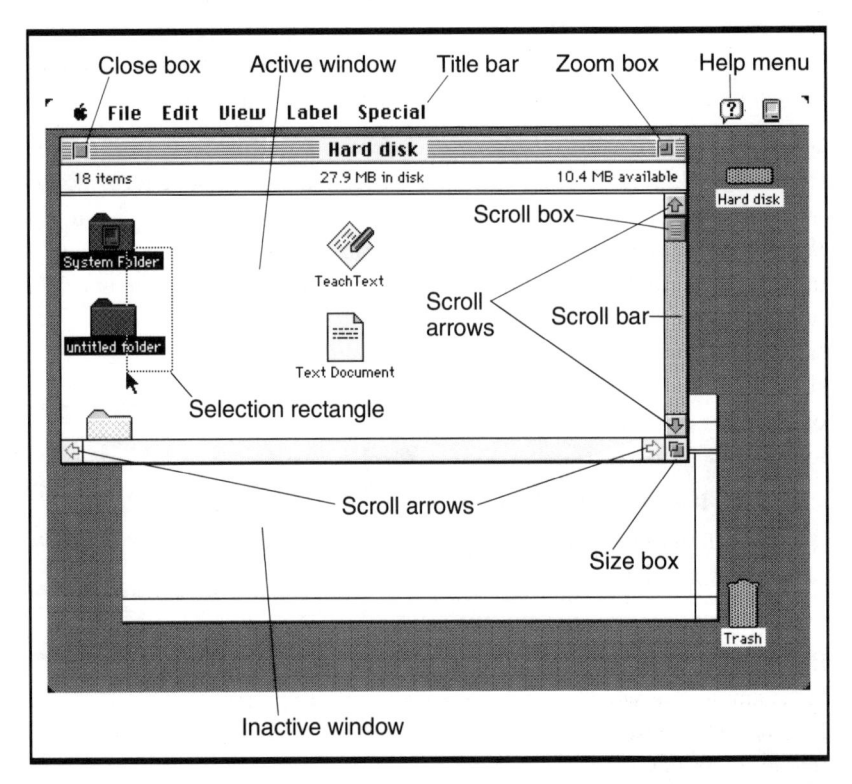

40 Chapter 2: Meet the Mouse and the Desktop

Here are the things you can do with the different parts of a window:

- To make a window active, click in it.
- To move a window around on the desktop, drag its title bar.
- To change the size of a window, drag the *size box* inward or outward.
- To zoom between the optimum window size and another size you have set, click the *zoom box*. The "optimum" size is shrink-to-fit around all the objects in the window. If there are more objects than will fit on the screen, the window zooms out as large as it can without covering the Trash and disk icons on the right side.
- To select multiple icons in a window, drag a *selection rectangle* across them. Click to one side of the group of icons, drag the dotted rectangle just as you would drag to select text, and release the mouse button when the icons you want are highlighted.
- To add another icon to a selected group, press the Shift key and click on the icon. This is called *Shift-clicking*. You can Shift-click to deselect one of a group of selected icons, too.
- To close the window, click on its close box.

If you have more things in a window than can be shown, scroll bars appear on the right and/or bottom edges. You don't have to worry about losing things in a window, even if you can't see all of them at once. If you want to make a sample window with a scroll bar, place several files or folders along the left side of a big window, then drag the size box in to shrink the window so an object is at least partially hidden, as the lowest folder in Figure 2.6. The following actions are then possible using scroll bars:

- To move slowly, click on the scroll arrows.
- To move quickly, a section at a time, click in the gray scroll bar above or below the scroll box.
- To jump to a distant section, drag the scroll box.

In all cases, the window moves the way you tell it to. If you click the up arrow, for example, the window moves up, and the objects inside it move down. Practice will accustom you to these scrolling movements. If you want to practice in a window with lots of icons in it, and you don't have any crowded folders yet, just double-click your System Folder icon and shrink its window

Tip

You can also scroll slowly by dragging an icon to the bottom or top of a window. Gently nudge the border of the window with the icon; if the icon is moving too fast, it zips right out of the window.

Doing Things to Windows **41**

down so only a couple folders show at a time. Then you can scroll both sideways and up and down.

Dragging Things to the Trash

The Trash can in the lower right corner of the desktop is where you put things you want to delete or get rid of. If you are done with something you worked on and don't want to leave it around, or if you have an extra copy of something, you put it in the Trash.

Warning

Empty the Trash once a day or so. If you forget to empty the Trash for a long time, you can get so many files in there that they bog down the Finder and eventually make it hard for the Mac's system software to do **anything** right.

You can drag an icon from anywhere on the desktop to the Trash can. The icon disappears and the Trash can bulges. If you ever want to see what is in the bulging Trash can, just double-click it; a Trash window opens, with all discarded items in it. Discarded items stay in the Trash until you choose Empty Trash from the Special menu. Even if you shut the Mac down and turn it off, when you start it up again, the Trash can will appear, bulging with your discarded items.

When you empty the Trash, an *alert box* tells you how much is in it and asks if you are sure you want to permanently remove it. Before you empty it, you should be sure there's nothing in there that you'll need again. Click the Cancel button and open the Trash window if you want to check the discarded items.

To recover a mistakenly discarded item, just drag its icon out of the Trash window and back to where it belongs. If you can't remember where it belongs, just select it in the Trash window and choose Put Away from the File menu. The Mac remembers for you!

If you know what is in the Trash and are sure you want to delete it permanently, press the Option key as you choose Empty Trash from the Special menu. The alert box doesn't appear. For more information on alert boxes, see the next section of this chapter.

42   Chapter 2: Meet the Mouse and the Desktop

Using Dialog and Alert Boxes

Dialog and alert boxes appear from time to time as you work with your Macintosh. These on-screen boxes help you make necessary choices, or warn you of risky actions, or prevent you from making destructive errors. Sometimes they seem like a bother, but if the Mac didn't have them, we'd all be a lot more bothered by the results of our own careless errors. They keep the environment we work in safe, sort of like warning signs on the handles of power tools.

Dialog Boxes

A *dialog box* takes charge of the screen after you choose a command with three dots after it. Usually the dialog box will help you specify how the command should be carried out. For example, if you choose Print… from the File menu in an application, or if you choose Print Window… from the File menu in the Finder, a dialog box that looks something like Figure 2.7 appears.

Notice that the box has no title bar like windows have. When you see a dialog box like the Print one, you look at the choices in it, change any that you want to be different from default choices that have been made for you, and then click either the button with the bold double outline (Print in this case; OK in many others) or the Cancel button.

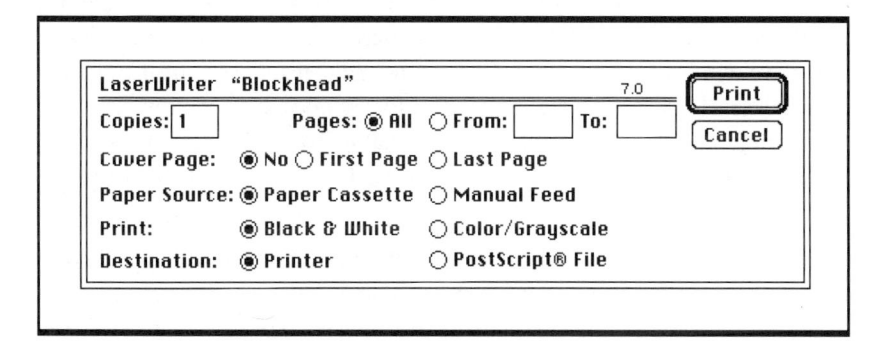

Figure 2.7
The Print dialog box

You *have* to click one button or the other to get out of this kind of dialog box. If you try to do anything else, like click in a window or choose another menu command, you just get a beep, and the dialog box stays there. For this reason, it is called a "must-do," or *modal*, dialog box. If you don't understand all the choices in a dialog box, it's usually safe to just leave things the way they are and click the bold outline button or press Return. If you want to learn more about the Print dialog box choices, see Chapter 3.

There are also dialog boxes that you can use or get out of without using. For example, in word processing applications such as Microsoft Word, you can choose a Find... command and a dialog box like the one in Figure 2.8 appears.

Figure 2.8
The Find dialog box

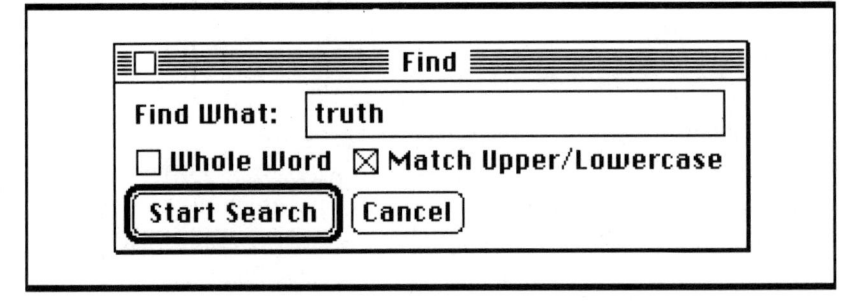

```
┌─────────────────── Find ───────────────────┐
│ Find What: │ truth                         │
│ ☐ Whole Word   ☒ Match Upper/Lowercase    │
│ [ Start Search ]  [ Cancel ]              │
└────────────────────────────────────────────┘
```

Once you've made your choices from this sort of dialog box, you have three options: You can go ahead with the action by clicking the button with the bold double outline, you can click Cancel to negate the command, or you can just click in another window.

If you click on another window, the new active window will come to the front, but the dialog box will still be available; if part of it is showing at the edge of the active window, you can click the box and make it active again at any time. This makes dialog boxes like Find almost like windows. They even have title bars. They are officially called modeless dialog boxes. I call them window boxes, or "less-than-must-do" boxes, because I can never remember the difference between modal and modeless.

There is a third type of dialog box, which you can see if you choose the Open... or Save As... command from the File menu. It lets you choose files from lists. For more information on this special type of dialog box, see "Working with Applications and Documents" in Chapter 4.

Chapter 2: Meet the Mouse and the Desktop

Alert Boxes

Alert boxes are like must-do dialog boxes, but they appear when you try to do something you really shouldn't. For example, if you try to drag the Trash can into a window on your desktop, an alert box like the one in Figure 2.9 appears.

You can tell how serious an alert box is by the icon on its left side. The Stop icon means you can't do what you tried to do. The Caution icon means you can do it, but there might be some drawbacks, or you might have to take some special steps. The text in the alert box explains these things, and there are buttons to either go ahead or cancel the action. If you see an alert box with a Note icon, it is just telling you some added information about the action you are taking. Read the text, then click the OK button to go ahead with the action.

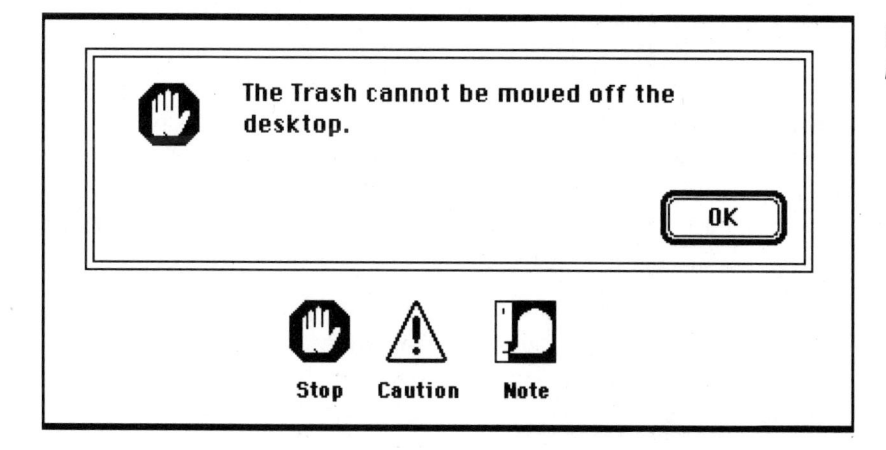

Figure 2.9
An alert box and alert icons

Using Dialog and Alert Boxes **45**

Troubleshooting Problems with the Mouse and Desktop

The following subsections cover the most common problems you can have when using the mouse, the desktop, the icons on the desktop, and the Finder windows you see on your desktop.

Clicking Doesn't Work

When you click the mouse button, the action doesn't take effect. This problem occurs most often when you're trying to click on something small, like a close box. The cause is usually that the tip or "hot spot" of the pointer is not over the thing you're trying to click on.

Move the mouse carefully to position the pointer, then try clicking again. In some rare cases, the Mac can be so busy thinking that it can't respond to the mouse click. Just repeat the clicking; it will surely work the second time. In very rare cases, static electricity or cosmic rays can freeze the screen: You can move the mouse pointer, but nothing else works. The only solution is to turn the Mac off, wait a few moments, then turn it back on.

If you get a beep when you try to click on something, or when you try to pull down a menu, it means you cannot do those things in the current situation. Most likely, there is a dialog box on the screen, and you have to click one of the buttons in it before you can do anything else.

Double-Clicking Doesn't Work

When you try to open something by double-clicking it, either nothing happens, or the thing just moves over a bit and doesn't open. The problem is that you moved the mouse a smidgen between the two clicks. Make sure you press down on the sides of the mouse with your thumb and other fingers as you tap lightly on the button with your index finger. Don't worry if you have some trouble double-clicking on your first few tries; it takes a little practice.

Stuff Hanging around the Trash

Icons of documents or folders that you have dragged to the Trash don't disappear (see Figure 2.10). Instead, they loiter around it like teenagers around a street corner. It's because you didn't drag them all the way to the Trash. Just drag each icon over the Trash until the Trash can is highlighted, then release the mouse button.

Figure 2.10
Stuff near the Trash can

Can't Empty Trash Because Item Is Locked or in Use

You try to empty the Trash and you get an alert box that tells you such and so an item can't be deleted because it contains items that are locked or in use.

If you can't figure out why an "in use" item is stuck in the Trash, save your latest work and quit all applications that are running. If that doesn't work, you may have to restart the Mac to delete the item; the system software still has a hold on it.

If you can't empty a Trash file because it is locked, try holding down the Option key while you choose Empty Trash from the Special menu. If that doesn't delete the file, take it out of the Trash and choose Get Info from the File menu. Click the locked check box to remove the X and unlock the file, then close the Information window, put the file back in the Trash, and empty it. If that doesn't work, restart the Mac and try again.

The Mouse Is Squeaky and Moves Erratically

If the mouse moves unevenly or squeaks at you (poor thing), or if the pointer doesn't move smoothly when you move the mouse, first shut down and turn off the computer. Then make sure that the mouse cable is connected firmly to the keyboard and the keyboard cable is connected firmly to the socket on the back of the computer. If that doesn't help, use the following procedure to clean the mouse:

1. Turn the mouse upside down in your hand.
2. Use two fingertips to press the ring that covers the ball. Then turn the ring counterclockwise, so the U mark moves from L for Lock to O for Open.
3. Tip the mouse over and catch the ring and the ball when they fall out.
4. Use a new cotton swab dipped in alcohol to clean off any lumps or ridges of grime on the three little plastic wheels inside the mouse, where the ball rolls.
5. Clean the ball with a lint-free cloth. If it's a little black ball, rather than a slightly bigger and heavier gray ball, get it super clean. Also, make sure your mouse pad or desk surface is clean all the time; quick, light mice are vulnerable to dust on the ball.
6. Ease the ball back into the mouse and replace the ring that holds it, starting with the U mark pointing at the O and turning it clockwise until it clicks into place, pointing at the L.

If you have lots of trouble with your mouse, get a good mouse pad for it. Different mice scurry better on different pads, so ask the dealer who sold you the mouse which pad is best. If a good pad doesn't help, try a different mouse, or maybe even a trackball. I don't like trackballs, but some people find them much easier to use.

Typing Does Not Enter Letters on the Screen

You may be in a situation that doesn't allow typing, or your keyboard may be disconnected or not working. Make sure you are in the window of an application that allows text, or in the text box of a dialog box. Click with the mouse pointer in the application's window or the dialog box's text box. If you are in a situation that allows entering text but the keyboard does not do it, shut down and turn off your Mac and make sure the keyboard cable is firmly connected to the socket on the back of the computer. Try cleaning it as described in the next section. If that does not help, see your dealer to find out if the keyboard or your computer needs repairs.

The Keyboard Isn't Working Right

If nothing happens when you do things with both the keyboard and the mouse, turn off the Mac and make sure the cables are plugged in all the way. If you have trouble with a certain key sticking or not making its letter appear on the screen, try cleaning the keyboard. Turn off the Mac and then unplug the keyboard and mouse. Turn the keyboard upside down and blow up in between the keys; clear the saliva out of your mouth so you don't spray moisture up in the works. Shake the keyboard up and down gently between breaths. If that doesn't help, or if you got something wet or sticky in the keyboard, like spilled root beer or peanut butter, you have to take the thing to a qualified repair shop.

The Screen Is Frozen, or You Are Stuck in a Bomb Alert Box

Either the screen is frozen so neither typing nor moving the mouse has any effect, or there is a bomb alert box on the screen and nothing is working. People call this being "hung," as in "hung up." Sometimes it's more dramatic; if the software has really crashed, you might see bizarre patterns of dots and lines rippling across the screen. Sometimes you even hear dreadful dut-dut-dut noises as the Mac gags on screwed-up code. But much more often, you just see an alert box like the one in Figure 2.11.

The first thing to do is keep calm. Don't let the icon mislead you; there isn't a little bomb that will go off inside the Mac unless you do something real

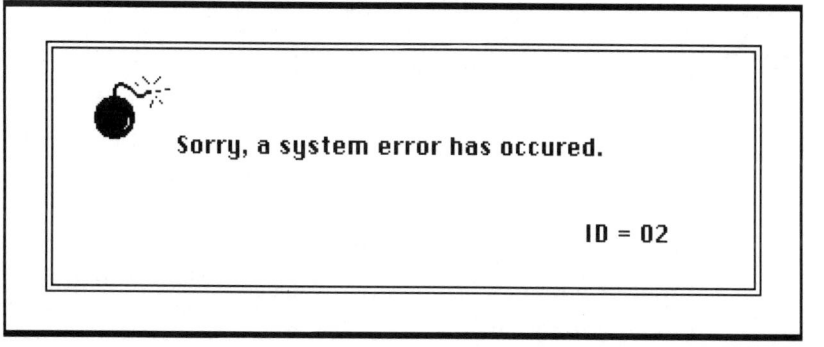

Figure 2.11
A Bomb alert box

quick. So keep cool; take a moment to gather a little information about what has happened. Try to recall the actions you took leading up to the error. Jot them down on a piece of paper. If an error message or a bomb alert box is on the screen, write down the message and the ID number if there is one. The message is usually a little more informative than the one in Figure 2.11 (by the way, system error 02 is an address error; usually caused by a bug in your application software).

Look for other screen clues as to what has gone wrong. If there is text left on the screen that you typed in, but didn't save, write it down on paper so you can reenter it later. If you work on a network or in an office with other Macintosh users, ask them to look at your screen and see if they are familiar with the problem. If you have to attack the problem on your own, try the following suggestions, starting with the ones that apply most clearly to your situation:

- Start afresh, if possible. If you are stuck in an application, try pressing Command-Option-Esc to quit the application you were using (press and hold down the Command and Option keys, then press Esc). If this works, save any documents you were working on with other applications, then restart the computer. If the screen is no longer frozen and you are in the Finder, choose Restart from the Special menu. If you are stuck in a bomb message box, click the Restart button. If that does not work, press the Reset button on the left side, right side, or front or right rear corner of your Mac (there are two buttons; the Reset button is closer to the or top). If you don't have a Reset button, such as on an LC, hold down the Command key and the Ctrl key, then press the big left-arrow key at the top of the keyboard.

- If the computer fails to restart, try again, using a floppy disk with a System Folder on it as your startup disk. If this works, reinstall the system software on your hard disk as explained in Chapter 1.

- If you have an external hard disk or a printer connected to your Mac and there is any chance that the peripheral device is causing your problem, turn it off for a minute or so, then turn it back on and restart your Macintosh.

- If you are not sure what the exact problem is, think of all the possible causes you can, focusing on what actions you took recently. Then try fixing the possible causes one at a time, beginning with the easiest possibility and working up to the hardest one. For example, if the printer isn't working, try adding paper and turning the printer off and on before you try to figure out how to install a new printer driver. If you just added a new control panel (a program that lets you adjust a Mac feature, such as sound) or extension (a program that expands the Mac's system software capabilities), remove it.

- Still no luck? You may need outside help.

Before you call Apple or your software manufacturer's support department, do a little preparatory work. Narrow down the problem as much as you can. Get out your product registration number so you can tell it to the support people and jot down the version of the System and Finder on your Mac. Then find out how much memory you have allocated to the disk cache and your applications (see Chapter 7) and determine the version of your problematic software. Also, jot down a list of the special customizing files (control panels, extensions, INITs or cdevs) on your computer; these are often the source of problems when they aren't compatible with each other, the system software, or your applications.

Icon Lost on Desktop behind Another Icon

You have a lot of icons on your desktop and one is lost behind one of the others. To find it without going around and moving all the others, just click in the window's open space and choose Clean Up Window. The icons will all sort out and you'll see your lost one.

Window Lost under Many Others

You let your desktop get all cluttered, and now you can't find a window because it is buried by others you opened later. The best solution is to press the Option key and click a close box in any window. All the windows close. Then start opening things in the hard disk window. It may be quicker to change to a list view of an upper level window, then just open the lists for the folders to work your way down to your lost folder. When you get to the folder you want, double-click it to open its window.

Three

Printing

• • • • • • • • • • • • • • • • • • •

Featuring

- ◆ Picking the right printer for your needs
- ◆ Using the Chooser to set up your printer
- ◆ Caring for a StyleWriter II, DeskWriter, LaserWriter, or ImageWriter
- ◆ Printing a document
- ◆ Background printing with the PrintMonitor
- ◆ Special printing setups in the Page Setup dialog box
- ◆ Printing what's in a window or a snapshot of what's on the screen
- ◆ Choosing and using fonts
- ◆ Using special accented characters
- ◆ Troubleshooting printing and fonts problems

First Steps

To set up printing in the Chooser: 59

Make sure your printer is plugged in, connected to your Mac correctly, and turned on. Turn on your Mac and select Chooser from the Apple menu. In the Chooser window, select the icon for the type of printer you intend to use, then choose the port (socket) the printer is connected to, or the name of your printer, depending on which of these appears on the right side of the window.

To make sure your printer is ready to print: 61

Make sure your printer is plugged in, connected to your Mac, and turned on. Check to make sure there is paper in the cassette or carrier, and make sure it is aligned and stacked properly. If the print quality is poor, you should check and replace the ink or toner cartridge.

To prevent start pages from appearing every time you turn on your LaserWriter: 65

Open the LaserWriter Font Utility; if you don't have it on your hard disk, open it on the Tidbits 2 floppy disk you got with your system software. Once you have clicked OK to get past the welcome dialog box, choose Start Page Options from the Utilities menu. Then click the Off button to turn off the start page option.

CHAPTER 3

To print a document you are currently working on: 66

Choose Print from your application's File menu, or (in most applications) press ⌘-P. Then you can make settings for how many copies you want to print, or if you don't want to print the whole document, how many pages of it you want to print. There are other settings, but you rarely need to change them. Just click the Print button or press Return, and printing begins.

To print a snapshot of what is on the Mac screen: 70

Press ⌘-Shift-3; a file called Picture 1 appears in the window of your hard drive. You can open Picture 1 in Teach-Text or any graphics application that can read PICT format files. Then just choose Print from the File menu to print the snapshot.

To install a font on your Mac: 75

Quit all open applications first; then open the windows for your hard disk and the floppy disk that has the font you want. If the font is in a folder and/or a suitcase, open them so you can see the icon for the actual font. Then drag the font icon to the System Folder on your hard disk, and click OK in the dialog box that asks if you want to put the font in the Fonts folder.

Printing is making copies of your work on paper. Paper copies are called *hard copies*. Printing out copies of your work is a vast improvement over typing documents on a typewriter, or writing out budgets on accounting paper, or making freehand drawings, because you can revise your work easily and make it look any way you want. If you print out a copy, then discover that it isn't quite right, you can change either its contents or its appearance, and print out a new copy. No fuss, no muss, no white-out or retyping.

One thing you need to remember about the ease and speed of computer printing: It uses up paper. To save paper and the trees that are cut down to make it, you should proofread and edit documents carefully on the Mac before you print them. If you find that you still create piles of first-draft hard copies that you don't want to use, recycle them; you can use the back sides for other rough drafts, and when you have used both sides, you can take the used paper to a recycling center.

Which Printer for You?

Printers can cost a lot of money, but you don't necessarily have to buy a top-of-the-line laser printer to produce acceptable hard copies. Just buy a printer that prints what you need to print, at a rate and a price that you can live with. If you don't have extensive printing needs now, but plan to increase your use of the printer, buy one that will meet your foreseeable needs.

The following paragraphs describe the types of printers available for the Mac and list their strengths and weaknesses. The specific printers covered are not the only ones on the market, and new printers appear all the time. Take the recommendations as guidelines, and find the printer that works best for you. I tend to favor Apple printers because they have such a great reputation for reliability, and because they are sure to work with the Mac system software, even if it changes significantly. Other printers may work fine today, but not so well with future versions of the system software.

Ink-Jet Printers

If you only need to print short documents with either standard text formats and fonts or standard graphic formats such as black-and-white MacPaint or PICT, you can use an ink-jet printer such as Apple's StyleWriter II or the

DeskWriter, made by Hewlett-Packard. Ink-jet printers aren't as fast as laser printers, and their output isn't quite as lovely, but they are cheap and reliable. They are easy to use and care for, too.

Ink-jet printers make images by spraying ultra-fine streams of ink onto the paper. They are relatively quiet and fast, in comparison to the ImageWriter and other dot-matrix printers that were once the low-budget printers of choice for Macs. The StyleWriter II is more portable than the DeskWriter and prints some types of images more clearly, including those with shades of gray. However, grayscale printing is slow on the StyleWriter II, and the DeskWriter can print some black-and-white documents a little faster, too. Still, the performance differences between the two printers are slight. I like the StyleWriter II a little better because it is so simple in design and function. But if you have used other computer printers, you may find the DeskWriter more familiar. In addition to the StyleWriter II and DeskWriter, there are other ink-jet printers that can print more fonts and some that print in color. But the StyleWriter II and DeskWriter are probably the best-known and most reliable choices.

Product at a Glance

StyleWriter II

Manufacturer:
Apple Computer, Inc.

System Specifications:
Resolution: 360 dots per inch
Speed: 2 pages per minute
Fonts: 15 TrueType

Description:
The StyleWriter II is a small, reliable printer for standard text and simple graphics purposes. It is not fast enough for high-production office printing needs, and it cannot produce photograph-quality grayscale output, but for many users, it is adequate, and its price is lower than almost all other printers.

Laser Printers

If you need to print lots of complex documents with different text formats and fonts, or if you want to print desktop publications or graphics in PostScript format, buy a PostScript laser printer such as an Apple LaserWriter or a laser printer made by any of the other major printer manufacturers. These printers use photocopying "engines" to crank out your documents much more quickly than other printers can. Their output is clean and crisp, and they give you a wide range of font and format options. Laser printers are suitable for almost any task, from rendering complex graphics to quick printouts of simple memos.

All this flexibility comes at a high price, of course. Fortunately laser printers come in many models, from less expensive ones with no memory, slow engines, and only a few fonts, to expensive models with many megs of RAM, twenty-page-per-minute engines, and dozens of built-in fonts.

Product at a Glance

LaserJet IVM

Manufacturer:
Apple Computer, Inc.

System Specifications:
Resolution: 600 dots per inch
Speed: 8 pages per minute
Fonts: 35 PostScript, 10 TrueType

Description:
The LaserJet IVM is a workhorse printer, a good choice for a network serving a number of users who all need to print lots of pages. It is also very good at making photograph-quality grayscale prints at the relatively high resolution of 600 dpi.

Dot-Matrix Printers

If you need to print carbon copies of documents, or if you want to use fanfold (continuous-feed) paper for things like data printouts or labels, buy a dot-matrix printer like an ImageWriter II. The ImageWriter forms letters by impact on a type ribbon, like a typewriter, so it can be used on carbon-copy or multiple-layered business forms, unlike ink-jet and laser printers.

The ImageWriter is noisy and much slower than either a StyleWriter II or a LaserWriter, and it cannot produce text or images that are as sharp as those of the other printers. However, it is cheap and it prints well enough for many simple home and office needs.

Setting Up Printing in the Chooser

Before you can print out your first Macintosh document, you have to connect the printer and select it in the Chooser. First make sure your printer's cable is connected to the proper port on the back of the computer. Then make sure the printer is properly configured, supplied with paper, and turned on. Install the necessary printer software that is correct and up-to-date for your specific printer. If you need help with these printer preparations, check your printer's owner's guide (the LaserWriter and StyleWriter guides are particularly clear and helpful), then see the section on the care and feeding of your type of printer later in this chapter.

To begin the process of setting up your Mac for printing on a connected printer, you select the Chooser from the Apple menu (click on the apple at the left end of the menu bar, and select Chooser). The Chooser window opens. What you see in it depends on whether your Macintosh is connected directly to a printer or to a network with one or more printers on it. The following procedure applies to Macintoshes that are connected directly to printers. If you are on a network and see a box for choosing a zone in the Chooser, get help from the network administrator or the most experienced Mac user on the network.

If your Mac is connected directly to a printer, the Chooser window should look something like Figure 3.1. Your Chooser window may show different printer types, or only one type of printer. The AppleShare icon may not appear, either. That's fine, as long as the Chooser shows an icon for your type of printer. Take these steps to set up your computer for printing:

1. Select the printer icon for the type of printer you have. A choice of printer ports or a choice of printers appears in the box on the right side of the window; the printer port usually appears at

Figure 3.1
The Chooser window

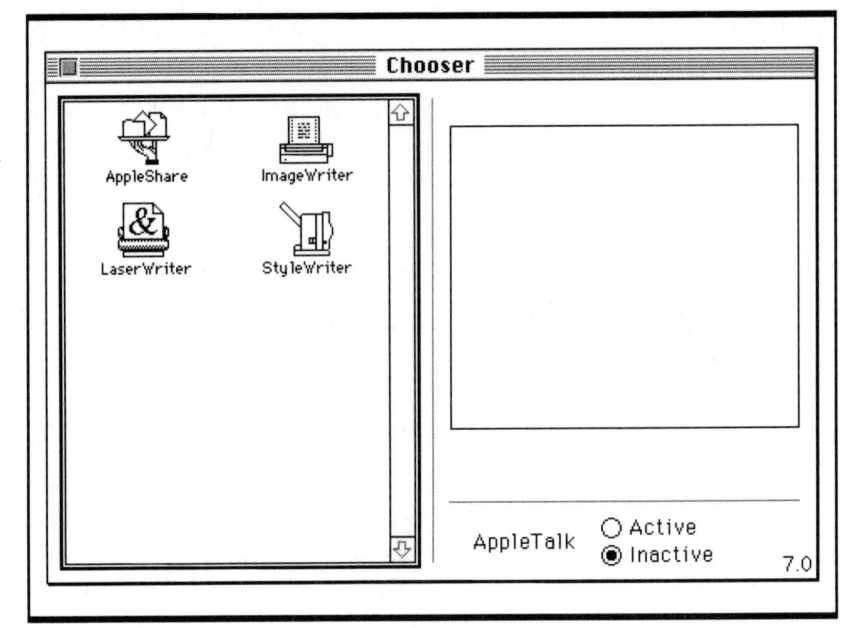

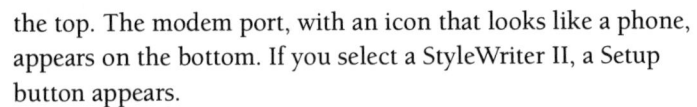

[Chooser window showing AppleShare, ImageWriter, LaserWriter, StyleWriter icons; AppleTalk Active/Inactive radio buttons; version 7.0]

the top. The modem port, with an icon that looks like a phone, appears on the bottom. If you select a StyleWriter II, a Setup button appears.

2. Select the port or printer that you connected your printer cable to. In most cases, this will be the printer port, although some printers may be connected to the modem port.

3. If your printer is an ImageWriter or StyleWriter, click the Inactive radio button for AppleTalk. If your printer is a LaserWriter or something compatible, it will be connected to your Mac via AppleTalk (LocalTalk or LocalTalk-compatible connectors). Click the Active button for AppleTalk so your Mac can talk to the printer over the cables. As soon as you make AppleTalk Active, buttons for Background Printing appear. Click the On button if you want to be able to keep working as your documents print on a LaserWriter.

4. Close the Chooser by clicking in the close box.

Note
The Chooser doesn't let you know when you have completed your choice of a printer; you just close the Chooser window and it goes away, without any confirming dialog box.

Chapter 3: Printing

Taking Care of Your Printer

Once you've purchased and set up a printer, you need to give it proper care to ensure that it lasts and that it performs at its best for you. The following sections tell how to care for some of the most common types of printers. If you have a different printer from the ones covered below, just use the information as a guideline and fill in any details you need with the help of your owner's guide.

Care and Feeding of a StyleWriter II

To turn on a StyleWriter II after plugging it in and connecting it to your Mac, you press the Power button, which is top-center on the front of the printer. When you press that button, the green Ready light under it glows, telling you that the printer is warming up; it stays on as long as the printer is ready to print.

Adding Paper

To add paper to the StyleWriter, first make sure the sheet feeder and paper support are firmly in place, sticking up from the back of the printer. Then load a stack of about 80 sheets of paper into the sheet feeder, making sure the stack is not higher than the point of the arrow on the left side-rail of the feeder panel. Also make sure the right edges of the sheets of paper are all lined up flush against the right side-rail of the feeder panel.

Changing the Ink Cartridge

To change the ink cartridge, you open the access door at the front of the printer: Pull the two half-round tabs that stick out near the top corners of the access door and flip the door down out of your way. Then pull the blue lever next to the ink cartridge up and pull the cartridge (the small, almost cube-shaped black plastic box) straight out towards you.

Carefully remove the head cap and the sealing tape from the business end of the new ink cartridge. Avoid touching those areas as you slip the new cartridge into place on the blue post inside the printer. The new cartridge sits a little slanted to one side until you flip the blue lever down; that makes it click into a vertical position. Close the access door firmly, and you're ready to print. You can run a test page or two to make sure the ink is working right.

Care and Feeding of a DeskWriter

To turn a DeskWriter on after you plug it in and attach the connector to your Mac, reach under the front left corner of the printer and flip the power switch to On. If you haven't run the printer for some time, it's a good idea to press the Prime button; this runs a tiny bit of ink out of the jets so the ink cartridge gets cleaned out and ready to print.

Adding Paper

To add paper, you simply pull out the drawer at the front of the printer and slide a block of paper in. Try to arrange the stack so the edges of the sheets are lined up; this keeps paper jams to a minimum.

Changing the Ink Cartridge

To change the ink cartridge on a DeskWriter, you just open the plastic cover at the front of the printer, then pull the cartridge (the little black box with the green arrow on top) toward the front of the printer and up. Remove the cover from a new cartridge and push it in firmly where the old one came out. Push the Prime button once or twice to get the jets running, and you're ready to print. If you want to save some money on ink cartridges and are willing to do a little ink-injection, you can learn to reload an old cartridge and reuse it. Although it seems like a good idea for the environment and your pocketbook, it is not a simple process, and you may not be able to get ink that's as good as the original. See *The Macintosh Bible* or talk to your local Mac user's group for more info.

Care and Feeding of a LaserWriter

LaserWriter printers are easy to use and care for. You can turn on your LaserWriter, add paper to the paper cassette, and even change the toner cartridge without any help from a printer expert. You can also complete the simple cleaning procedure that is the only maintenance a LaserWriter normally needs. Many other laser printers such as the Hewlett-Packard LaserJet are quite similar in design and as easy to operate and care for; just see the owner's guide for details about the care and feeding of your particular laser printer.

To turn on your LaserWriter after plugging it in and connecting the cable to your Mac, you reach around to the back and click the power switch; it is usually near the lower left corner as you face the back of the printer. The LaserWriter hums up to speed, and in a moment you hear the engine take a test run. If you haven't turned off the test sheet option as explained under "Turning Off Start Pages" later in this section, the printer spits out a test page to prove that it's ready to go to work.

Adding Paper

To add paper to the paper drawer or *cassette*, all you have to do is reach under the front of the printer and pull the drawer out, just like pulling out a desk drawer, except that you pull it all the way out. If the drawer has a plastic cover, take it off.

Get a block of paper (the number of sheets depends on your printer) and clunk the edges on your tabletop so all the sheets line up in a nice smooth stack. Then hold one end of the block in your right hand and slide the other end of the stack down into the back end of the drawer, under the two retainer tabs that stick out towards you. The block of paper will slide down in there easily if you push the little wall spring on the side of the drawer back with your left thumb. Push the front corners of the block of paper down gently, past the metal corner brackets. On most LaserWriters' paper cassettes, there are pictures that show you how to slide the paper in.

Check to make sure the stack of paper isn't taller than the dotted line with an arrow that is on the side of the drawer. If the stack is too tall, take some sheets out. If the front end of the stack is uneven, tip the back end of the drawer up and jiggle the drawer until all of the sheets' edges are in line—this will keep the paper from jamming. Put the lid back on the drawer if there is a lid, then slide the drawer back into the printer all the way. When it's in there right, the yellow paper-out light goes off and the green ready-to-print light goes on. That's all there is to it.

Changing and Testing the Toner Cartridge

To change the toner cartridge, turn the printer off, then pull up the cover release lever or press the cover release button and open the access door to the LaserWriter. On the NT and LS, the front opens; on others the top lifts up. If there is a little plastic flap on a spring at the top of the cartridge, hold it firmly with your thumb and fingers, then gently pull the cartridge up and out of the printer. If there is no little flap on your toner cartridge, just grip the body of the cartridge and slide it out and up.

Put the used cartridge down on a piece of newspaper. Remove the new cartridge from its package and pull the tape tab so the plastic tape slides all the way out of the cartridge and breaks off. Throw that messy tape thing away. Rock the new cartridge end-to-end in order to spread the toner around inside there (some models need to be rocked fore-and-aft).

Then hold on to the plastic tab on the top of the new cartridge and slip the cartridge into the same place the old one came out of. Most cartridges have little pictures on top of them that make it all very clear. When the new cartridge is in place, close the cover of the printer. Then wrap up the used cartridge in the new one's wrapper and contact a local cartridge recycler. You can usually locate one through a business supply store or your local Mac user group. Recycling cartridges saves money as well as natural resources.

To run a cartridge through its paces and see that it's working OK, do the following:

1. Find the document called Cleaning Page (it's on the Installation Disk you got with your LaserWriter) and select it in the Finder.
2. Choose Print from the Finder's File menu. The printer puts out a test page with a broad diagonal black line across it.
3. Set your printer up for manual feeding of paper, then put the test sheet into the manual feed slot, face up so the printer can write on the back side of it.
4. Select the Cleaning Page document and choose Print from the Finder's File menu again. This time, click the Manual Feed button in the Print dialog box. Your test page disappears into the

printer and comes out with the big diagonal line across the back side of the paper.

5. Check the quality of the black on the back-side diagonal line. It should be evenly dark throughout. If there are bands of faded gray or thin lines of white, it's time to replace the cartridge.

Turning Off Start Pages

If you are using a LaserWriter and do not want the start page (the test page with the LaserWriter letterhead) to spit out every time your printer starts up, here is a way to turn off start pages:

1. Find the LaserWriter Font Utility. If you don't have it on your hard disk, you can find it on the Tidbits disks you received with your system software.
2. Make sure your printer is connected to your Mac, turned on, and chosen in the Chooser. Then double-click on the LaserWriter Font Utility icon to open it. A dialog box tells you what the utility can do with fonts.
3. Click OK in the Font Utility dialog box. It goes away and a message box tells you that the utility is checking the characteristics of your printer. Then a new menu for the utility appears.
4. Choose Start Page Options from the Utilities menu. A small dialog box displays On and Off buttons for the printer start page.
5. Click the Off button and the OK button. The box goes away after the command has been sent to your printer.
6. Quit the Font Utility.

The start pages will no longer come out of the LaserWriter every time you start it up. If you need to see a start page, just follow the procedure above and click the On button in the Start Page dialog box.

Care and Feeding of an ImageWriter

To turn the ImageWriter on after plugging it in and connecting the cables to your Mac, you press the Power button on the right part of the printer's lid, then press the Select button.

Adding Paper

To insert the first page of the paper roll, you pull off the vented cover at the top of the printer, then pull up the flaps that cover the tractor-feed poles. Place the first perforations on the paper over the poles. If the paper doesn't lie flat, adjust the width of the tractor-feed poles: Pull up the little black lever behind the right set of poles, then move those poles to match the distance between the perforations at the edges of the paper.

Changing the Ribbon

To change the ink ribbon in an ImageWriter, you have to open the cover on the top of the printer (squeeze the sides in to release the latches). Then pull the little latch on the right side of the ribbon cartridge and tip the cartridge up and to the left to remove it. Put the new cartridge in place, making sure the ribbon passes behind the black plastic post. Press the cartridge down until the little latch clicks into place. Close the cover down and press it until it snaps into place, and you're ready to print again.

Printing a Single Sheet

If you need to print out something on a single sheet of paper, but don't want to remove and reengage the fanfold paper on the feeding pins, just back the paper up as far as it will go without coming off the pins. Do your manual feed of the single sheet. Then roll the fanfold paper back into the works again. If the fanfold paper is only engaged on the first pair of pins and none of the others, the ImageWriter doesn't know it's there.

Printing Documents

To get a hard copy of a document from a printer after you have connected it and set things up in the Chooser, you open the document with the application you used to create it, then choose Print from the File menu (or press ⌘-P; that is the keyboard shortcut in most applications). The Print dialog box opens. It will have different options depending on what type of printer you have and what application you are using. Some of the most common options for a LaserWriter are shown in Figure 3.2.

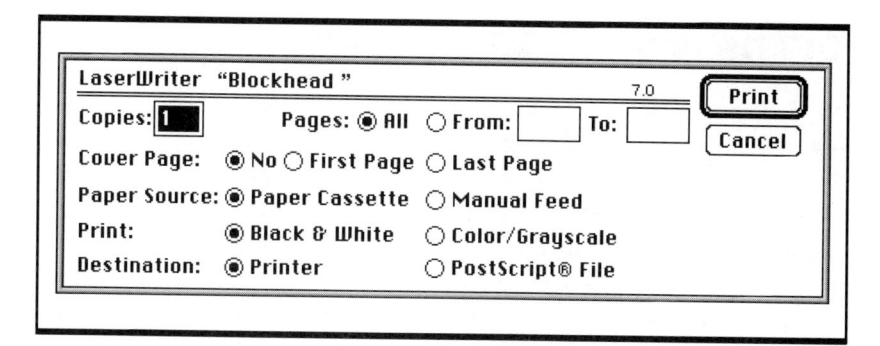

Figure 3.2
Print dialog box

```
LaserWriter  "Blockhead"                    7.0    [ Print  ]
Copies: [1]      Pages: ● All  ○ From: [  ] To: [  ]  [ Cancel ]
Cover Page:   ● No  ○ First Page  ○ Last Page
Paper Source: ● Paper Cassette  ○ Manual Feed
Print:          ● Black & White  ○ Color/Grayscale
Destination:    ● Printer        ○ PostScript® File
```

The default settings are usually the ones you want to use. You can, however, make the following changes to the LaserWriter settings for special print jobs:

- Copies: Set the number of copies of the document you want. Keep in mind that it is much cheaper and more energy-efficient to photocopy documents than to print multiple copies, as long as a photocopier is available.

- Pages: Enter numbers in the From and To boxes to print only a portion of the document. This is the most-used option in the dialog box. If you want to print the last few pages of a document, just enter the From page number and leave the To box blank.

- Cover Page: Click the First or Last Page button to add a cover page to the beginning or end of your print job. This lets others using the printer see whose it is and what it is.

- Paper Source: Click the Manual Feed button if your paper cassette or fanfold paper-feeding mechanism is broken, or if you want to feed nonstandard paper or an envelope into the printer.

- Print: Select Color/Grayscale only if you have a color printer.

- Destination: Click the PostScript File button to make a PostScript format file on your current disk rather than a hard copy. Be aware that this process can take *much* longer than printing.

When you have made your choices, click the Print button. Message boxes tell you how printing is going.

Using the PrintMonitor

If you are printing to a LaserWriter or StyleWriter II over an AppleTalk cable and you have the PrintMonitor extension in your System Folder, you can continue work while printing is going on in the background. If you don't have the PrintMonitor in the Extensions folder in your System Folder, you can drag its icon there from the Printing disk. This disk is included with the system software disks you received with your Macintosh. Make sure you have turned on Background Printing in the Chooser so the PrintMonitor is ready to work. Then, when you send a document to the printer, choose Print-Monitor from the Applications menu (that's the menu under the little application icon in the upper right corner of your screen) to see the status of your printing job, as shown in Figure 3.3. If there are other jobs being printed, yours appears in a waiting list.

Figure 3.3
The PrintMonitor window

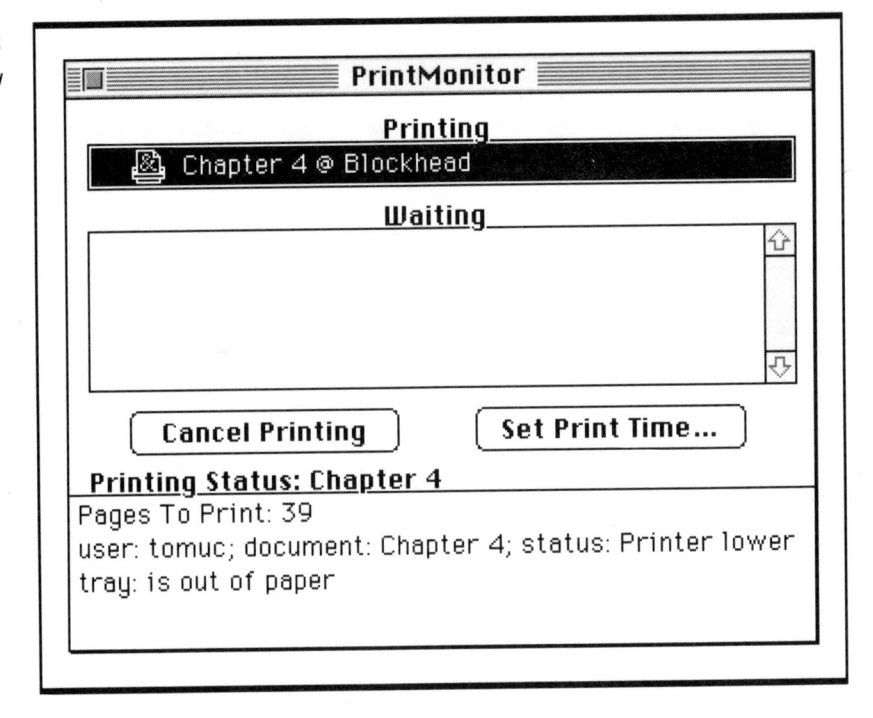

Chapter 3: Printing

You can click buttons to cancel your printing job or set a time for it to print later. When your job is finished, the PrintMonitor quits automatically. If you no longer see the PrintMonitor listed in the Applications menu, you can assume that your job is finished. If the printer cannot finish your job due to printing problems, such as running out of paper, the PrintMonitor icon flashes at the right end of the menu bar.

One odd quirk about the Print Monitor is that you don't have to close its window. When the print job finishes, the PrintMonitor disappears from the Applications menu, all by itself. This can be a bit confusing if you are looking at the window, see your job finish, then try to close the window; the PrintMonitor menu refuses to go away until you switch to another application.

Note

The DeskWriter and other popular printers have utilities like the Print-Monitor that put printing in the background. These utilities work much the same way, but you should see your printer's user manual for details.

Using Page Setup for Special Printing Needs

If you use the Chooser to change to a different printer while you are running an application, you must choose Page Setup from the File menu before you try to print documents again. When the dialog box shown in Figure 3.4 appears, just click OK and you can print on the newly chosen printer.

You can also use the Page Setup dialog box to achieve a number of special printing options. The options vary depending on your printer. For example, if your Mac is connected to a LaserWriter printer, you see a dialog box like the one in Figure 3.4. You can make the following settings for a LaserWriter:

- Paper: Choose paper sizes and business envelope settings. The choices are these: US Letter (8.5" × 11"), US Legal (8.5" × 14"), A4 Letter (8.5" × 11.7"), B5 Letter (7" × 10"), Tabloid (11" × 17"), A3 Tabloid (11.7" × 16.5"), and two envelope choices.

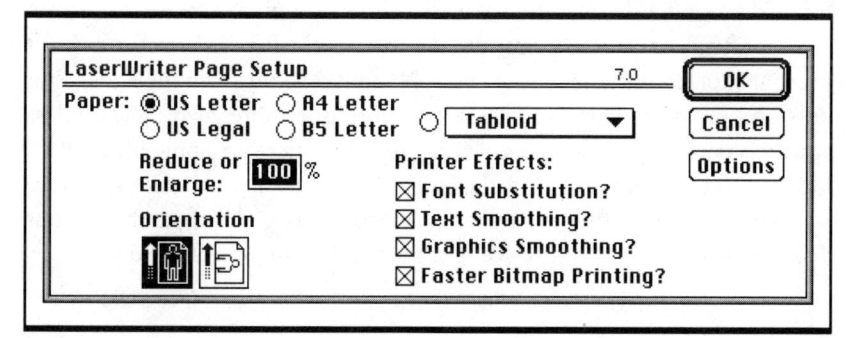

Figure 3.4
The Page Setup dialog box

- Reduce or Enlarge: Change the size of the printed output.
- Orientation: Change to horizontal printing for spreadsheets and other wide images.
- Printer Effects: Turn enhancements on or off for special effects or speed.
- Options: Click this button for image enhancement features, such as flipping, inverting, and precision-smoothing.

For more information on these options, choose Page Setup from the File menu in the Finder, then turn on balloon help and point at the options you want to know more about.

Printing a Window in the Finder

When you are in the Finder you can print the contents of the active window by choosing Print Window from the File menu. The Print dialog box opens. Click the Print button and the total contents of the window (including items in scrollable lists that aren't showing at the time) will be printed out by the current printer. This is a good way to make a hard copy of a long list of folders and files, so you can look at the list all at once rather than scrolling up and down it in a window. Just keep in mind that a very long list (like one that shows every item on your hard disk) can take quite a while to print out.

Printing a Snapshot of the Screen

If you'd like a hard copy of whatever is showing on your screen at a given moment, you can take a snapshot (screen dump) of it. Then you can print the snapshot. To start the process, press ⌘-Shift-3 (hold down the ⌘ and Shift keys and press 3). This Command-key shortcut requires two hands unless you are a concert pianist with long fingers. It produces a graphic file in PICT format, names it Picture 1, and places it on your current startup disk. Picture 1 is listed among the files and folders at the top level of the hierarchy on your disk; in other words, you can see it in the window for your hard disk.

To look at the snapshot, you must open Picture 1 with TeachText or any graphics application that can read PICT files. To print the snapshot, choose Print from the File menu of the application you are using to look at Picture 1. Click OK in the Print dialog box. (If you don't understand some of these details about files, folders, and graphic formats, don't worry. Files and folders are explained in Chapter 5, and graphic formats are explained in Appendix A.)

You can also copy a snapshot to another document. First select a portion of the snapshot in TeachText or your graphics application. Then choose Copy from the Edit menu to place the selection in the Clipboard. You can then paste the selection from the Clipboard into other documents. For more information on copying and pasting, see Chapter 15.

Using the Right Fonts for Your Printer

A font is a particular design of letters that are all used together to print text. In printing jargon, a font is just one set of characters (a typeface) in one size and style only. For example, Helvetica 18-point bold refers to Helvetica type that is 18 points in size (a point is approximately $1/72$ of an inch) and in the bold style. On the screen, it looks more or less like Figure 3.5.

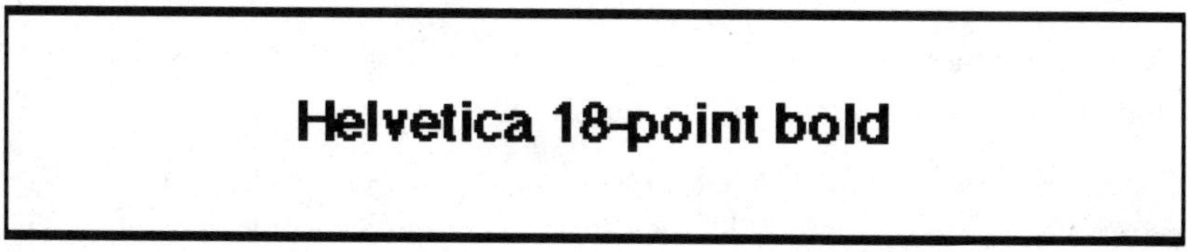

Helvetica 18-point bold

Figure 3.5
Helvetica 18-point bold

In the Macintosh environment, a font has come to mean all the different sizes and styles of a typeface: the name *Geneva* refers to bold, italic, and plain type of the Geneva typeface, in sizes from 9-point to 48-point or more. So all of the styles and sizes in Figure 3.6 are considered parts of the Geneva font.

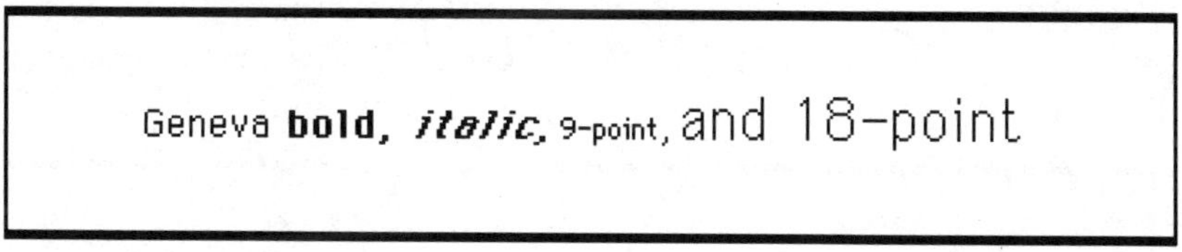

Geneva **bold,** *italic,* 9-point, and 18-point

Figure 3.6
Varieties of Geneva

Kinds of Fonts

Your Mac comes with a number of standard TrueType fonts. Among these are Courier, which looks like typewriter type, Times, which looks like the type in a magazine, and Helvetica, which is a sans serif font, meaning that it has no ornaments at the tips of the letters. Figure 3.7 shows an example of the difference between a serif font and a sans serif font.

Figure 3.7
A serif font and a sans serif font

> Times font, with easy-to-read serifs
>
> Helvetica, a legible sans serif

Sans serif fonts make good headlines and short call-outs that you want people to see from a distance and grasp quickly. They are also clear and legible on the Mac screen. Serif fonts are better for long stretches of printed text; most readers find them easier on the eyes. So you may well want to do your word processing work on the Mac using a sans serif font like Helvetica, then change all the text to a serif font like Times before you print it out for others to read.

Along with the three serif and san serif fonts, you get Symbol, which is included for scientific notation like that in Figure 3.8.

These basic fonts are adequate for most word processing and spreadsheet applications. If you use them fully, varying sizes and styles, you can create documents with a fine, professional appearance, even if you are not printing them out on a LaserWriter. For example, you can mix larger bold Helvetica headings with smaller plain Times text in a report or a resume. Fonts like Times

Figure 3.8
Symbol font

> ωH∀τ TλΣ Hεςκ?

Chapter 3: Printing

and Helvetica look fine when printed out on almost any printer. If you stick to these fonts, you will be able to print any document you create on almost any printer that can handle your application's output.

Your Mac may also have a number of other fonts installed. There may be *bit-mapped fonts*, which are good for screen viewing and printing on dot-matrix printers like the ImageWriter. At the other extreme, you may have purchased and installed publication-quality PostScript *outline fonts*. Outline fonts are composed of programmed instructions for drawing the precise outline of each letter, then filling it in. They are used typically on a PostScript printer like the LaserWriter, but they can also be used on the highest-quality commercial printers, such as the Linotronic.

If you venture out from TrueType fonts into the world of bit-mapped or PostScript outline fonts, you may be able to create documents with more variety of appearance, but remember that many special fonts may look good when printed on one kind of printer but awkward or even illegible when printed

Which Category of Font Is That?

If you want to know what fonts you have in each of the different categories, just open your System Folder, then open the Fonts folder. In it you may see font files and/or suitcases containing fonts. If you open a suitcase you'll see the font file icons inside it. Use icon view (choose by Icon from the View menu) to see the different icons for different categories of fonts. A bit-mapped font always has just a single letter *A* in the icon, and a size number after the name of the font, like 10, 12, or 18. A TrueType font has a large letter *A* with a couple of smaller shadows receding behind it, to indicate that the font has all sizes. There is no size number after the name. Outline fonts, such as PostScript ones, can have all kinds of icons. Adobe PostScript fonts have horizontal lines behind a white letter *A*, for example. Others have printer-like icons. But they never have size numbers after the name, whatever the icons look like.

by other printers. Some may look strange on your screen, too. For example, if you use bit-mapped fonts with city names, such as New York, Geneva, or Monaco, they print out quite nicely on dot-matrix printers such as the ImageWriter. Each bit in the bit map is assigned to a dot in the dot-matrix printout. These same fonts will not look good at all if you print them out on a LaserWriter that does not have the exact bit map for the font, size, and style you are using. The LaserWriter has to make up a bit-map estimation of what the font should look like, and it often comes out with jagged edges and weird lumps.

On the other hand, some high-quality PostScript outline fonts that make beautiful 24-point letters on a LaserWriter produce jagged gibberish on non-PostScript printers. They may look bad on your screen, too, unless you use a type-management utility such as Adobe Type Manager. ATM, as it is fondly called by font-folks, can be obtained almost for free with a coupon that you get when you purchase system software of version 7.1 or later. ATM allows you to use a vast selection of fonts, because it can either convert PostScript outline fonts to TrueType (which is really just another type of outline font) or adapt outline fonts to bit-mapped ones, so they look as clean as possible on your screen and in printouts on some non-PostScript printers. However, if your computer does not have much memory, if its CPU is slow, or if your printer doesn't have any memory, the printing process may become extremely slow, and you can even get weird, gratuitous changes of font in the middle of a print job.

You must also keep in mind, when you are working with converted or adapted fonts, that they change the spacing that you had with the original font, so that the line and page breaks in a document often change. For example, if you have been using a PostScript outline Times font and you begin using TrueType Times, the lines and pages will not always break the same. If you experiment with different fonts of varying quality, you can have difficulty finding a printer that will print all of the different fonts well. With that in mind, make the best possible use of the fonts you have, and add fonts to the Fonts folder in your System file judiciously, keeping to well-known outline fonts if possible. If your printer prints TrueType well, and your Mac has a bunch of nice TrueType fonts, use them. If you have a PostScript printer with a bunch of nice PostScript outline fonts in its memory, get ATM and the same bunch of nice PostScript outline fonts for your Mac, and stick with them. If you *must* change fonts often, obtain a font-juggling utility such as Suitcase or MasterJuggler from a software vendor to keep them all straight.

Installing Fonts

To install a font onto your Mac from a floppy disk, use the following procedure if your Mac is running on system software version 7.1 or later:

1. Quit all applications and exit to the Finder. Pull down the Applications menu to make sure you have left no applications open.
2. Open the window for your hard disk and the window for the floppy disk that contains the new font.
3. Drag the font icon to the System Folder on your hard disk. Do not open the System Folder window and drag the font into the window. A dialog box asks if the font should be placed in the Fonts folder.
4. Click the OK button in the dialog box.

If you are installing a bit-mapped font, you need to drag all available sizes of the font to the System Folder. You only need to drag one icon for an outline font to the System Folder, because the font is scalable or variable-size; one size stretches to fit all, in other words.

Warning

Moving fonts in and out of the System Folder is not so simple if your Mac is running on an earlier version of the system software. If you want to do lots of font-intensive work, update your system software to version 7.1, or get help from a real ace in font management.

Removing Fonts

To get rid of a font that you no longer use or that has been replaced by a new font of the same name, use the following procedure:

1. Open the System Folder on your hard disk.
2. Find and double-click the Fonts folder.
3. Locate the font you want to remove and drag the icon out of the Fonts folder window. You can copy the font to a floppy disk or throw it in the Trash. Do not leave the font in the System Folder outside the Fonts folder.

If you have removed a set of PostScript outline fonts from your System file so that your Mac and printer will use the TrueType font of the same name, you may have to adjust the format of documents that were created using the PostScript outline fonts to keep the line and page breaks where you want them. If you have both TrueType and PostScript fonts of the same name on your Mac, it will use the PostScript fonts first.

Using the Right Fonts for Your Printer

Using Key Caps to Compare Fonts

If you are considering a change in font, you can use the Key Caps desk accessory get an idea of what a new font will look like before you put it in your document. The KeyFinder in the Norton Utilities is similar and even easier to use. Either desk accessory will be especially useful if you are using TrueType fonts, or if your fonts have been adapted by a type-managing program to look their best on your screen. The TrueType and adapted fonts you see in Key Caps closely resemble the fonts as they appear on the printed page. Bit-mapped fonts may not look the same on the screen as they do in print.

To see how a font looks before you use it, follow this procedure:

1. Choose Key Caps from the Apple menu. The keyboard window appears, as shown in Figure 3.9.
2. Choose a font from the Key Caps menu. The fonts listed are those installed in your System file.
3. Type characters or click on them in the keyboard window. They appear in the text box at the top of the window.
4. Press the Shift key, the Option key, and the Option and Shift key together to see all the special characters that are available with a font. If a rectangle appears in the place of a key cap, it means that there is no character for that keystroke.

If you find a special character or a font that suits your needs, do a test printing to make sure it comes out looking the way you want before you create a large

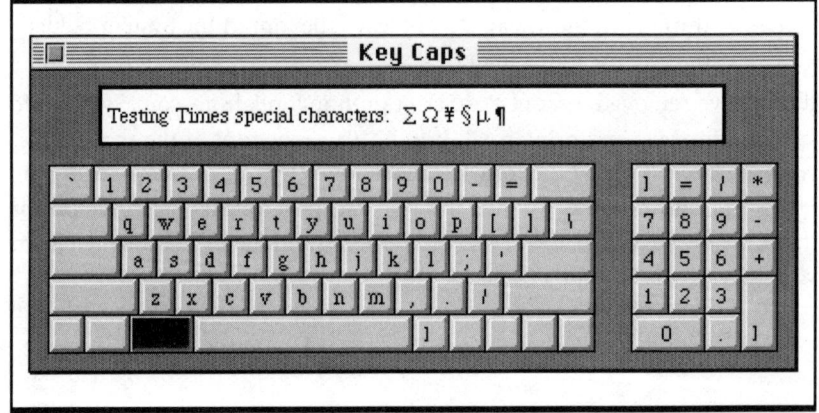

Figure 3.9
Looking at a font in the Key Caps window

document using it. There are often slight differences between the way characters appear on the screen and the way they print out, and there are often variations of the printed characters between different printers. You have to experiment to find the best combination for your work.

Using Accented Characters

No matter which font you use, you may have trouble creating certain characters that are used in languages other than English. These include accents, tildes, and other special marks that appear over standard characters. To use accents and other special marks when you are using a Domestic U.S. Keyboard file, enter the following keystrokes:

Accent Mark	Key Combination
Grave accent (`)	Option-`, then the accented character
Acute accent (é)	Option-e, then the accented character
Circumflex (^)	Option-i, then the accented character
Tilde (~)	Option-n, then the accented character
Umlaut (ü)	Option-u, then the accented character
Cedilla (ç)	Option-c

If you type an accent with a character that does not accept it, the accent mark appears, then the character appears in the next space.

Troubleshooting Printing

The following sections describe solutions to the problems that can occur when you are trying to print out documents from within Macintosh applications or from the Finder.

Your Printer's Icon Does Not Appear in the Chooser

When you open the Chooser to set up printing to your printer for the first time, the printer's icon is not in the left panel of the Chooser window. You probably have not installed the printer software you need for your printer. Make sure you have the latest version of the printer software (the printer driver, as it is called) and that you have installed it correctly, either by using the system software installer, or by dragging the icon of the printer software to the closed System Folder on your hard disk.

Your Mac Refuses to Talk to the Printer

You have chosen the icon of your printer in the Chooser, but either the name of the printer doesn't appear (if it's a networked printer), or nothing prints and you see a message box telling you that there is no printer or the printer could not be found. Either the printer is off or unplugged, or it is not ready to print (on a StyleWriter, the Ready light is off; on an ImageWriter, the Select button is off).

Fix the plugs, turn the printer on, and press the Select or Ready button. If the printer is on, it may be hung; turn it off and back on again. If the printer is on a network, make sure the network is functioning, and check to make sure nobody has changed the name of the printer. If none of those efforts help, contact a qualified technician.

Jagged Text

You wrote some great text and converted it to a font that looks fine on the screen, but when you print it out, it is all ugly and jagged around the edges. Here are the most common causes and their solutions:

- You are using a city-name (bit-mapped) font and printing on a LaserWriter, and you do not have the bit map for that particular font in your System Folder. Change the font, or install the bit-mapped font for the one you want.

- You do not have Font Smoothing and/or Font Substitution selected in the Page Setup dialog box for the application you are using. Select them.

- You are using an ImageWriter or StyleWriter and you haven't selected Best Quality in the Print dialog box. Select it.

- You are using PostScript outline fonts on a non-PostScript printer, and you aren't using Adobe Type Manager, or you haven't turned it on in its control panel. Install ATM and turn it on.

Right-Justified Paragraphs Have Ragged Right Margins

You are getting varied spacing with the font you are using. If your application has a fractional-width spacing option in the Page Setup dialog box, select it. If the application does not support fractional-width spacing, you have to install all of the bit-mapped font sizes you are using.

Characters Overlap on ImageWriter Printouts

When you print out documents to an ImageWriter, the characters are too close to each other, and some overlap others. You must choose Page Setup from the File menu in the application you are printing from, and deselect the Fractional Widths option. You may also have to choose the Tall Adjusted option in the Print dialog boxes if the character spacing still comes out uneven.

You Can't Remember the Keystroke for a Special Character in Your Current Font

If you need to enter a special character, like a *u* with an umlaut, or a little heart, or some mathematical symbol, and you can't remember which key does the trick, you can use Key Caps for a reminder. Just choose Key Caps from the Apple Menu (or KeyFinder, if you have Norton Utilities). If you want to keep referring back to Key Caps for different special characters, move the Key Caps window down to the bottom of your screen, then use the size box in your application window to resize the window, so you can see the Key Caps window under there. If any other windows are open, you have to resize or close them to get them out of the way.

Text Switches to Geneva Font for No Apparent Reason

This is a spooky problem. You are working along, not thinking about fonts at all, and you either print a large document out, or do some memory-intensive process like a big spell-check or a repagination, and suddenly, your text starts converting from whatever font you chose to Geneva font.

The problem is that the Mac has run out of memory, so it can't use the outline font you chose. You have to free up some memory for your work in the application. You may be able to quit other applications, or cut down the number of special startup customizing files in your System Folder. You may have to reduce your RAM cache in the Memory control panel. See Chapter 7 for more information. Or you may just have to bite the bullet and go to your Apple dealer and install some more RAM.

Text in a Particular Font Size Is Jagged

Text in most of your document looks fine when you print it out, but if you change to an unusual font size for some of the text, it comes out jagged. This is because the size you changed to is not installed on your Mac, and it is having to do a bit-mapped approximation of that size. Either change the text to a font size that appears in outline form in the menu or install the font in your System Folder so it is available. If you are using ATM and PostScript outline fonts, check the troubleshooting chapter in the ATM *User Guide* for more information.

PrintMonitor Window Won't Go Away

You look at the PrintMonitor window to see how your print job is doing, and pretty soon the print job is finished and disappears from the window. Then when you try to quit the PrintMonitor, or you close the window, you find there is no Quit option in the Find menu and the menu and the icon in the Application menu refuse to go away. This is because the PrintMonitor appears and disappears automatically. To get rid of it, you need to choose another Application from the Applications menu. The moment you get into that application, the PrintMonitor disappears from the Applications menu. If it doesn't disappear, it means that a print job is waiting in the background for enough memory to begin printing.

Paper Jammed inside Printer

You sent a job to the printer and not all of the pages came out. If your printer has a little light with a jammed-paper icon next to it, the light is blinking merrily. No matter which kind of printer you have, press the release button and open the cover of the printer. Find one end or the other of the paper and pull it out gently. For good hints on how to get jammed paper out, see your printer's owner's guide—all the Apple printers have great descriptions of how to get jammed paper out.

If you have a StyleWriter (the original, not a StyleWriter II) and the paper feeder won't feed the paper, make sure the release button on the feeder is pushed down so the feeder panel has snapped forward. Then make sure the release lever on the front of the printer is pushed all the way in. Finally, make sure the two halves of the printer, the engine half and the feeder half, are pushed firmly together, and slide the latches at the sides toward the front of the printer.

Paper Won't Feed into Printer Properly

The paper jams or gets skewed or crumpled as it leaves the paper tray and goes into the printer. If the paper feeder is overloaded, take out the extra paper and try printing again. If there are still problems, flip the whole stack of paper over; some types of paper have a slick side and a textured side, and if the slick side is up, they don't feed well. Make sure the edges of the paper are not dog-eared, and that they are all lined up so the stack is smooth-sided.

Printer Status Lights Blinking or Off

The status lights on different printers mean different things. On all printers, though, a blinking paper light means it's time to add paper, and a blinking Ready light means that the printer is working on a job. If all the lights are off, the printer isn't getting power. Check to make sure it is plugged in, and that the outlet has power. If the Ready light on a LaserWriter blinks, pauses, and blinks again, over and over, there is something wrong with the PRAM that controls printing from the Mac.

Text or Images Print Off-Center on Page

The text or images of a document you printed run off one side of the page. First check the margin settings in the application that made the document. You may have to select all of the text or all of the images, then set the margins. If that doesn't help, check the paper size that is selected in the Page Setup dialog box; if you select a larger paper size than the paper you are using, the printed matter runs off the bottom of each page.

If the margins and paper size are correct, check the paper feeder to make sure it isn't overloaded. Check to see that you are using good quality paper (16- to 24-pound cotton bond), and see that the stack of paper is lined up right, too.

Ink Smudges on Back Side of Pages Printed on LaserWriter

There are gray blots and clouds on the backs of pages you print out of your LaserWriter. The insides of the printer engine are getting coated with excess toner. You need to clean things out. See the "Care and Feeding of a Laser-Writer" section for information on running a Cleaning Page.

Page Prints All Black, or with White Streaks through Letters

The quality of your printed pages is going downhill. Either they come out all black, or white streaks run down the pages, or lines appear on the paper, running through the text or images. Your ink or toner cartridge is almost empty, or it has been sitting still for a long time and needs to be fiddled with.

Remove it as described in the "Care and Feeding" section for your type of printer earlier in this chapter. LaserWriter owners, rock the cartridge side to side or forward and back. Original StyleWriter owners, clear the ink cartridge, turn off the Power button, then hold the Ready button down while you press the Power button. Finally, release both the Power and Ready buttons. StyleWriter II owners, turn the printer off and then on again. Desk-Writer owners, just press the Prime button for a few seconds.

If fiddling with your ink or toner cartridge doesn't help your print quality, it's time to replace the cartridge. See the "Care and Feeding" section for your printer type.

ImageWriter Paper Gets out of Line for Page Breaks

If you are using an ImageWriter and the paper gets misaligned so the page breaks don't appear between the sheets of paper, use the following procedure to realign your paper properly:

1. With the printer turned on and the Select light off, press the line-feed button until the page-break perforation is exactly lined up at the top of the printer head.
2. Do your printing. When printing long documents, you may have to pause the printer and adjust the paper to make up for any inaccuracy of the page breaks.
3. When the printer finishes a document, turn the Select button off and press the form-feed button. This advances the paper to the next page and aligns the page-break perforation correctly.
4. Turn the Select button back on, then tear off the last page of your document, leaving the extra sheet sticking out of the ImageWriter.
5. Use extra sheets for children's art or scratch paper. Or add them to your collection of perforated edge-strips, and recycle them.

Part Two

Exploring the Mac

• •

The second part of this book tells you how to get the most out of System 7, the software that runs the Mac. You'll learn how to get to your work easily and quickly, how to keep your work well organized, how to store it on hard and floppy disks, and how to make good use of the Mac's memory to help process your work. Once you've mastered these basics, you'll learn to customize the Mac to serve your own special needs.

Four

Working with Applications and Documents

◆ ◆ ◆ ◆ ◆ ◆ ◆ ◆ ◆ ◆ ◆ ◆ ◆ ◆ ◆ ◆

Featuring

- Definitions of applications and documents
- Installing an application
- Opening an application or an alias
- Opening a document
- Saving your work
- Opening an application from the Apple menu
- Switching between applications
- Finding a lost document
- Switching between documents
- Using list views of documents and folders
- Troubleshooting problems with applications and documents

First Steps

To install an application from master floppy disks: 91

Insert the first disk, called the Program, Setup or Installation floppy disk, from the set of master disks that the application came on. You can make backup copies for safekeeping if you want. Open the window for the first disk of the set and open the Install or Setup icon. You may have to enter your name and organization in a Personalizing dialog box; then choose to install just the files you need to do your work, or if you have the room and aren't sure which files you'll need, install all of them. Once you have clicked the Install button, all you have to do is insert the floppy disks the Mac asks for.

To open an application: 93

Simply double-click the icon for the application. With some applications, you can click the icon for a document created in the application to open the document and the application simultaneously.

To open a document: 94

Choose Open from the File menu, then find the name of the document you want to open in the list box of the Open dialog box. Select the document and click Open, or just double-click the name for the document.

CHAPTER 4

To save a document for the first time: 96

Choose Save from the File menu and enter a name for the new document. If you want to put the document in a folder other than the current one or a new folder, use the buttons and the file list box that are in the Save dialog box. When you have the right name and location for the file, click the Save button. For all succeeding saves, all you have to do is choose Save from the File menu or press ⌘-S.

To find a misplaced document: 101

You need to be in the Finder to find a document, and it's best if the window for your hard disk is active. Choose Find from the File menu, then enter as much of the name of the document as you can remember accurately. If you know the date, size, or other information about the document, click the More Choices button and specify that information. Then click the Find button. If the Finder displays a document or folder that has a name similar to the one you want, but it isn't the right one, you just choose Find Again from the File menu, so the Finder will search until it finds the document you want.

Now that your Mac and your printer are set up, and you're comfortable with the mouse and the desktop, you're ready to get down to work with applications and documents. No matter what specific tasks you do with your Mac, and no matter which applications you use to do those tasks, you need to learn the basic techniques for using applications and documents. This chapter shows you how to install your applications, how to open applications and documents, and how to save the work you've created with your Mac.

Introducing Applications and Documents

Applications are the tools you use on the Macintosh to do your work. As you work, you and the applications produce *documents*. If your task is writing text, you will use a word processing application and produce text documents. If your task is creating art or illustrations, you will use drawing, drafting, painting, or photo-editing applications that create graphics documents. If your task is making snazzy presentations, you will use QuickTime and a video-editing application or photo CDs. If your task is financial reporting or forecasting, you will use applications that create spreadsheets or database documents. If your task is fooling around, you will use games like Tetris and Dark Castle, and you will create high scores by making little shapes fit together or by escaping the flaming eyeball. But sooner or later you'll get back to work with applications and documents.

Applications and documents are different kinds of *files*. These electronic files are much more versatile and powerful than the files you stuff in a file case. In fact, everything your Mac does relies on files like applications and documents.

On the desktop, you see icons for applications, documents, and folders. If your Mac is running under At Ease, you see just two big folders, one for applications and one for documents. Otherwise, you probably see lots of folders with documents and applications in them. You can put documents and applications inside a folder by dragging the icons over the folder icon. Then, when you open up the folder by double-clicking it, you see the icons of the applications and documents in the folder's window. Folders can also be put inside other folders; this nesting of folders is further explained in Chapter 5.

Applications have icons that indicate what they do. For example, a painting application may show a hand painting on a diamond-shaped piece of paper, as the MacSplot icon in Figure 4.1 does. By convention, most documents look like a rectangular sheet of paper, often with one corner bent over. Text documents have text on them, graphics ones have some sort of artwork.

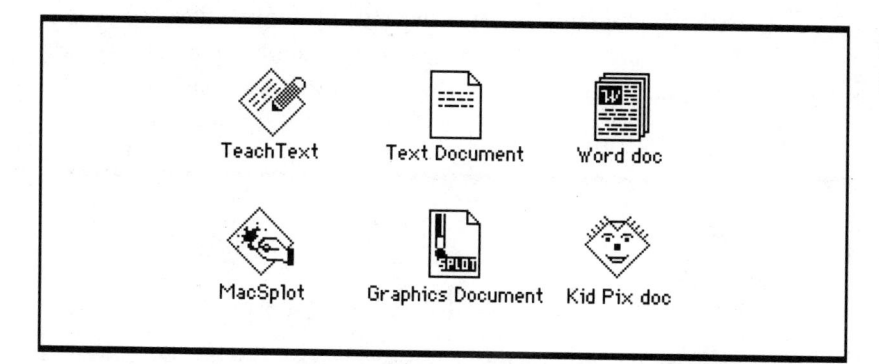

Figure 4.1
Application and document icons

There are also application and document icons that look very different from the conventional ones. However, you can usually tell what an application does by looking at its icon, and you can get some sort of hint about the nature of a document by looking at its icon.

Installing an Application

To install an application on your Mac's hard disk, you insert the floppy disk that contains the application (often called the *program disk* or *setup disk*) into your computer's floppy disk drive. If you want to play it safe, make backup copies of the application and its supplemental items, as described in "Backing Up System and Application Disks" in Chapter 6.

1. When you're done copying, insert your working copy of the application disk, and double-click the disk icon when it appears on the desktop. If you see an icon in the window called Install or Setup, double-click it.

2. With some applications, a dialog box then asks you to personalize your copy of the program. Enter your name and the name of the organization you work for in the text boxes. You have to

click in the organization box with the mouse to move the insertion point into it. Click OK when you are done.

3. If a dialog box opens asking you what you want to install, choose the program and the essential supplemental files that go with it, such as Help, Dictionary, Plug-in, and Preference files. Figure 4.2 shows a few icons of these files. If you are familiar with the program, you can leave out any Tutorial files and Samples files on the floppy disk. See the application's user guide if you need help deciding what is essential and what isn't.

Figure 4.2
Supplemental files for Word, Photoshop, and Excel

MS Dictionary   Plug-in Tool   Default Brushes   Add-in Functions

4. Click the Install or OK button when you have decided what to install. The installer program does its work. The screen usually displays a sliding bar that indicates how copying is going. The installer may put up a message box asking you to insert another disk (if two or more are required to install the program). Feed the Mac the disks it asks for.

Some programs are a bit more primitive: When you put the program disk into the computer and open the disk icon, all you see is the icon for the application and maybe a sample document or two. Open your hard disk icon, then resize the two windows so both can be seen at the same time. Find the icon for the application in the floppy disk window. Drag this icon to the hard disk window. If there are icons for supplemental files in the floppy disk window, find out from your application's user manual if you need to copy them onto the same disk as the application.

If you want to install some supplemental files onto your hard disk along with the application, it's good to create a new folder on the hard disk for them. (If you don't know how to create a folder, see Chapter 5 for more information.) Then drag the application and all its supplemental files into the folder. Name the folder after the application, so you don't lose it.

For example, if an imaginary application called MacSplot had a Custom Patterns file, you could create a new folder in your hard disk window and name it MacSplotters. Then you could drag the application icon and the Custom Patterns icon into the MacSplotters folder. If you have lots of applications, you can create an Applications folder and put all of the folders for the different tools inside it. When you finish copying an application off a floppy, you can drag the application's disk icon to the Trash so the disk ejects.

Opening an Installed Application or an Alias

To open an application, you double-click on the icon for it. Some applications (especially ones that take some time to open up) display an opening message, but soon you see the application's document window. There are other visual clues that you are "in" an application now instead of in the Finder; the most obvious is the application's special icon in the upper right corner of the screen. The menu options are also different from the ones on the Finder's desktop, and the application's pointer, insertion point, or cursor is often different from the arrow seen on the desktop.

Once you have installed an application, you can make an *alias*, or copy, of the application's icon. On the Mac, an alias has nothing to do with a nickname or an assumed name for a criminal. It is more like a substitute or a stand-in for an icon. It allows you to keep copies of the icon in places where they'll be convenient. Since an alias is only a copy of the icon, very little storage space is used up by the alias. This is better than keeping several copies of an application in different folders, which wastes large amounts of disk storage space, and which can lead to confusion if each version is set up differently.

To make an alias, select the original icon and choose Make Alias from the desktop's File menu. Then drag the alias to the folder where you keep your current documents created by that application. Or you can put an alias onto the desktop with your hard disk icon. If you double-click the alias it opens the application quickly.

Opening a Document

The most direct way to open a document is to double-click its icon. If the application that made the document is not open, it starts up, opens a window, and displays a page or section of the document you double-clicked on. There is another simple way to open a document from the desktop if you are looking at a Finder window containing both the document icon and the icon of the application that made it. Drag the document icon over the application one, and the document will open. This works with the alias of an application icon, too.

You can even drag a document onto the icon or alias of a different application from the one that created it, and if that application can read the format of your document, it will open the document. This avoids problems you can run into when you try to double-click an imported document that you don't have the application for. For example, if you drag a TeachText document onto the Microsoft Word icon, the document opens in Word. Or if you have several different types of graphics documents, all of which can be opened by Photoshop, you can put an alias of Photoshop in the same folder with all the different documents, then drag each one to the Photoshop alias to open it.

If you have opened an application, you can open a document from inside it. Choose the Open command from the application's File menu. A dialog box appears; find the name of the document in the current folder list and double-click it. You can look in folders other than the current one by pulling down the folder hierarchy menu shown in Figure 4.3. Just move the pointer to the title of the current folder list and press the mouse button.

Tip

If you bury a file way down in some obscure folder and can't remember how to get to it, just cancel out of the Open dialog box, go to the Finder, and choose Find from the File menu. When you find the file, double-click it.

The hierarchy of folders in the folder hierarchy menu is inverted; this means that for the sample shown in Figure 4.3 the memos folder is inside the Correspondence folder, which is on the Hard disk. Figure 4.4 shows a picture of the hierarchy of folders, with the desktop at the top.

If you are not sure how to get to the document you want, choose Desktop from the folder hierarchy menu, or click the Desktop button in the dialog box. Then start your search by double-clicking on the name of your hard disk in the list box. It helps if you have a simple, clear hierarchy, so you don't have to hunt down through five layers of folders. The one shown in Figure 4.4 is over-simplified, but if you can limit yourself to about five to ten folders on any one level, and keep your most-used documents just one or two levels down from the hard disk, you'll be happier and more productive. For more information on organizing files and folders, see Chapter 5.

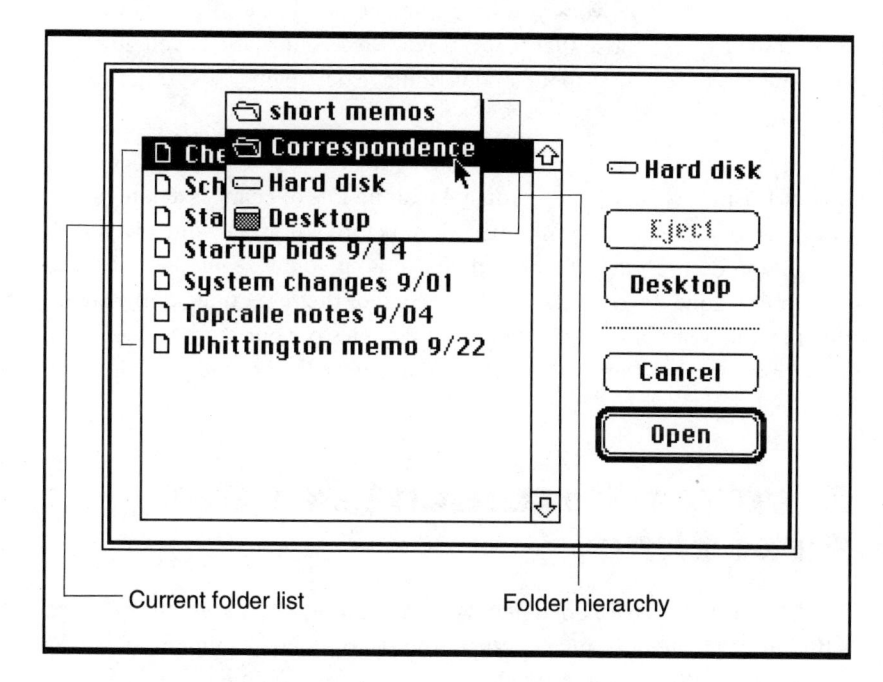

Figure 4.3
Pulling down the folder hierarchy menu in an Open dialog box

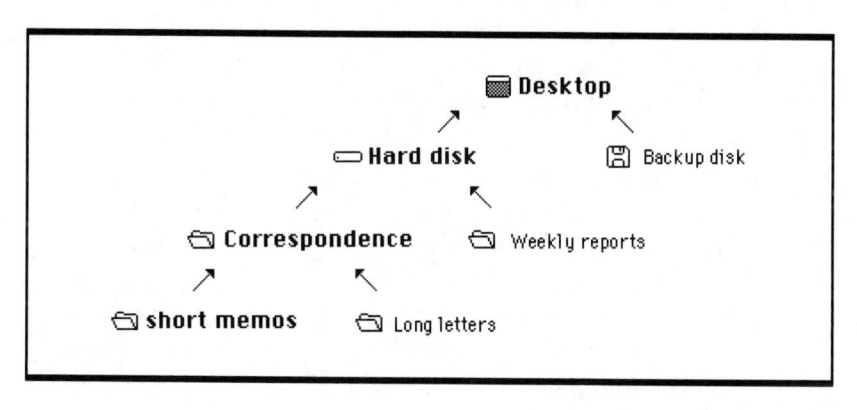

Figure 4.4
Hierarchy of folders with short memos inside Correspondence on Hard disk

Opening a Document **95**

Saving Your Work on a Document

When you have found and opened a document you can either create new work in it, or edit the work you have done before. Either way, you want to make sure you don't lose that work. If you save your work as you go along you never have to worry about a power outage destroying everything you've done that day.

Note
For more information on backing up your work, see Chapter 6.

The key lesson is: *Save often*. If you are creating a text or graphics document, save at least every half hour. If you are making lots of changes at a high rate of input, save every fifteen minutes. Save before you leave your Macintosh even if you do not intend to be gone for long; if you are switching between two applications, save before you leave each of them to go do a little something in the other one. And make backup copies of your work at least once a day, especially if there is any chance of power fluctuations or hard disk trouble.

Saving a Document for the First Time

The first time you save a document you are creating, you have to name it and tell your Mac where to put it. When you open a new document, either by starting an application without choosing an existing document, or by choosing New from an application's File menu, the new document has a generic name, such as Untitled or Document 1. If you see a generic title in the title bar of the window you are working in, use the following procedure to save your work:

1. Choose Save from the File menu. A dialog box opens, as in Figure 4.5. It displays a list of the contents of your hard disk or your current folder (the folder you are working in). There is a text box for naming the document, with the generic title highlighted in it, and buttons for saving, canceling, opening a new folder, and switching to the desktop. For more information on these features, see the "Special Saving Techniques" section that follows.

Chapter 4: Working with Applications and Documents

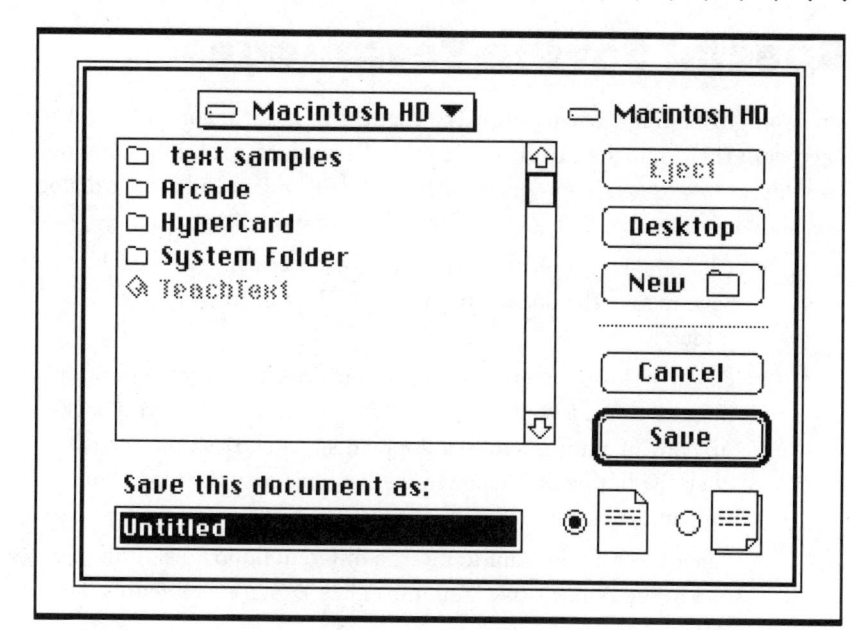

Figure 4.5
The Save As dialog box

2. Type in a name for your new file. The new name replaces *Untitled* in the text box.
3. Click the Save button. The disk drive whirrs as it writes your document onto the disk, and then the document window returns, with the new name in the title bar.

Saving As You Edit

As you work on a document, the changes you make are stored in the temporary memory of your Mac. To put this work in a permanent storage place, choose Save in the File menu, or in most applications, press ⌘-S. If you save often, each save takes only a moment, so your work pace is not interrupted.

There is only one situation in which you should not save your work. If you realize that everything you have done since the last time you saved is all a big mistake, *do not* save your work. Instead, close the window, and when you see a dialog box asking if you want to save changes before closing, click the No button.

Special Saving Techniques

There might be times when you make changes to a document and want to keep both the original and edited versions of that document. For situations like this, choose the Save As command from the File menu and use the dialog box shown in Figure 4.5. These are the different possibilities:

- Click the New Folder button, enter a folder name, and click Save to save the document in a new folder inside the current folder.
- Click Desktop if you want to save the document on the desktop instead of inside your current folder. If you want to save a backup copy of a document to a floppy disk, click Desktop, then click the floppy disk name in the list box, click the Open button, and click Save.
- Click Eject if you want to insert a different floppy disk from the one in the floppy drive. You must click Desktop before this button becomes active.
- Enter a new name for the document if you want to have two copies of it; the previous version, and a new version with your latest changes.
- Pull down the folder hierarchy menu if you are inside a folder and want to save the document to the desktop or another folder. Choose the Desktop from the folder hierarchy menu if you are not sure where the desired folder is. You can start seeking it from the desktop down.

Managing Your Applications

Once you've acquired a few applications, you'll find yourself casting about for quicker and easier ways to open and move among them. By using the Apple and the Applications menus judiciously, you can make sure your applications are right where you need them.

Opening Applications from the Apple Menu

You can set up your Mac so you can open your most-used applications from the Apple menu. Remember, the Apple menu is the one under the little apple icon at the far left end of the menu bar, and it is available at all times. You can put aliases of applications in the Apple menu. An alias of an application, as explained earlier in this chapter, is a stand-in for the icon of the application.

To make an alias for an application so you can put it in the Apple menu, all you have to do is find the original icon of the application, select it, then choose Make Alias in the File menu. Then open the window for your System Folder on your hard disk, find the Apple Menu Items folder, and drag the alias for the application to the Apple Menu Items folder. Pull down the Apple menu and you'll see that the alias is there. Notice that the Apple menu gets longer as you add things to it. It can even run off the bottom of the screen; you just have to scroll down to the hidden items at the bottom. The advantage to having an application's alias in the Apple menu is that you can use it to open the application. The Applications menu only shows applications that are already open (see Figure 4.6).

Tip
To put the aliases of your most-used applications at the top of the Apple menu, add a space before the first letter of an alias title. You can add an apostrophe to the front of a title to move it to the end of the list.

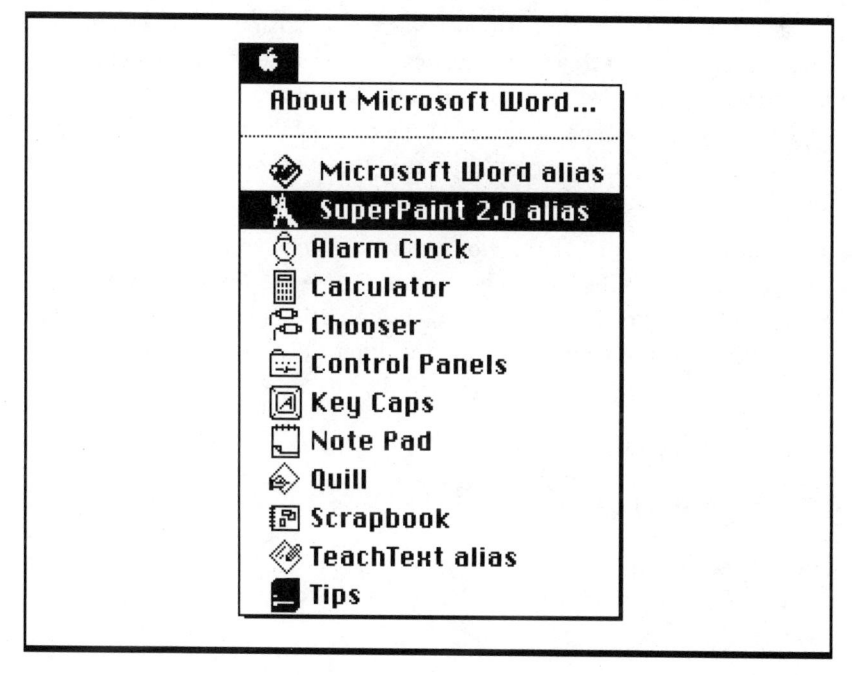

Figure 4.6
Application aliases in the Apple menu

Managing Your Applications **99**

Switching between Applications

If your Mac has enough internal memory (RAM), you can open more than one application at a time and switch quickly between applications. You need at least 4 megabytes (4MB) of RAM to run the system software and two applications on top of it. Many memory-hungry applications require even more RAM to run two at a time.

To open two applications, start by opening one. Open the second one from the Apple menu if you have placed an alias of it there. If there is no alias for the second application in the Apple menu, choose Finder from the Applications menu, which you pull down from the first application's icon at the far right end of the menu bar. Find the second application's icon on your desktop. If the desktop is cluttered with windows opened by the first application, choose Hide Others from the Applications menu. When you find the second application's icon, double-click it. You can also double-click the icon of any document created by the second application, and it will open a window for that application with the document displayed.

To switch between two or more open applications, choose the one you want from the Applications menu. If you arrange the windows of the different applications carefully, you can also switch from application to application by simply clicking in the different windows. For example, if you open a Teach-Text window in the lower left portion of the screen and have a paint or draw application window open in the upper right part of the screen, you can click in the upper right and lower left corners of the windows to switch back and forth between the applications.

If you want to hide one application's windows when you switch to another one, just hold down the Option key as you choose the dominant application from the Applications menu. The other application's windows are hidden, but you can get at them by choosing the dimmed name and icon of the application from the Applications menu.

Managing Your Documents

The Mac also gives you several ways to find, open, and move among your documents. These are described in the following sections.

Finding Misplaced Documents

If you have a large number of folders and you can't remember where a document is, you can use the following Finder procedure to seek out your document and select it for you.

1. Choose Finder from the Applications menu. This menu is under the application icon on the far right end of your menu bar.
2. Click in the window for your hard disk to make it active. If you can't find the hard disk window, choose Hide Others from the Applications menu, then double-click your hard disk icon to open its window.
3. Choose Find from the File menu on the desktop.
4. Type the name of the document you want to open, or as much of the name as you can remember.
5. Click on the More Choices button if you want to be more specific about the document you are searching for. For example, if you know the name of the document starts with the letters *Sche*, you can enter those letters in the Find dialog box, click More Choices, then pull down the menu under "contains" and change it to "starts with."
6. Click the Find button when you have narrowed your search as much as possible. A dialog box tells you how the search is going, then the Finder opens the window that contains the document and selects it for you. Double-click it to open it.
7. If more than one document matches the pattern of characters you are searching for, and your first search turns up a document you don't want, choose Find Again from the File menu on the desktop. The Finder runs around your folder hierarchy again until it finds another document that fits the pattern you specified.

Switching between Documents

Many applications let you open more than one document at a time. To find out if opening multiple documents is allowed in an application, first open one document, then pull down the File menu. If the Open command is dimmed, you cannot open another document. If the command is dark, choose it, then double-click a second document in the Open dialog box. The second document appears in its own window, and in most cases, the two document windows are staggered in such a way that you can see the edge of the inactive one behind the active one.

When working with multiple documents make sure you save your work in each one. If you do some work in a document and go on to another one without saving, it is easy to forget all about the first document until there is a power surge or a system problem that makes you restart and lose your work. The best policy is to save your work in each document before you leave it to work in another one.

Tip
To switch from one window to the other, so you can work on one document and then the other, click on the edge of the inactive window. It becomes active, and you can go to work immediately.

Changing Your Desktop View of Documents and Folders

There are a lot of ways to look at the documents and folders in a window on the desktop. Each view of the items is useful for different reasons; don't use the same view for all situations. Here is a list of the views as they appear in the Views menu, and the most obvious situation called for by each.

- by Small Icon: Shows little icons and titles for files and folders. Good for showing lots of different types of files and folders in one window.

- by Icon: Shows a full-size icon and title for each file or folder. Good for showing a few icons of different kinds, especially if kids or other less dexterous users are going to be using the window.

- by Name: Lists folders and files with the names sorted alphabetically. Good for long lists of documents you want to sort alphabetically.

- by Size: Lists folders and files sorted by size, largest first. Good for finding out which folders and documents need cleaning out when you are running short of disk space.

- by Kind: Lists folders, applications, and documents in separate, alphabetized groups. Good for finding and listing documents;

gives you a clear view of your hierarchy of folders and documents. In Figure 4.7 you can see a listing by kind of a simple folder and file hierarchy.

- **by Label**: Lists folders and files sorted by the labels you assign to them. Good for organizing long lists of similar files, so you don't mix them up.
- **by Date**: Lists folders and files sorted by last modification date, most recently modified first. Good for determining which documents need to be backed up.

If any of these views are not available in the View menu, you probably need to make an adjustment in the Views control panel, as explained in "Views Control Settings" in Chapter 8. Only the by Name view is always available.

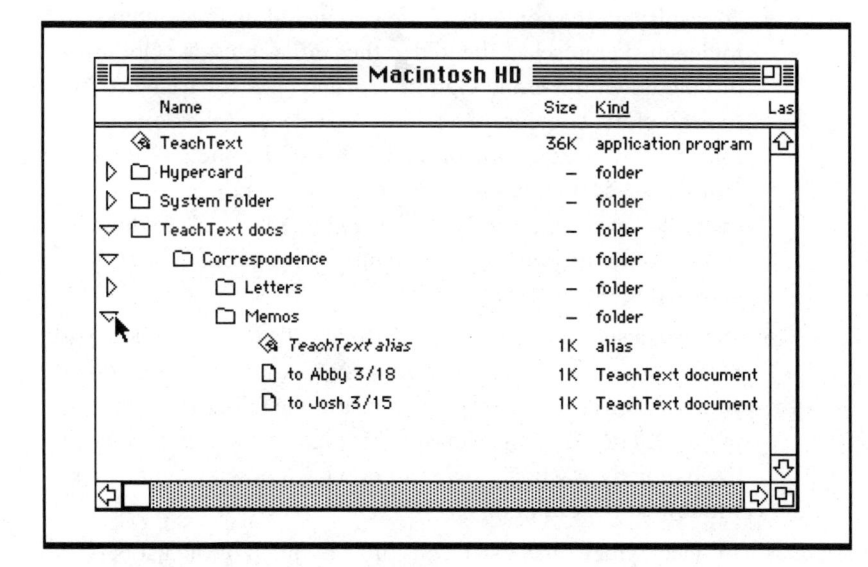

Figure 4.7
A list by kind of a simple file and folder hierarchy

Using List Views

To get the most out of list views, you may need to expand and collapse the lists of what is in the folders. Sometimes you want to see what is in a folder, and sometimes you want to hide the contents of a folder so they don't fill the screen and prevent you from seeing the top levels of your folder and file hierarchy. The more complex and extensive your hierarchy is, the more you need to manipulate the lists. Here are a few of the most useful techniques:

- To see as much information in a list window as possible, expand the window with the size box in the lower right corner of the screen (not the zoom box in the upper right corner) until it fills the whole screen. Also, use the Views control panel (see "Views Control Settings" later in Chapter 8) to hide any column of information you don't need, such as the Label column.

- To display the contents of a folder in the list, click the triangle in the left margin of the list. To hide the contents, you click the triangle again. When the triangle points down, the contents show, when it points to the right, the contents are hidden, as shown in Figure 4.7.

- To display *all* the contents of a folder, including the contents of folders inside it, select the folder, then either press ⌘-Option-→ or hold down the ⌘ and Option keys and click the triangle. To hide all of the contents of a folder, you select it (click on the folder's icon up at the top of the whole list of contents), then either press ⌘-Option-← or use ⌘-Options and click the triangle. The next time you display the contents of this folder, you will see only the immediate contents of it; the contents of enclosed folders will be hidden.

- To move a selected icon to a folder that is listed on a remote part of the hierarchy, use the previous techniques to hide as much as you can between your selected icon and the folder you want to put it in. Then drag the icon *slowly* to its destination. If you drag it too quickly, it will zip right out of the window to some other window or the desktop.

- To select widely dispersed icons, hide as much of the list between them as you can, then click on the first icon and Shift-click the others. This technique is great for selecting documents in a bunch of different folders; you don't have to open and close all those windows.

- To select a file or folder from a long list without having to scroll until you find it, just type the first few letters of its name, without any pause between letters. Presto; the icon of the file or folder appears, selected.

- To select several icons in one folder, start a selection rectangle in the left margin and drag a bit to the right and then down through the list of icons. You can keep dragging down a long list, even if it runs out of sight at the bottom of the window.

- To change the way items are listed, click on the column header for the listing you want. For example, if the items are listed by kind, you can click the Last Modified column header and the window will change to a By Date listing. The column header of the current list type is underlined.

- To adjust the list view display and to show additional information in list views, see "Views Control Settings" in Chapter 8.

Troubleshooting Problems with Applications and Documents

These are the problems you may have in working with your applications and documents and using the System 7 Finder.

Lost in FinderSpace, or, "What View Am I Looking At?"

You switch to the Finder and either no windows are open, or you are looking at a window that doesn't make any sense to you at all.

To get away from the lost feeling that the blank desktop gives you, just double-click your hard disk or floppy disk icon. Its window opens, and you can then open any of the folders shown.

To figure out what kind of a list view you are looking at in a window, you just check out the column titles up near the top of the window, and see which one, Name, Size, Kind, Label, or Last Modified, is underlined.

If you are looking at a window with a title you don't recognize, and you can't figure out what folder you're in, just press the ⌘ key and use the mouse to pull down the hierarchy menu hidden under the title of the window. This trick doesn't work in application windows, but all you have to do in an application is choose Open from the File menu, then pull down the folder hierarchy in the title of the list box. Once you know where you are, click Cancel to make that dialog box go away. See "Opening a Document" earlier in this chapter for details.

A Column Is Missing from a List View Window

You are looking at a list view, and one of the columns is gone, such as the Label column, or the Size or Kind column. To bring back the column, open the Views control panel and click on the appropriate check box. (See Chapter 8 for information on control panels.) If you want to see the sizes of folders as well as files, you have to click on the Calculate folder sizes check box.

An Application Is Not Available

You see an alert box that looks like Figure 4.8. In most cases, this means you double-clicked a document icon, and your Mac can't find the application that created the document.

The solution is to open the application first, then open the document, but that only works if you have the application that created the document. If you don't, try opening the closest application you have, then opening the document from inside that application. For example, if you are trying to open a MacWrite document but don't have MacWrite, you can open Word, then open the MacWrite document. Word will convert the MacWrite document to Word format as it opens the document. Similarly, you can use Photoshop to open all kinds of paint and draw documents. If you have PageMaker, you can open almost anything with it.

Application Won't Quit As Expected

You try to quit an application after finishing work in it, and either the screen hangs, or the Mac puts you right back in the application. The cause of the problem is that you still have a utility or desk accessory open. Check the items in your Apple menu. The Scrapbook is a common culprit. When you find the open utility or desk accessory, close it, then quit your main application.

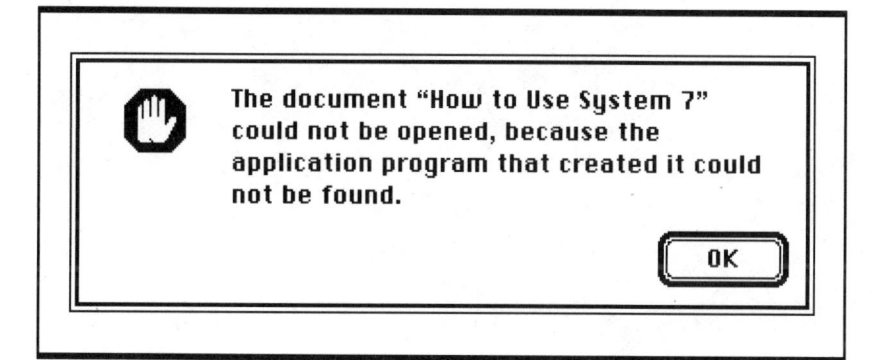

Figure 4.8
Application Not Available alert box

Troubleshooting Problems with Applications and Documents

File Lost After Moving in a List View

You moved a file to a folder in a window that was displaying a list view, and now you can't find that file. Use the Find command in the File menu to find the lost file, then move it carefully, making sure that the target folder is highlighted before you "drop" the file. It is easy to miss a target folder in a list view, especially if you use the small icons of files and folders in order to squeeze as long a list as possible into the window.

Five

Using Folders to Organize Your Files

◆ ◆

Featuring

- ◆ Description of the Macintosh hierarchical file system (HFS)
- ◆ How to make and name folders
- ◆ How to nest folders to make a hierarchy
- ◆ How to use list views to look into folders
- ◆ Troubleshooting problems with file and folder hierarchies

First Steps

To make and name a new folder: 113

Make sure you're in a window of your hard disk or an already existing folder so you have a place to put the folder you make. Choose New Folder from the File menu or press ⌘-N. When the folder appears it is called "untitled folder," but the name is selected, so you can enter a new name immediately. You can make a folder on the desktop, too; just select an icon on the desktop to deselect all windows, then choose New Folder from the File menu.

To make a hierarchy by placing files and nesting folders: 114

First you need to organize your groups of related files in folders; you do this by dragging each file to the folder that makes sense, releasing the mouse button when the destination folder becomes highlighted. You can select related files in a window by dragging a selection rectangle across them; then you can drag one of them to a folder, and the others in the group will follow. If several folders contain similar or related data, you can nest them all inside a single folder. You simply drag each related folder to the destination folder and drop it when the destination folder becomes highlighted.

CHAPTER 5

To look inside folders that are in other folders: 117

> You have to open the top level folder first. Then either double-click the top level folder and then double-click the one inside, or use a list view (you choose by Name or by Kind from the View menu) and click on the triangles in the left margins to open and close the folders all in the same window.

To change the order in which files or folders are listed: 118

> You can put special characters (characters other than letters and numerals) in front of the names of files or folders to reorder them for logic or personal preference. Put a space in front of the name of any file or folder that you want to see at the beginning of a list. To make a file or folder go to the end of a list, put an accent mark (`) or caret (^) before the name.

This chapter tells how to keep your work organized on your Macintosh. A Mac can store a lot of documents and applications on its hard disk. But it is up to you to organize your files so you can use the computer efficiently. Remember, all applications and documents are just files, as far as the Mac knows. And as long as you don't mess with its System file, it doesn't care *what* you do with all the other ones. But it can slow both you and the Mac down if files are scattered all over and neither of you can find them when they are needed. So you need to organize your files.

You organize files by putting them in *folders*. That's simple enough; it's just like when you accumulate a bunch of related papers on your real-world desk and then store them in a folder. However, when you have several folders of stuff cluttering up your desk, you put them in a pile or stick them in an alphabetized file case.

Note
Whenever you work with the hierarchy of files and folders, remember that "up" is toward the desktop, and "down" is deeper into the layers of folders inside other folders.

On the Mac, it's a little different. You put related files in a folder, but when you accumulate lots of folders, you can put some of them inside another folder.

Now, you *could* do that with real-world folders, but the folder holding the other folders would get unwieldy. By contrast, the Mac can handle folders inside folders with ease. The folders inside folders create a nice organization of layers; you can put a document file or an application in any folder, at any level of the folder organization.

Apple calls the whole thing the Macintosh hierarchical file system, or HFS for short. The *hierarchy* refers to the layers of folders. Folders inside other folders are at "lower" levels of the hierarchy. Folders you see when you open your hard disk are near the top. The desktop itself is at the peak of the pyramid, above the hard disk and any floppy disks that appear on it. Figure 5.1 shows a picture of how the hierarchy is set up.

Figure 5.1
Hierarchy of folders on disks under the desktop

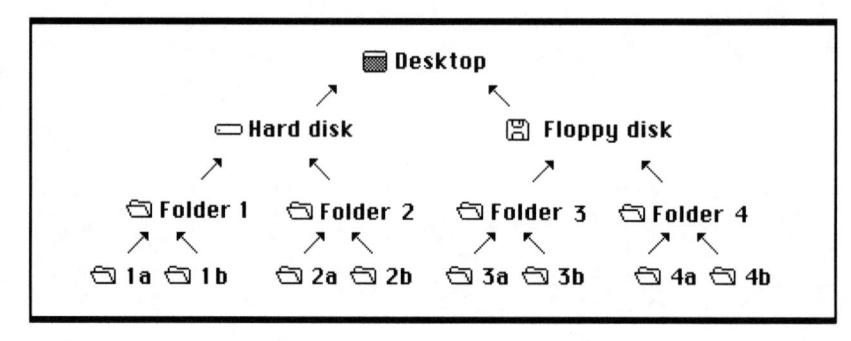

112 Chapter 5: Using Folders to Organize Your Files

There aren't any names for the folders in the picture; but naming is an important part of organizing your work, and it is explained later in this chapter.

Creating Folders

OK, so folders are the basic building blocks of the hierarchical file system. To make them, you need to be in the Finder with your hard disk window open. If you aren't already there, choose the Finder from the Applications menu. Choose Hide Others from the Applications menu if the desktop is cluttered with open windows. If there are still lots of Finder windows open, just press the Option key and click in the close box of any Finder window, and all of them will close. If, when the clutter clears, you find that your hard disk window isn't open, double-click the hard disk icon. If the hard disk window is inactive, click in it to make it active.

To make a folder in the active window, choose New Folder from the File menu or press ⌘-. (the ⌘ key and a period). The folder appears, highlighted, with the name "untitled folder." There is a frame around the name of the folder, indicating that it is selected so you can type in a better name.

You can also put folders on the desktop; all you have to do is select any icon on the desktop (so no window is active), then choose New Folder from the File menu. However, the folders and the stuff in them have to be stored on a disk *somewhere*, so I prefer to build all my hierarchies inside disk windows. Besides, it's confusing to clutter up the desktop with stuff that is of uncertain origin. Better to put each folder that holds a hierarchy in the window of the disk where it is stored.

Naming and Nesting Folders to Make a Hierarchy

To name a newly created folder, you just type in the new name when you see the frame around "untitled folder." To change the name of an existing folder or file, you click on the name (*not* the folder) and wait for the frame to appear around it. Then either type in a new name, or select part of the old name and replace it. For more information on selecting and replacing text, see "Deleting and Replacing Text" in Chapter 9.

To put a file such as a document into a folder, drag the icon of the document to the folder. When the folder becomes highlighted, release the mouse button, "dropping" the document into the folder. To put several files in a folder, drag a selection rectangle through them, then drag one of the icons to the folder. The others follow.

To put a folder into another folder, or "nest" it, drag the icon of the "egg" folder to the icon of the "nest" folder and drop it in. Open up the nest folder and the egg one will be inside there.

For an example of the basic techniques of nesting folders to make a hierarchy, create a few new folders, such as those shown in Figure 5.2. If your computer is new and you haven't rearranged things on your hard disk, you'll probably already have a System Folder (remember, you *do not* nest it anywhere or move stuff in or out of it unless you know exactly what you are doing), a HyperCard folder, and TeachText. If you do not have any documents in your hard disk window, create and save two with TeachText or your word processing application of choice. (If you don't know how to create and save a word processing document, see Chapter 9, "Word Processors.")

Figure 5.2
Some folders and files in a hard disk window

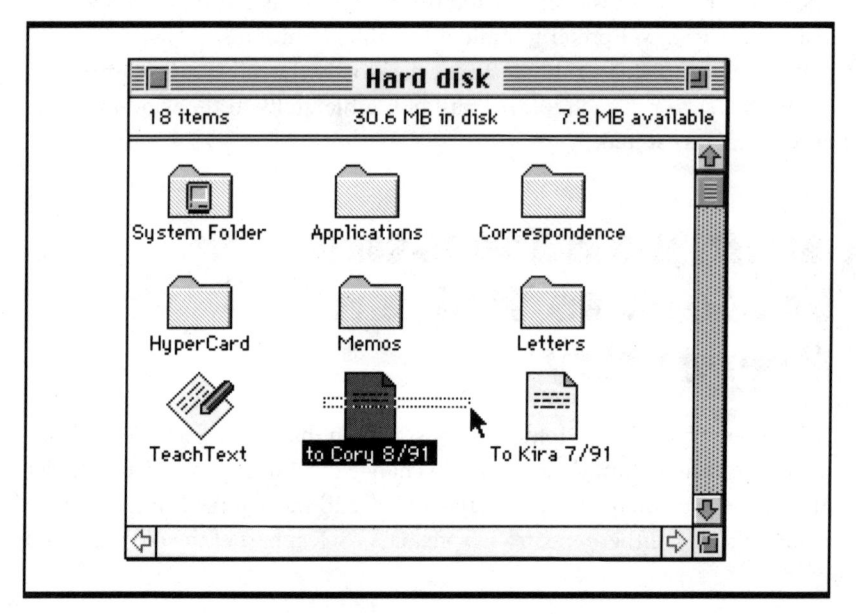

Chapter 5: Using Folders to Organize Your Files

The names of the files and folders in this sample are simple, clear, and easy to organize into a logical hierarchy. The two memos, "to Cory" and "to Kira," belong in the Memos folder. The Memos and Letters folders belong in the Correspondence folder, since they are for two different kinds of correspondence files.

The HyperCard folder, which contains the HyperCard application, belongs in the Applications folder. TeachText, another application, goes there too.

So, to create the hierarchy shown in Figure 5.3, just follow these steps:

1. Select the two memos and drag them to the Memos folder.
2. Select the Memos and Letters folders and drag them to Correspondence.
3. Select the HyperCard folder and TeachText and drag them to the Applications folder.

Now all you see in the Hard disk window is three folders: Applications, Correspondence, and the System Folder.

This simple hierarchy would be adequate to organize 20 or 30 memos and letters in the correspondence folder, and 10 or 15 applications. To help you remember when you created a particular file, you can add a date after it, as shown for the memos above. You don't need to add a last modification date; you can see that in a list view, as explained below.

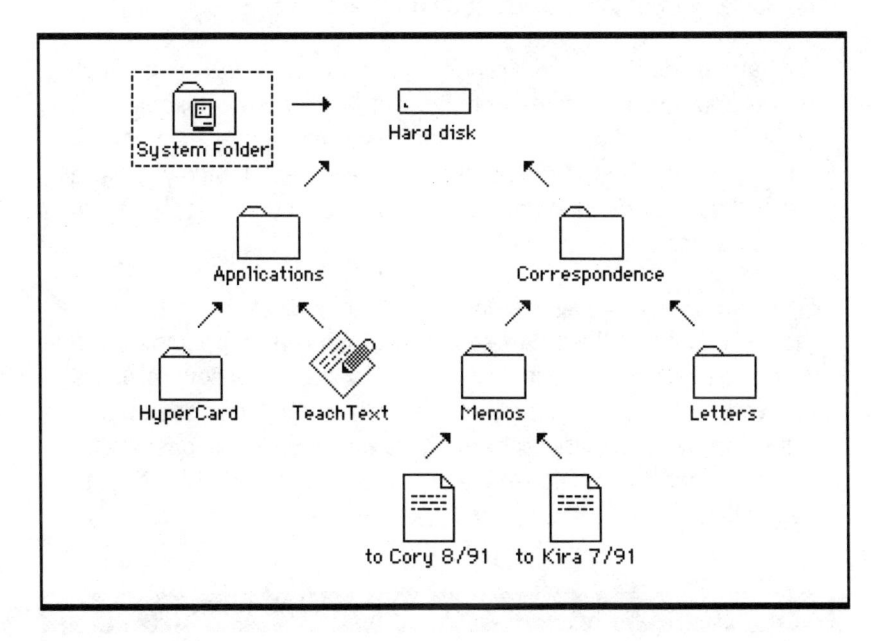

Figure 5.3
Building a sample hierarchy of folders and files

Naming and Nesting Folders to Make a Hierarchy

If you build up a large number of files in any folder, you can split them into subfolders. Although there is almost no limit to how many layers and folders you can nest, it is best to keep each level to less than ten folders, and to limit the hierarchy to three or four levels, so you can find things easily. You would never have trouble finding files down inside a sample hierarchy like the one in Figure 5.3, because the names of all the folders describe what is in them.

Keeping things in a clear, simple hierarchy doesn't mean you have to be rigid. For example, it's OK to have both files and folders in a folder, like having the HyperCard folder and TeachText (an application file) in the Applications folder.

Some Sample Organizing Schemes

You can organize your files any way you want, but here are a couple of schemes that are used by large numbers of Mac users.

By Project: Put all the documents for a particular project in a single folder. Within that folder, you can put text documents and graphics into different folders, or put both text and graphics documents into different folders, each of which contains everything pertaining to a particular part of the project, such as chapters of a book.

By Date: If you do financial reporting or accounting, you can put all of the spreadsheets for a specific client or group of clients in a single folder, and within that folder, make folders for each week, month, or year. Or you can have one large folder for each year, and have folders for the documents pertaining to each client inside the annual folder.

By User: If several users store their data on the same hard drive (as on a network), they can each have their own large folder, and organize the documents in it however they want. Or if several users are working on the same project, they can all keep their documents in the same folder; in this scheme, you may have to use passwords and access restrictions, to make sure users don't undo or overwrite each other's work.

Using List Views to Work with Folders

If you want to see several layers of your folder hierarchy at once, in order to find out if the naming and nesting is clear and logical, just open the window for your hard disk and choose by Name or by Kind from the View menu. You'll see something similar to Figure 5.4. The sample shows the name, size, and kind of each file or folder. If you scroll the list to the right, you can see the time and date that the files and folders were last modified.

This view gives you an outline of the files and folders; the logic of the naming scheme is obvious when you see it in outline form. This is the key to good organization of your folders and files. If the folder names make a clear outline in a list view, you won't lose things in the hierarchy. If the names of the folders don't make a sensible outline, or if files are in folders that don't make sense, the hierarchy needs work. If you don't fix it up, and if you add more and more files and folders, higgledy-piggledy, the thing will soon become such a mess that you can't locate anything without using the Find command in the File menu.

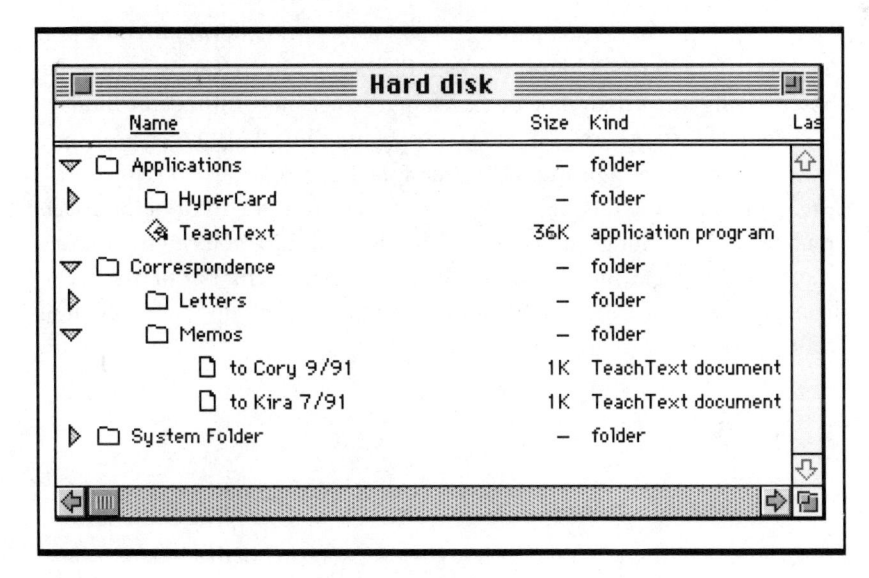

Name	Size	Kind
▽ 📁 Applications	—	folder
▷ 📁 HyperCard	—	folder
◈ TeachText	36K	application program
▽ 📁 Correspondence	—	folder
▷ 📁 Letters	—	folder
▽ 📁 Memos	—	folder
📄 to Cory 9/91	1K	TeachText document
📄 to Kira 7/91	1K	TeachText document
▷ 📁 System Folder	—	folder

Window title: Hard disk

Figure 5.4
A list view of a sample folder hierarchy

For example, if you wrote a short letter one day, and decided to put it in the Memos folder, even though it wasn't really a memo, you might forget that it was there later, and go looking for it in the Letters folder. And if it turned out to be a very important letter, you would go through some anxious moments before you found it in the Memos folder.

Or if you named the folders Shrtntes.B52 and Lngstff.B17 instead of Memos and Letters, you might forget what in the world those names meant.

Save yourself the trouble. Build your hierarchy with clear, simple names, and put files in the appropriate folders. If you can tell that a name is wrong in a list view, you can select and change it. If a file is in the wrong folder, you can move it, even if the folder where you want to put it is not in view. Just drag the icon of the file to the top or bottom of the screen, then drag it slowly to scroll the list view. For more information on list views, see "Using List Views" in Chapter 4.

If you want to change the order in which files are listed in a folder, you can put special characters (things other than letters or numbers) in front of the files' names. To move a file to the front of a list, put a space or exclamation point in front of the name. To move a file to the end of a list, put an accent (`) or caret (^) in front of the name. This technique is good for straightening out the way numbered files are listed.

For example, if you list some files named File 1 through File 12, you'll find that files 10, 11, and 12 appear between File 1 and File 2. Not cool. To move those two-digit files to the end of the list, put an accent in front of the number for each file, so they become File `10, File `11, and File `12. If you have a long list with many two-digit numbers (like File 1 through File 37), just put a space in front of the one-digit numbers so they go to the front of the list. If you have a HUGE long list, like File 1 through File 325, you can put a space in front of the single digits and an exclamation point in front of all those two-digit numbers. But a file list that long should be broken up into a bunch of smaller folders.

Chapter 5: Using Folders to Organize Your Files

Troubleshooting Problems with Files and Folders

The following sections cover the problems you can have when using files and folders to build your file hierarchy.

Can't Determine Where Current Folder Fits in Hierarchy

You are looking at a window that shows the contents of a folder, but you can't figure out what folder the current one is inside (the *parent* folder, as they say). Press the ⌘ key and press on the title of the current window. A menu like the one in Figure 5.5 pops down, with the layers of the hierarchy above your current folder, listed in reverse order. That means the parent folder is listed first, then the parent of that folder, and so forth, to the hard disk.

Figure 5.5
The folder hierarchy pop-down menu

File or Folder Is Lost

You can't remember where a file is. Or you just dragged a file or folder into a window with a list view, and it disappeared. Choose Find from the File menu at the desktop (you have to be in the Finder to find stuff). A dialog box opens, with a text box ready for you to enter the name of the file or folder you want to find. You don't have to enter the whole name; all the Finder needs is enough letters to distinguish the item you've lost from all the other ones.

If you enter only part of the name and the Finder turns up a different file or folder from the one you want, just choose Find Again from File menu or press ⌘-G to find the next item that matches the pattern of letters you entered in the Find text box.

If you want to find and list a group of files that share something in common, you can use an expanded Find dialog box. First choose Find from the File menu, then click the More Chances button in the small dialog box. The larger dialog box appears, with three boxes containing pop-up menus across the top. Click on the boxes to see the choices in each pop-up menu. Choose limiting categories from all three pop-up menus, always working from left to right.

For example, if you want to find and list all of the files you modified yesterday (you *know* you want some information out of one of those files, you just can't remember which one), first choose "date modified" from the left pop-up. Leave "is" for the center pop-up, and select the day part of the date and use the down arrow to change it to yesterday's date. Click the Find button, and the files appear, highlighted in a list view. If they are inside a folder, the folder's list opens automatically so you can scroll down the list and see all of the files. This is a slick way to list related files. Just check out the different choices in the left pop-up menu to see all the ways you can limit the search.

Can't Find a Buried Folder Window

You have about ten windows open on your desktop, and they are completely covering the window of a folder that you want to see. The simple solution is to close all the other windows, but this means switching between programs and it may also mean closing up something you want to get back to soon. Not to worry; there are alternative paths to your buried window.

First, choose Hide Others from the Applications menu. That gets all your open document windows out of the way. Then, if the window you want is partly in view, just click on it to bring it to the front. If it is still completely hidden, see if you can find an icon for it quickly, then just double-click the icon to bring the window up front. For instance, if your hard disk icon is in view (and you should set things up so some edge or corner of it is *always* in view) and the folder you want has an icon in the hard disk window, double-click on the hard disk icon. If the folder is down inside the hierarchy, you can choose by Kind or by Name from the View menu, then quickly open the folders you need to in order to get at your desired folder. When you get to the folder, its icon will be highlighted if its window is open.

Can't Change a File's Name

If you try to select the name of a file and the frame doesn't appear around it, so you can't edit the name, the file or disk that contains it is locked. To unlock a file, you need to choose Get Info from the File menu, click the Locked check box to uncheck it (thereby unlocking the file), then close the Info window. Now you can select the name of the file and change it when the frame appears around it.

If the file is unlocked and you still can't select the name, it must be on a locked floppy disk. Eject the disk and slide the lock tab over the hole. Then reinsert the disk, open it, and select the name of the file you want to change. See Chapter 6 for more information on locking and unlocking floppy disks.

New File or Folder Is Selected When You Try to Change a File or Folder's Name

You select a file or folder, but when you start to type characters to change its name a new file or folder becomes selected. The problem is that you selected the item, but didn't select the title. You have to click on the title itself and wait for the frame to appear around it. *Then* edit the title. When the item is selected rather than its title, you are telling the Mac to find and select a new item when you type in letters.

Six

Storage: Hard and Floppy Disks

◆ ◆ ◆ ◆ ◆ ◆ ◆ ◆ ◆ ◆ ◆ ◆ ◆ ◆

Featuring:

- ◆ Introduction to hard and floppy disks
- ◆ All about bytes, kilobytes, and megabytes
- ◆ A guide to different disks for different folks
- ◆ How to connect and care for your hard disk
- ◆ How to save and back up your work on disks
- ◆ How to insert, eject, initialize, lock, unlock, erase, and name floppy disks
- ◆ Floppy disk precautions
- ◆ Startup disk, system disks, application disks, and data disks defined
- ◆ How to back up files on a floppy disks
- ◆ Copying an entire disk
- ◆ Troubleshooting problems with hard and floppy disks

First Steps

To back up your work on floppy disks: 134

Before you can make backup copies of your work, save all current work on the documents you want to back up and close the windows showing them. Then you can either copy the files directly onto floppy disks, or start a backup utility to do the work for you. If you use a backup utility, all you have to do is look in the file catalog (created when you make your first backup) and select the files you want to back up afresh. Select the type of floppy you want, click a button that starts the backup process, and simply insert the floppy disks that the utility tells you to.

To defragment your hard disk: 135

Before you defragment a hard disk, you must back up all important documents, applications, and preferences files. Preferences files are found either in the Preferences folder in your System Folder or in applications' folders. Once you have backed everything up, start a defragmenting utility such as Speed Disk and check the disk for file fragmentation. Then just click Optimize and wait for the utility to do its work.

To insert a floppy disk: 137

Hold the disk with the label side up, gripping the plastic edge so the metal door is away from you. Insert the disk in the disk drive slot and push it with your fingers until it clicks down and into place. If you have inserted the disk correctly and are in the Finder, the disk's icon appears on the screen.

CHAPTER 6

To eject a floppy disk: 137

You need to get to the Finder so you can see the floppy disk's icon on the desktop. Then you can either drag the floppy disk icon to the Trash or select the icon and choose Put Away from the File menu. You can also choose Eject Disk from the Special menu, but this leaves a ghost icon for the disk behind. If you don't want that ghost to haunt you, reinsert the disk and drag its icon to the Trash.

To prepare a new floppy disk for use: 139

You should make sure a disk is unlocked and is either blank or free of any data that anybody else needs before you prepare it for use it in your Mac. Insert the disk in the floppy disk drive, and when the dialog box appears, click the Initialize or (for older Macs) the Two-Sided button. When the initializing process is finished, you can name the disk and open its icon on the desktop.

To copy an entire floppy disk: 142

Insert the floppy disk you want to copy to and open it to make sure you don't want any of the files on it. Close the disk and choose Eject Disk from the Special menu. With the ghost icon of the target disk still on the desktop, insert the source disk. Drag the icon of the source disk onto the ghost icon of the target disk and click OK in the dialog box. As copying proceeds, you may have to switch the disks in and out a couple times before the copying is done.

Disks are what you store things on when you use the Mac. They contain the tools you use and they give you space to save the work you produce. Your work is stored in the form of electronic blips on the surfaces of the disks, somewhat like music is stored on magnetic cassette tape. You need disk storage because the main portion of your computer's memory, the random access memory (RAM), is lost when you turn the computer off. So if you do not store your hard-earned blips on disks, you lose them.

This chapter describes the two different types of disks, hard disks and floppy disks, and tells how to prepare and use them, how to make backup copies of them, how to lock and erase them, and how to check the amount of space you have to store things on them. It also tells you how to solve the most common problems you can have with disks.

Introducing Hard Disks

A *hard disk* consists of one or more platters for storing information. The platters are sealed inside a disk drive, either inside your Mac or inside a separate, external hard disk drive that you connect to your computer. You can't get into the drive and look at the platters, but the computer can read things off of them and write things to them. On the desktop, the icon for your hard disk drive, or *hard drive*, is typically a horizontal rectangle with a name under it, like the one in Figure 6.1. It may look more like your particular model of Mac or hard drive, but if it's the startup drive, it will always be in the upper right corner of the desktop. In fact, if you move it, it will go right back to its corner the next time you shut down or restart the Mac.

Figure 6.1
A hard disk icon

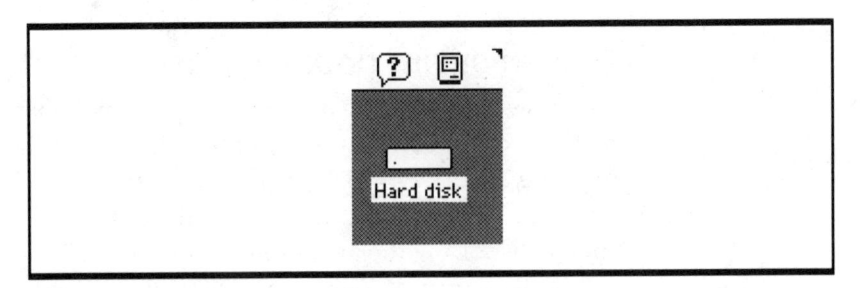

Chapter 6: Storage: Hard and Floppy Disks

You cannot drag the startup hard disk (the one with the system software that's running the Mac) to the Trash. If you have other hard drives connected to your Mac, either by direct cables or by network connections, you can drag their icons to the Trash and undo the logical connection to them.

Introducing Floppy Disks

A *floppy disk* is a thin, round, floppy piece of plastic. The plastic disk behaves somewhat like the magnetized plastic used for cassette tape. It is inside a sturdy plastic case with a metal door. You can put floppy disks into your Macintosh and take them out; the computer reads things off a floppy disk and writes things onto it. On the desktop, the icon for a floppy disk looks like Figure 6.2. It appears under your hard disk icon when you insert the floppy disk in the disk drive. You can move the floppy disk icon anywhere you want on the desktop, but it's easiest to leave it over there on the right side, where you can find it when you have windows open on the left side of the screen.

Figure 6.2
A floppy disk icon

You can drag a floppy disk icon to the Trash to eject the disk from the floppy drive, unless the floppy disk is your startup disk (the one with the system software that's running the Mac) or a disk with something on it that is in use. The first time you eject a floppy disk by dragging it to the Trash you may feel a twinge of fear; you can't help wondering if throwing a disk in the Trash might delete things on the disk, or at least get them a little messy around the edges. Fear not. Throwing a floppy disk in the Trash is merely a symbolic act. The actual disk pops out of the disk drive, without any coffee grounds or bad odors clinging to it.

Tip
Keep your open windows over on the left side of your screen, so you can always get at the icons for your hard disk, floppy disks, and the Trash.

Bytes, Kilobytes, Megabytes

Different types of disks can store different amounts of data. For instance, hard disks can store much more information than floppy disks. Information in computers comes in tiny units called *bytes*: 1024 bytes make a kilobyte (K), 1024 kilobytes make a megabyte (MB). A standard 3.5-inch floppy disk can hold either 800K or 1.4MB of information. Hard disks can store 40MB or more, and their capacities are growing all the time, even as the actual hard drives become smaller and smaller. One gigabyte (G) hard drives, which hold 1024MB of data, are considered low-capacity by some Mac hot-rodders.

To put the storage figures in simple, concrete terms for you and me, though, a floppy disk can store about a book's worth of information; a typical hard disk can store a hefty encyclopedia or more. In terms of graphics, a floppy disk can hold one or two typical color photographs, and a hard disk can usually hold more than a hundred, if they haven't been heavily edited.

To distinguish 800K from 1.4MB floppy disks, look at the corners. If the disk has a single little square hole in the upper right corner of the case, it's an 800K disk. If it has two little square holes, one in each upper corner of the case, and an HD symbol in the lower left corner, it's a 1.4MB disk. Figure 6.3 shows examples of both kinds of disk.

All late-model Macs have SuperDrives that accept 1.4MB disks, while older Macs can use only 800K floppies. If you work with two or more Macs and some have SuperDrives and others don't, you should buy and use 800K disks and use them on all of the machines.

Figure 6.3
Two different 3.5-inch floppy disks

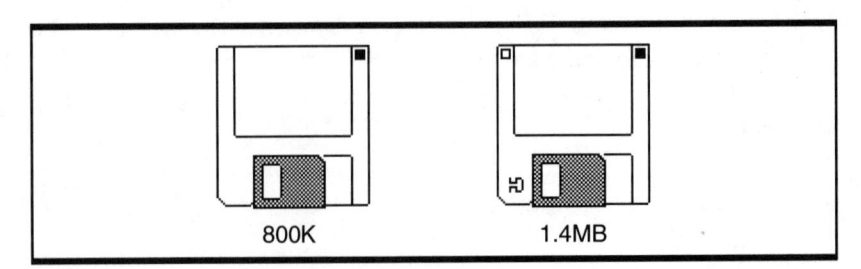

You can't transfer data on 1.4MB disks from a Mac with a SuperDrive to a Mac without a SuperDrive, unless the 1.4MB floppy is formatted as an 800K disk. And what's worse, if you format a 1.4MB floppy as an 800K disk on an old Mac Plus, then put lots of important data on it and stick it in your SuperDrive Mac, it asks you if you want to reinitialize the disk and erase all the data. This is not good. What's worse, even if you *do* want to reinitialize a 1.4MB disk that you formatted on an 800K drive, the SuperDrive often can't manage it! There is a primitive workaround to both these problems; just tape over the hole in the left corner of the case, so the SuperDrive will think the floppy is a standard 800K one. But for less fuss and bother, just stick to using standard 800K disks from the start.

Which Disk for You?

If possible, purchase a Mac with a built-in hard disk, or purchase an external hard disk drive that connects to the SCSI port (socket) on the back of your Macintosh. It is best to use floppy disks only for storing backup copies of the work you produce and the applications you use. Keep your working tools and the things you create or modify daily on a hard disk. Your Mac can write things to and read things from a hard disk much more quickly than a floppy disk, and you can keep so much more on a hard disk that you shouldn't try to get along with just floppy disks unless your work requires using only one application that can run on an older (and therefore smaller) version of the system software, and you create only a few small documents each day. If you try to do more than that without a hard drive, you'll go nuts switching floppies in and out of your Mac. You can use two floppy drives, and keep your startup disk on one of them, but you'll still have to do a mess of disk swapping as you work.

So, you should get a hard disk if you possibly can. But do you want an internal or an external hard disk? If you have a compact, portable, or PowerBook Mac, you want an internal drive, to keep the machine portable. On the other hand, if you have two Macs in different locations and you have to run data back and forth a lot, get an external drive, so that it is the only thing you have to transport.

There are many small, light, fast, and quiet external drives on the market. Another advantage to an external drive is that if you have trouble with it, you can take it to a shop without having to turn over your whole Mac. On the downside for external drives, the service can be poor, and if the Mac system software changes, you can have problems getting compatible driver software to run your external drive properly. So if you buy an external drive, get one from a company that has a reputation for good service and perfect compatibility with the Mac system software.

There are other features you want in any hard drive. Large capacity is the most critical; you will *always* need more disk space in the future, no matter how much is in a hard disk you buy. Fast access and data transfer are important too, especially if you buy an external hard drive and plan to move up to a faster Mac, keeping the hard drive to use with it. Any good new hard drive will also have automatic head parking, so the little heads that read and write on the disk move a safe distance away from it when you aren't using them.

What Is a Small, Light, Fast, and Quiet Hard Drive?

Hard drives are developing rapidly, so it is hard pin down the relative terms for size, weight, speed, and quietness. But at the time of this writing, drives made by La Cie, one of the best-respected companies in the market, have standard-setting statistics. Many have 2.5-inch disks and can fit easily in your shirt pocket. There are several models that weigh less than 10 ounces and all of them have access times of 16 milliseconds or less. These drives have no noisy fans, so they make less than 32 decibels of noise. That makes them inaudible if there is any background noise or music in the room. Hard disks that are 1.8 inches in diameter and weigh one ounce are being built for some special uses. Drives will continue to get smaller, lighter, and faster, but you should make sure any new drive you get has enough capacity for your needs.

Care and Feeding of a Hard Disk

Hard disks don't require much care, normally. All you have to do is make sure you shut down properly before you switch off your Mac; see Chapter 1 for more information on starting up and shutting down. If you avoid dropping your hard disk down the stairs and pouring cleaning solvent into it, it should give you many years of carefree service.

However, if you do have major problems with a hard disk, they can cause real nightmares, like losing all your data and applications. So you should follow a few basic rules and precautions.

Connect and Initialize the Hard Drive Properly

If you are using an internal hard drive, all you have to do is make sure the disk is initialized before you start using it. Most disks are initialized by the factory or shop that installed them; but if yours isn't, the system software will ask you to initialize it the first time you access the disk. Click Initialize to finish the job.

If you are connecting an external disk drive to your Mac, connect the SCSI (Small Computer System Interface) cable as described in the drive's documentation. Make sure you set the ID number to something other than 0 (zero) or 7. Many people set their SCSI drive ID at 6, which makes it the first thing the Mac accesses after its own memory and internal hard drive (if there is one).

Some SCSI drives require that you install a terminator. Plug the terminator into the hard drive's cable socket (it usually looks just like an extra plug), then plug the connector cable into it. Some hard drives have the terminator built into the hardware; your owner's guide will tell you if the drive needs a terminator or not.

Once a new external hard drive is connected to your Mac, turn on the hard disk, then the Mac, and see if the hard disk icon appears on the desktop. If it doesn't, initialize the disk by running the Apple HD SC Setup program, which

Warning
Before starting up a new external hard drive and your Mac, check with an expert on hard drives or with the dealer who sold you your drive to make sure you have terminated it properly; improper termination can cause data loss.

is on the Disk Tools disk you received with your system software. If this program cannot format your particular brand of hard disk, you should have received a floppy disk with the hard disk, and this floppy should have a utility (a small application) on it that can initialize the hard disk. Follow the instructions for the utility in your hard drive's documentation.

When you have connected and initialized an external hard drive, the icon appears on the Mac desktop. You can double-click it to open the drive's window and use it for all your storage needs.

Turn the External Drive On First, and Turn It Off Last

You have to turn your external hard drive on before you turn your Mac on, and you have to leave the external drive on until after you shut down the Mac and turn it off. It's usually OK to turn on the drive and the Mac simultaneously, unless the hard drive is extremely slow in coming up to speed. Just make sure you shut down and turn off the Mac before you turn the hard drive off. The one exception to this rule is that you must use the Mac to park the heads of a few oddball SCSI drives. I recommend that you avoid using these oddball drives, however.

Although you must shut down your Mac and turn it off before turning off the hard drive, you must also make sure you never turn off the Mac while the hard drive is reading or writing data. This can't happen as long as you make sure you shut down before you turn the Mac off. See Chapter 1 for more information on shutting down.

Be Kind to Your Hard Disk

Don't slide, move, tip, punch, slap, or bump your hard disk while it is at work. If the heads bump the disk while it is spinning, they can cause major damage (known as a "head crash"). Even when the hard drive and the Mac are off, you should be careful with the drive whenever you move it; dropping a drive can damage the heads.

Use the hard drive at comfortable room temperatures only. If you move the drive from a hot or cold place to a comfy-temperature place, let it acclimatize for an hour or so before you turn it on.

Keep only one System Folder and one copy of the system software on your hard disk at a time. The Mac system software is not good at competing with itself. The Finder tends to get lost. It may race around in wild, endless loops looking for things that aren't there, or it may try to access things it thinks are at two different places at the same time. Kafkaesque situations like those are tough on hard disks, just as they are tough on humans.

Clean the filter screens in the vents on your hard drive. You can do it yourself with a strong vacuum that has a narrow mouth, like a Dust Buster. Or you can take the hard drive to a qualified technician once a year or so and have it cleaned professionally. Keep papers, clothes, food, and other stuff away from the vents while the drive is on, too; it needs to breathe easily.

Rebuild your desktop once a week or so. All you have to do is hold down the Command key (⌘) and the Option key as you start up or restart the Mac, then click OK when a dialog box asks if you want to rebuild. Just keep in mind, as the dialog box says, that any comments in Info boxes for files and folders on the hard disk will be erased.

Check the hard disk's window now and then to see how many megabytes of data are on the disk, and how much space still remains. See "Checking Disk Capacity" later in this chapter for more info on the subject. When your disk gets to about two-thirds full, see if you can save some data to floppies, or copy off some applications or games that you don't or shouldn't be using much. You can also use a compression utility such as StuffIt or DiskDoubler to reduce the size of your files, but you always pay a price in time (the time it takes to compress and decompress files) for what you save in space. If you have been running the disk at more than two-thirds full for some time, and moving lots of things onto it and off of it, consider defragmenting, as explained later in this chapter.

Keep an eye out for little warning signs, like the Mac taking a long time to switch from an application to the Finder, or unexplained appearances of the message, "The application is busy or missing," or unexplained appearances of bomb boxes. These things call for rebuilding the desktop, as explained above. After you rebuild, check to see how full the hard disk is, and if you still need space, copy more stuff to floppies or delete it.

Note
You can't trust the advertised capacity of your disk drive; in reality, once they are formatted and prepared for use, most drives hold about five to ten percent less than the manufacturers claim.

Save and Back Up

I know, I know, you've been told before. I also know that you are human, like me. We humans tend to overlook things like saving and backing up, especially when we are in a hurry, and when we are in a hurry we tend to push the Mac a little bit too hard, just the way we tend to pull shoelaces a little too hard when we are rushed.

But shoelaces are cheap. Your applications and all your data are much more valuable, much more difficult to replace. Save your work every ten or fifteen minutes, so you never have to redo much in the event of an electrical surge or s system software problem.

Backing up is important too. First off, the term "back up" has nothing to do with putting the Mac in reverse. It means to make a backup or reserve copy of data on the Mac. Back up your work at least once a week if your hard disk is less than half full, and back up your work once a day if your hard disk is more than two-thirds full. If your hard disk gets more than three-quarters full, or if it starts giving you "Out of Space" messages when you do things like save, or if you notice that it takes more time than usual to switch to and from the Finder, or if the Finder is taking a long time to find things, BACK UP RIGHT NOW!!!! Don't stop to tie your shoes, and don't hurry up to finish just one more edit of that document you are working on. DO IT NOW.

Note
Most backup utilities let you make a catalog of folders and files you need to back up regularly. All you have to do is choose the folder name from the catalog, click a Back-up button, and let the utility do the rest for you.

Backing up your work can be either very simple or very complex, depending on how paranoid you are. If you are just working on one project at a time, and you just want to make sure you have a copy of your latest work on the project, all you have to do is copy the whole project once a week or so, then back up the last chapter you did major work on once every day or so. If you have trouble remembering to do this, you can automate the process with a utility such as FastBack or Redux. I like Backup, which comes with the Norton Utilities package. It is simple and quick to use.

If you can afford to put some extra money into your Mac, you can buy an inexpensive second hard disk drive and do your backups to it. Copying files from one hard disk to another is much faster than copying to floppy disks, and you can keep all the backups for each project in one nice, big folder, rather than scattered among a bunch of floppies. Some people even back up their applications on a second hard drive, but I think it's safe enough to keep a backup copy of the original program floppy.

The backup procedure is similar for most of the utilities that do it. For example, to back up a folder containing your latest work using Norton's Backup, you use the following steps:

1. Save your work and close any documents you intend to back up.
2. Find the backup catalog for the folder you want to back up. I keep all these catalog files in a folder inside the Norton Utilities folder, so I can get at them easily.
3. Double-click the catalog to open Backup and display a file list with the selected folder at the top.
4. Open the folder and make sure you want to back up everything in it. Click in the left margin of the list to check or uncheck folders and files.
5. Check the Backup to: setting to make sure you are going to back up to the kind of floppies you have in hand.
6. Click the Update button and insert the disks that Backup asks you to.

Backup tells you how long the backup might take in the worst case; the further along it gets on the job, the shorter that time estimate gets, in most cases. In my experience, the backup jobs of 1MB to 2MB folders only take a few minutes.

Whether you use a hard disk or floppies for backup, make sure you have a large amount of memory set aside in your Mac's disk cache. The rule of thumb is to allot at least 32K of memory to the disk cache for each megabyte of RAM your machine has. Allot much more if you use memory-hungry applications or ones that create relatively large (200K+) documents. The larger the disk cache, the faster you can copy things, and the easier it will be for the Mac to do the copying in the background, which allows you to go on working in your current application.

Defragment the Hard Disk Before It Fills Up

If you have filled your hard disk to three-quarters of its capacity, or if you have been running it at about two-thirds full for a few months, or if you have done lots of file moving over several months, even with a hard disk that is half full or less, the disk will become fragmented. This means that the individual files on the disk get scattered all over it, rather than staying together.

Fragmenting happens because the disk's driver software places data on the disk wherever it can find space, and the space on the disk is divided up into small units. As a disk gets near to full, files are put into all the little leftover units of space between other files. As you add and delete more new files, the little leftover units of space get more and more scattered, so your files wind up in little fragments all over the disk. Then when the Finder comes looking for a file it has to do a lot of hunting around and collecting fragments to make the whole file. This is hard on the Finder, and it means the disk has to do a lot more spinning to get your work done.

If it takes a long time for the Mac to open an edited file, or if you see the message "The application is busy or missing," even though you know the application is right there in front of you and not busy at all, then you can bet you need to defragment your hard disk.

Tip
Back up all your essential data and customizing files on your hard disk before you defragment it.

The simplest, most primitive way to defragment a hard disk is to copy all of it to another hard disk or to floppy disks. Then initialize the fragmented disk, and copy everything back onto it. If you can rent or borrow a hard disk that is the same size as yours and copy everything over to it and back again, this is not only simple, but quick. Copying everything to floppies takes quite some time and effort, especially if you haven't been backing up your work regularly.

You can also get a utility, such as Speed Disk (one of the Norton Utilities) or Silverlining, and let the utility defragment and reorganize your files in the optimum sequence for performance, without moving them off the disk. The only problem with these defragmenting or *optimizing* utilities is that they take a lot of time to do their work, especially if you are defragmenting a large disk that is nearly full, and which hasn't ever been defragmented before. See the utility's documentation for information on using it, and how to make it work as fast as possible.

A good compromise between optimizing and primitive defragmenting is to copy everything off your disk onto a borrowed or rented hard disk, then install the optimizing utility, then copy everything back. Once the disk is in good order, the utility doesn't take much time to prevent future defragmentation. You can even divide up your hard disk into partitions, which further prevents fragmentation (see your hard drive documentation for more information on partitioning). I prefer to keep everything on one partition, but I use the defragmenting utility pretty often, to guard against built-up fragmentation.

Chapter 6: Storage: Hard and Floppy Disks

To carry out a standard defragmentation using Speed Disk and assuming that you have put the disk in good order and defragmented it at least once before, use the following steps:

1. Back up your data, applications, preference files, and custom dictionaries.
2. Go to the Finder and find the Speed Disk icon. Increase the memory allocation as much as possible; for example, if you have 4MB of RAM and your system software uses 2.5MB, set the Speed Disk allocation at 1.3MB.
3. Start the Speed Disk utility; this means double-clicking the Norton Utilities icon, then clicking the Speed Disk icon in the window that appears.
4. Make sure the drive you want to defragment is selected when the Speed Disk window opens, then click Check Drive.
5. If the disk is close to full and has moderate fragmentation or worse, click the Optimize button. If it is your startup disk, you have to restart the Mac using the Norton Utilities Applications disk, then start Speed Disk and click the Optimize button.
6. Wait. It may take quite awhile, depending on how big your disk is, and how fast your Mac's CPU is.

Care and Feeding of Floppy Disks

The main things you do with floppy disks are insert them, eject them, name them, and copy things onto and off of them.

To "feed" or insert a floppy disk into your Mac, hold the disk label side up, metal part away from you, and slide the disk into the drive. It clicks firmly into place, and if the Macintosh screen is displaying the desktop, the icon for the inserted floppy disk appears.

To eject (or spit out, as some say) a floppy disk when you can see its icon on the desktop, drag the icon to the Trash. This does not delete or erase anything on the floppy disk. It just tells the computer to spit out the disk. You can also select the disk icon and choose Put Away from the File menu, but this method is much less convenient.

Tip

If you cannot select the name of a floppy to change it, the floppy must be locked. Eject the floppy, unlock it, then reinsert the floppy and change the name.

To change the name of any floppy or hard disk, select the name under the icon on the desktop and type a new name, which replaces the old name automatically. Give each disk a distinct name that reflects what is on it. You can use any character except the colon (:) in a disk name, and you can use spaces as well.

To copy things onto a floppy disk, just drag their icons to the floppy disk icon on the desktop, or into the floppy disk's open window. To copy things from a floppy disk, open the disk's window and drag the icons to the window of the folder or disk you want to copy them to. If you copy a file that has been compressed with a utility such as StuffIt, you may have to decompress the file before you can use it.

Compressed Files and How to Use Them

Compressed files are ones that have been made smaller by a special utility. You can fit more of them on a floppy or hard disk, and they can be sent more quickly over a modem, saving phone bills and money spent on an information service. But before a compressed file can be used, you must decompress it. Two well-known utilities that compress and decompress files reliably are StuffIt Deluxe and DiskDoubler.

The icons of files that have been compressed show the logo of the compressing utility, and most have a suffix, such as .sit, added to the name. Once you have moved a compressed file from a floppy disk to your hard disk, where you presumably have more room, you can just double-click the file to decompress it. Even if you don't have the compression utility on your hard disk, the file can usually decompress itself. If you are using an installer program to install an application that is compressed, the installer will usually decompress the files for you; this takes place at the end of the installation, and you may see a dialog box that tells you how the decompression process is coming along. It can take from a minute to half an hour or more to decompress files, depending on how large they are and how fast or slow your Mac is.

Chapter 6: Storage: Hard and Floppy Disks

Floppy Disk Precautions

Floppy disks don't require much care, but keep them away from the following things:

- Magnets: Toy magnets, paper clip holders, telephones, TV or computer-monitor magnets, stereo-speaker magnets, and electric motors. If you have an external disk drive and a compact Mac, keep the drive away from the left side of your Mac; there are strong magnetic fields by the power supply on that side. Keep disks away from the left side of ImageWriter printers, too.
- Heat and cold: Use floppies and the floppy disk drive only when both are at room temperature.
- Static electricity: Avoid touching the metal door on a floppy disk with your fingers (especially if you just walked across a deep pile wool rug), and don't put disks in plastic bags.
- Grease, dust, water: Never open the metal door and touch the floppy itself. Don't store floppies in damp or dusty places.

Preparing a Floppy Disk for Use

Before you can use a brand-new blank floppy disk, you have to format or initialize it so your Macintosh can write to and read from it. Initializing is sort of like setting up the compartments on the disk for the Mac to store things in. It has nothing to do with putting your initials on the disk. Use the following procedure to prepare a new disk or erase everything off an old disk to make a fresh start. Whatever kind of disk you are working with, make sure it is unlocked; for information on unlocking a disk, see "Locking and Unlocking a Floppy Disk" later in this chapter.

1. Insert the disk in the floppy disk drive. If it's a new or damaged disk, a dialog box tells you that the disk is unreadable and asks if you want to initialize it. If it's an old disk you want to erase, make sure it's selected, then choose Erase Disk from the Special menu; the Initialize dialog box then appears.
2. If you inserted a 1.4MB disk, click the Initialize button. If you inserted an 800K disk, click Two-Sided. An alert box warns you that the initialization process will erase everything on the disk.

3. As long as you are sure you did insert a new, blank disk, or a disk that you want to erase completely, click the Erase button. A message box soon appears, telling you how the formatting is going. The box closes and the disk's icon appears on the desktop when formatting is complete.

Floppy Disks for Different Uses

The following sections describe the different types of disks that you use to start up your Mac, to run it, and to do your work.

The Startup Disk

A startup disk can be either a hard disk or a floppy disk. For normal Mac use, it should be a hard disk. It must contain the System Folder with all the system software in it, and the disk must be in your Macintosh or in an external drive that is properly connected to the Mac and turned on, before you can turn on the Mac and start it up. In other words, it's the disk with the software that tells your Mac what to do when you turn it on. It gets the system running, then presents the desktop so you can go to work.

System Disks and Application Disks

When you purchase a new Mac, you receive a number of floppy disks with the system software on them. These are like backup copies for the system software that is normally installed on the Mac's hard drive. When you purchase applications for your computer, you receive one or more floppy disks that contain the application program and any additional software you need to use it. You often receive floppy disks with installation software, to help put the application and all the other stuff on your hard disk.

If you lose or damage your system or application disks, then lose or corrupt the system or application software you have on your hard disk, you are stuck. You have to purchase and install new software before you can go back to work. Avoid this fiasco; make backup copies of the system disks and any application disks you have purchased. See "Backing Up System and Applications Disks" later in this chapter.

Data Disks

Data disks are the floppy disks you use to store your work. If you have no hard disk, you must save all your work to data disks as you create it. If you have a hard disk, save your work to it, and use data disks or a second hard disk to back up your work once a day or so.

Backing Up Files on System and Application Disks

Back up (make copies of) your valuable system and application files on disks to prevent loss of the tools you need most for your work. You can also back up data files by the same method, although most people use a backup utility, as explained in "Save and Back Up" earlier in this chapter.

If you know you want to copy *all* of the files on a system or application disk, there is a shortcut; use the procedure in "Copying an Entire Floppy Disk" later in this chapter. Copying the whole floppy to another one is especially good if you are backing up an application that has been compressed with a utility such as StuffIt. But you can use the following procedure to copy some uncompressed application files or system software you need off a disk.

1. Insert the system or application disk in the floppy disk drive.
2. Double-click the disk icon to open a window displaying its contents.
3. Double-click the icon for your hard disk to open its window if it isn't open. Resize and arrange the two windows so they fit on the screen.
4. Click in the hard disk window, then choose New Folder from the File menu to create an untitled folder in the hard disk window.
5. Rename the folder to reflect the name of the application or system software you want to back up.

6. Click in the window of the system or application floppy disk, then drag a selection rectangle across all of the files and folders you want to back up.
7. Drag all of the files and folders to the untitled folder in the hard disk window. A message box tells you how copying is going.
8. If there is more than one windowful of files and folders in the system or application disk window, repeat the selection and copying process.
9. Close the window for the system or application floppy disk. Drag the disk icon to the Trash to eject the floppy disk.
10. Insert a new disk and initialize it. See "Preparing a Floppy Disk for Use" earlier in this chapter for more information.
11. Drag the newly named system or application folder from the hard disk window to the new floppy disk icon. A message box tells you how copying is going.
12. When copying is complete, open the floppy disk icon and check the contents. Then close the window, drag the floppy disk icon to the Trash to eject it, and label the floppy disk.
13. Store the backup disk in a safe but handy place, preferably not the same place where you store the original system or application disk.

Copying an Entire Floppy Disk

If you have two floppy drives in your Mac, or an external and an internal floppy drive, it is quite simple to copy the entire contents of one floppy disk to another floppy disk. You just put the two disks in the two drives, and when the two floppy disk icons appear on the desktop, you drag the source disk icon to the target disk icon. The source disk is the one with the stuff you want to copy, and the target is the empty disk you're aiming to fill. A dialog box appears, asking if you want to replace the contents of the target disk with those of the source. Just click OK, and the Mac does the copying. Anything that was on the target disk is erased.

It's a bit more of a trick to copy a whole floppy to another one if you have only one disk drive. Use the following steps to limit disk-swapping to a minimum.

1. Insert the target floppy disk, open its window, and make sure it has nothing on it that you want to keep.
2. Close the disk's window, but leave the icon selected.
3. Choose Eject Disk from the Special menu. The target disk spits out of the disk drive, but a ghost icon remains on the desktop.
4. Insert the source disk. When its icon appears, drag it to the ghost icon of the target disk, as shown in Figure 6.4.
5. Click OK in the message box that asks if you want to replace the contents of the disk with those of the source disk.
6. Switch disks when the Mac asks you to.

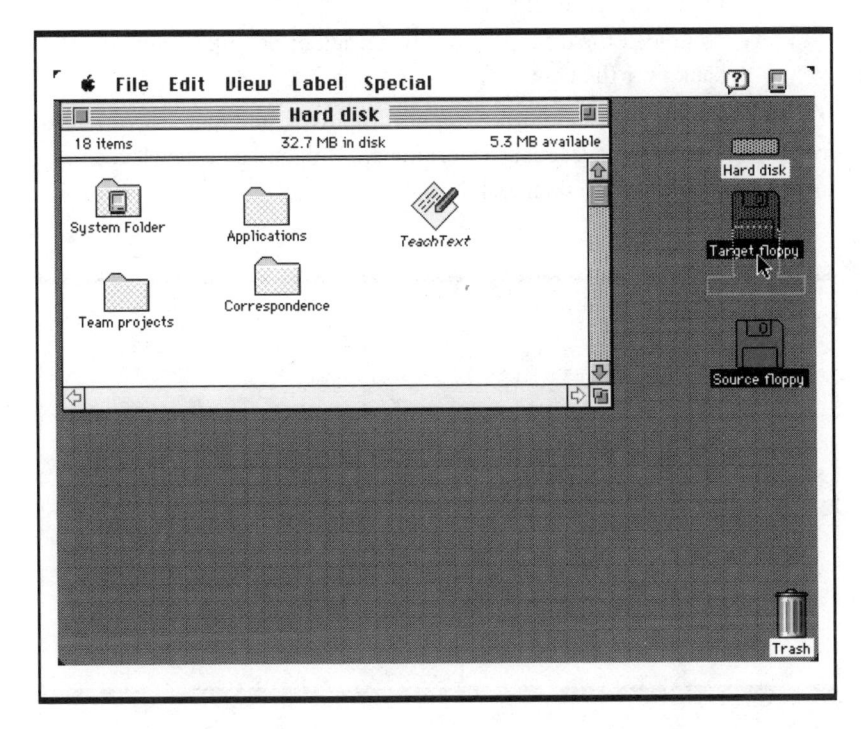

Figure 6.4
Copying an entire disk

Copying an Entire Floppy Disk **143**

Locking and Unlocking a Floppy Disk

To lock or *write-protect* a disk so you cannot add to, change, or delete anything on it, use the following procedure:

1. Eject the disk from the computer if it is inserted.
2. Hold the disk face down, with the metal end away from you, and look closely at the locking tab that is now in the lower right corner.
3. Use your fingernail or the tip of a ball-point pen to slide the locking tab toward the edge of the disk cover, as shown in Figure 6.5. A small hole opens.
4. To unlock the disk, use your fingernail or pen tip to slide the tab back over the hole.

It is wise to lock all system disks, application disks, and data backup disks for projects that you have finished working on. Unlock a data disk if you need to add information to it, then lock it again.

Figure 6.5
Locking a floppy disk

Erasing a Floppy Disk

If you have a disk with old information on it that you no longer need, you can erase it and reuse the disk. Insert the disk in the drive and open the icon to make sure there's nothing you want on the disk. Then close the window and choose Erase Disk from the Special menu. A dialog box asks if you want to completely erase the disk. If you are erasing a 1.4MB disk, click the Initialize button. If you are erasing an 800K disk, click the Two-Sided button.

Checking Disk Capacity

To see how much storage space you have used and how much is left on any hard or floppy disk, open the icon for disk and look at the information bar (shown in Figure 6.6) that is just under the title bar of the disk's window.

In this bar you can see how many items are on the disk, how many bytes they take up, and how many bytes are left. The example in Figure 6.6 is an 800K floppy disk with 2 items taking up 79K of space, leaving 707K available. Notice that the two figures don't add up to 800K. About three percent of each disk is used up by hidden files that the Mac needs to keep tabs on what is in the disk and what you have done with it. Similarly, on a hard disk, about five percent to ten percent of the disk capacity is taken up by formatting and hidden files.

Tip
If you can't see the information bar, choose by Icon or by Small Icon from the View menu.

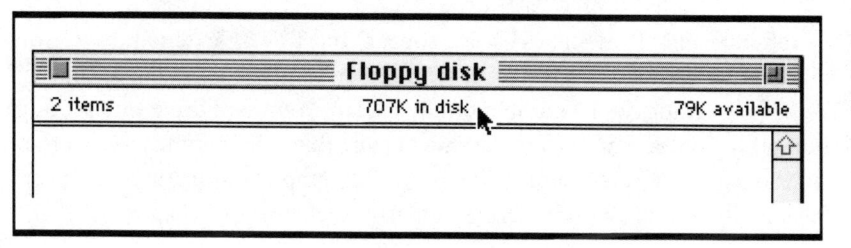

Figure 6.6
An information bar for a floppy disk

Troubleshooting Problems with Hard and Floppy Disks

These are the problems you are most likely to have with hard and floppy disks, and how to solve them without causing damage to the applications and data you have stored on disks.

Hard Disk Icon Does Not Appear on Desktop

The problem is that either the Mac can't communicate with the hard drive, or that the hard drive isn't working.

First, try turning everything off and checking the power plugs and cable connections; then turn everything back on. If the hard drive is an internal one, all you have to do is turn the Mac off, check the plug, wait about a half minute or so, then turn it back on. If the drive is an external one, make sure you turn it on *before* you turn on the Mac.

If the hard disk that isn't appearing on the desktop is your startup disk, you'll just get a question mark disk icon, and no desktop at all. Turn the Mac off and start it with a startup floppy disk, such as the Disk Tools disk you got with your system software. If the Mac starts OK and the hard disk icon appears, you need to reinstall the system software on your hard disk.

If the hard disk icon still does not appear, and it is an external drive, you probably have it set to a bad SCSI ID number. Find the little dial or thumbwheel for setting the ID number on the back of your hard drive, and set it to something other than 0 (zero) or 7, and something different from any other SCSI device you have attached to your Mac. For more information, see "Connect and Initialize the Hard Drive Properly" earlier in this chapter.

If you try all of the above and still don't see the hard disk icon, you may have to rebuild the desktop. See "Be Kind to Your Hard Disk" earlier in this chapter for help with rebuilding your desktop. If that doesn't help, it's time to take the Mac to a qualified technician for service. If you have an early Mac Plus and you experience lots of trouble with an external SCSI drive, you might have a faulty ROM (Read Only Memory) chip; the thing can't talk to the SCSI drive properly. Make sure the technician checks out the ROM on your old Mac.

You Can't Remember What Disk Your Current Folder Is On

If you are looking at the window of a folder in the Finder and you can't remember if the folder is on your hard disk or a floppy disk, or if you can't remember the name of the floppy disk in the floppy drive, just press the Command key (⌘) and pull down the menu under the window's title. The name of the disk will be the bottom item on the menu.

A Disk Is Too Full

You are trying to move or save a file to a hard or floppy disk, and you get an error message box that says the item could not be moved because the disk is full. If you are trying to move something to a floppy disk, you can open the disk's window and delete items to make more room. If you are trying to move or save a file to your hard disk and you get this message, WATCH OUT!!!! You are putting your hard disk and your system software at risk. You need to clear a lot of stuff off of your hard disk (until it is only about ⅔ full) and you probably need to defragment the hard disk if you have not already done so. See the section, "Defragment the Hard Disk Before It Fills Up" earlier in this chapter.

Hard Disk Has Crashed

You bumped the hard disk or the electricity surged or something, and the Mac is hung up or making weird noises. Keep calm. The first thing to try is just turning off the Mac, then the hard drive (if it is external). Wait a minute or two, or until the lights stop dimming and flaring if there are electrical surges, then turn the hard drive (if it is external) and the Mac back on. Hold down the ⌘ key and Option as you turn on the Mac.

This rebuilds the desktop. If the hard disk refuses to start up, take the following steps:

1. If it is an external hard drive, make sure the cables are connected firmly. If the drive has a terminator, make sure it is firmly connected, too.

2. If the hard disk is your startup disk, start the Mac with a floppy disk such as Disk Tools (which you got with your system software) or the Norton Utilities Application disk.
3. Use Disk First Aid or the Norton Utilities Disk Doctor to check and repair the hard disk.
4. If that didn't help, reinstall the system software on your hard disk.
5. Still no go? Reinstall the hard drive's driver software (see your hard disk documentation for help).
6. If all else fails, you have to zap your Mac's PRAM. If you are still running on a floppy disk, press the ⌘, Shift, and Option keys and choose Control Panel from the Apple menu. Click Yes when asked if you want to zap the PRAM. This resets the Mac so it should work with your hard disk.

If none of these solutions work, take your Mac and hard disk to a qualified technician.

The Mac Is Slow to Load an Edited File, or It Tells You Wrongly That an Application Is Busy or Missing

These two problems may just mean that you are loading a big file, or that an application is not where the Mac expects it to be, but if you notice the two symptoms cropping up often, and without obvious reason, you can bet your hard disk is fragmented. See the section "Defragment the Hard Disk Before it Fills Up" earlier in this chapter for information on how to fix the problem, before it starts causing crashes and data loss.

The Mac Can't Read or Write a File You're Trying to Copy to a Floppy Disk

When you try to copy a file to a floppy disk, you see an error message that says the file couldn't be read or it couldn't be written and it was skipped. Before you do anything else, look closely at the error message. If it says the file cannot be read, then you have a problem with the source file or the hard disk. If it says the file cannot be written, there is a problem with the target floppy disk.

First just try copying the file again. If that doesn't work, and the problem is with the source on your hard disk, use a utility such as Disk First Aid, or one of the Symantec disk-repair utilities, to see if you can save the file. If the problem was with the target floppy disk, eject it, reinsert it, and copy something else to it, then try copying the file you want. If you keep getting the same error message, or you get a message that says the disk is damaged, back up everything on the floppy disk, then erase it and try to copy something to it again. If it still acts up, discard it. It is damaged, and you may lose any future data you put on it.

The Mac Can't Read from or Write to a Disk Because of a Disk Error Caused by Bad Media

You are trying to open a file on a hard or floppy disk, or you are trying to copy a file to or from a disk, and you see an error message that says there is a disk error due to bad media. Either there is something like a piece of dust on the disk, or it has been damaged in some way. If it is a floppy disk, try this low-tech procedure first: Eject the disk, tap its edge on your palm, reinsert it, then try the read or write action you wanted.

No luck? Use a disk repair utility, such as Disk First Aid (which comes with your system software, on the Disk Tools disk), or the Norton Utilities Disk Doctor, to check the disk for errors that can be fixed easily. Usually, media errors can't be fixed by these utilities. There is one other thing you can try, though. If you have a disk defragmenting utility, such as Norton's Speed Disk, it may be able to move things around and save the file. Just use the optimizing or defragmenting feature to defragment the disk with bad media error.

If you do manage to fix the disk error or work around it, save any important data you have on the disk to a backup disk, immediately. If the media problem was on a hard disk, and it crops up more than once, see a qualified technician to see if your hard disk can be repaired or at least reformatted in such a way that the media problem doesn't come back and haunt you.

The Mac Thinks It Can't Read a Floppy Disk

If you insert a floppy disk that you know has information on it, you may nonetheless see an error message that says

>   This disk is unreadable:
>   Do you want to initialize it?

There may be a bit of dust on the disk. Click the Eject button in the error message box, then grasp a corner of the disk and tap the edge of the case against your palm briskly. Slide the metal door open and shut a couple times (without touching the floppy inside), to make sure it works. Put two fingertips on the metal hub in the middle of the back of the floppy and turn the thing a bit. Reinsert the disk.

If you get the "unreadable" message again, the disk is probably damaged. One last-ditch effort you can make is to hold down the ⌘ and Option keys as you insert the faulty disk; Click the Yes button when a message box asks if you want to rebuild the desktop file. Sometimes a disk has a glitch in its desktop file code. If you still get the "unreadable" message, you can try to reinitialize the disk, erasing all the contents, but initialization may fail, and even if it doesn't the disk is a poor risk; the best thing to do with it is throw it away.

If there are files on the disk that you need, you can use a utility such as Disk First Aid, which is on the Disk Tools disk you received with your system software, or Norton disk-recovery utilities. Place the recovered files on another disk, then throw away the damaged disk so you don't lose any more data on it.

A Floppy Disk You Want to Eject Is Hidden by Open Windows

If open windows on your desktop hide the icon of a disk you want to eject, choose Put Away from the Finder's File menu or press ⌘-Y. Don't eject the hidden disk by choosing the Eject Disk command from the Special menu, or you may have problems later with the floppy ghost icon, which is shown in Figure 6.7.

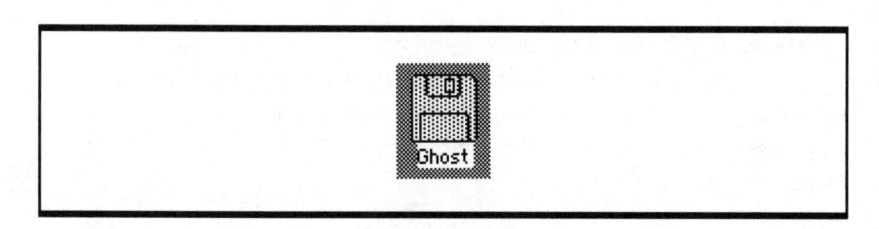

Figure 6.7
Floppy ghost

The Mac Demands a Disk You Ejected

You ejected a disk with the Eject Disk command from the Special menu in the Finder. Although this seems like a logical way to eject a disk, it leaves a ghost behind (as explained in the previous problem), and when you perform some other Finder action later, the Finder asks for the disk that belongs to the ghost. Eject disks by dragging them to the Trash or by selecting their icons and choosing Put Away from the File menu.

Floppy Disk Icon Does Not Appear on Desktop

You have inserted a floppy disk, but its icon does not show up on the desktop. To kick the floppy disk out, press ⌘-1 (for an internal drive) or ⌘-2. If that doesn't work, use the paper-clip method described in the next problem. When you get the floppy disk out, restart the computer and try again. If the problem recurs, take your Mac to a qualified technician; the Mac or disk drive is sick.

Floppy Disk Stuck in Disk Drive

No matter how you try to eject a disk, whether you drag it to the Trash or choose the Put Away or Eject Disk command, the thing just sticks in there. Often the drive will make painful choking and hacking noises, but to no avail. First, try pressing ⌘-1 (for the internal floppy drive) or ⌘-2 (for an external floppy drive). If that doesn't spit it out, try shutting down and turning the Mac off, then turning it on with the mouse button held down.

Still no luck? To dislodge a really stuck floppy, use the custom-made power-user's tool; a straightened paper clip. Seriously, you have to get a paper clip (the large, heavy-duty ones are best) and straighten one end of it out. Stick that end into the tiny hole to the side of your disk drive, and press straight in on the button that's in there. It takes a firm, but gentle push, and you have

Troubleshooting Problems with Hard and Floppy Disks

to make sure the end of the paper clip is pushing directly against the little lever in there. If the disk won't come out all the way when you press that lever repeatedly, don't try to yank the disk out with pliers or your bare hands; you could destroy the disk drive by yanking it. Take the Mac to a qualified technician instead.

Can't Find a Seldom-Used File on a Forgotten Floppy

You forgot which floppy a file is on, and you can't even remember the name of the file for sure. Use the Find command with More Choices in the Finder's File menu, and use any clues you can remember, like the last modification date or any part of the name. Search through your floppies one at a time, and when you find the dumb file, make an alias of it and put the alias in some logical place on your hard drive. Then, if you need the file again and forget what floppy it's on, you can just double-click the alias and the Mac will ask you for the floppy by name.

You Are Switching Floppy Disks Over and Over

You keep seeing a little message box that asks you to insert a floppy disk; at the same time, the Mac spits out the floppy that is in the drive. What a pain. People call this problem a switch-disk nightmare. To stop it, try pressing ⌘-. (period) at least once, and several times if it doesn't work the first time.

Seven

Memory: Checking and Adjusting Your RAM Use

◆ ◆

Featuring

- ◆ What RAM is and why you always need more
- ◆ How to monitor your Mac's memory needs in any situation
- ◆ How to adjust the amount of memory allocated to an application
- ◆ How to adjust the amount of RAM set aside in the disk cache
- ◆ Troubleshooting problems with memory

First Steps

To check on memory use: 157

Go to the Finder and choose About This Macintosh from the Apple menu. When the window appears, look at the data at the top to see how much memory is built into your Mac, how much memory you have overall, if you have virtual memory, and how large the biggest unused block of memory is. You can also look at the bars in the lower part of the window to find out how much memory is allocated to the system software and how much is allocated to each application. You can then check the dark parts of the bars to see roughly how much of the allocated memory is being used by each application and the system software.

To see exactly how much RAM your system software and applications are using: 158

Go to the Finder and choose About This Macintosh from the Apple menu. When you see the window showing memory bars, choose Show Balloons from the Help menu, then just point to each of the memory bars and read the exact number of kilobytes of RAM that are currently being used.

CHAPTER 7

To change the amount of memory allocated to an application: 159

Before you can adjust an application's memory allocation, you have to quit it and go to the Finder. Then you need to find the icon for the application and select it. When the icon is selected, choose Get Info from the File menu and look in the lower right corner of the application's Info window for the memory settings. If you want to allocate more or less memory to the application, select the Preferred size number and edit it. You shouldn't set the preferred size to be any less than the suggested size unless you can't avoid it.

To adjust the disk cache: 159

You should quit all applications before you begin to adjust your Mac's disk cache. Then choose Control Panels from the Apple menu, and open the Memory control panel. Click the Defaults button to see what the default setting for memory is. Then click the up and down arrows to set the cache size to a different number of kilobytes. Unless your Mac is very short of RAM, you'll want the setting to be higher than the default for improved performance. After you close the Memory control panel, you need to restart your Mac to have the new disk cache setting take effect.

This chapter explains how to make the best use of the memory in your Mac. A computer needs memory to retain information temporarily; it keeps data and applications on its memory chips as it uses them. When you start an application or open a document, the information is brought out of storage on your hard disk (or a floppy disk) and the computer puts the parts it needs into the memory chips. When you save your work on a document or quit an application, your Mac puts the information that is in its temporary memory back into the more permanent storage space available on a disk.

What RAM Is

There are several different types of memory on different chips in the computer, but the most important type for your purposes is *random access memory* (RAM). The Mac can access the different parts of this memory in any order, and can therefore use the memory to do whatever an application requires.

Tip
You should install 25 percent more RAM than you think you need to do your current work. That way, when you upgrade your applications and require more RAM, your Mac will still be able to meet their needs.

The more RAM you have, the more you can do with your computer. This chapter tells you how to make the most of what you have, but there is no substitute for having enough RAM to start with. If you have 2 megabytes (2MB) of RAM in your Macintosh, for instance, you can only open one program that requires 1MB of RAM to operate. In fact, you have to have a minimal version of the system software to leave 1MB for an application. You may be able to open a small desk accessory or a second application that doesn't use much RAM, but even this can cause problems when your major application tries to do a memory-intensive operation such as repaginating a text document, cutting or pasting a complex graphic image, or recalculating a large spreadsheet.

If you have 4MB of RAM, you can open at least two applications and keep a desk accessory open on the side, if none of the three requires excessive amounts of memory. Or you can use one application and let it take over a large portion of the computer's memory, so it works as efficiently as possible, without having to "hit the disk" (access the hard disk) for information. If you have 8MB or 10MB of RAM, you can use large, memory-hungry applications and never run out.

When you have enough RAM, your Macintosh works silently and quickly; when you hear the hard disk whirring often during your work, you know you need to install more memory or adjust the allocation of the memory you have. Before adjusting your computer's memory, give serious consideration to increasing the RAM to at least 4MB, or as much as you can afford. See your Apple dealer for a memory upgrade. The memory chips, of the SIMMs (Single In-line Memory Modules) are becoming less and less expensive, so the upgrade may cost you less than five percent of the cost of your computer. Once you have installed as much memory as you can afford, use the remainder of this chapter to make the most of the memory you have.

Monitoring Your Memory Use

To see what your memory needs are and how you should adjust for them, use the About This Macintosh window. To open the window, go to the Finder (choose the Finder from the Applications menu at the right end of your menu bar), and choose About This Macintosh from the Apple menu. A window more or less like the one in Figure 7.1 appears; the applications and memory figures will vary according to how much memory you have and how you have allocated it.

Use the About This Macintosh window to learn the following things:

- To determine how much memory your Mac contains, see the Total Memory amount (8,192K in the example).

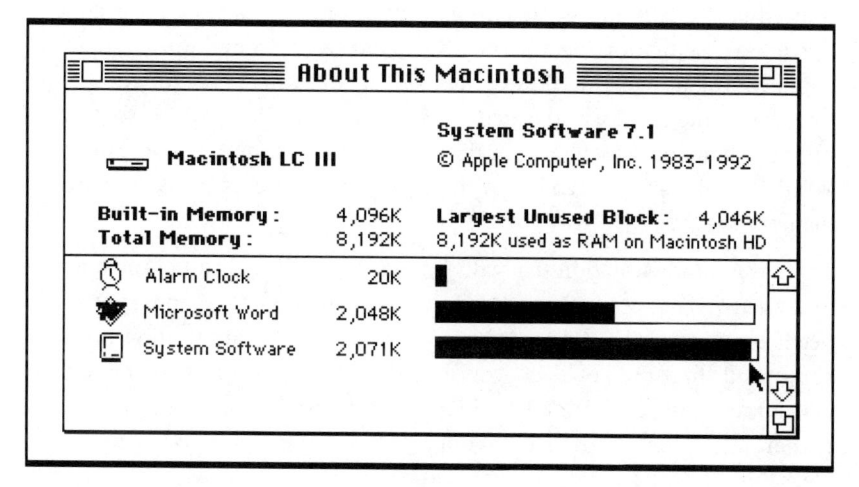

Figure 7.1
About This Macintosh window showing memory information

Monitoring Your Memory Use **157**

- To see how much memory is available to open another application, see the Largest Unused Block amount (4,046K in the example).
- To see how much memory is allocated for the use of each open application or DA, see the amounts listed next to them (2,048K for Microsoft Word and 20K for Alarm Clock in the example).
- To estimate how much of its allocated memory an application is using, look at the black bars and the white spaces (Word is using just over half of its allotted memory in the example).

If you want to know exactly how much memory the system software or an application is using, just choose Show Balloons from the Help menu (the menu with a question mark in a balloon), then hold the pointer on the System Software or the bar of an application in the About This Macintosh window. A balloon appears; text in it tells you about the bar and tells you how much memory the application or system software is using. To get rid of the balloons, choose Hide Balloons from the Help menu.

Adjusting Application Allocations

If you want to open an application that needs more memory than the largest unused block, you may be able to do it by adjusting memory. For example, if you have a situation like the one shown in Figure 7.1 and want to open an application that needs 4,100K of memory (whew, what a memory hog), you can reduce the memory allocated to Microsoft Word by 100K or so, freeing up enough memory to open your third application. In the example, Microsoft Word is only using about half of its allocation; it seems to have plenty of memory to spare.

Warning
If you open a number of large documents in an application, or if you invoke some memory-intensive processes, your application can run out of memory and crash.

There is another situation that calls for adjusting the amount of memory allocated to your applications. If you have opened all the applications you need, but in the About This Macintosh window your application memory bars are all almost full of black, you should see if it is possible to increase their allocations. Look at the number of K's in the largest unused block of memory. Is there more than 1MB (1,000K) of RAM available? If so, you need to increase the allocations for your applications.

Use the following procedure to increase or decrease the amount of memory that is allocated to an application:

1. Quit the application if you are using it.
2. In the Finder, select the icon for the application. If you have trouble finding it, select the icon for an alias of it, choose Get Info from the File menu, and click the Find Original button in the Info window. If there are no aliases, choose Find from the File menu and enter the name of the application.
3. When you have selected the icon for the application, choose Get Info from the File menu. The Info window opens, as shown in Figure 7.2.
4. Select the number in the Preferred size box in the lower right corner of the Info window.
5. Enter a new number. Do not enter a number lower than the suggested size unless you have tried all other methods of memory adjustment. If you set the allocation even slightly less than the suggested amount, save your work often and avoid memory-intensive procedures when using the application.
6. Close the Info window. If you have entered a Preferred size that is smaller than suggested, a dialog box appears, asking if you want to do this. Click Cancel unless you are sure you want to take the risk.

The next time you start the program it will set aside the amount of memory you have allocated for its use.

Adjusting the Disk Cache (RAM Cache)

The *disk cache* (or RAM cache, as it is often called) is a portion of your Mac's RAM set aside to speed up frequently used operations such as opening and quitting applications or desk accessories and switching between applications. Some operations inside applications can run from the disk cache rather than the hard disk, too. This all happens behind the scenes, without requiring you to do anything except increase the disk cache for it. So you should set the disk cache to be as big as possible, depending on how much RAM you have and how much of it you require to open applications. Even if the disk cache is a relatively small portion of your total RAM, it can improve your

Figure 7.2
Increasing an application's memory allocation

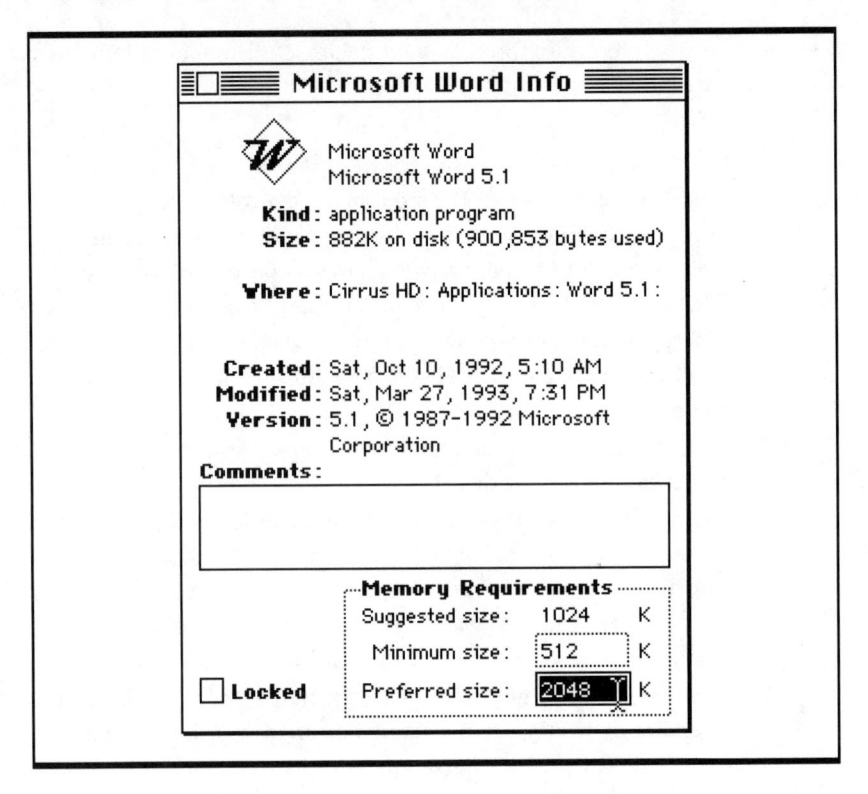

```
┌─────────────────────────────────────────┐
│ ≡▭≡      Microsoft Word Info      ≡≡≡  │
│                                          │
│    [W]   Microsoft Word                 │
│          Microsoft Word 5.1             │
│                                          │
│    Kind : application program           │
│    Size : 882K on disk (900,853 bytes used) │
│                                          │
│   Where : Cirrus HD : Applications : Word 5.1 : │
│                                          │
│  Created : Sat, Oct 10, 1992, 5:10 AM   │
│  Modified : Sat, Mar 27, 1993, 7:31 PM  │
│  Version : 5.1, © 1987-1992 Microsoft   │
│            Corporation                   │
│ Comments :                               │
│ ┌────────────────────────────────────┐ │
│ │                                    │ │
│ │                                    │ │
│ └────────────────────────────────────┘ │
│          ┌─ Memory Requirements ──────┐│
│          │ Suggested size :   1024  K ││
│          │ Minimum size :    [512]  K ││
│  ☐ Locked│ Preferred size :  [2048] K ││
│          └────────────────────────────┘│
└─────────────────────────────────────────┘
```

Mac's performance greatly, as long as you keep it at least up to the default settings. To manage your disk cache setting, use the following procedure:

1. Quit any applications you are using.
2. Choose Control Panels from the Apple menu. The Control Panels window opens.
3. Double-click the Memory icon in the Control Panels window. The Memory control panel opens, showing the current size of your disk cache.
4. Click the Use Defaults button to see what the default setting is; if your setting is different than the default, the number in the Cache Size box changes.
5. Click the up and down arrows, as shown in Figure 7.3, to adjust the disk cache size. Set the cache to be larger than the default if possible.
6. Close the Memory control panel and close the Control Panels window.

160 Chapter 7: Memory: Checking and Adjusting Your RAM Use

7. Choose Restart from the Special menu. Your Mac shuts down and starts up again; when the desktop returns, the new disk cache setting will be in effect.

The setting you choose for your disk cache size should reflect how much memory you have and how much of that memory you need to open applications. For example, if you have 4MB of RAM and normally use only one or two applications, increase the disk cache size to 192K or 256K. If you use a spreadsheet application, you can improve performance with even higher settings. On the other hand, if you have only 2MB of memory and want to use every bit you can for opening one or two memory-hungry applications, you can lower the disk cache size one setting below the default (32K instead of 64K). This may slow down your Macintosh, however.

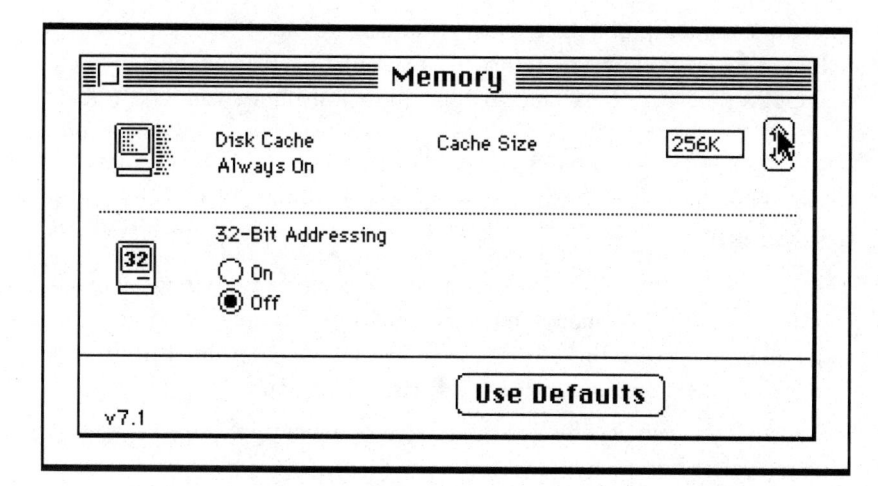

Figure 7.3
Increasing the disk cache size

Troubleshooting Problems with Memory

The following sections cover the most common problems you can have with memory and memory allocations in your Mac. Although different solutions are suggested for each problem, keep in mind that the first and often the best solution to memory problems is to install more RAM.

Out of Memory Messages, or Memory Bars Full

This is a common problem, and a very unpleasant one. If you see messages telling you your Mac can't do things like recalculating, repaginating, or opening applications because it doesn't have enough memory, you have a RAM shortage. You may not get "Not enough memory" messages. You may notice, when you look in the About This Macintosh window, that your application memory bars are all close to full and the largest unused block of memory is less than 1MB.

This is a warning sign; if you don't take care of the memory shortage, you will soon start getting "Not enough memory" messages. You might even start getting bombs and freeze-ups of the screen. Before things get that bad, try one or more of the following solutions. The easiest solutions are listed first.

- If you can get along without having so many applications open, close one.
- If you are sure you should have more available memory than the largest unused block indicates, quit all your open applications and start them again; you may have isolated bits and pieces of unused memory (fragmented memory, as it is called). Restarting the applications will free the whole block of unused memory. To prevent this fragmentation, always start your largest, most-used applications *before* starting others.
- If you have a huge item like a complex graphic or a long spreadsheet in the Clipboard, select a small item, like a dot or one

letter of text, and copy it twice into the Clipboard to flush out the large item (the second copy flushes the large item from the Undo memory, too).

- If you only have 2MB of RAM, upgrade to 4MB, or more if possible. That's easy to say, but it may be hard for you to afford. One thing is for sure; you will never regret adding more RAM to your Mac. The more RAM the merrier, as they say.

- If you have lots of extra sounds and fonts in your System file, or if you are running lots of unimportant special customizing files (INITs), delete them to reduce the amount of memory your system software uses. You can also quit any background desk accessories and turn off File Sharing (in the Sharing Setup control panel) if it is on. Only turn Sharing and those INITs on if you need to use File Sharing or some special customizing power. It always makes sense to keep your System file as small and unencumbered as possible. This reduces memory problems, and helps the Mac work at top speed.

- If you have no other choice, you can reduce your disk cache. Do this as a last resort, especially if it means reducing the cache size below the default setting. See "Adjusting the Disk Cache" in this chapter for details.

If you need to do things that require more memory than you have, such as use more applications or use applications that demand lots of memory, the only sure-fire solution is to install more RAM. Even if you don't use every bit of it all the time, you will find that the Mac works better and faster with the extra memory.

You See a Message That Says Your Application Has Unexpectedly Quit

This problem is almost always due to the fact that there is not enough memory allotted to the application. See "Adjusting Application Allocations" in this chapter, and increase the allocation so there is enough for the application and enough extra to hold the largest possible document. If the application had plenty of memory for itself *and* the document you were trying to open or repaginate or whatever, then the error is due to an internal problem in the application; if you get the same message every time you try to use a certain feature or carry out a certain task, contact the customer support people for the application.

The Mac Bombs at Startup or as a Screen Saver or Other Control Panel Takes Over

There can be a number of reasons for these bombs, but the most common is that some special customizing files (INITs) or control panels (cdevs) are overtaxing the specific portion of the Mac's RAM that is set aside for the system software. This portion of RAM, the *system heap*, can expand and contract as needed; you can watch it grow and shrink in the About This Macintosh window. But sometimes special customizing files and control panels can make concurrent demands of the system heap, causing crashes and bomb messages.

To prevent these problems, you can try increasing the size of the system heap with a utility such as HeapFixer or Bootman, but this may provide only temporary relief, depending on what is causing the memory overload. In some cases, increasing the system heap can actually interfere with the system software's ability to grow and shrink the heap, which will hurt the Mac rather than helping it.

The more permanent solution to system heap overload is to remove all of your special customizing files and non-Apple control panels, then reinstall them one at a time, testing each addition to find out which is the lemon. Some types of control panels just don't get along together, because they are both trying to customize the same elements of the system software; for example, screen capture programs and screen savers are often incompatible, as are menu-customizing programs and macro or keystroke-shortcut programs.

Eight

Customizing Your Mac

• • • • • • • • • • • • • • • •

Featuring

- ◆ An introduction to the contents of your System Folder
- ◆ How to automate the startup of often-used applications or documents
- ◆ Choosing and installing customizing extensions and control panels
- ◆ Opening and closing control panels
- ◆ Adjusting the desktop pattern, time, and date
- ◆ Adjusting the brightness of the screen
- ◆ Turning color on and off and adjusting the colors you see in the Finder
- ◆ Adjusting keyboard and mouse
- ◆ Customizing your view of items in Finder windows
- ◆ Adjusting your disk cache
- ◆ Troubleshooting customization problems

First Steps

To open an application or document automatically every time your Mac starts up: 170

Open the System Folder's window on your desktop. Next, open the folder that contains the application or document you want to open at startup. Make an alias of the application or document, and drag the alias to the Startup Items folder in the System Folder. The next time you start up the Mac, this application or document will open automatically.

To install a customizing extension (INIT) or control panel: 171

Make sure the customizing file is compatible with your version of the system software, and that it doesn't conflict with any of the applications you use frequently. Look at the Read Me file that comes with the customizing file, call the manufacturer, or check with experienced folks in your User's Group. When you are assured that the extension or control panel will work on your Mac, insert the floppy disk containing it in your Mac, open the floppy disk's window, and drag the icon for the customizing file to the icon for the System Folder in your hard disk window. Make sure the System Folder is closed when you do this. When a dialog box appears to tell you where the file must be stored, click the OK button and let the Mac put the file in the right place. You may need to restart the Mac for the extension or control panel to go into effect.

CHAPTER 8

To open a control panel so you can change the settings: 172

Choose Control Panels from the Apple menu. Then double-click the icon for the control panel you want to use. When the control window opens, use the pop-up menus, text boxes, and buttons in it to adjust the controls according to your taste or specific needs. Close the control window and go back to work. In most cases, the changed settings take effect immediately.

To adjust basic desktop functions: 173

Choose Control Panels from the Apple menu, then double-click the General Controls panel icon. In the control window that opens, you can redesign your desktop pattern with the enlarged view provided. You can also click buttons and arrows to change the rate of insertion point blinking from slow to fast, change the number of times menu commands blink when you select them, or change the time and date settings.

This chapter is about customizing your Mac to make it a comfortable, efficient environment to work in. The system software lets you change many aspects of your Mac's operations—from your screen colors to your mouse's double-click speed—by altering the settings in its *control panels*. You can change these settings at any time, or you can leave them at the default settings selected by Apple at the factory.

If you want to customize your Mac even more than you can using the system software alone, you can add various special customizing files that run automatically at startup time. Special customizing files go by several names (INITs, cdevs, extensions, control panels), and they perform any number of functions, from preventing your screen from "burning in" to organizing your fonts.

Looking Around Your System Folder

You customize your Mac from within the System Folder, so it pays to learn a bit about it before you start fooling around. To open your System Folder, double-click on your hard disk icon, then double-click on the System Folder in your hard disk window. You should see a window that looks like Figure 8.1. The following list describes the different items inside your System Folder, and what goes inside each item:

- System file: Contains fonts and sounds. If you want to use different fonts, see Chapter 3. Use the Sound control panel to change the error beep and other sounds.

- Finder: Contains the system software that makes the desktop work. You can't get in there to look at it. You can't add to it or change it, unless you are a programmer with special programming tools. So leave it alone.

- Apple Menu Items folder: Contains any items you want to have easy access to. You can reach the contents of the Apple Menu Items folder at any time by pulling down the Apple menu. The things that make the most sense to add to this folder, in addition to the standard items such as the Control Panels and the Alarm

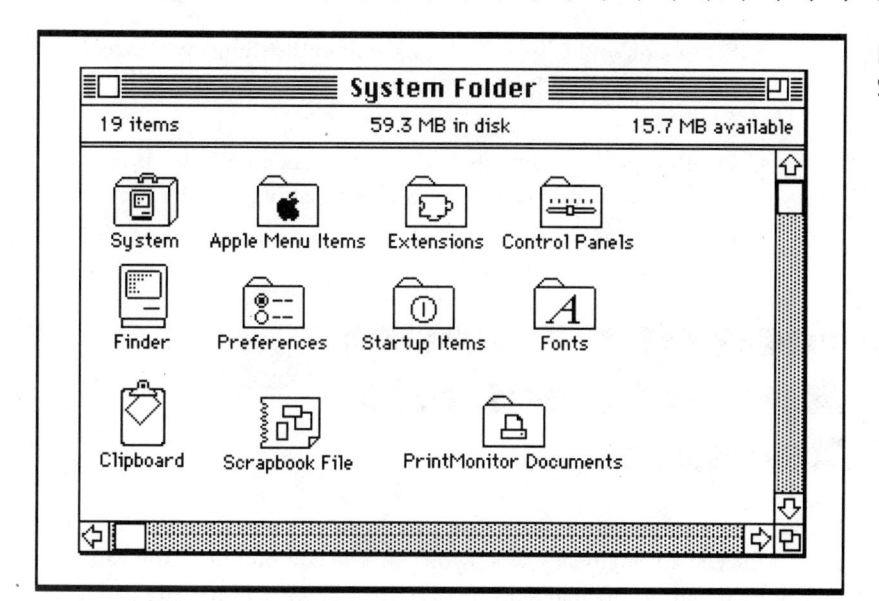

Figure 8.1
System Folder contents

Clock, are other handy desk accessories, aliases for much-used applications and control panels, and small documents, such as tips you want to remember.

- Extensions folder: Contains special customizing files that extend the power of the system software for such special needs as networking, background printing, and virus prevention.
- Control Panels folder: Contains small programs that change the look, sound, and behavior of the desktop, monitor, mouse, and keyboard of your Mac. You can also add special customizing files to the Control Panels folder.
- Preferences: Contains the preferences files for applications, so that each time you start one, it comes up looking like it was when you left it.
- Startup Items folder: Contains the items you want to have start up automatically each time you turn the Mac on. You can put applications or their aliases in it, or you can put in documents or special customizing files that do things like automatically empty the Trash at startup.
- Fonts folder: Contains all kinds of fonts, including bit-mapped, TrueType, and PostScript ones.

Looking Around Your System Folder

- Scrapbook and Clipboard files: Contain the things you save in the Scrapbook and the last thing you cut or copied to the Clipboard.
- PrintMonitor Documents folder: Holds documents for printing in the background (for Apple and compatible printers with memory only).

Specifying Startup Applications and Documents

If you use the same application every day, you can tell your Macintosh to open it for you automatically when you start the computer up. You can even pick a document to open at startup. Use the following procedure to specify items for startup:

1. Open the System Folder. The files and folders inside it are displayed.
2. Open the folder containing the application or document you want to specify for startup.
3. Drag the item you want to specify for startup to the Startup Items folder in the System Folder. If you want to open an application at startup, it is usually best to make an alias of the application and place this in the Startup Items folder. This saves memory in the System Folder and allows you to leave your applications in folders that have the supplementary files they need to run.

The item or items you put in the Startup Items folder will be opened automatically the next time you start up your Mac.

If you ever want to stop an item from opening at startup, open the Startup Items folder in the System Folder and drag the icon for the startup item out of both the Startup Items folder *and* the System Folder. The next time you start up your Mac, the item will not open automatically.

Using Special Customizing Files

You can add special utilities to your System Folder to do a number of valuable chores as you start up your Mac and use it. These files are sometimes referred to as special customizing files, or *INITs*, because they become part of the initialization process the computer goes through when you start it up. These files do *not* belong in the Startup Items folder. They belong in either the Extensions or Control Panels folders, depending on how they work.

Special customizing files that work in the background and never need adjusting are usually *system software extensions*. There are extensions that do simple things, such as Quote INIT, which substitutes curly quotes for the standard Macintosh vertical ones. There are also extensions that perform complex jobs, such as Disinfectant, which guards against viruses.

Any special customizing file that you can control or adjust by making settings is a *control panel*. You can look through your control panels at any time by choosing Control Panels from the Apple menu. You can add control panels that do many different jobs and adjust them to do their jobs in ways that suit your needs.

You can obtain the more common extensions and control panels from software dealers, or by ordering them from the catalogs that post listings in popular Macintosh periodicals such as *Macworld* and *MacUser*. New and more esoteric utilities of this kind can be obtained from electronic bulletin boards of user groups, or from online information services such as CompuServe and America Online. Once you have obtained a special customizing file that is either an extension or a control panel, use the following procedure to install it:

1. Check the file to make sure it is compatible with your system software. Either contact the maker of the special customizing file, or use the Compatibility Checker you received with your system software. It is critical that you have special customizing files that are updated to work with the version of the Macintosh system software you are using.

2. Insert the disk and open its icon. If necessary, open the folder with the icon of the special customizing file you want to install. Then open your hard disk window.

3. Drag the special customizing file icon to the System Folder (do not open the System Folder window and drag the special customizing file into it). A dialog box appears, telling you that the file you are installing must be stored in the Extensions or Control Panels folder.

4. Click OK in the dialog box. The file is copied into the appropriate folder inside your System Folder. If a dialog box appears, telling you the file cannot go into effect until you restart your Mac, quit all open applications and restart.

Some extensions do not work properly if they are inside a folder in the System Folder. If your Macintosh does not start after installing an extension, or if the extension does not work properly, hold the Shift key down while starting the computer (this disables all extensions), and then move the extension from the Extensions folder to the System Folder itself. Restart the computer and try out the extension. If you still have trouble, see the Troubleshooting section at the end of this chapter.

If you find that you do not need a particular customizing file, or if one causes system problems or problems with an application, you can remove the special customizing file from the System Folder. If you are not sure which folder the file is in, choose Find from the File menu and search for the file. When you find the file, drag it out of the System Folder completely. You cannot throw the file in the Trash until you have started your Mac again; startup files remain in use until you shut down and start up again.

Using Control Panels

You can change the way your Mac looks, sounds, and behaves at any time by choosing Control Panels from the Apple menu, then changing the settings in any of the different control panel windows.

You follow the same basic procedure to open a control panel window for any setting:

1. Choose the Control Panels command from the Apple menu at the far left end of your menu bar. The Control Panels window

opens and displays the icons for all the things you can customize on your Mac.

2. Double-click the icon for the item you want to change.

3. When the control window opens, make the settings you want in each panel. Close each control window before opening another.

For example, you can double-click the General Controls icon in the Control Panels window to see settings for basic desktop items. The General Controls window displays several panels, which contain dialog boxes for the different settings. In Figure 8.2, the hour setting in the Time panel is selected.

The following sections cover all of the most commonly used control panels and their settings. The Labels settings are covered in Chapter 5, "Using Folders to Organize Your Files." For information on specialized settings such as Easy Access and Sharing Setup, see the *Macintosh Reference* manual you received with your Macintosh.

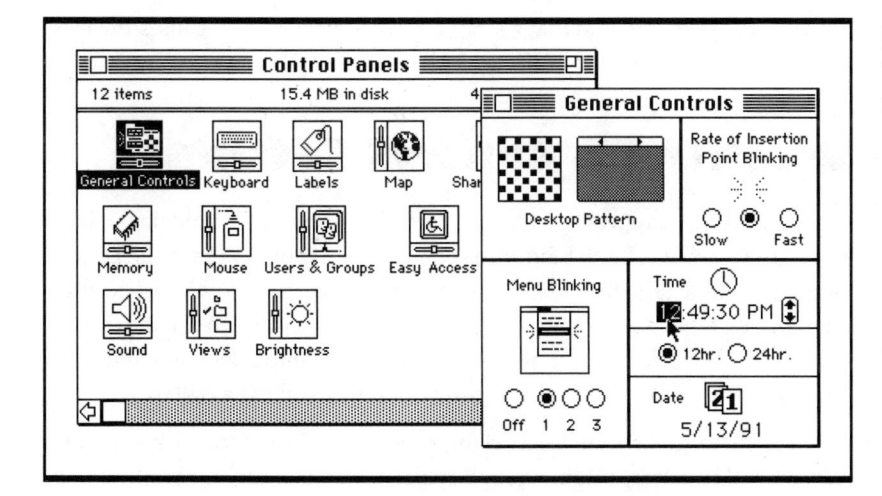

Figure 8.2
The Control Panels window and the General Controls window

General Controls Settings

You can make the following adjustments to your Macintosh environment by changing settings in the dialog boxes of the General Controls window:

- Change the desktop pattern by clicking the small white bar above the unenlarged pattern, or by modifying the enlarged pattern. Click in the unenlarged pattern to see your choice take effect on the desktop immediately. *Recommended setting:* Leave gray or solid color pattern.

- Change the rate of insertion point blinking by clicking in the *radio buttons* for either Slow or Fast blinking. *Recommended setting:* Medium blinking rate.
- Change the number of times a menu command blinks when you select it, by clicking in the radio buttons. *Recommended setting:* 1 or 2.
- Set the time by clicking on the various time increments, then clicking or pressing on the up and down arrows to correct the time.
- Choose the 12- or 24-hour clock by clicking in radio buttons.
- Set the date by clicking on the various time increments, then clicking or pressing on the up and down arrows that appear.

Of all the General Controls settings, the time and date are probably the only ones you need to adjust. Experiment with the desktop pattern if you want, but you will probably find that a simple, shaded background causes the least eye strain.

Brightness Control Settings

This control panel appears on Macs that do not support color and do not have a brightness control knob built into the monitor. If you don't see the control panel icon, adjust the brightness of your monitor with the knob that is either on the side of the monitor or under the front of the screen. To use the control panel, double-click the Brightness icon in the Control Panels window; a horizontal slider for brightness adjustment appears in a dialog box.

Drag the slider to the right for a brighter screen, to the left for darker. *Recommended setting:* Barely bright enough so your screen is slightly brighter than whatever is behind the computer; a strong contrast between screen brightness and ambient light can strain your eyes.

Color Control Settings

If your monitor (display screen) and your Mac are capable of showing colors, there will be a Monitors control panel (shown in Figure 8.3) and a Color control panel. First double-click the Monitors icon to see a dialog box that lets

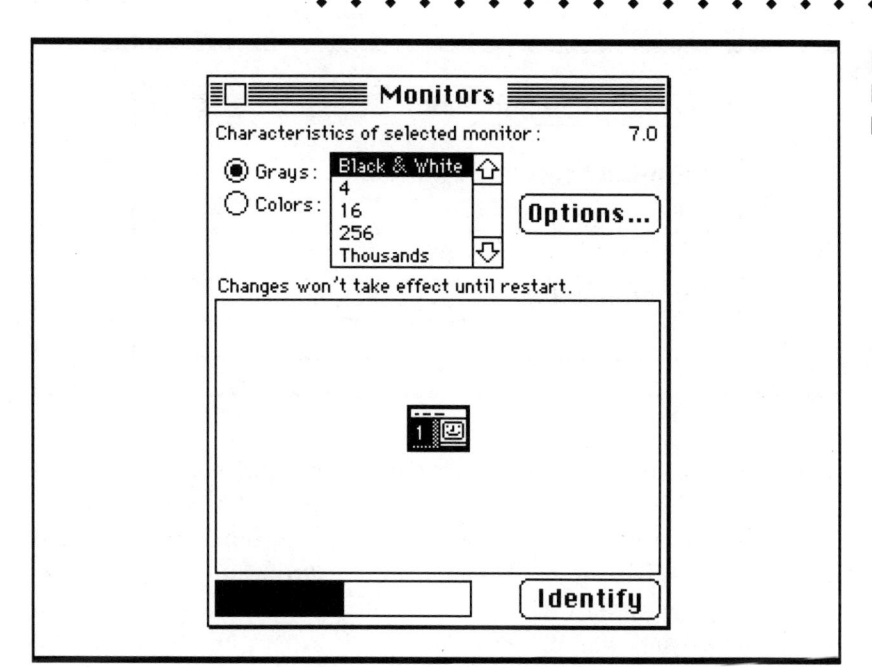

Figure 8.3

Monitors control panel, set for black and white

you switch your monitor from shades of gray to color. If you have more than one monitor, click the icon for the one you want to adjust in the lower part of the dialog box.

To see black and white only, you click the Grays radio button, then click Black & White in the list box. If your monitor can display shades of gray, click the number of shades you want to see.

To see color, click the Colors radio button, then, in the list box, click the number of colors you want displayed. In most cases, 256 colors works best. If you have a special high-resolution monitor and a color expansion card, you may want to display more colors, but some applications will not be able to take advantage of the colors anyway. If you have a Mac with a slow CPU, you may want to choose fewer colors; the more colors, the slower the Mac runs when doing graphic-intensive work.

After turning on color in the Monitors control panel, open the Color control panel shown in Figure 8.4 to select highlight and window trim colors. Press on the little triangles in the Highlight and Window color pop-up menus to see the choices of color, gray, or black and white.

Figure 8.4
The Color control panel

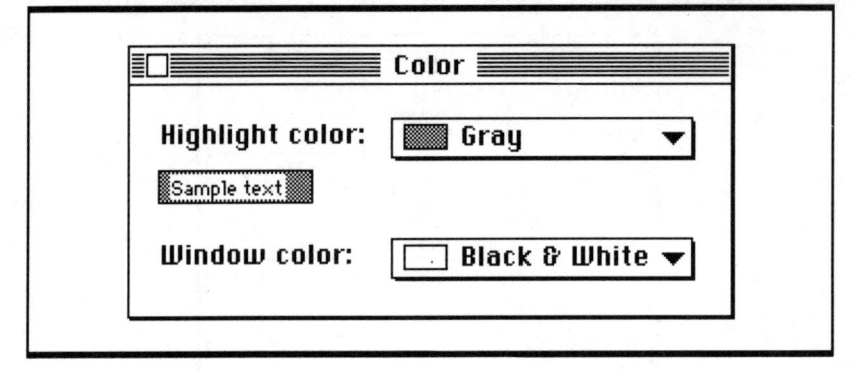

If none of the colors suits you, choose Other from either pop-up menu and use the color wheel to come up with your own custom color. You can get anything from hi-liter yellow to chocolate brown, but remember that it's hard to read text inside a dark or deeply saturated color. *Recommended setting:* Gray highlight, and whatever window trim you like (I prefer black and white to flashy colored window trim, because my eyes do better with the plain vanilla shapes you get if you choose black and white).

To change the color of your desktop, open the General Controls panel after turning color on in the Monitors control panel. You'll find a color bar under the desktop patterns (see Figure 8.5). You click a color to select it, then drag

Figure 8.5
Color bar in General Controls panel

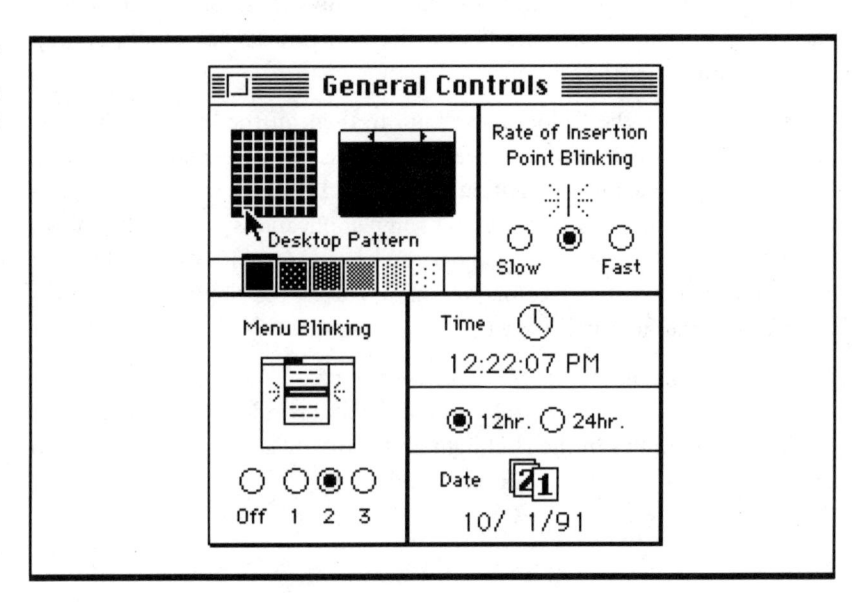

176 *Chapter 8: Customizing Your Mac*

the pointer around in the magnified view of the desktop pattern (the one on the left) to fill in all the dots. Then click in the nonmagnified view of the desktop on the right side of the panel and the new desktop color will go into effect.

If you want to make a custom color, double-click any of the color squares in the color bar, then click a color in the color wheel that appears (see Figure 8.6). Drag the scroll box up and down to change the brightness of the colors.

When you have the color you want, click OK, then drag the pointer around in the magnified view of the desktop pattern to fill in all the dots. Click in the unmagnified view to put your new color into effect.

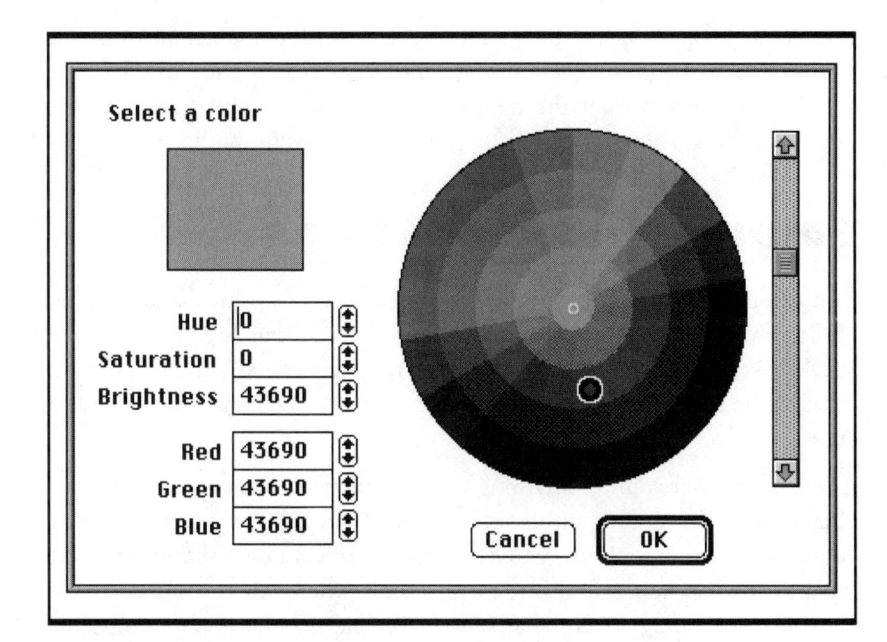

Figure 8.6
The color wheel

Keyboard Control Settings

Double-click the Keyboard icon to see the settings for your keyboard. Boxes appear with settings for key repeats and domestic or international keyboard designs. You can make the following adjustments:

- Change the rate at which a key repeats if you hold it down. Click in the radio buttons for a slower or faster rate. *Recommended setting:* Second fastest.

Using Control Panels **177**

- Set how long you have to hold down a key before it repeats, or turn the repeat feature off. Click in a radio button to make a choice. *Recommended setting:* Second shortest.
- Set the keyboard to Domestic (U.S.) or International; if there are other options, they appear in the central panel of the window.

If you are a seasoned typist but tend to rest your fingers on the keyboard, turn off the repeat feature.

Mouse Control Settings

Double-click the Mouse icon to see the settings for double-clicking and tracking on your mouse. Click in the appropriate radio button to select the speed at which you want the mouse to track, and the speed required for double-clicking. *Recommended settings:* Second fastest for both.

Sound Control Settings

Double-click the Sound icon to see settings for speaker volume and the type of sound you hear when the Macintosh alerts you (normally a beep). Set the Speaker Volume slider so the volume of the alert sound suits you. Scroll through the list of possible sounds and click on the one that bothers you the least.

If you want other sounds, anything from laughter to fierce growls, you can obtain a sound-installing utility and add whatever alert sound you want. If your Mac has a microphone, you can even record your own sounds and add them to the list. You can also remove sounds when you get sick of them. *Recommended settings:* Volume at 1 or 2. The alert sound is up to you, but keep in mind that anybody else using your computer or working in the same room has to put up with the sound you select.

Views Control Settings

Double-click the Views icon to see a dialog box (shown in Figure 8.7) for changing the look and the types of information in list views that appear in Finder windows. For more information on views, see "Changing Your Desktop View" in Chapter 5.

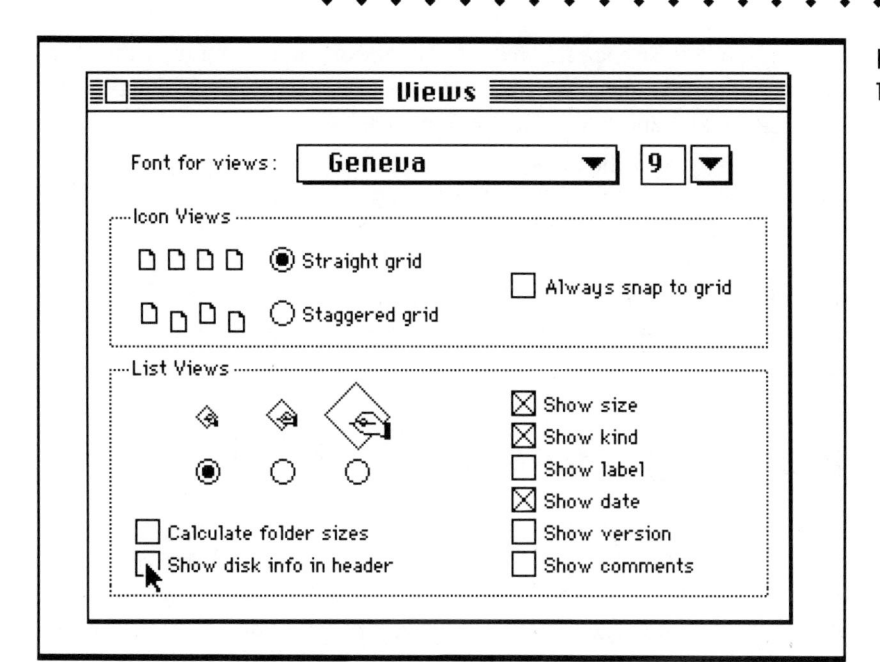

Figure 8.7
The Views control panel

You can make the following settings in the Views control panel:

- Font for views: Allows you to set a font and font size for all views. *Recommended setting:* Geneva 9-point, because it is the clearest font at the smallest standard size, allowing you to see the maximum information in a window at one time.

- Icon Views: Allows you to set for staggered or straight grid and turn snap-to-grid on or off. *Recommended setting:* Straight grid, snap-to-grid off. If you use full icon views in most windows, opt for staggered grid so you can pack more icons with large titles into each window.

- List Views: Allows you to set size of icons displayed, set which information you want listed, turn folder size calculation and disk information header on and off. *Recommended setting:* Smallest icons in lists (allows maximum information in window at one time). Turn on Show size, kind, and date. Turn on disk info header if you are running short of disk space; turn on folder size calculation only when you are short of disk space and you want to see which folders need cleaning out. Folder size calculation slows the Finder down.

Using Control Panels **179**

Of course, if you have special needs or tastes, you can use settings other than the recommended ones. For example, if you have dozens of similar documents in a folder and you want to distinguish between a few "hot" ones you are working on and all the "cool" ones that aren't important anymore, you can click the Show label box in the Views control panel, then select the documents in the Finder, and choose Hot or Cool from the Label menu to tag them. If you list these documents in a window and choose the by Label option from the View menu, the Hot documents will be neatly separated from all the Cool ones and listed first. You can even open the Labels control panel and make up new labels of your own.

Memory Control Settings

Double-click on the Memory icon to see a dialog box for setting the disk cache, which is the amount of random access memory (RAM) reserved for common operations and much-used data. It speeds up your work considerably. Click the up and down arrows to raise or lower the number of bytes. *Recommended setting:* 32K per megabyte of total RAM in your Mac. For more information, see Chapter 7, "Checking and Adjusting Memory."

Closing Control Panels

When you have made all the adjustments to your environment that you want, click in the close box in the last control window, then click the close box in the Control Panels window. You do not have to do anything else for the settings to take effect. All settings are stored in a special part of the Macintosh's memory (PRAM) that is not lost at shutdown, and so they remain in effect even when you turn the computer off and turn it back on.

Customizing Icons

If you want, you can make your own icon for a folder or file you use often, so it will stand out on the desktop. Just use the following procedure:

1. Create or copy a small image in a paint or draw program (for information on graphics applications, see Chapter 10). Images that are a size of about 35 by 40 pixels work best.

2. Select the image and copy it to the Clipboard by choosing Copy from the Edit menu.
3. Go to the desktop and select the folder or file you want to assign the new icon to.
4. Choose Get Info from the File menu. The Info window opens.
5. Select the file or folder's old icon in the upper left corner of the Info window.
6. Choose Paste from the Edit menu. Your new icon appears.

You can also copy an icon from another file or folder's Info window and paste it into the Info window of your target file or folder, but remember that you may confuse the icons of the target and the source on the desktop.

Troubleshooting Customization Problems

These are the problems you may have when customizing your Mac.

Just Started the Mac, and Everything Looks Different

You just turned the Mac on, and when the desktop came up, it didn't look right. The things you have customized, like the desktop pattern, the location of windows and icons, and the list views inside windows, are different. The problem is that your Mac is running different, outdated system software. Unless you have just installed new system software and removed all the preference files from your previous system software, you must have gotten two System Folders onto your hard disk, or you must have started from a floppy startup disk.

To remove an extra System Folder from your hard disk, you must start up from a floppy disk such as the Disk Tools one that you received with your system software. Then you look at the contents of the two System Folders on your hard disk and remove the one that is not set up the way you want it. Drag the whole folder to the Trash, or copy it to a floppy disk. Then restart your Mac without inserting the floppy startup disk.

The Screen Went Dark

If you have a screen saver, just press any key or move or click the mouse. If that doesn't help, see "Screen Stays Dark" in the Troubleshooting section of Chapter 1.

A Control Panel Is Missing

Either your Mac is not capable of doing the things that the control panel deals with (you won't have a Color control panel if your Mac is black and white, for example) or you have not installed the software for the feature that the control panel deals with (network software must be installed, for example, before the Sharing Setup and other networking control panels show up).

A Column Is Missing from a List View Window

You are looking at a list view, and one of the columns is gone, such as the Label column, or the Size or Kind column. To bring back the column, open the Views control panel and click on the appropriate check box. If you want to see the sizes of folders as well as files, you have to click on the Calculate folder sizes check box.

New Control Panel or Extension Causing Problems

Your Mac won't start, or you have numerous unexplained problems (anything from lost functions to bombs) in applications and in the Finder after installing a control panel or an extension. If an extension causes problems when placed in both the Extensions folder and the System Folder, or if a control panel causes problems, try changing its name. In some cases, just changing the name of an extension so it begins with *A* or *Z* will solve the problems. During initialization, two extensions may be clashing; if you change the name of one, it will start earlier or later than the other.

If neither moving an extension nor changing its name solves your problems with it, you have to remove the extension or control panel from the System Folder, as explained in "Using Special Customizing Files" in this chapter.

If you are installing several extensions, it is best to install one at a time. Then test your most-used applications and the Finder between installations, so if you have problems, you can remove just the last-installed extension.

If you want to use more than two or three extensions and control panels, obtain a utility to help you manage them, such as INITPicker, Conflict Catcher, or Extensions Manager. Such utilities let you select the files you want to run either at startup or in a control panel. Some also tell you how much memory each file is using, and protect against clashes between extensions.

Part Three

Applications for the Mac

The third part of this book describes the major tools you can use for your work on the Mac. Each chapter introduces one type of tool and tells what features make it especially useful. Taken together, the different chapters cover the full range of types of work that you can do on a Mac, from writing a memo to drawing a logo, from creating a spreadsheet to laying out the pages of a newsletter.

In each chapter, there are guidelines to help you find the best application for your specific needs and some recommendations of specific products that are well known and well liked. For each type of application, one or more examples are given of how to do the basic tasks of opening a document, entering things, correcting things, saving your work, and printing. Using the basic principles from the examples, you can quickly master the application that's best for your specific type of work.

Nine

Word Processors

• •

Featuring

- ◆ Choosing the right word processing application for you
- ◆ How to open a new document in Microsoft Word and MacWrite Pro
- ◆ How to enter text in Microsoft Word and MacWrite Pro
- ◆ How to edit text in Microsoft Word and MacWrite Pro
- ◆ How to format text with the ruler in Microsoft Word and MacWrite Pro
- ◆ How to change the style of text in Microsoft Word and MacWrite Pro
- ◆ How to save and print documents in Microsoft Word and MacWrite Pro

First Steps

To open a new document in Microsoft Word or MacWrite Pro:
193
204

Start the application first, by double-clicking the icon for the application or double-clicking the icon for any Word document. If you open the application, it presents you with a blank window for a new document. If you open an existing document, you need to choose New from the File menu to open a fresh window for your new document.

To enter text in Microsoft Word or MacWrite Pro:
195
205

If you are just beginning a document, just type at the keyboard and the text appears at the top of the document window. If you want to add text to an existing document, click with the I-beam to place the insertion point, then begin typing. You do not need to press Return at the end of each line of a paragraph. You use Return to start a new paragraph or separate lines of text.

To edit text in Microsoft Word or MacWrite Pro:
196
206

Select any text you wish to change; then type new text to replace the selected text or press Delete to remove the text.

CHAPTER 9

To move or copy text in Microsoft Word or MacWrite Pro:
196
207

To move selected text in Microsoft Word, you can drag and drop it, releasing the mouse button when you have placed the pointer where you want the text to begin. In Word you can also copy a block of selected text by holding down the ⌘ key as you do the drag-and-drop procedure. In either Word or MacWrite Pro, you can move and copy selected text by using the Cut, Copy, and Paste commands in the Edit menu.

To undo a mistake in Microsoft Word or MacWrite Pro:
197
207

If you need to undo a mistake you have made in typing or editing, choose Undo from the Edit menu.

To change the style of text in Word or MacWrite Pro:
202
210

First select the text. Then choose the style you want from the Format menu in Word, or the Style menu in MacWrite Pro. If you want to continue typing after changing the style of selected text, but you want to change back to ordinary text, place the insertion point after the changed text and choose Plain Text from the Format menu (in Word) or Style menu (in MacWrite Pro). Then you can begin entering ordinary text again.

Word processors are tools you use to write text and format it so it looks right. Good word processing applications make it easy to write what you want to, whether you want to write something simple or complex, and they make it easy to change the format and style of the text so it looks just like you want it to.

Since none of us writes porfectly, a word processor should also make it easy to select, edit, move, and remove text. Fortunately, the Mac interface makes all these jobs easy. All the application has to do is use the Mac to good advantage.

Some word processors can do much more, though. They can check your spelling, for instance, and tell you that *porfectly* should be *perfectly*. They can let you change the format of your text with a single command. They can show two separate parts of your text in split windows. They can let you put in things like pictures, tables, and lists. Some can let you transfer graphic files into the text, or let you translate text into formats used by other word processing applications, like DOS ones, for example. They can let you outline your work, and change the outline as you work. Similarly, they can let you keep a running index, a table of contents, or even footnotes that move with the text that they refer to.

If you're lucky, you can get one that lets you make custom commands and keystrokes to use as shortcuts for the tasks you perform most often. It's a happy day for any of us writers when we discover a word processor that takes the drudgery out of our repetitive tasks.

Which Word Processor for You?

There are so many word processors that you can go crazy trying to shop for one, so it pays to do a little thinking before you wander down to the local software shop. First, decide what you expect to be writing, then look at the recommendations below and decide which kind of word processor comes closest to filling your needs.

Word Processors for Big Writing Jobs

If you write long documents with changing formats and lots of lists and tables, try Microsoft Word; it has the power to do all kinds of writing tasks, and it is usually fast and reliable. Some of the powerful features are a bit hard to use, but in the newer versions, the power is more accessible. Microsoft Word has been the leading word processor for Macs for so long that many other applications, including DOS ones, can accept files from it. Word can import data from lots of other applications, too.

If you work on a network with lots of DOS machines and people write with WordPerfect, you can use WordPerfect for the Mac, too. It is powerful and fairly easy to use, but it doesn't let you do as many different things as Word, and it is noticeably slower when carrying out some common tasks.

Product at a Glance

Microsoft Word 5.1

Publisher:
Microsoft Corporation
Upgrades from 5.0 and 4.0: Available, but not free

Requires:
Macintosh Classic or better
System 6.7 or later
1MB of RAM if running System 6.7, 2MB of RAM if also running Grammar Checker; 4MB of RAM if running System 7, 5MB if also running Grammar Checker
One 800K disk drive; hard disk with 5MB to 7MB of free space recommended
Printer that is compatible with fonts installed on Mac

Description:
Word is a very powerful tool. You can use it to do just about anything you want to do with text. There are great ways to change the style of your text as you write, and ways to customize text in a given style after you have finished the writing. There are handy ways to find text, move text, and change the font style and size of text. You can also put text into tables, around pictures, in columns, headers, footers, and footnotes, or just about anywhere else on the page you want it. It isn't always easy to learn how to do all of these things, but once you learn how to do a task, there are always shortcuts, so you can do the task more quickly the next time around.

A Word Processor for Everyday Jobs

If you write straightforward letters, reports, or short newsletters, and you don't have to compose long or complicated documents with lots of unusual style changes, consider MacWrite Pro. It is wonderfully easy to use, and the features it has are all readily available, so you don't have to wander around in a maze of menus and dialog boxes looking for the option you need. You just write, edit, and format your text with the tools that are right at hand or in convenient palettes, and MacWrite Pro never gets in your way. You can also use frames for text and graphics, so you can do many basic page layout tasks as you do your word processing. Since MacWrite formed the first standard for Mac word processing, you can transfer many types of data and translate many different documents into and out of it.

The only problem with MacWrite Pro is that there are a few limitations to the features. You can't split a window to view two parts of a document at once, and you can't automate indexing, for instance. Special jobs like printing envelopes are difficult to handle, and there is no way to create shortcuts for often-repeated tasks.

Product at a Glance

MacWrite Pro

Publisher:
Claris Corporation
Upgrades from MacWrite II: Available, but not free

Requires:
Mac Plus or better
System 6.0 or later
1MB or RAM if running System 6.7 or earlier, 2.5MB of RAM if running System 7 or later
Hard disk with 2MB of free space
Printer that is compatible with fonts installed on Mac

Description:
MacWrite was one of the first applications for the Mac, and MacWrite Pro still has a fresh, clear feel to it that is hard to beat. You can write letters and memos without any fuss or bother. It has added features that make it a good tool for producing newsletters, brochures, and straightforward reports, too. It can be used for longer documents, but it does not have a well-developed arsenal of tools and shortcuts for complex or repetitive word processing tasks.

Bargain Word Processors

If you only need to do a few simple jobs with a word processor, you don't have to spend hundreds of dollars on an application. For writing letters and short memos or reports, you can use WriteNow; it is fast, easy to learn, and powerful enough to take care of a surprising number of basic writing needs. It also has a number of features you normally expect in more complicated applications, such as a spelling checker and a word finder that can search forwards and backwards.

If you are really a penny-pincher you can use TeachText, which comes with your system software. It has almost no features, but you can write a simple letter and edit the text in the most basic fashion. Just don't expect to do any fancy formatting, spell checking, or much of anything else. There are other small word processing applications that you can use for notes, letters, and address lists, but they are a far cry from WriteNow or MacWrite Pro.

The bargain word processors are not covered in the rest of this chapter, but you can use the sections on Microsoft Word and MacWrite Pro as guidelines, and read your application's user manual for details.

Using Microsoft Word

The following sections describe how to create a simple document using Microsoft Word. You can follow the procedures just as they are written and make a document like the example, or you can use them as guidelines to create your own document. The basic steps of opening a document, creating and editing text, and saving and printing your work are the same for all kinds of documents, from short memos like the sample to full-length manuscripts. Once you have become familiar with the basic steps, see the Microsoft Word *User's Guide* for details about the application's specialized features.

Opening a New Document

Take the following steps to open a new document in Microsoft Word:
- If you have not started Microsoft Word, double-click the Word icon, as shown in Figure 9.1, or double-click an alias for it.

Figure 9.1
The Microsoft Word icon

- If you have started Microsoft Word and are looking at an existing document, choose New from the File menu.

The Word document window, shown in Figure 9.2, opens with menu titles in the menu bar and the Word icon at the right end of the menu bar. In the title bar of the window is the name Untitled1. This name will change the first time you save the document and give it a title.

Nothing appears inside the window but a vertical line blinking near the top left corner and a thick horizontal line beneath the blinking one. The blinking vertical line is your *insertion point*. The thick horizontal line marks the end of the document. You may see a vertical line with sprouts at the end; this is the *I-beam*, a special kind of pointer you will soon learn to use in Word. You

Figure 9.2
The Microsoft Word document window

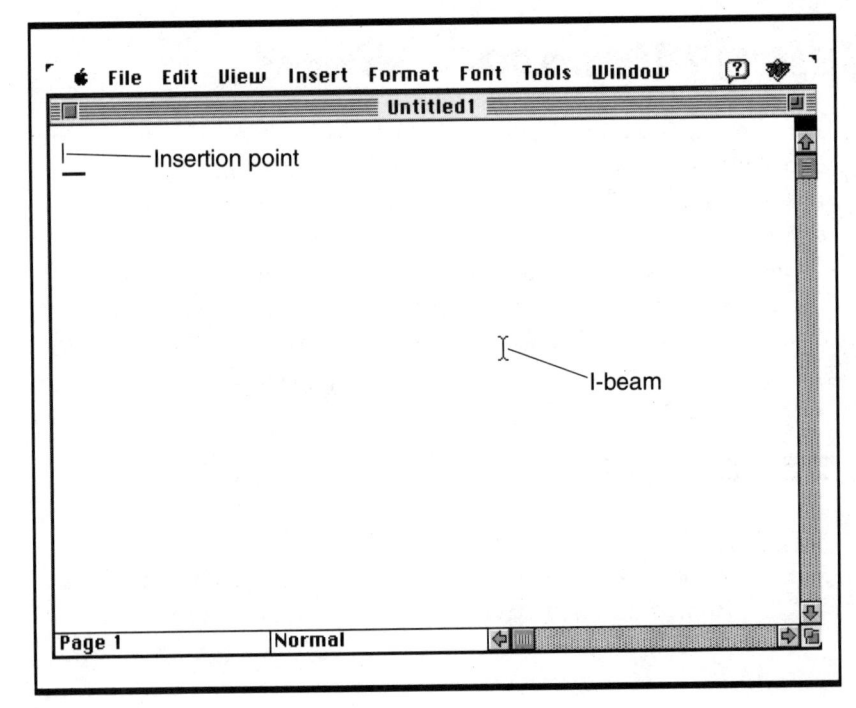

Chapter 9: Word Processors

may also see a ruler or a ribbon at the top of the document window, as shown in Figure 9.10, or a toolbar with nifty icon buttons may appear across the top or along one side of your Mac screen, but you do not need to do anything with any of those three gadgets. All you need to deal with is the blinking insertion point, for now.

Entering Text

To enter text at the insertion point, you just start typing. Use the following hints to help you write the example memo shown in Figure 9.3.

1. After each short line at the top of the memo, press the Return key to go on to the next line.
2. Press Return twice to create a blank line between lines of text.
3. When typing a paragraph of text, do not press Return at the end of each line; Word *wraps* the text for you, breaking each line between words, at the right margin.
4. You do not need to enter two spaces between the end of one sentence and the beginning of the next. Word spaces the sentence breaks for you when it prints the file.

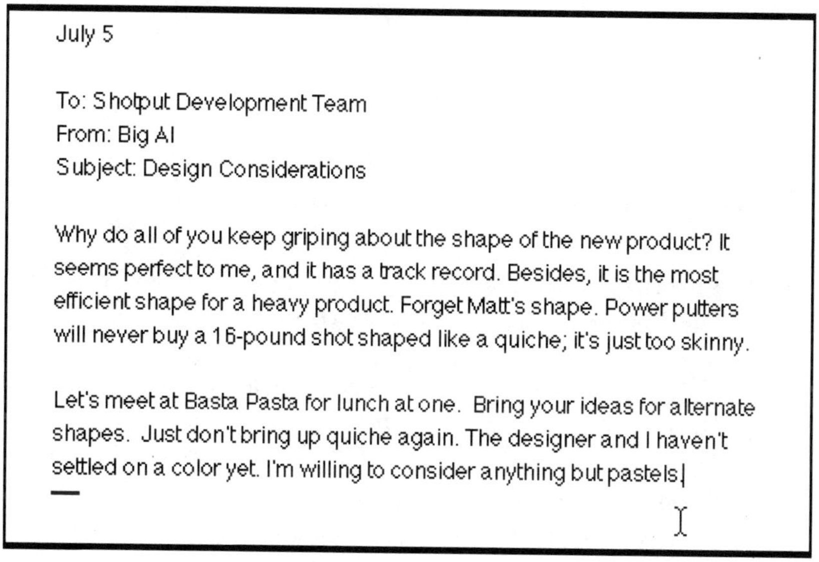

```
July 5

To: Shotput Development Team
From: Big Al
Subject: Design Considerations

Why do all of you keep griping about the shape of the new product? It
seems perfect to me, and it has a track record. Besides, it is the most
efficient shape for a heavy product. Forget Matt's shape. Power putters
will never buy a 16-pound shot shaped like a quiche; it's just too skinny.

Let's meet at Basta Pasta for lunch at one. Bring your ideas for alternate
shapes. Just don't bring up quiche again. The designer and I haven't
settled on a color yet. I'm willing to consider anything but pastels.
```

Figure 9.3

An example of a memo written in Word

Using Microsoft Word

Figure 9.4
Adding text

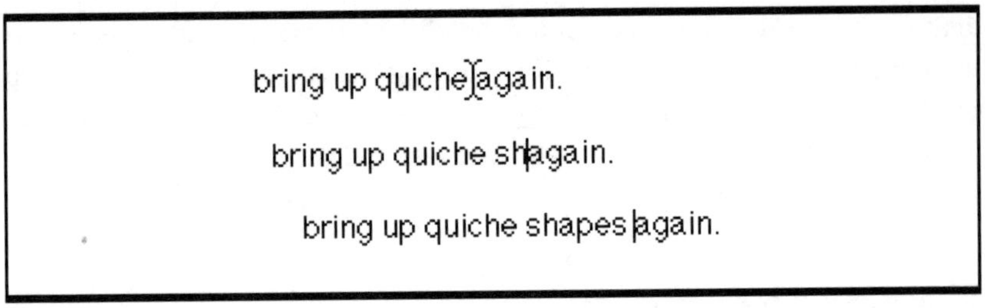

> bring up quiche|again.
>
> bring up quiche sh|again.
>
> bring up quiche shapes|again.

Editing Text

You use the special *I-beam* pointer, the vertical line with sprouts at the end, to add to and edit the text you have entered. To edit existing text, you need to select it first. This is the most basic rule in text processing: *Select first, then operate*.

- To add text, as shown in Figure 9.4, move the I-beam pointer to where you want to add the text and click. Then type the text in.
- To replace text, as shown in Figure 9.5, first select it by dragging the I-beam over it. Then type in the new text.

Figure 9.5
Replacing text

> just too **skinny**.
>
> just too fl|.
>
> just too flat|.

- To delete text, as shown in Figure 9.6, first select it by dragging the I-beam over it. Then press the Delete key.
- To move text to a nearby location, use the drag-and-drop method shown in Figure 9.7. First, select the text by dragging the I-beam over it, and move the I-beam into the selected area so it turns into a pointer, as shown in the top panel of Figure 9.7. Then drag the pointer and the flickering insertion point that comes with it to the place where you want to insert the text.

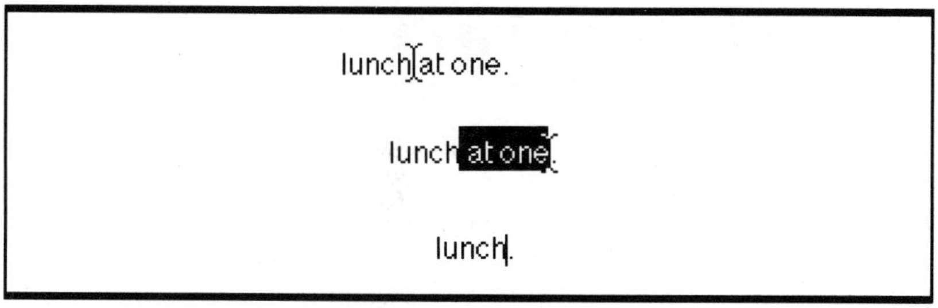

Figure 9.6
Deleting text

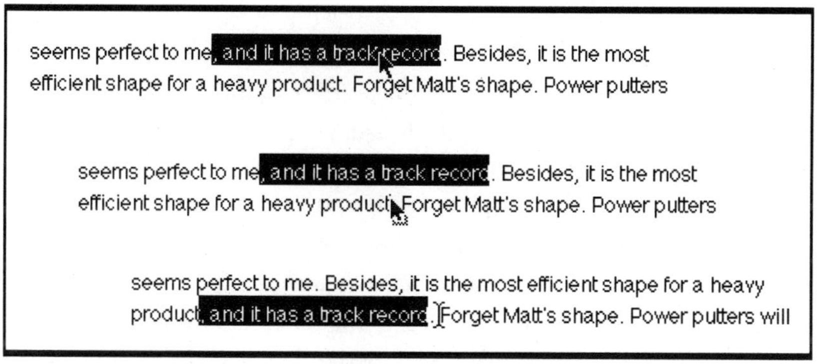

Figure 9.7
Dragging and dropping selected text in Word

Release the mouse button to drop the text into place. (To move a block of text to a distant location, see the next section of this chapter.)

- To copy a block of text, use the drag-and-drop method, but hold down the ⌘ key as you drag the selected text.
- To extend a selected block of text, move the I-beam to the new end point for the block you want to select. Then Shift-click (hold the Shift key down and click the mouse button) to extend the selection.
- To select lines of text, move the I-beam to the left of the text, until it becomes an arrow pointing to the right. Click to select a single line, double-click to select a paragraph.
- To undo a small typing or spelling mistake, you back up over it and retype the text. Use your Delete key to back up. To undo larger mistakes, choose Undo from the Edit menu. The command in the menu changes to reflect your last action. For example, if you just entered some text, the command is Undo Typing.

Using Microsoft Word **197**

Moving, Copying, and Replacing Text via the Clipboard

Word, like most Mac applications, provides several commands in the Edit menu to move and replace blocks of text that are not near each other. These commands take text out of your document, hold it temporarily in the *Clipboard*, a special storage place in the Macintosh's memory, and put it back into your document. Use the following Edit commands to handle any large block of text you have selected:

- To remove a selected text block from a document and store it temporarily in the Clipboard, choose Cut from the Edit menu.
- To make a duplicate of a selected text block and store it temporarily in the Clipboard, choose Copy from the Edit menu.
- To replace a selected text block with a block you have just cut or copied into the Clipboard, choose Paste from the Edit menu.
- To move a selected text block to a different place, choose Cut from the Edit menu. Then scroll to the location where you want the text to appear, place the insertion point, and choose Paste from the Edit menu.
- To delete a block *without* storing it in the Clipboard, choose Clear from the Edit menu, or just press the Delete key.

Note
For more information on the Clipboard and how to cut and paste things, see Chapter 15.

When using the Clipboard, keep in mind that it can only hold one item at a time. For example, if you copy a large text block into the Clipboard so you can paste it somewhere else, but then cut two words of text before pasting the large block, you lose the large block of text. On the other hand, if you copy text into the Clipboard, you can paste it into your document in several different places; text stays in the Clipboard no matter how many times you paste. The only ways to lose the text in the Clipboard are cutting and copying new text or shutting down your Mac.

Using the Ruler to Format Text

The Word ruler allows you to make formatting changes to your documents visually. By dragging and clicking on the markers and icons shown in Figure 9.8,

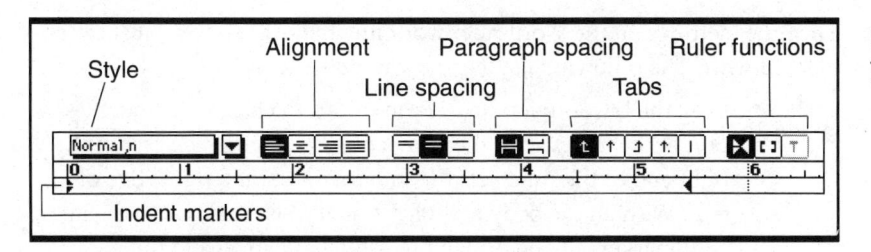

Figure 9.8
The Microsoft Word ruler

you can set or change your document's indents, tabs, and line spacing. If you make settings with the ruler before you type a block of text, the block will show all your ruler settings. If you want to change the format of a block of text you have already typed, select the whole block, then make your ruler settings.

To get a sense of how the ruler works, let's change the first-line indent of our shot-put memo:

1. If the ruler is not showing at the top of the document window, choose Ruler from the View menu.
2. Select both paragraphs of the memo.
3. Drag the upper left indent marker to the half-inch mark to set the indent for the first line of each paragraph. Your memo should now look like Figure 9.9.

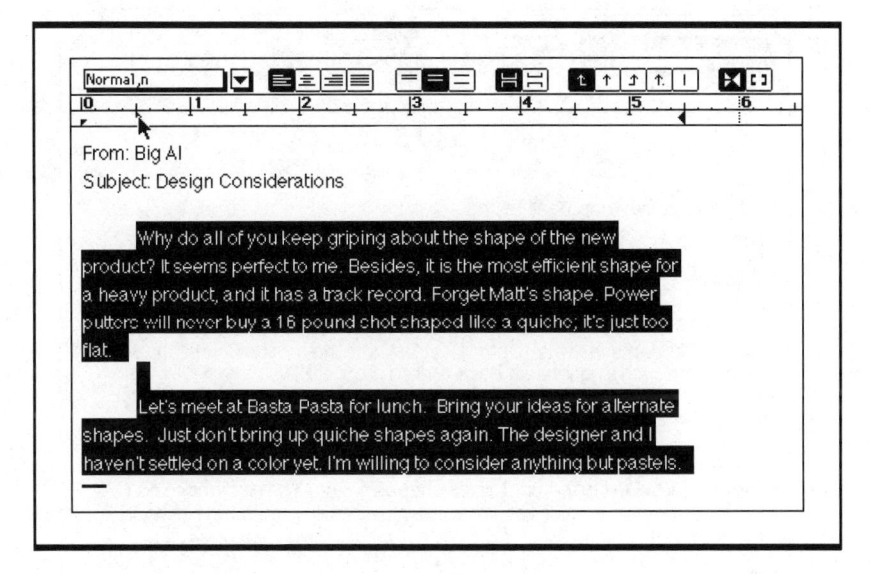

Figure 9.9
Changing the first-line indent

Using Microsoft Word **199**

The other settings on the Word ruler work much like the one we just experimented with. The following list tells how to make each setting:

- Drag the lower indent marker in or out to change the indentation of the left edge of the text. The large triangle marker at the right end of the ruler sets the indentation of the right edge of text. With all the body text of the memo selected, move the indent markers in and out and watch what happens to the body text. When you move the left indent marker, notice that the first-line indent marker always moves too, so you keep your first-line indent.

- Drag a tab marker to each point on the ruler where you want to set a tab. There are left align, center, and right align tabs, as well as a tab for entering a decimal point. To remove tab settings, drag the marker off the bottom of the ruler. In the sample memo, you can set a tab for a sign-off at the end, as shown in Figure 9.10. Place the insertion point after the last word in the

Figure 9.10
Sample memo in Word with format changes

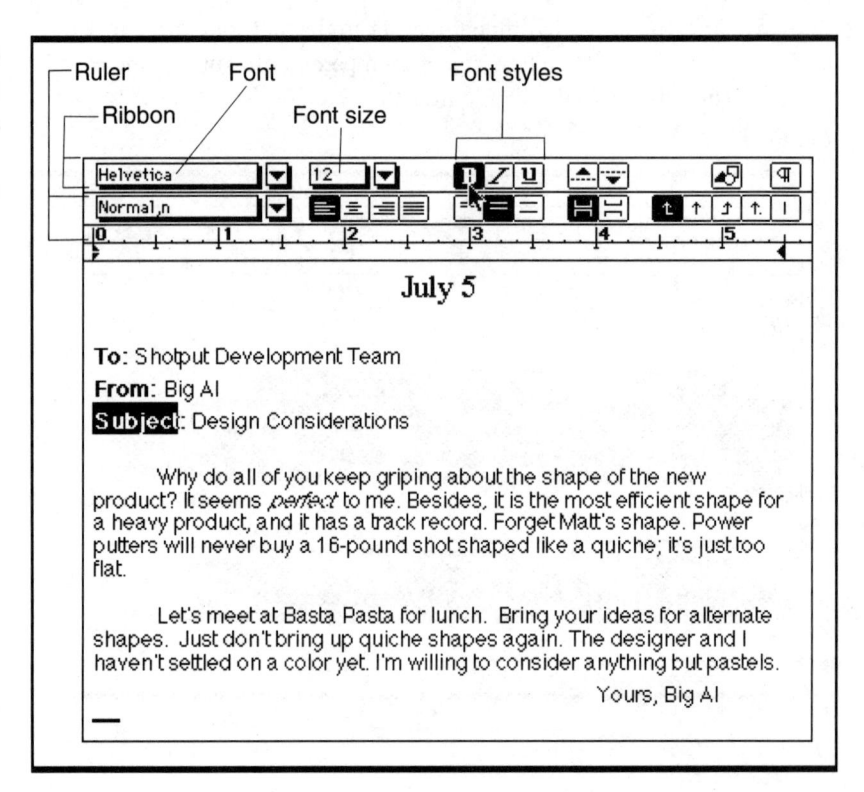

memo and then drag a left align tab (which is selected by default) to about the 4-inch mark on the ruler. Then press Return to start a new line, press the Tab key, and type a sign-off, like **Yours, Big Al**.

- Click on the different alignment icons to align the text at the left margin (as shown), or to center the text, or align it on the right margin. Try selecting the date at the top of the memo and clicking the icon for centered text (the second alignment icon from the left).

- Click on the different line spacing icons to select narrow, medium, or wide spacing between lines of text. Typically, the choices are 12, 18, and 24 points. To see what the memo looks like with narrow spacing, select all of the body text and click the narrow spacing icon (the one on the left).

- There are buttons at the right end of the Word ruler that change the ruler's functions. Click on the fat parentheses button and you can drag two margin icons to change the limits for the margins. Click the fat T button (if it is visible) to change the margins and column widths for a table. See your Word documentation for details on tables; they work well in Word.

- There is also a text box at the left end of the Word ruler that shows the style you are now using. Press on the little down-pointing triangle next to the box to see a list of other styles. You can choose a style and see its ruler; at the same time, the current paragraph changes to that style. See the Word *User's Guide* for more information on styles.

If you select a large block of text and notice that the ruler becomes grayed, it means that there are different formats mixed in the selected text block. To find out where the exceptions are, reduce the size of the selected block by Shift-clicking. If you reduce the block by a few lines at a time and watch for the ruler to change, you can quickly locate the problem. Word has hidden formatting characters that you can see if you need them to find a formatting change. Just choose Show ¶ from the View menu in order to display the hidden characters.

Changing Text Style

To change text from a plain appearance to bold or other styles, first select the text, then choose the style you want from the Format menu. Make sure you don't confuse the Style command in the Format menu with text styles; you can change all kinds of things with the Style command, as explained in the Word documentation.

For an example of a style change in the sample memo, let's give emphasis to the word *perfect* in the first paragraph.

1. Select *perfect* and the space before it.
2. Choose Italic from the Format menu. The word becomes italicized.
3. If the end of the word leans over and runs into the next one, just select the last couple of letters and the space, type the letters over, and hold down the Option key as you press the spacebar.

To deitalicize the word, choose Plain Text from the Style menu.

You can change the font or font size of text by using the same method and selecting the new font or size you want from the Font menu.

You can also use a *ribbon* (a band that goes across the top of the window like the ruler) with buttons for changing font, font style and size. Press ⌘-Option-R to see the ribbon at the top of the document window, as in Figure 9.10. Let's use the ribbon to make some changes to the memo.

1. Select the date.
2. Click on the downward-pointing triangle next to the font box and choose Times from the pop-up menu.
3. Click on the triangle next to the font size box and choose 18 point from the list.
4. Select each of the first words of the header lines (To, From, and Subject) and click the Bold button in the ribbon. Your memo should now look like Figure 9.10.

These are all little touches, but they can add strength and clarity to your work. For more information on them, and on the other icons in the ribbon and ruler, see the Microsoft Word *User's Guide*.

After you have changed the text style, font, or font size of a word, keep in mind that any text you enter immediately after that word adopts the changed text style. So if you put the insertion point at the end of an italicized word, all new text you enter will be italicized, too. To prevent this, choose Plain Text from the Format menu after placing the insertion point.

Saving and Printing a Document

To protect your work, save it often, like every ten to fifteen minutes. All you have to do is choose Save from the File menu, or press ⌘-S. The first time you save a document, you must name it and choose where to place it in your folder hierarchy.

To print a hard copy of your document, first save it, then choose Print from the File menu, or press ⌘-P. The Print dialog box opens. Unless you want to do something special, leave all the settings as they are and click the Print button (or just press the Return key) to start printing. If you have a LaserWriter or compatible printer that allows background printing, the PrintMonitor will take over your print job in a moment or two, and you can go right back to work while printing proceeds. For more information, see Chapter 3.

Note

For more information on saving, see "Saving Your Work on a Document" in Chapter 4.

Shortcuts, Shortcuts

As you use Word, you'll find that there are almost endless ways to take shortcuts for repetitious jobs. Sometimes learning how to do a shortcut takes more effort than it saves you, but if you just learn the simplest and most useful tricks, you'll find your work goes a lot easier. Using keyboard shortcuts for commands is a good example; ⌘-S is a great shortcut for the Save command, and ⌘-P is a good shortcut for Print. Just look at the menu commands for their keyboard shortcuts. Or you can choose Commands from the Tools menu to make up keyboard shortcuts for almost any command you want.

If you would rather use the mouse to click a button for a command than use the keyboard, you can turn on the toolbar. It has buttons for most of the commands you tend to use often, and you can add buttons for other commands by choosing Customize from the menu under the down-pointing triangle at the right end of the menu. See the Word *User's Guide* for more information on these shortcut options.

Using Microsoft Word **203**

Using MacWrite Pro

Using MacWrite Pro is a lot like using Word. If you've worked through the exercises in Word, you'll notice that many procedures are identical in the two programs. As before, you can follow the procedures just as they are written and make a document like the example, or you can use them as guidelines to create your own original document. Once you have become familiar with the basic steps, see the MacWrite Pro *User's Guide*. It is a superb manual, a shining example of clarity and good organization. The online help (available from the menu under the question mark balloon) is brief but clear and to the point, too.

Opening a Document

Take the following steps to open a new document in MacWrite Pro:

- If you have not started MacWrite Pro, double-click the MacWrite Pro icon as shown in Figure 9.11, or double-click an alias for it.
- If you have started MacWrite Pro and are looking at an existing document, choose New from the File menu.

Figure 9.11
The MacWrite Pro icon

A window opens with the MacWrite Pro menu titles in the menu bar and the MacWrite Pro icon at the right end of the menu bar, as shown in Figure 9.12. In the title bar of the window is the name Document1. This name will change the first time you save the document and give it a title.

When the window first opens, all you see in it is a vertical line blinking near the left side and a cursor that is a line with sprouts at the end. The blinking

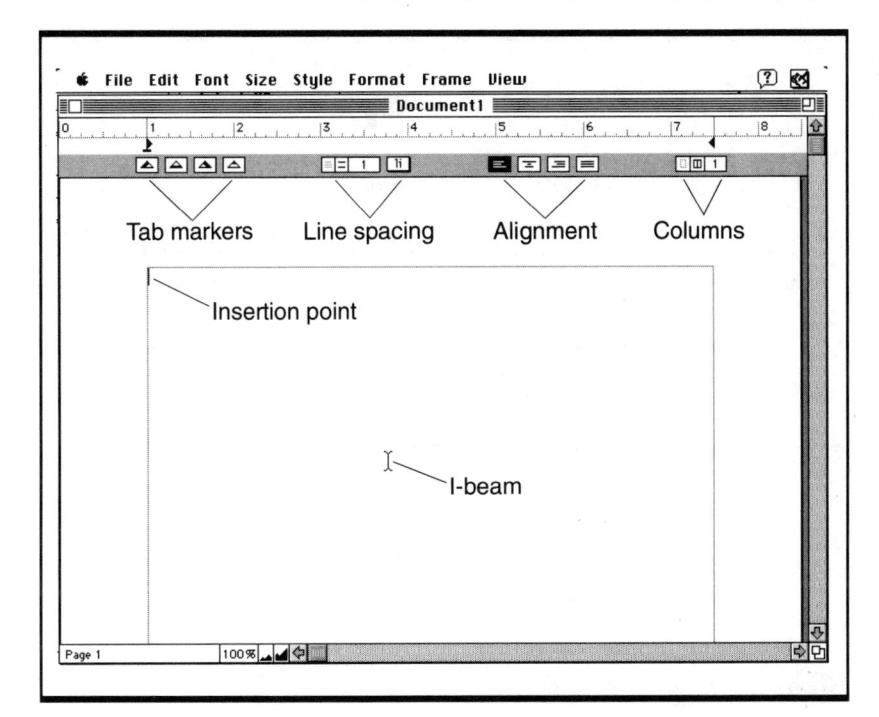

Figure 9.12
The MacWrite Pro document window

vertical line is your *insertion point*. The line with sprouts is a special kind of pointer you will soon learn to use in MacWrite. You don't have to do anything with the ruler or the bar with the tab markers and other stuff before you start entering text in MacWrite.

Entering Text

To enter text in MacWrite, simply type at the keyboard, and your text appears at the insertion point. Write the example memo shown in Figure 9.13; the following hints may help.

1. After you type each short line of the memo header, press the Return key to go on to the next line.
2. Press Return to create a blank line between lines of text.
3. When you type a paragraph of text, do not press Return at the end of each line. MacWrite Pro *wraps* the text for you, ending each line between words at the right margin and starting a new line below.

Figure 9.13
An example of a memo written in MacWrite Pro

July 5

To: Shotput Development Team
From: Big Al
Subject: Design Considerations

Why do all of you keep griping about the shape of the new product? It seems perfect to me and it has a track record. Besides, it is the most efficient shape for a heavy product. Forget Matt's shape. Power putters will never buy a 16-pound shot shaped like a quiche; it's just too skinny.

Let's meet at Basta Pasta for lunch at one. Bring your ideas for alternate shapes. Just don't bring up quiche again. The designer and I haven't settled on a color yet. I'm willing to consider anything but pastels.

---

4. You don't have to enter two spaces after the period at the end of each sentence. MacWrite Pro will make spaces at the sentence breaks for you when it prints the file.

Editing Text

MacWrite Pro has many of the same editing features as Word, so as you work through this section, you can look back to Figures 9.4 to 9.6 for guidance. As with Word, you use the special *I-beam* pointer, the vertical line with sprouts at the end, to add to and edit the text you have entered. And, of course, to edit existing text, make sure you *select it first*.

- To add text, place the I-beam pointer and click where you want to begin adding text. Then type the text in, as shown in Figure 9.4.
- To replace text, first drag the I-beam over it to select it. Then type in the new text, as shown in Figure 9.5.
- To delete text, first select it by dragging the I-beam over it. Then press the Delete key, as shown in Figure 9.6.
- To extend a selected block of text, place the I-beam at the new end-point you want to select. Then Shift-click (hold the Shift key down and click the mouse button) to make the selection grow. To decrease the size of a selected block of text, Shift-click at the new end-point within the selection.

- To extend a selection to the end of a line, press ⌘-Shift-→. Use ⌘-Shift-← to extend the selection to the beginning of a line.
- To undo a small typing or spelling mistake, you back up over it and retype the text. Use your Delete key to back up. To undo larger mistakes, choose Undo from the File menu. The command in the menu changes to reflect your last action. For example, if you just entered some text, the command is Undo Typing.

You can also use the commands in the Edit menu to move and replace blocks of text. These commands take text out of your document, hold it temporarily in the Clipboard, a special storage place in the Macintosh's memory, and put it back into your document. MacWrite Pro's commands for working with the Clipboard are identical to those in Word, so for more information, turn to the section on "Moving and Replacing Text via the Clipboard" in Word, earlier in this chapter.

Using the Ruler to Format Text

MacWrite also has a ruler you can use to make formatting changes quickly and easily. Figure 9.12 shows the ruler's icons and markers. To see how the ruler works, let's change the first-line indent of the shot-put memo.

1. If the ruler is not showing at the top of the document window, choose Show Ruler from the View menu.
2. Select both paragraphs of the memo.
3. Drag the first-line indent marker (the one that looks like an upside-down T) in to set the indent for the first line of text in each paragraph. Your memo should now look like Figure 9.14.

The other settings on the MacWrite ruler work a lot like the first-line indent. The list below tells how to make each setting. The two buttons for setting columns are not covered, because it makes no sense to put a memo into columns; if you're doing a newsletter, though, you'll find those buttons very handy.

- Drag the left margin marker (the triangle at the left margin) in or out to change the left margin of the text. The triangle marker at the right end of the ruler sets the margin for the right edge of

Figure 9.14
Changing the first line indent with the MacWrite Pro ruler

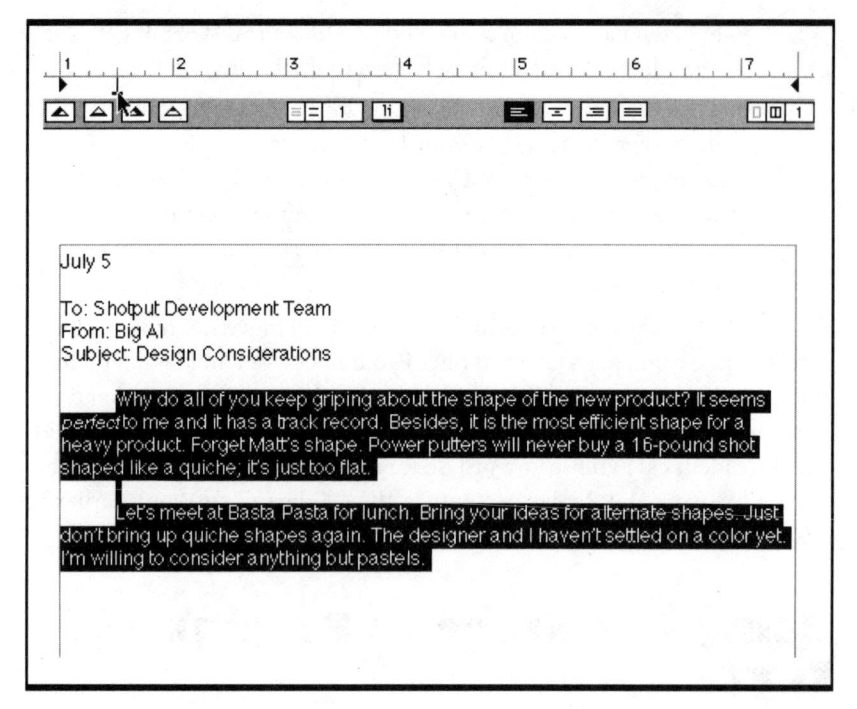

text. With all the body text of the memo selected, move the margin markers in and out and watch what happens to the margins. When you move the left margin marker, notice that the first-line indent marker always moves too, so you keep your first-line indent.

- Drag a triangular tab marker to each point on the ruler where you want to set a tab. There are left align, center, and right align tabs, as well as a tab for entering a decimal point. The dark part of each tab triangle tells you the alignment. Ain't that cute? To remove tab settings, drag the marker off the bottom of the ruler. In the sample memo, you can set a tab for a sign-off at the end, as shown in Figure 9.14. Place the insertion point after the last word of the memo, and then drag a left align tab (the triangle with the dark left side) to about the 5-inch mark on the ruler. Then press Return to start a new line, press the Tab key, and type a sign-off, like **Yours, Big Al**.

- Click on the different alignment icons to align the text at the left margin (as shown), or to center the text, or align it on the left margin. Try selecting the date at the top of the memo and clicking the icon for centered text (the second alignment icon from the left).

- Click on the different line spacing icons to select narrow (single), or medium (1.5) spacing between lines of text. Typically, with 12-point fonts, the choices are 16 or 17 points. To see what the memo looks like with medium spacing, select all of the body text and click the right icon. The text box changes to show that you went from single spacing to one and a half. If you select something in the header of the memo, as in Figure 9.15, the line spacing goes back to one.

If you select a large block of text and notice that there are different formats mixed in the selected text block, just make the setting you want for the whole block, and the parts that are different will straighten themselves out. Sometimes you have to change the setting and change it back to have it take effect. If you need to see hidden formatting characters to figure out what formatting is where, choose Show Invisibles from the View menu.

Figure 9.15
Sample memo in MacWrite Pro with format changes

Changing Text Style

If you want to change text so it has a different style, such as bold, first select the text, then choose the style you want from the Format menu. For example, let's emphasize the word *perfect* in the first paragraph of the memo.

1. Select the word and the space before it.
2. Then choose Italic from the Style menu. The word becomes italicized.
3. If you are using an older version of MacWrite II and the end of the word leans over so far it runs into the next one, just select the last couple of letters and the space, type the letters over, and hold down the ⌘ key as you press the spacebar. That makes a bigger space on the screen, like the one shown in Figure 9.15.

To deitalicize a word if you change your mind about emphasizing it, choose Plain Text from the Style menu.

To change the font or font size of text use the same method and select the new font or size you want from the Font and Size menus. In the sample memo, select the date and use the Font and Size menus to change it to Times 18-point. Then select each of the first words of the header lines (To, From, and Subject) and either choose Bold from the Style menu or press ⌘-B.

These font style changes are minor, but they can make a difference in the overall effect of your document. For more information on them, see the MacWrite Pro *User's Guide*.

After you change the text style, font, or font size of a word, keep in mind that any text you enter immediately after that word adopts the changed text style. If you put the insertion point at the end of an italicized word, for example, all new text you enter will be italicized, too. To prevent this, choose Plain Text from the Style menu after placing the insertion point.

Saving and Printing a Document

Save your MacWrite documents every ten to fifteen minutes as you work on them. Just choose Save from the File menu, or press ⌘-S. The first time you save a document, you must name it and choose where to place it in your folder hierarchy. For more information on this, see "Saving Your Work on a Document" in Chapter 4.

To print a hard copy of your document, first save it, then choose Print from the File menu, or press ⌘-P. The Print dialog box opens. Unless you want to do something special, leave all the settings as they are and click the Print button or just press the Return key to start printing. If you have a LaserWriter or compatible printer that allows background printing, the PrintMonitor will take over your print job in a moment or two, and you can go right back to work while printing proceeds.

Note

For more information on printing, see Chapter 3.

Troubleshooting Problems with Your Word Processor

The following subsections cover the problems you are most likely to have while working with word processing applications. The solutions given in some of these sections apply specifically to Microsoft Word and MacWrite Pro. If you use a different word processing application, you can still use the suggestions as general guidelines.

Not Enough Memory

You get the message "Not enough memory to open the application" when you try to open your word processor. If you have auxiliary tools you don't use with your application, see if you can remove or disable them. For example, if you have Microsoft Word, take the Grammar file out of the Word Commands folder that is in the same folder as the Word application. Take out any converter files that you don't need for converting files to other formats, too.

If you still do not have enough memory, try increasing the memory allocation in the application's Info box; Chapter 7 contains information on how to do this. If you cannot give the application enough memory because there is not enough RAM in your Mac, then you have to take the Mac to a qualified technician to install more.

Text Appears in Wrong Style

You have a paragraph of text in one style, and you place the insertion point on the next line after the paragraph, and when you type in new text, it appears in the wrong style. The problem is that the invisible paragraph mark on the line below the existing text has a change of style embedded in it.

To keep the style of the paragraph above, first choose Show ¶ from the View menu (if you are in Word) or Show Invisibles (if you are in MacWrite Pro). Then select the paragraph marker on the line below the existing text and change the style to the one used for the preceding paragraph. To change the style if you are in Word you can either choose the one that's right from the list at the left end of the ruler, or choose Style from the Format menu and choose the style from the list there. If you are in MacWrite Pro, choose the style from the Style palette. If it is not showing, choose Show Styles from the Style menu.

Text Disappeared

The most likely problem is that you have deleted the text or replaced it with a space or a single letter. Before you do anything else, choose Undo from the Edit menu. If that doesn't bring the text back, scroll up and down to see if the text has simply been pushed out of view. If it is really gone, you can choose Save As from the File menu and give the document a temporary name. Then open the original document, and if the text is in it, select it, copy it out and paste it into the temporary version. Finally, use Save As to replace the old version with the updated temporary one.

If even that method fails to turn up your missing text, you have no choice but to type the text in again. Save often to avoid problems like this in the future.

Indents Not Printing As Expected

You created a document without using the ruler to make indents at the beginning of each paragraph, and when you print out the document, some of the indents are different sizes than others. To make sure your indents are consistent in size, you must make them all with tabs, or set the first-line indent in the ruler and use the Return key to start each new paragraph.

Mixed Formatting

You have typed in a long paragraph that is all supposed to be in the same style, but parts of it have strange formatting that you don't know how you put there. The simplest solution is to select the whole block of text and apply a single style to it. Then go through the text and select any pieces that still have incorrect font styles or other attributes and correct them.

Phrase Split by Word Wrap

A phrase that you want to keep together (something like St. Nick or Henry VIII) gets split at the end of a line. Just select the space between the two words and press Option-spacebar. This makes a nonbreaking link between the two words.

Ten

Graphics Applications

Featuring

- Choosing the right graphics application for you
- How to open a new document in Kid Pix and MacDraw Pro
- How to draw lines and shapes in Kid Pix and MacDraw Pro
- How to fill spaces with shades or patterns in Kid Pix and MacDraw Pro
- How to undo and erase mistakes in Kid Pix and MacDraw Pro
- How to place stamps in Kid Pix
- How to enter and manipulate text in MacDraw Pro
- How to save and print documents in Kid Pix and MacDraw Pro
- Troubleshooting problems with graphics applications

First Steps

To open a new document in Kid Pix: 222

If you have not started the application already, double-click the Kid Pix icon. If Kid Pix is already running and you are looking at a document window, choose New from the File menu, and a window for the new document will open.

To create a picture in Kid Pix: 223

Click on a tool in the tool palette on the left side of the window. Then, if there are a number of possible choices for how the tool can work or what it can look like, choose the option you want from the palette at the bottom of the window. Then you can either click or drag to create the images you want in the window.

To open a new document in MacDraw Pro: 227

If you have not started the application already, double-click the MacDraw Pro icon. If MacDraw Pro is already running and you are looking at a document window, choose New from the File menu, and a window for the new document will open.

CHAPTER 10

To create graphic images in MacDraw Pro: 227

Select the tool you need by clicking it in the tool palette on the left side of the window. Then check the fill and line indicators to make sure the color (shade, on monochrome Macs), pattern, and gradient are what you want. Use the pop-up menus for each to set up the tool the way you want it. Then click or drag with the tool in the document window to create and fill the shapes you want.

To move and edit objects you have created: 228

Click on the arrow tool at the top of the tool palette. Then click with the arrow's point on the object you want to edit or move. When the handles appear on the corners of the object, you can move or alter it.

To zoom in and out of a magnified view of a MacDraw Pro graphic: 231

Click on the large and small landscape icons in the lower left corner of the window. If you want to see a very highly magnified view of one section of your graphic, click on the fractional zoom icon (the one to the right of the two landscape icons). Then move the magnifying glass pointer to the part of your graphic you want to see up close and click.

Graphics applications are the tools you use to create images. Good graphics applications make it fun to be creative, whether you are doodling with a spray can or making three-dimensional engineering plans.

All graphics programs should make it easy for you to revise and manipulate the images you have created. The greatest advantage the computer has over other art media is the ease with which you can undo and redo your work. If a graphics application makes good use of the Mac's mouse, menus, and dialog boxes, it can be almost as much fun to use for revisions as for the original creative effort.

The better graphics applications let you draw straight and curved lines, shapes, patterns, and shades of gray. They usually give you a way to copy public domain *clip art* and alter it according to your taste. Most current graphics applications allow the use of color, if your Mac supports color. Some specialize in certain types of graphics, such as paintings, drawings, or photographs.

Look through the applications listed in this chapter and find the one that seems best suited to your needs.

Which Graphics Application for You?

You can choose from several distinct types of graphics applications. There are bitmapped painting programs, such as Kid Pix and MacPaint, and there are object-oriented drawing/illustrating programs such as MacDraw Pro, Illustrator, and Freehand. Some applications, such as SuperPaint and Canvas, can handle both bitmapped and object-oriented graphics.

A Great Beginner's Graphics Application

If you are new to computing with a Mac, or if you are just starting to work in graphics, there's one program that is miles ahead of all the others. It's called Kid Pix. It costs much less than other basic painting or drawing applications, but it lets you do a lot of fun things with bitmapped painting tools. It is a great tool for anyone new to the Mac, because it encourages you to use the mouse, menus, and the basic elements of Mac windows, and it shows you right away how easy it is to get things done on a Mac. For an example of how to make a picture with Kid Pix, see the "Using Kid Pix" section later in this chapter.

Workhorse Applications That Paint and Draw

If you want to sketch out simple bitmapped images *and* create fine object-oriented images that require precision and control, you should choose a graphics application that allows you to work with both types of graphics. SuperPaint and Canvas are the two leaders in the field. If your Mac has a monochrome monitor, less than 4MB of RAM, and a relatively slow CPU (if it's a Plus, for instance), you should use SuperPaint 2.0. If you have a high-powered Mac and lots of RAM and a color monitor, it makes more sense to use SuperPaint 3.0 or higher, or the more expensive Canvas.

Product at a Glance

Kid Pix

Publisher:
Broderbund Software
Add-on available: Kid Pix Companion

Requires:
Mac Plus or later
System 6.7 or later
1MB of RAM on monochrome Macs; 2MB of RAM on color Macs. If running System 7 or later, 2MB of RAM on monochrome Macs; 4MB of RAM on color Macs.
One 800K disk drive and a hard disk with at least 5MB of free space
Compatible with any printer that can handle Mac graphics, although print quality will vary

Description:
One of the best and least expensive beginners' graphics applications for young and old Mac users. Kid Pix offers a wide variety of tools for creating paint documents, and makes it easy to get at all the tools, including preformed stamps, comical erasers, and fractal trees. But Kid Pix is more than a toy; the lessons and concepts that you learn as you explore and enjoy Kid Pix will help you make the best use of any other Mac application you work with.

These applications can churn out good quality artwork, and they let you either paint or draw, as your needs dictate. You can create illustrations that are suitable for publication in either application, but each has its limits. SuperPaint has problems with several file formats that are often used in the publishing industry, and Canvas is relatively hard to learn.

High-Power Drawing Applications

If you want to create complex illustrations for publication, ones that require precision and fully controlled use of lines, shapes, shading, and color, then you should buy an object-oriented drawing program such as MacDraw Pro, Illustrator, or FreeHand. These applications allow you to manipulate lines in very sophisticated ways. Every straight line has endpoints, and every curved line has a number of points that define the *path*. These points act as handles, which you can adjust to a very fine degree. You can also specify the stroke width, color, and pattern of a line.

The business advantage of MacDraw Pro, Illustrator, and other high-end drawing programs is that they produce graphics that can be reproduced at any resolution, from 72 DPI (dots per inch) on a Mac Classic screen to 2540 DPI on a Linotronic printing press used for publishing. The graphics are usually EPS (encapsulated PostScript) files, which means that they can be exported to many page layout applications, both for Macs and other computers, and they can be printed on most high-quality printers in the publishing world. EPS files can also be output directly to negative or positive film for printing or silk-screening.

MacDraw Pro and Illustrator can handle text in all kinds of ways, too. You can type in text, then change the font, shape, size and color. You can also align text to a curved path in Illustrator, or make it fit inside a closed path so it conforms to the shape. MacDraw Pro has much more limited powers of text and image manipulation, but it is relatively easy to learn. For an example of how to make a simple headline graphic for a newsletter, see the "Using MacDraw Pro" section later in this chapter.

> **Product at a Glance**
>
> ### MacDraw Pro
>
> **Publisher:**
> Claris
> Upgrade from MacDraw II is available, but not free
>
> **Requires:**
> Macintosh Plus or better; Classic/LC or better recommended
> System 6.7 or later
> 2MB of RAM on 6.7; 4MB of RAM on 7.0 or later
> One 800K disk drive and a hard disk with at least 1.5MB of free space; 40MB hard drive recommended
> Compatible with any printer capable of printing standard Mac output, but print quality will vary
>
> **Description:**
> MacDraw Pro is a powerful object-oriented graphics tool. It has a straightforward interface that is a direct descendent of the original MacDraw, which helped make the Mac popular from the start. You can use the simple, clear drawing and filling tools to create images, and you can edit any existing image after selecting it. MacDraw can be adapted to do all kinds of specialized tasks, from making a frame for a block of text to designing a computer circuit board.

Learning to manipulate curves and layered images in an application like Illustrator is tricky at first, and it may seem that it takes you too long to get your idea into a workable form. Once you do have the basic form of a graphic in place, however, you will be amazed at how easily and precisely you can edit and develop it into a polished work of art. Your initial time investment can lead to huge payoffs as you build more and more complex graphics.

Using Kid Pix

Using Kid Pix is the Macintosh dream come true. It's so simple it begs you to play around and be creative. In fact, I recommend Kid Pix to anybody who has just bought a Mac. Using Kid Pix is the easiest and most entertaining way to learn about the mouse and the other basic elements of the Mac interface. The following procedures will give you a peek at the many joys of Kid Pix, but you'll have to explore on your own to find all of its wonderful little tricks, jokes, and funny noises. If you have Kid Pix already and enjoy using it, you should also get the Kid Pix Companion. It adds to the fun and creative diversions of the basic Kid Pix software.

Opening a Document

Take one of the following actions to open a document in Kid Pix, depending on your situation:

- To open a new document if you have not started Kid Pix, double-click the Kid Pix icon, as shown in Figure 10.1, or double-click an alias for it.
- To open a new document if you have started Kid Pix and are looking at an existing picture, choose New from the File menu.

Figure 10.1
The Kid Pix icon

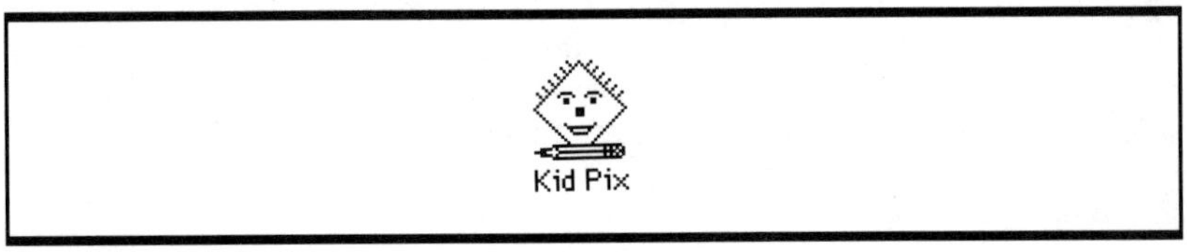

A window opens with the ultra-simple set of Kid Pix menu titles in the menu bar, the Kid Pix icon at the right end of the bar, the tools palette on the left side of the window, and the options for the selected tool at the bottom of the window, as shown in Figure 10.2. Since the pencil tool is selected by default, the cursor looks like a short, fat pencil, and the pencil tool in the tools palette is highlighted.

If this is the first time you have ever used a Mac, or if you are helping a young or uncoordinated user learn about the Mac, you can make the experience almost fool-proof by pulling down the Goodies menu and choosing Small Kids Mode. This hides most of the menus and sets the screen so you can't run off the edge of the Kid Pix window and switch into the Finder or another application by mistake. You can always get the menus back by choosing Show Menu Bar from the Kid Pix menu, which is the menu on the right when you are in Small Kids Mode.

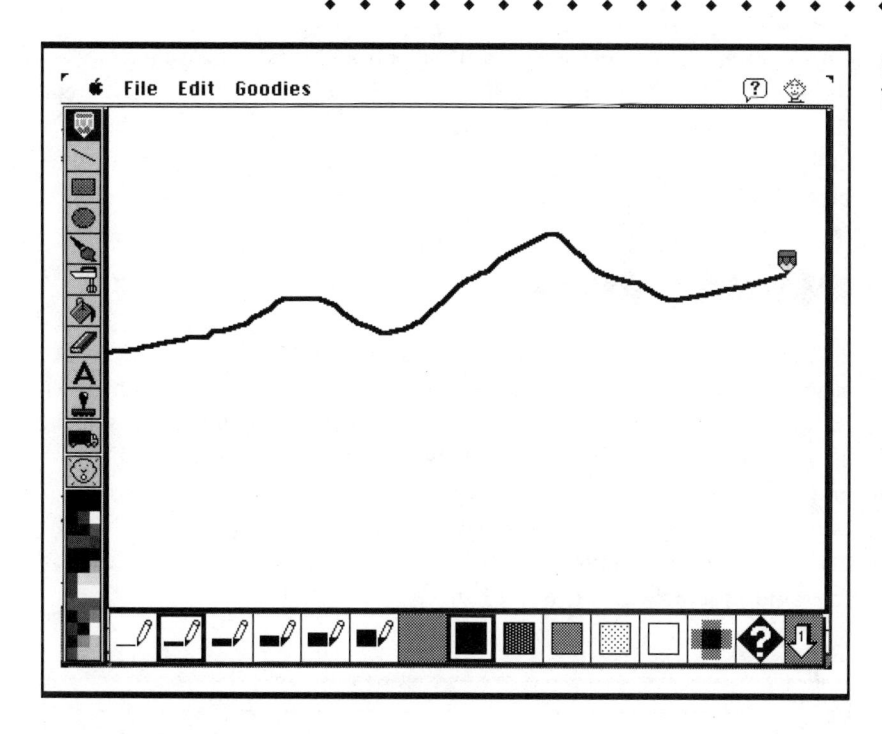

Figure 10.2
The Kid Pix window

Drawing Lines

To draw a line, just press the mouse button and drag the fat pencil around on the screen. It makes a scratchy noise as it draws. To make wider, thinner, or textured lines, just move the pointer down to the boxes at the bottom of the screen (it turns into an arrow down there) and choose a different box. Fool around a little. Then go on to the section "Undoing and Erasing Mistakes" and erase your experiments. When you have a clean window, draw a nice horizon with some mountains, as shown in Figure 10.2.

Undoing and Erasing Mistakes

To undo the last line you drew, choose Undo from the Edit menu, or click the undo guy (the guy with his mouth open) at the bottom of the tools palette. To erase things, move the pointer to the tools palette on the left side of the screen and click on the chalkboard eraser tool (it looks more like a brick or a short board; it's under the paint can and above the letter *A*). A whole set of eraser options appear in the boxes at the bottom of the screen. The ones on the left can be dragged around the screen like erasers. There are different sizes and shapes, but they all erase white swaths across the screen when you drag them. The other eraser options are for either clearing the screen completely, or for creating mysterious images as you erase.

Placing Stamps

Tip
To make an image larger than the standard one, hold down the Option or Shift key while you click with the stamp pointer.

To add preformed images of things to your Kid Pix graphic, click the rubber stamp tool in the tools palette on the left side of the screen (it's below the letter A). Then browse through the stamps that appear on the bottom of the screen. To see stamps other than the ones shown, click the down arrow at the right end of the palette. Click on your stamp of choice, then click with the stamp pointer wherever you want the image to appear in your picture. Use the rubber stamp to put a cactus, a horse, some palm trees, or whatever you want into your mountain scene, as in Figure 10.3.

Figure 10.3
A Kid Pix graphic

224 Chapter 10: Graphics Applications

Painting with the Wacky Brush

To add a tree to your picture, use the wacky brush. When you click on it (it's the one with a blobby end, just below the round shape in the tools palette) you see a bunch of new options at the bottom of the screen, many of which don't make sense until you try them.

1. Click on the wacky brush to make it the active tool.
2. Click on the tree icon in the second set of options (click the down arrow at the right end of the palette to see the two sets of options).
3. Then click in the picture. Kid Pix paints a fractal tree (every one is different from the last) and makes a wonderful chime sound.
4. To put foliage on the tree, as shown in Figure 10.3, use the bubbly option for the wacky brush (it's the fourth option from the left in the first set of options) and drag the wacky brush around in the upper branches of the fractal tree.

Painting an Area with the Paint Can

To fill an area with a pattern, click on the paint can in the tools palette, then click on a pattern in the palette that appears across the bottom of the screen. Then move the paint can pointer to the space you want to fill (the tip of the pouring paint is the hot spot, if you have to fill a small area) and click.

You can fill an area with graded bands of gray, like the sky in Figure 10.3.

1. Choose the paint can from the tools palette.
2. Click the question mark option in the pattern palette.
3. Move the paint can to the area you want to fill, hold down the Option key, and click the mouse button.

Shades of gray look best on a grayscale or color monitor, and they print out best on a high-resolution printer, but you can some interesting effects with grays on a monochrome screen and a 72 DPI or 300 DPI printer.

Saving and Printing a Kid Pix Document

> **Note**
> For more information on using the Save command, see "Saving Your Work on a Document" in Chapter 4.

To protect your priceless Kid Pix art, save it often, about every fifteen minutes when you are working on it. All you have to do is choose Save from the File menu. The first time you save a document, you must name it and choose where to place it in your folder hierarchy, or it will be called "Untitled Kids" and placed in the same folder with the Kid Pix application.

To print a hard copy of your graphic, first save it, then choose Print from the File menu. A print dialog box opens. Unless you want to do something special, leave all the settings as they are and click the Print button or press the Return key to start printing. If you have a LaserWriter or compatible printer that allows background printing, the PrintMonitor will take over your print job in a moment or two, and you can go right back to Kid Pix while printing proceeds. For more information, see Chapter 3.

Using MacDraw Pro

MacDraw Pro creates objects you can deal with as units, rather than images that are simply collections of bits. Now, this may not mean much to you if you aren't familiar with graphics applications, but if you compare the way MacDraw Pro works with the way Kid Pix works, it's fairly easy to understand.

For example, if you make a hill shape and put a house shape on it in Kid Pix, you can't select the house and move it to a nicer location on the hill. If you try to select the house, you select the part of the hill that is behind it, too. This is because the whole graphic is a single bitmap—a collection of dark and light bits, exactly as you see them on the screen. To move something on a bit-mapped graphic, you have to erase it, fix the background, then recreate the erased object in the new place where you want to see it.

However, if you make a hill shape in a draw application such as MacDraw Pro or Illustrator, you can create a house or some other image, then move it around and edit it without changing the background at all. That's because each image is a separate graphic object. It's more like the shapes are cut-outs that you can place on a felt board and then play around with. The following procedure explains how to use MacDraw Pro to work with objects and create a simple newsletter heading. See the MacDraw Pro *User Manual* to learn more information on how to create, edit, and delete graphic objects.

Opening a Document

Take one of the following actions to open a document in MacDraw Pro, depending on your situation:

- To open a new document if you have not started MacDraw Pro, double-click the MacDraw Pro icon, as shown in Figure 10.4, or double-click an alias for it.

- To open a new document if you have started MacDraw Pro and are looking at an existing picture, choose New from the File menu.

Figure 10.4
The MacDraw Pro icon

A window opens with the MacDraw Pro menu titles in the menu bar, the MacDraw Pro icon at the right end of the bar, the tool palette on the left side of the window, and the pop-up menus for colors, fill patterns, and gradients at the top of the window, as shown in Figure 10.5.

The window has the name "Untitled1 - Layer #1." The name of the document will change the first time you save it and give it a title. The layer number will change if you make drawings with more than one layer. If you are just learning about MacDraw Pro, it is best to work in only one layer. The arrow tool in the upper left corner of the window is selected by default, so the arrow pointer appears in the window. The arrow works like the pointer in the Finder; you can select and drag things with it.

In general, the way you create images in MacDraw Pro is to go through the following steps:

1. Choose a tool that will do what you want.
2. Choose the color, line, fill, or gradient you want.
3. Create the image you have in mind.

Figure 10.5
The MacDraw Pro window

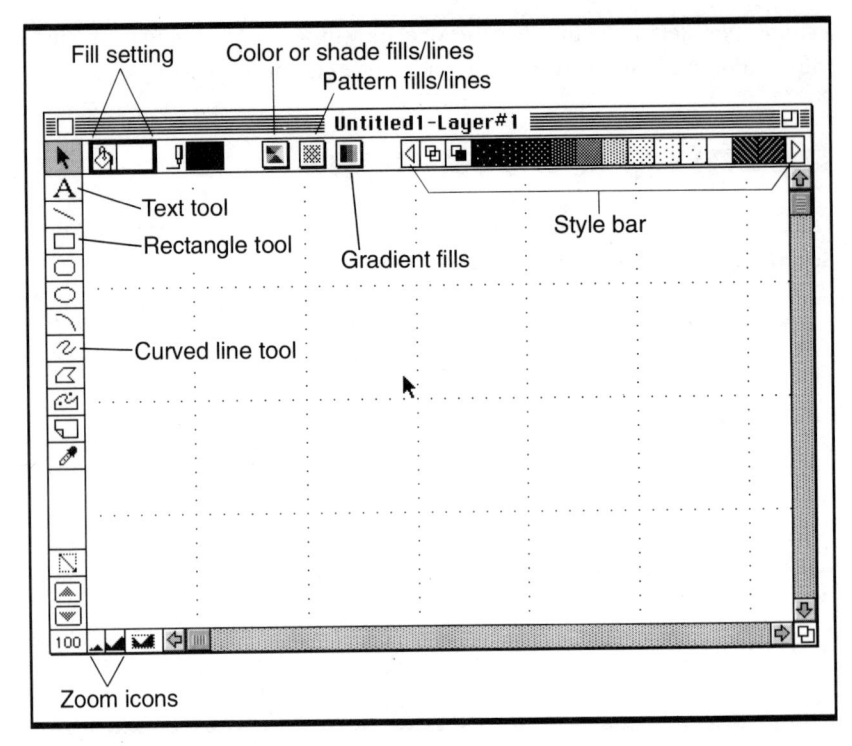

[Diagram of the MacDraw Pro window with labels: Fill setting, Color or shade fills/lines, Pattern fills/lines, Text tool, Rectangle tool, Gradient fills, Style bar, Curved line tool, Zoom icons]

In the sections that follow, we'll use MacDraw Pro to create a simple title graphic for a newsletter. If you follow the procedures listed to create this graphic, you will make the same general choices over and over. After you create any object, you'll notice that little boxes or *handles* appear at the corners of it. If you want to move or edit any object you have created, you have to use the arrow tool to select the object so those handles appear. Then you can move the object or use other tools to edit it.

Creating a Shape

To create a shape you choose the shape tool you want from the tools palette on the left side of the window, then you draw the shape. When the shape is complete, you can edit it to get it just the way you want it.

To see how this works, let's make a nice skyline for a newsletter title graphic.

1. Select the curved line tool (it looks like a backwards S) in the middle of the tool palette. Note that the pointer becomes a pen.

228 Chapter 10: Graphics Applications

2. Click the pen icon at the top of the window to see what shade lines the pen draws. If the box next to the pen isn't black, open the pop-up menu for colors (they'll just be shades of gray if your Mac doesn't support color) and choose black.
3. From the Pen menu in the menu bar, choose 2-point to make the line that the pen draws 2 pixels thick. Leave the line type set to plain.
4. Place the tip of the pen on one of the dots of the grid that is at an intersection of a vertical and horizontal dotted line, then draw down, to the right, and back up to the horizontal line where you started. This makes a nice valley view, as shown in Figure 10.6. If the gridlines aren't visible, choose Show Gridlines from the View menu.

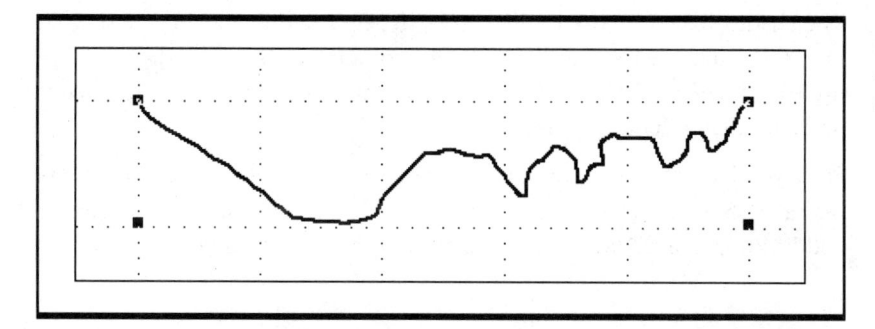

Figure 10.6
A line that creates a valley shape

5. If you are not pleased with your first attempt at drawing a valley, just choose Undo from the Edit menu and try again.
6. Check the ends of the line to make sure both of them are exactly on the dotted horizontal grid. You can magnify the drawing by clicking on the large landscape icon in the lower left corner of the window; this zooms your view in close.
7. If your valley line ends too high or low, click the small landscape icon and zoom out to a normal 100 percent view. Then use the Delete key to erase the original line and draw a new one.

Tip
If you have trouble ending a line on the grid, try starting on a dot and ending on a dot.

So now you have a nice valley line in the window. The actual shape of the line can be any way you want it, but it will work best if it has no loops or zigzags.

Using MacDraw Pro **229**

Creating a Fill

Once you have a shape, you can fill it with whatever pattern, shade, or graded shades you want. Here's a way to fill your valley with shades of gray that look almost like a sunset:

1. Make sure the valley shape you just drew is selected; click it with the arrow tool to make the handles appear at the corners.
2. Click the paint can icon at the top left corner of the window to see what fill is set. Probably none will be set, so the box to the right of the paint can will be blank.
3. Drag down from the gradient fills icon to open the pop-up menu for gradient fills and choose the box that shows shades that vary from black at the top of the box to white at the bottom of the box. The shape fills with the gradient.

The shades may be more or less clear, depending on what Mac and what monitor you are using, but they should look more or less like those in Figure 10.7. If you have a good printer the shading will probably come out better on paper than it looks on the screen.

Since you have put a fair amount of work into your graphic, save it by choosing Save from the File menu or Pressing ⌘-S. For more on saving, see "Saving and Printing a MacDraw Pro Document" later in this chapter.

Figure 10.7
The completed MacDraw Pro graphic

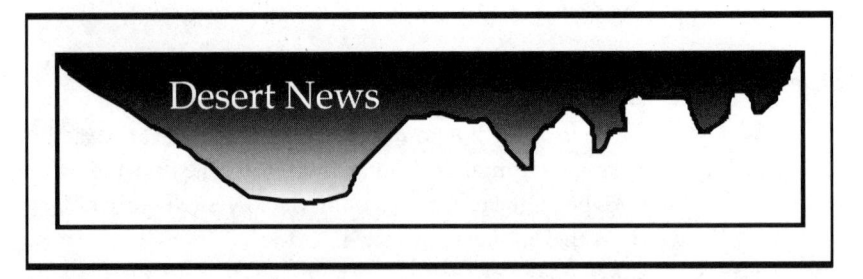

Adding Text to a Graphic

If you want to use a graphic for a title to a newsletter or a letterhead, you have to put text into it. MacDraw Pro makes this easy for you. You can place the text, then treat it like any other shape you have created.

1. Click the text tool in the tool palette on the left side of the window. It looks like a large *A*.
2. Place the I-beam at the point in the graphic where you want the text to begin. Near the top left corner is a good spot. Click the mouse to select that spot, but don't start typing yet.
3. Before you start typing, choose a font and size for your text, using the Font and Size menus. One possibility is to use Palatino font and 18-point size. Just choose whatever you want.
4. You also need to write in white text to make it show up, so don't start typing until you have clicked the pen icon at the top of the window, then chosen white from the color pop-up menu.
5. Now you can finally type in your text.
6. If the text is in the wrong place, you can drag the whole text box to the right place.
7. If the text is too large, make sure the text tool is selected, then drag across the text in the text box and choose a smaller font size from the Font menu.
8. To get a better idea of how the text will look when you print it, use the zoom icon (the large landscape down in the lower left corner of the window) to magnify the image to 200 percent. Click outside the graphic to deselect the text box. Select the text again if you need to edit.

If you aren't satisfied with the text, feel free to play with it. Then you can check the results in a magnified view. You may want to print out a text copy of the graphic at this point, but keep in mind that this wastes paper. I prefer to keep checking the graphic in 200 percent zoom view, rather than printing lots of test copies.

Placing a Frame around a Graphic

You may want to set your title graphic apart from the other elements of your newsletter. To do this, you can frame the graphic by using the MacDraw Pro shape tools.

1. Click the rectangle shape tool, just two tools down from the text tool.

2. Click the paint can fill icon, then choose the overlapping white square thingies at the top left corner of the patterns pop-up menu. Those overlapping squares indicate that whatever shape you draw will have no fill, so you can see the stuff behind it.

3. Check the line setting next to the pen icon to make sure the lines of the frame you draw will be black. Use the Pen menu in the menu bar to choose a thicker or thinner frame if you want.

4. Drag the mouse diagonally from the upper left corner of the graphic down to the lower right corner, then release the mouse button to make your frame.

5. Check the corners of the frame and the corners of the graphic to make sure you don't have any blank spots or protrusions; you can fill blank spots with short fat black lines, and you can hide protrusions outside the frame with short fat white lines.

Your graphic is now ready for inclusion in your newsletter layout. It should look like Figure 10.7, back a few pages. Not only can you import the graphic into any page layout application, you can come back and edit the document if you decide to change the name of the newsletter or something. Such flexibility is rare in the graphic arts.

Tip
Put the colors and fills you use most often, such as black and white, near the left end of the style bar, for instant access.

If you do lots of work with MacDraw Pro and find that you are always having to choose the same patterns and shades from the pop-up menus at the top of the window, you can place those patterns in the style bar that's to the right of the pop-ups. To add a color, pattern, or gradient, just open the menu and drag it away from its normal position (this makes it a *tear-off* menu). Then drag the item you want to the place where you want to have it in the style bar.

Saving and Printing a MacDraw Pro Document

To protect your well-crafted MacDraw Pro graphic, save it often, about every fifteen minutes when you are working on it. All you have to do is choose Save from the File menu. The first time you save a document, you must name it and choose where to place it in your folder hierarchy, or it will be called "Untitled1" and placed in the same folder with the MacDraw Pro application. For more information on using the Save command, see "Saving Your Work on a Document" in Chapter 4.

To print a hard copy of your graphic, first save it, then choose Print from the File menu. A print dialog box opens. Unless you want to do something special, leave all the settings as they are and click the Print button or press the Return key to start printing. If you have a LaserWriter or compatible printer that allows background printing, the PrintMonitor will take over your print job in a moment or two, and you can go right back to MacDraw Pro while printing proceeds. For more information, see Chapter 3.

Troubleshooting Problems with Graphics Applications

The following subsections cover the most common problems you may encounter when working with graphics applications.

Paint or a Fill Spread beyond Intended Area

You poured paint or a texture into what you thought was a closed area, but the stuff escapes and goes all over the place. The problem is that there is a leak somewhere: a space between the ends of two lines, or a corner where the sides don't meet. First, choose Undo from the Edit menu to clean up the mess instantly. Then look for the leak, using a magnified view at any points where holes are likely. When you find the leak, close it off, then try your paint-pour or fill over again.

Text in a Bitmapped Graphic Is Jagged

Bitmapped graphics can only make approximations of outline fonts; if you copy text from a word processing application into your graphics, or if you use fonts that you don't have a bitmap for, the text will look jagged in the printed graphics. The solution is to stick to fonts that print well as bitmaps, such as those with city names. Otherwise, use an object-oriented application for all text work.

You Can't Place or Create an Object Exactly Where You Want It

The problem is that your application (usually a draw application) is placing everything on a grid. You have to turn off that grid-aligning option. In MacDraw Pro, you choose Turn Autogrid Off from the Layout menu. In other applications you have to go to a dialog box by choosing grids from an Options or Preferences menu. Once you have turned the grid off, you can move objects wherever you want. Just keep in mind that it is harder to line things up when the grid is turned off.

Printed Graphic Looks Bad

This usually means the printer is not capable of printing with good enough resolution to show the effects you have created. If you are using an object-oriented application, try saving your graphic in PICT or MacPaint format and printing it. If your application and monitor can show grayscale, you may be able to print graphics in black and white (choose Black & White in the Print dialog box), but the results may be pretty dotty and muddled. The best solution is to print the grayscale graphics on a high-resolution printer.

Eleven

Page Layout Applications

Featuring

- Choosing the right page layout application for your needs
- How to plan and sketch the layout of a newsletter
- How to open a new document in PageMaker
- How to do page setup in PageMaker
- A description of the elements of the PageMaker document window
- How to create master pages in PageMaker
- How to place text and graphics in PageMaker
- How to zoom in and out of magnified page views in PageMaker
- How to adjust text and graphics layout in PageMaker
- How to wrap text around a graphic in PageMaker
- How to save and print documents in PageMaker
- Troubleshooting problems in PageMaker

First Steps

To open a new document in PageMaker: 245

If you have not started the application already, double-click the PageMaker icon. When the PageMaker menu appears, choose New from the File menu. If PageMaker is already running and you are looking at a window with a document in it, just choose New from the File menu. Then fill in the page setup specifications in the Page Setup dialog box, and set up your overall format on the master pages that appear in the document window.

To set up pages in PageMaker: 246

Choose New from the File menu to open the Page Setup dialog box, then fill in the text boxes and click the buttons for your choices. Typically, you will want to leave most of the settings at their defaults. You need to specify the number of pages, and you can turn off the Facing Pages if you have a small-screen Mac. You can also reduce all of the margins other than the inside one to .5" to increase the space for graphics and text on the pages.

CHAPTER 11

To set up master pages in PageMaker: 249

Click on the icon for the left master page, then choose Column Guides in the Layout menu to set up your columns in the column guide box. Set the number of columns you want and how much space you want between them. Follow the same steps to set up columns for the right master page. You can add page numbers to both right and left master pages, too; just make a small text block on each master page where you want the numbers, then press ⌘-Option-P to designate page numbers for all pages.

To place text in PageMaker: 251

Click the icon of the page where you want to place the text. Then choose Autoflow in the Utilities menu, if you want the text to flow on from column to column. Press ⌘-D and use the Open dialog box to find and select the text file you want to place. When you click OK in the dialog box, you can click with the "loaded" cursor in the document window; the text flows down from where you started it.

To place a graphic image in PageMaker: 252

Follow the same procedure as for placing text; go to the page you want, then press ⌘-D and select the file you want. Then place the graphic with the loaded pointer. The graphic appears in the same size and shape as it was created, even if it does not fit in the space provided.

Page layout applications are tools for putting together text and graphics to make nice-looking documents. But that doesn't really tell the whole story of page layout on the Mac.

Page layout is what put the Mac on the map. When PageMaker for the Mac came out, a revolution in publishing began. It is called desktop publishing, and it has succeeded because you can do page layout much faster, cheaper, and more creatively on a Mac than you can by cutting up pieces of paper and sticking them on big pasteboards. You waste a lot less paper, too, unless you do dozens of test printouts.

The effects of desktop publishing have been amazing. Instead of dozens of people slaving away to create paste-ups, now there are single individuals, often working at home, creating the page layouts for everything from church calendars to major periodicals and full-length books. Desktop publishing is a major cottage industry, and the Mac is the desktop publisher's computer of choice.

The growth of this cottage industry is not just due to the economics. It's also due to the fact that it's fun. A desktop publisher can collect a bunch of graphics files that have been created by a gifted artist or illustrator, and a bunch of text files written by talented writers, and shape them into a document that has even more impact than the ingredients that went into it. This is highly satisfying work. Even if the document is just a newsletter made up of corny articles and clip art (public domain cartoons and simple graphics), the process of creating pages is a gratifying one; you can watch a page take shape before your eyes, and you have great power to manipulate the different elements to make it look the way you want.

You can use page layout applications to do simple things like writing letters and adding letterheads, or you can do huge, complex jobs like full-color professional publications. You have complete control of all phases of the production, from editing text to the final printout. The feeling you get from this control is downright exhilarating, especially when the printout actually looks just like you wanted.

Which Page Layout Application for You?

There are only a few serious contenders in the world of page layout applications. There are inexpensive page layout applications such as Personal Press that are good for simple, short documents. Then there are the big applications, such as PageMaker and QuarkXPress, for all kinds of publishing needs, and there is FrameMaker, which is especially good for long technical documents.

An Inexpensive Page Layout Tool for Small Jobs

If you don't want to do all kinds of fancy publishing tricks, and you have a low-end Mac and a tight budget, try Personal Press. It works great for short documents like newsletters, fliers, and business cards. Aldus made this application to take care of all the people who don't want to learn about automatic kerning and such things. To make a layout, you just choose a template and fill in the text and graphics where you want, and you're done. You can crank out your weekly newsletter without having to relearn the whole art and science of page layout each week. Personal Press can make nice-looking documents on low-cost printers, too. You can play around a bit with the elements as you lay them out, but you don't have the freedom or the power to create a completely unique look for your documents.

Publish It Easy is another low-end layout tool that gives you much more flexibility and power, but it is sometimes confusing and sometimes crash-prone, which are the last things you want if you are new to the page layout game.

Page Layout Applications for Big Jobs

QuarkXPress versus PageMaker: the battle has been raging since the conception of the two leading page layout programs. Discussing these programs with a user from another camp can be like discussing religion with your Aunt

Maude. You can both give strong arguments for your side, but no one leaves satisfied that they have discovered the one and only truth. To me, the important truth is that both applications are very good, and they will both continue to improve, each trying to catch up with the new features the other adds.

PageMaker is easier to learn and you can change your layout easier than you can in Quark. PageMaker also has the ability to link separate documents and create an index and table of contents for the entire linked group. This is an important feature for producing multichapter books. Quark, however, is known for its great precision in handling text and graphics, especially color graphics. Aldus, the manufacturer of PageMaker, has better technical support, according to many users. PageMaker also has better online help and a better manual. PageMaker has a broader user base, and therefore you are more likely to find someone to advise you on PageMaker than on Quark. I could go on and on but Aunt Maude is getting tired.

What it boils down to is this—if you are doing mostly high-end color work, demand precision typographic control, and have the time to invest in learning Quark, then go for it. Otherwise, I would choose PageMaker mostly for its ease of use and Aldus' outstanding technical support.

Product at a Glance

PageMaker

Publisher:
Aldus Corporation
Upgrade from PageMaker 4.0 is available, but not free

Requires:
Macintosh LC, Classic, or better; LC II or better recommended
System 6.7 or later; System 7.1 or later recommended
4MB of RAM and a 20MB hard drive with 7.5MB of free space required; 8MB of RAM and an 80MB hard drive recommended
PostScript or QuickDraw laser printer with Mac-compatible fonts installed

Description:
PageMaker 4.0 is a full-powered page layout application that has been a leading force in the desktop publishing revolution. It makes the job of placing text and graphics an enjoyable creative effort, rather than a tedious bore. Once you learn how to set up master pages in PageMaker, you can manipulate, edit, and rearrange the elements of your pages with intuitive ease. If you have special needs or problems, you can always get help from other users, from PageMaker's excellent documentation, or from Aldus support.

One other application is worth mentioning: FrameMaker. It is a powerful and well-integrated page layout tool that works best on long technical documents. It is not too easy to learn, however; and it requires a powerful Mac and a lot of memory and storage to run at a reasonable speed.

Using PageMaker

This section and the subsections that follow tell how to create a newsletter with PageMaker, from opening the document to printing the finished publication. The procedures are arranged in the same order you would go through them to create any publication, but the example is short and relatively simple so you can get through it quickly.

The basic steps of the procedure are:

1. Make a rough sketch and locate text and graphics files.
2. Create master pages that serve as templates for all other pages.
3. Place text and graphics on page one.
4. Refine the format of text and graphics on page one.
5. Place extra text on page two.
6. Print.

Of course, you will be saving your work frequently during the whole procedure. PageMaker encourages and often requires lots of creative effort. Losing the product of your creativity is especially frustrating, so save often.

Making a Rough Sketch and Collecting Files

Before you start in on the layout procedures in PageMaker, you should make at least a rough sketch for your newsletter and get the necessary text and graphics files together. There are a lot of choices you have to make as you set up your page design, and if you make a sketch before you start and know what the pieces are going to be, the pieces all fall into place much more easily.

For instance, if you know you want a newsletter that looks something like the one in Figure 11.1, you can plan for three columns of text on standard letter-size paper, with some graphics and a logo at the top. You can make the

> **Note**
> See Appendix A for details on graphics file format compatibility.

margins and page numbering standard, plain vanilla. To keep the page from being too boring, you can plan for part of one story to span a couple of columns, like the one in the lower right corner of the sketch.

To build up a newsletter like this, you'll need some text files and some graphics files. You can use the practice files in the PageMaker Tutorial folder that you received with the application. Make sure the Tutorial folder is installed on your hard disk; it should be in the same folder with PageMaker. When you prepare to do an original PageMaker document of your own, you will have to get the text and graphics files together, preferably in one or two folders on the same hard disk with PageMaker. You can also use the file libraries that PageMaker has set up; these make it easy to access all your files and keep them in order. Check to make sure all files are compatible with PageMaker and the printer you plan to use.

Figure 11.1
A rough sketch of a newsletter layout

Chapter 11: Page Layout Applications

Opening a Document

Take one of the following actions to open a new document in PageMaker, depending on your situation:

- To open a new document if you have not started PageMaker, double-click the application's icon, as shown in Figure 11.2, or double-click an alias for it. When the PageMaker menu appears, choose New from the File menu.

- To open a new document if you have already started PageMaker and are looking at a document window, just choose New from the File menu.

No matter which action you take, the Page setup dialog box appears, as shown in Figure 11.3.

Figure 11.2
The PageMaker icon

Figure 11.3
The Page setup dialog box

Using PageMaker 245

Making Preliminary Page Settings

Before you even get into PageMaker, it asks you to make some settings for page size, margins, and orientation. Make these settings according to the basic look you decided upon when you made your sketch. Although the settings are not really part of the page layout, they set limits within which all the page layout decisions must fit, so don't take them lightly. The following steps describe how to make page setup settings for the newsletter I sketched in Figure 11.1.

1. Leave Page set to Letter. That's a good standard size for a newsletter.
2. Leave Page dimensions set at 8.5 by 11 inches.
3. Leave the Tall radio button selected for orientation.
4. You want your document to start with page 1, but change the number of pages to 2 so the sample newsletter can be two pages long.
5. In the Options boxes leave Double-sided selected. The newsletter will be printed on both sides of one page.
6. Uncheck the Facing pages box. This lets you see more of your page, especially if you are working on a small-screen Mac.
7. Leave the Inside margin at 1 inch so newsletter readers can punch holes for binder rings.
8. Change all the other margins from 0.75" to 0.5" wide. This gives you more room for text.
9. Set the printer resolution to match your printer; see your printer's user guide if you don't know how many dots per inch it can print.
10. Click OK. The PageMaker document window opens, as shown in Figure 11.4.

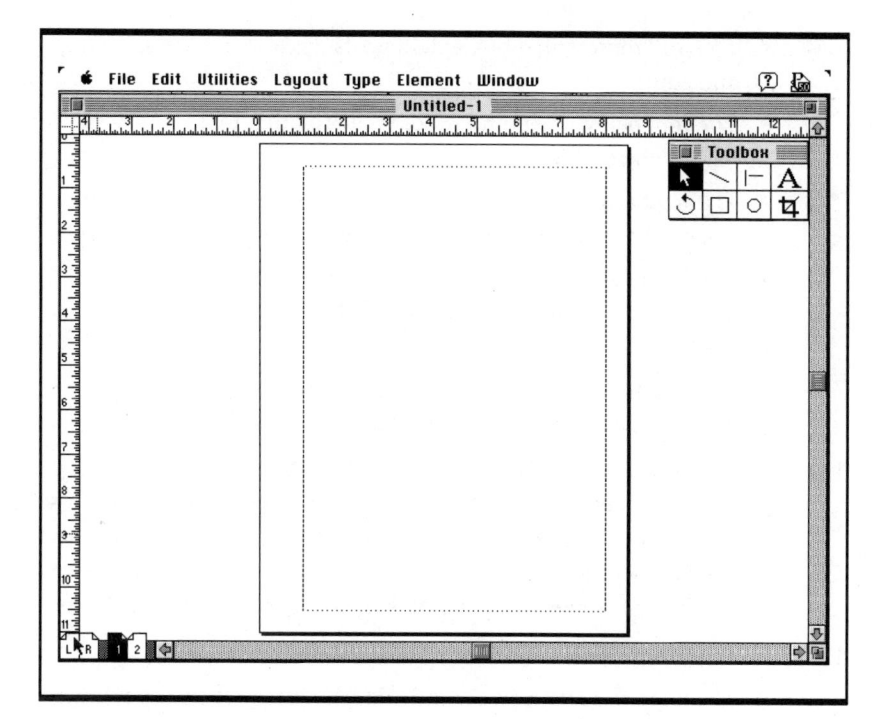

Figure 11.4
The PageMaker document window

The PageMaker Document Window

The PageMaker document window displays a small Toolbox, and a number of helpful features around the borders.

The Toolbox is a *floating palette*, which means it can be dragged with the pointer by the title bar to the position that's most convenient for you. It contains icons for tools you can use to do graphic work and select elements of the page you're creating.

- The pointer tool (the arrow-shaped tool) is for selecting text blocks and graphics.
- The tool to the right of the pointer is the diagonal-line tool. This tool draws straight lines at any angle.
- The next tool to the right is the perpendicular-line tool for drawing vertical and horizontal lines and lines at a 45-degree angle.

Using PageMaker **247**

- The tool represented by the letter *A* is the text tool for selecting and editing text.
- The tool below the pointer tool is the rotating tool for turning placed objects around an axis.
- The next tool to the right is the square-corner tool for drawing squares or rectangles. Hold down the Shift key to draw a square.
- The circle-shaped tool is for drawing circles and ovals. You get circles by holding down the Shift key when you draw with this tool.
- The odd tool under the A is a cropping tool; you can cut graphics down to smaller sizes with it.

The document window can also display other palettes. Choose Style palette from the Windows menu if you use styles to speed up formatting. Choose Color palette if you use Color. Choose Control palette to place, skew, and rotate objects precisely. use the Library palette to access stored graphics and text files. See the PageMaker *Reference Manual* for details on these palettes.

There are a number of other key elements of the document window:

- There are rulers are on the top and left sides of the window. You can set the units of measurement the rulers are in by choosing Preferences from the File menu and making choices in the dialog box.
- The menu bar is above the window. Take a minute to explore the menus by clicking on the words and holding down the mouse button while you read.
- Scroll bars appear on the right and bottom of the window. Click on the arrows, move the scroll box, or just click in the scroll bar to move the document up or down in the window.
- Page icons appear in the bottom left corner of the window. You can click on the L and R icons to get to you left and right master pages (pages you set up as templates for all the rest). Click on the numbered pages to get to your actual working pages.
- The margins of your page are indicated by a magenta rectangle if you have a color monitor, or by dashed-line rectangle if you have a black and white monitor.

- The area outside of your page is called the pasteboard. This is where you place things you don't want showing on the current page but may want to get later for another page. Sometimes I put notes to myself here so I remember to check something later; the note doesn't show up on the page when I'm printing.

Creating Master Pages

Now that you know your way around the document window, you're probably champing at the bit, just itching to slap some text and graphics into that first page. Rein in. Hold your horses. Remember that this is *page layout*, not just page fill-up. You need to set up master pages, so things that repeat on every page don't have to be placed over and over. Whatever you place on the master pages will show up on all the other pages in your document.

Master pages can save you lots of time. This is especially true if you plan to use the same format for a whole bunch of documents, like issues of a newsletter. When you start a new issue you can paste in your master pages from a previous issue, and you'll have a lot less work to do. So take a few moments and use the following procedures to create master pages for the sample newsletter.

To create three columns as in the sketch, take these steps:

1. Click on the L in the page icon in the lower left corner of the document window. The L stands for Left. Your left master page appears in the middle of the window.
2. Choose Column guides from the Layout menu. The Column guides dialog box appears.
3. Change the number of columns to 3.
4. Leave the space between columns as it is and click OK. Column guides appear, dividing the area inside your margins into three equal vertical spaces.
5. Click the R page icon and repeat the above steps for the right master page.

Now that you have your columns, you can add page numbers. Even though the newsletter document only has two pages, number them. The newsletter may grow in the future and you'll want the numbers included in the design. If you set up the numbering on the master pages, all pages of your newsletter will be paginated, no matter how many you add.

1. Click in the L to get back to the left master page.
2. Select the text tool in the Toolbox and drag a little text block (a dotted rectangle) just outside the lower left hand corner of the margin area.
3. Look at your rulers as you drag. The dotted lines there show where your cursor is. If you start dragging at 10½" on the vertical ruler and 7/16" on the horizontal ruler, the block should come out about right.
4. If you are working on a small screen, press ⌘-1 to get a closer look at the placement of the text block. When you release your mouse button after dragging the text block, an insertion point appears.
5. Press ⌘-Option-P. On the left master page you'll see LM for left master page. The L should wind up right below the left margin guide, as shown in Figure 11.5. Use the pointer tool to select and drag the page number to exactly the right place.
6. Click on the R page icon and drag a text block just outside the lower right margin corner.
7. Press ⌘-Option-P. RM for right master page appears in the text block; the R should be under the right margin guide line.

The correct page numbers will automatically replace the LM and RM on the actual pages of the document.

When you are satisfied with your master pages, choose Save from the File menu or press ⌘-S. Save your work often in PageMaker; there is nothing more frustrating than working out some great solution to a formatting problem, only to lose it to a power surge. For more information on saving, see "Saving and Printing a Document" later in this chapter.

Figure 11.5
A page number symbol placed on the left master page

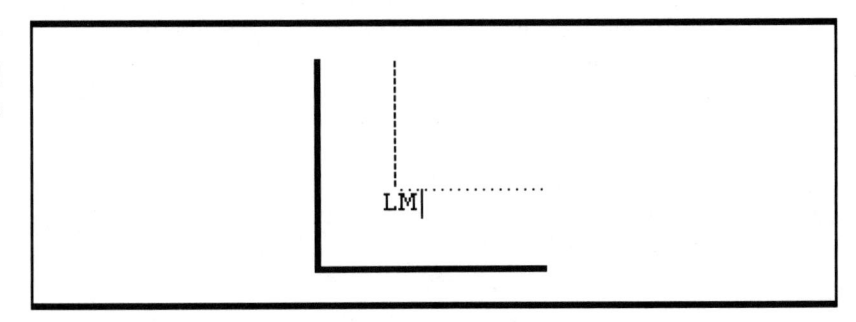

250 Chapter 11: Page Layout Applications

Placing Text

The following procedure tells how to place text in the sample newsletter columns, but it is the same basic procedure you use no matter what kind of document you are creating. In this case, you will place the text in all of the three columns, but you will leave some space at the beginning for your newsletter logo.

1. Click the page 1 icon in the lower left corner of the window. A right page appears with nothing on it but the column and margin guides and the page number. Books normally start each chapter with a right page; that's why PageMaker makes the first page a right one.
2. Choose Autoflow from the Utilities menu. This will place all of the text you bring in from someplace else, filling your column guides to make three nice columns. Even if it overflows onto another page of your document, it will *all* flow in.
3. Choose Place from the File menu or press ⌘-D. The Open dialog box appears. You probably see a list of folders in the Aldus PageMaker folder.
4. Double-click the Tutorial folder, then double-click the Lesson 1 folder.
5. Select the Sample Text file and click OK.
6. Your cursor becomes a "loaded" text icon. It looks like a carpenter's square with a curvy arrow in it. If you ever select the wrong file, click in the Toolbox to unload the icon.
7. Line up the left side of the icon with the left margin guide, about two-thirds of the way down the left column. This will leave space for your logo.
8. Click the mouse button. Your text flows into the columns until the entire text file is placed.

Your page will now look like it's filled with three columns of gray bars, with some blank space at the top of the left column, and some at the bottom of the right column, as in Figure 11.6. It isn't too exciting, but it's a good start. It gives you a clear idea of how much room you have for graphics and a second story.

Figure 11.6
Text placed on the first page

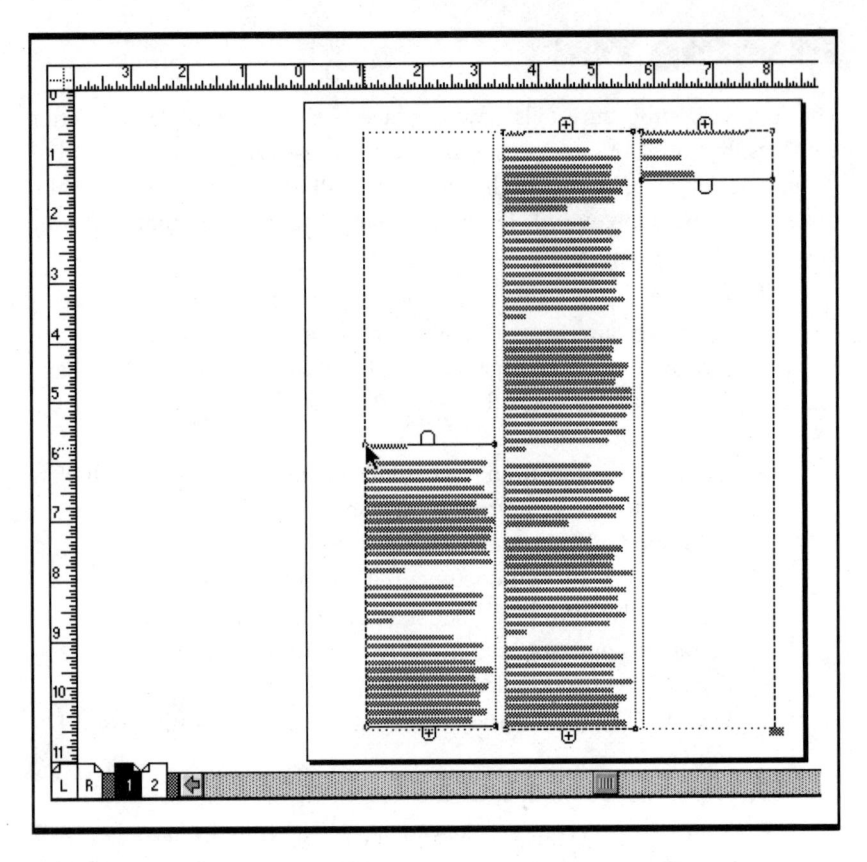

Placing a Graphic

Placing graphics in PageMaker is just like placing text. The following procedure is for putting a nice logo at the head of your sample newsletter. You will place and size a graphic in the available space, but you won't be able to put it in the place you want it until you adjust the text layout.

1. Press ⌘-D and select the Logotype.tif file in the Lesson 1 folder, then click OK.
2. Click with the loaded pointer at the top left corner of your newsletter, in the left column where you left some open space. The graphic appears at the same size and shape it was created. This isn't the size and shape I sketched in Figure 11.1, so let's change it.

Chapter 11: Page Layout Applications

3. Drag the handle (the little square) in the lower left corner of the graphic to the left, to make a long rectangle like the logo in the sketch. When you are done, it should look like Figure 11.7.
4. Select the sized graphic and move it as close as you can to where you want to place it. In the sample, you can't put the graphic at the top right corner of the page yet, so just line up the top edge with the top margin guide.
5. Save your file.

So how do you place that graphic where you want it? You have to move the text out of the way, but first you need to learn how to look at things up close.

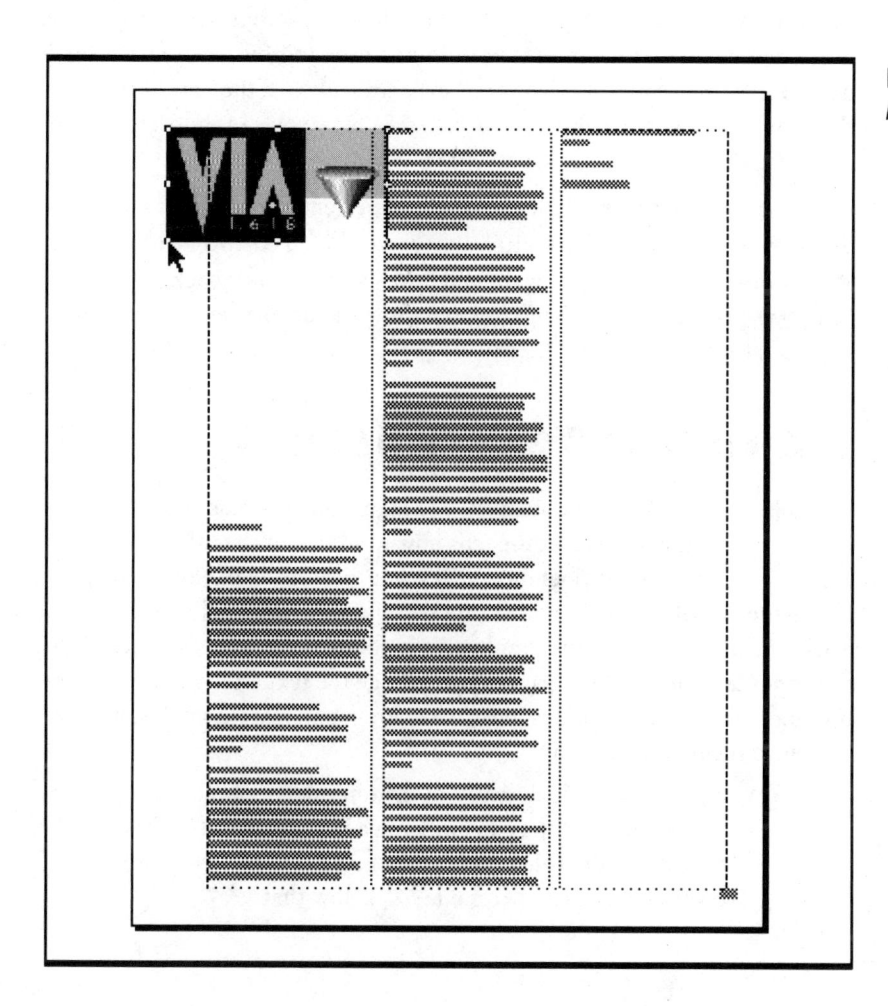

Figure 11.7
A placed graphic

Changing Your View of the Page

Once you have placed something, you will need to look at it up close to make sure the text reads correctly and is placed so the paragraphs break nicely at the ends of columns. There are a couple of great tricks for zooming in and out of magnified views in PageMaker. In the View submenu of the Layout menu there are commands for making the current page fit in the window, appear at actual size, or appear at 25, 50, 75, 200, or 400 percent of the actual size.

For example, let's take a closer look at the text you just placed. Choose Actual size from the Page menu or press ⌘-1 (for 100 percent) to see your text at the size it will print at. To get back to the default view, choose Fit in window from the Page menu, or press ⌘-W. To zoom in and out even faster, hold down the ⌘ and Option keys on the keyboard and click the part of the page that you want to see up close. Presto change-o. Now you can almost read your text! Is it all still Greek, or is that Latin?

If you want to see a part of your page at 200 percent (twice actual size) hold down ⌘-Option-Shift and click where you need to zoom in. Use the ⌘-Option-Shift-click action again and it toggles your view back to 100 percent size. These view-shifting commands work no matter which tool is selected at the time you use them.

Adjusting Text Blocks

After placing a graphic, you often need to adjust the text blocks to fit around it better. The following procedure tells how to adjust for the title graphic you added to the newsletter document. First you need to make an open space across the top of the page, and fit the text onto the page below that space. This will make room for the graphic, so it doesn't have to be squeezed into the upper left corner of the page. Then, to line the text and graphic up, you use ruler guides. These guides look like column and margin guides, but you can move them around easily.

1. Drag a ruler guide down from the top ruler. Just move the pointer into the top ruler and drag a horizontal dotted line down. Align the ruler guide with the bottom of your graphic. Now drag another ruler guide ¼" below that.

2. Adjust the three text blocks in the three columns by dragging them. Work from left to right. Select a block by clicking it with the arrow tool, then put the pointer tool in the little windowshade handle at the top and drag the top line of the text block up or down to the lower of the two ruler guides.

3. If you have long columns of text, they will run off the bottom of the page. To adjust the text, first click on the long block, then drag the bottom windowshade handle up to the bottom margin of the page. To check the text for bad line breaks, zoom in by pressing ⌘-1. The shortened text block looks like the one in Figure 11.8.

When you shorten a text block, PageMaker keeps track of the text you just hid. It either flows into the next column, or it is loaded into the bottom windowshade handle to place elsewhere. If your selected text block has a plus sign in the windowshade handle, it means that there is text from the same story after this text block, in the next column or on the next page. If the windowshade handle has a triangle in it, as shown in Figure 11.8, then you know that there is more text from that story yet to be placed in your document.

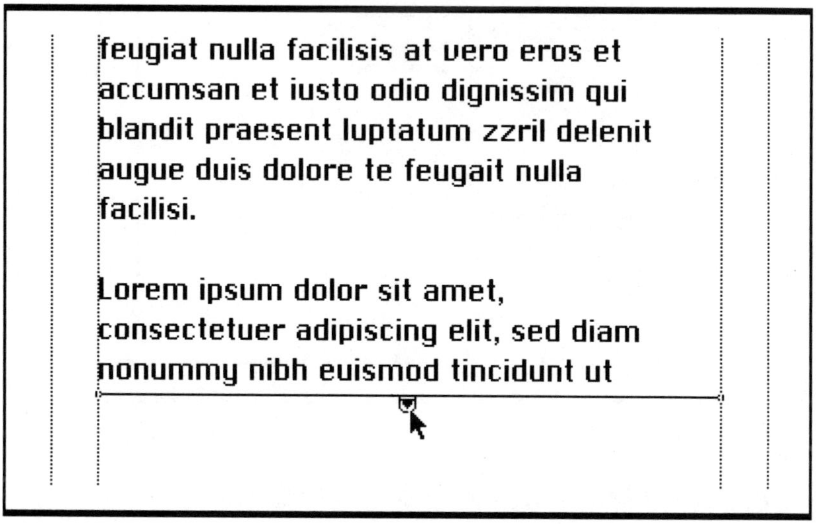

Figure 11.8
Adjusted text block with handle

Drag the windowshade to the bottom of the column if you have room. If there is still a "loaded" triangle in it, click in that loaded windowshade handle, then move to a new column or a new page and use the loaded pointer to place the leftover text. The page should look like Figure 11.9.

Figure 11.9
The newsletter with its text adjusted

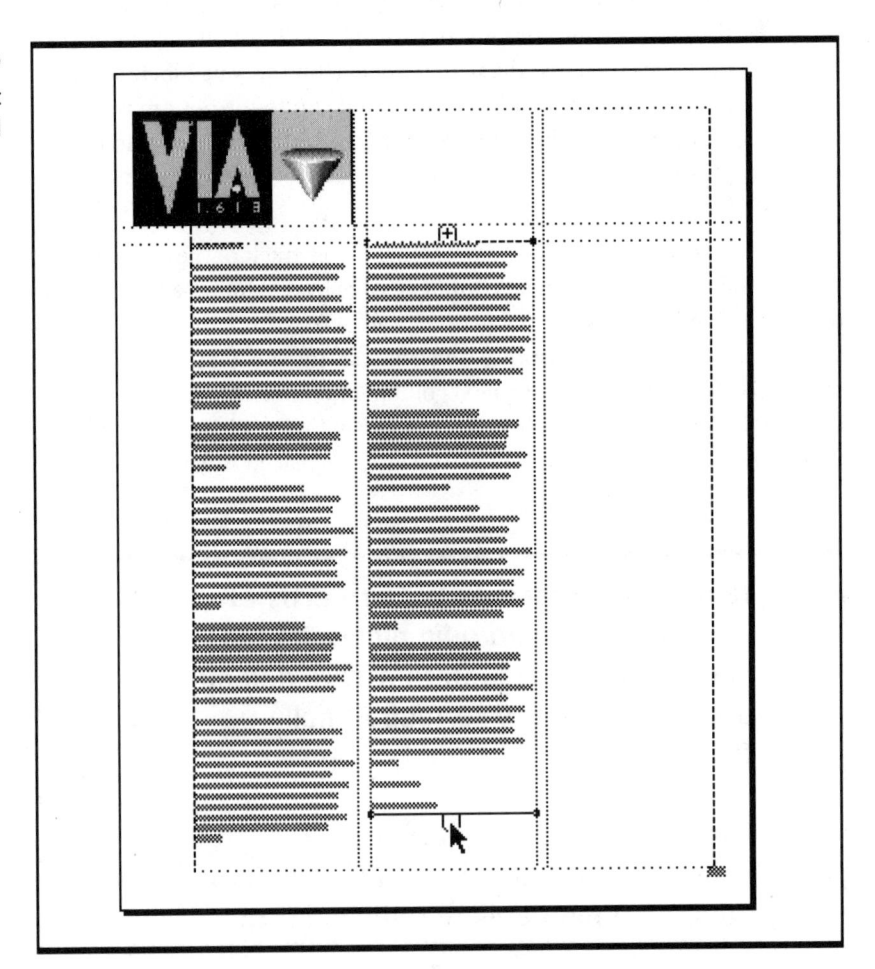

Adjusting the Layout of a Document

OK, you've gotten your feet wet moving those text blocks. It's time to really start dragging things around, so you can achieve the layout in the sketch shown a few pages back in Figure 11.1. This section tells how to move elements of text and graphics around on a page to improve the page's appearance and impact. The techniques used for the example newsletter can be used on any document; the key thing is to use the layout to give your material more impact.

To get the look of that sketch, you need to move the logo to the right and add a thick line across the top of the page. Then you'll move all of the text up so you can add a little graphic to the lower left column and create a new text block that spans the two right columns down at the bottom.

You should be looking at your page in Fit in window view. Start your layout work by moving the graphic and raising the bottoms of the three columns of text:

1. Select the graphic and move it to the right side of the page. Keep it inside the ruler and margin guides.
2. Select the left column text block and drag the lower windowshade handle up about an inch. This will make space for your little graphic.
3. Shorten the text block in the center column up about half of the page to make room for your two-column story. Use the loaded handle at the end to place the leftover text in the right column.
4. If you wind up with a loaded windowshade handle, as shown in Figure 11.10, select it and click with the loaded text icon on the page 2 icon. Then place the extra text in the first column of that page. Come back to page 1 when you're done.

Now that you have moved the text out of the way, you can put in the new story that spans two columns.

1. Press ⌘-D to give the Place command.
2. Select the Sample Text file again, then click OK. Of course, if you were making a real newsletter, you'd select another article, but this is just make-believe.
3. Drag a text block across the open space in the two left columns, starting at the column guide in the upper left corner of the space, about a half inch below the bottom of the existing text. The story fills in the two-column space.
4. If there is extra text, click the loaded windowshade handle, then click the page 2 icon and place the extra text in a different

Figure 11.10
Adjusting the layout

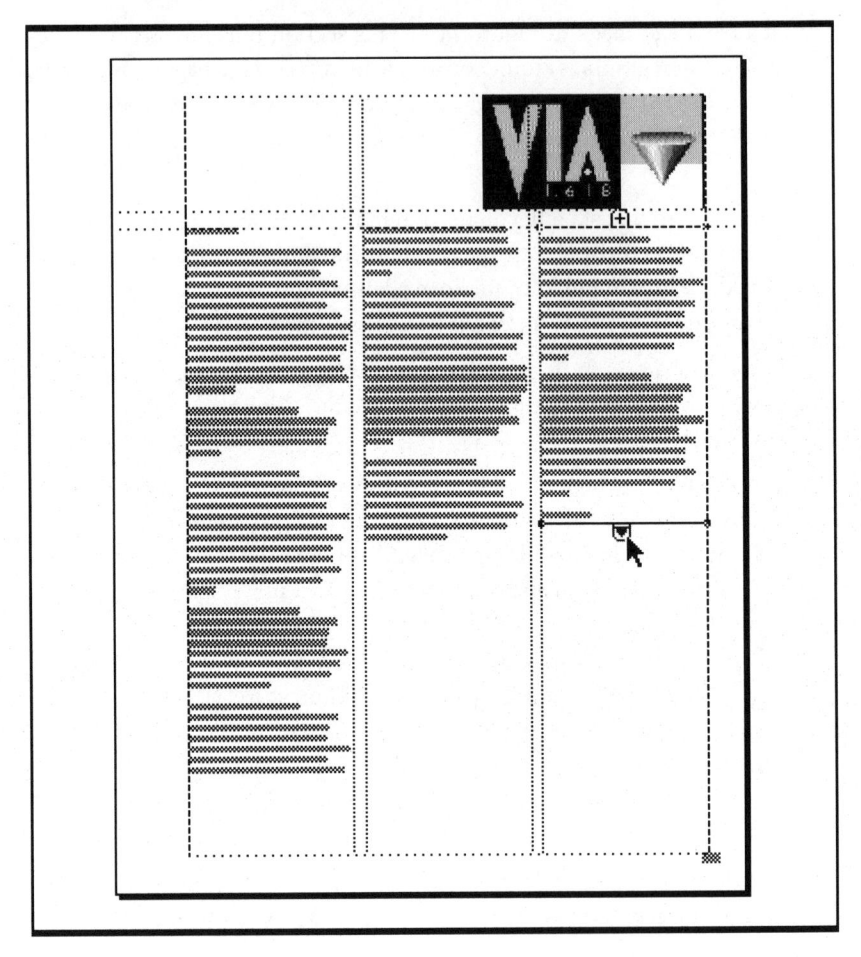

column from the other leftover text block. Then click the page 1 icon to go back there.

Now that you have all your text in place, you can work on the graphic. Use the following procedure to add a thick line or *rule* across the top of the newsletter, running into the graphic there.

1. Click on the perpendicular-line tool. Draw a line by clicking next to the graphic and dragging to the left.
2. When your line is long enough, release the mouse button. The line should still be selected (you can tell by the selection handles on either end).

258 Chapter 11: Page Layout Applications

3. Choose Line from the Element menu. A submenu appears.
4. While still holding down the mouse button, drag to the right and down until 8 pt line is selected, then release the mouse button.
5. To run the line into the logo graphic, select it with the pointer tool and move it to the right until it touches the logo.

Go back to Fit in window view (⌘-W). Does your page look more or less like Figure 11.11? If everything looks good so far, save your work by choosing Save from the File menu or pressing ⌘-S.

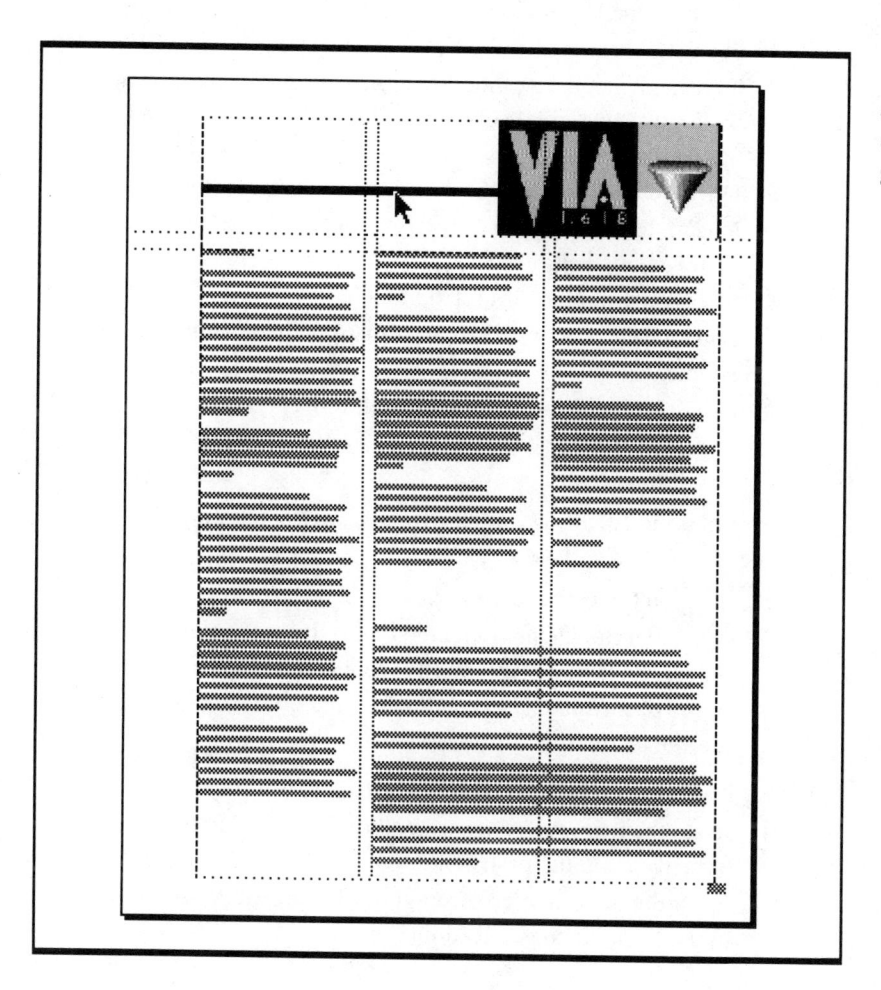

Figure 11.11
Adding a two-column story and adding a rule to the logo graphic

Changing Text Style for Headings

To make the headings for the stories in your newsletter look good, you need to work on the fonts. The following steps show how to make the headings stand out and still fit in the format you have set up.

1. Hold down the ⌘ and Option keys and click on the first line of type in the first (far left) column. You see the heading, which looks puny.
2. Click on the text tool.
3. Select the heading.
4. To make it stand out, pull down the Type menu and go into the Style (not Type style) submenu. Choose Subhead 1 from the Style menu.
5. Use ⌘-Option-click to get back to Fit in window view, then use it again to zoom in on the heading for the two-column story. That heading begs for changing, too.
6. Select the heading with the text tool.
7. Enter a title of your choice, or something like "Title for an Article."
8. Pull down the Type menu and go into the Style menu, where you can choose Subhead 1 again. Oooh, those titles look professional.

Now let's add a nice dividing line between your two-column story and the rest of the text. Just take these steps:

1. Click on the perpendicular-line tool.
2. Pull down the Element menu, go into the Line submenu, and choose the medium-thick (3 pt) dashed line.
3. Drag a dashed line between the heading of the two-column story and the text of the other story.

Finally, you can add a title to your newsletter by following these steps:

1. Select the text tool from the Toolbox and type **My Newsletter** somewhere on the pasteboard.
2. Select the title, then go through the Type menu to the Style submenu and choose Headline.

3. Select the pointer tool from the Toolbox and select the title.
4. Drag the title to the open space to the left of the newsletter logo. Move it around until it looks right. You can even select the text and make it larger, like I did.

Hey, that front page is looking pretty good. For a really classy touch, though, you can go on to the next section and see how to add a little graphic and wrap text around it.

Adding a Graphic and Wrapping Text around It

The following procedure tells how to add a graphic and form the body text to fit around it. This can be a good way to add interest and clarity to your layout, and not use up too much space. You may want to use more informative graphics than the one in the sample, but the method is always the same.

Start with these steps to place the graphic:

1. Press ⌘-D for the Place command.
2. Select the Logotype.tif file in the Lesson 1 folder again and click OK.
3. Click with the loaded icon just below the text on the left margin of your page.
4. Place the pointer on the lower right corner handle and drag inward to shrink the graphic down to about half the width of the column.

The graphic probably extends down too far, but don't worry, you'll move it up soon. First, follow these steps to turn on text wrap:

1. While the graphic is still selected, choose Text wrap from the Element menu. You see the Text wrap dialog box.
2. Click on the middle wrap option, as shown in Figure 11.12. The Text flow setting changes to Wrap-all-sides, which means that the text will flow around all sides of the graphic, wherever it will fit. In this case, it will only fit on the right side of the graphic. PageMaker automatically selects the standoff dimensions.
3. Click OK.

Figure 11.12

The Text wrap dialog box

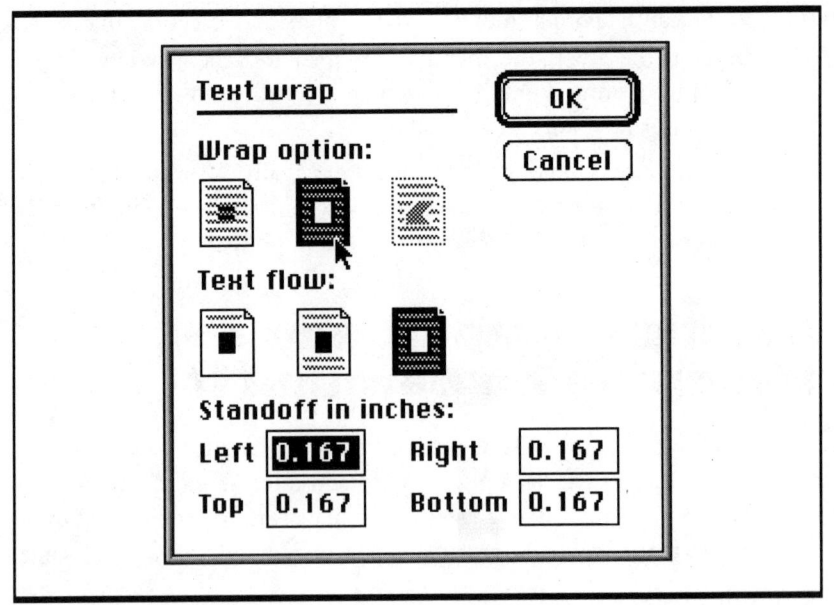

The dialog box goes away and now your graphic has two sets of selection handles. One set controls the graphic and the other controls the text wrap. The text wrap boundary looks like a dotted line with handles (little black diamonds) at the corners.

1. Use ⌘-n-Option–Shift-click to zoom up close to the graphic.
2. Move the pointer into the middle of the graphic and drag it up until the bottom is lined up with the bottom margin guide.
3. Drag the bottom windowshade for the text block down to the bottom margin.

Your graphic should look like Figure 11.13.

Make sure you check the text that follows your new graphic on the page. Part of your story may have flowed to another column or a heading may have been

Figure 11.13
Text wrapped around a graphic

pushed out of place. Fix any text problems, then save your work by pressing ⌘-S. The front page should look like Figure 11.14. Happy with how your newsletter looks on screen? If you are, you can start printing.

Saving and Printing a PageMaker Document

To protect your PageMaker work, save it often, about every fifteen minutes when you are working on it. All you have to do is choose Save from the File menu or press ⌘-S. The first time you save a document, you must name it and choose where to place it in your folder hierarchy, or it will be called "Untitled" and placed in the same folder with the PageMaker application.

To print a hard copy of your document, first save it, then choose Print from the File menu or type ⌘-P. The Print to dialog box appears. Select your

Note

For more information on using the Save command, see "Saving Your Work on a Document" in Chapter 4.

Using PageMaker **263**

Figure 11.14
The finished sample PageMaker document

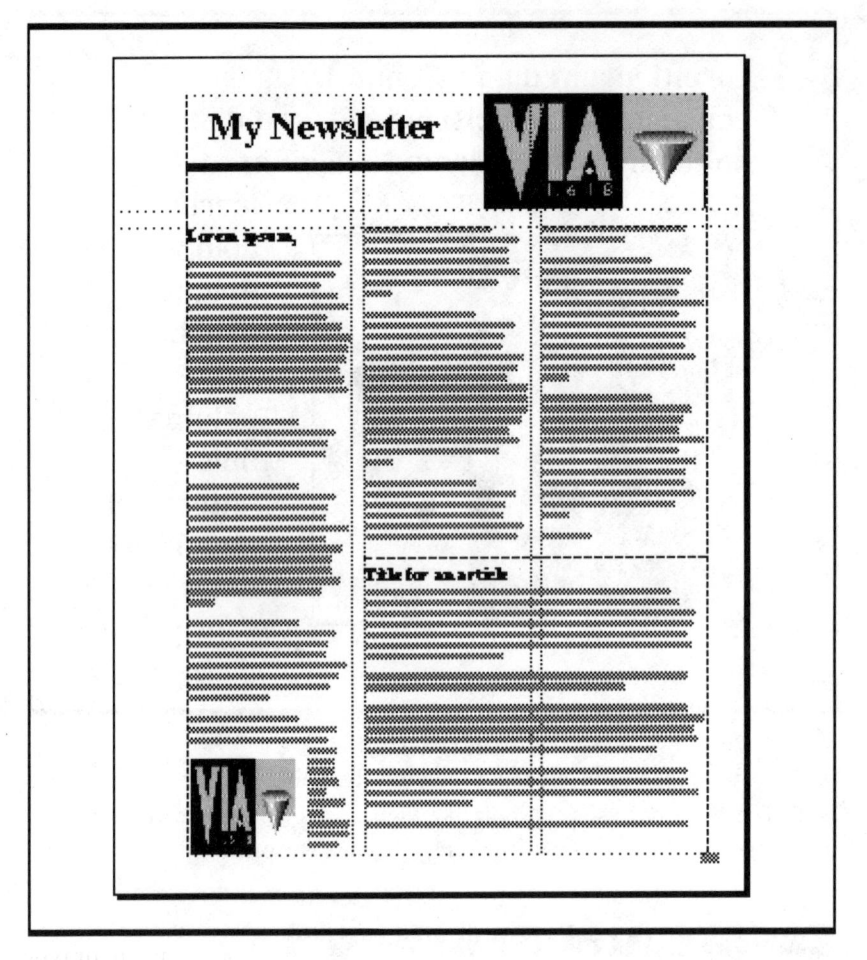

printer type from the Printer box menu at the bottom of the dialog box. If this box is blank, printing will not start. If you want one copy of page one only, press the Tab key twice until the second page range box is selected. Then type 1 in there. Click Print to begin printing.

Troubleshooting Problems in PageMaker

The following subsections cover the problems you are most likely to have while working with PageMaker and other page layout applications.

Missing Text

Remember that text blocks in the same story are linked or threaded together. If you change one text block, it affects the others. If you are missing some text, look on the next page or next column; chances are it flowed from the text block you changed to another text block in that next column or on that next page.

Can't Find the Center of a Page or Column

Want to find the center of the page or a column? Draw a rectangle the width (or height) of what you are trying to find the center of. The selection handle in the middle of the rectangle will be the center of the column or page.

Can't Find an Object Left on the Pasteboard

You can't find some text you were sure you left on the pasteboard? Hold down the Shift key while you select Fit in window from the View menu, or type %-0 (zero). This fits the whole pasteboard in your window. When you find the text, move it near to the page you want to put it on, then zoom in to a closer view and drag the text to where you want it.

Can't Calculate Measurements in the Middle of the Page

To measure something on your page, go up to the upper left corner of your PageMaker window where the two rulers meet and click on the space with the dotted lines in it. Then drag along one ruler or the other until the zero point is aligned with your graphic or whatever it is that you want to measure.

Can't Select a Hidden Element

To select something that is behind some other element, hold down the ⌘ key while you keep clicking, until the item you want is selected. This problem occurs most often when you place a large graphic or long text block and it runs right over a small block of text. After you ⌘-click to select the covered-up item, drag it out to the pasteboard, then place it where it won't get covered up again.

Added Text Doesn't Thread to Next Text Block

You are trying to add text to the end of a text block with the text tool, but the text doesn't thread into the next text block; it just goes on down the page mindlessly. The problem is that you put the insertion point below the bottom or beyond the side of the text block you were trying to add to. Select the new text, choose Cut from the Edit menu, place the insertion point carefully inside the text block, then choose Paste from the Edit menu.

When You Type in Text It Is in the Wrong Font

The default font is wrong. To change it, click on the pointer tool (not the text tool, as you might expect), then go through the Type menu to the Font sub-menu and choose the font you want to have as your current default. It will be the font you see when you type, unless you change the font just before entering text. If you bring in text from an application with different defaults, you'll get those defaults inside the text blocks, however.

You Can't Move the Ruler or Column Guides

You probably want to get your guides out of the way so you can do some detail work, but they won't budge. Pull down the Options menu and see if Lock Guides has a check in front of it. Select it if it does, and the guides will come unlocked so you can move them. Move them back home after you're done with your detail work, and you can choose Lock Guides again to make them stay put for your other work.

Loaded Icon Appears When You Try to Drag Windowshade Handle

All you were doing was trying to move a windowshade up or down, for crying out loud, and now you've got this loaded icon on your hands. The problem is that you clicked in a windowshade handle with a plus or a triangle in it, when what you meant to do was drag the handle. Don't aim that loaded icon at anybody, whatever you do. Just move it up into the Toolbox and click the pointer (or any other tool). Then go back to that windowshade handle, and this time, hold the mouse button down firmly as you drag the handle up or down.

The Story Doesn't Appear in the Edit Story Window

You choose Edit story from the Edit menu so you can see the whole story you are working on, instead of all those pieces in text blocks. But instead of seeing the whole story, you see nothing, or just a little fuzzy patch. The problem is that no part of the story is selected. Close the empty window, click with either the text or pointer tool in any part of the story, then choose Edit story from the Edit menu again. There you go; it wasn't in the twilight zone after all.

Difficult to Line Things Up on Margin, Column, or Ruler Guides

You can't get anything to stick to those guides; things like text blocks and loaded icons just drift off the guides, right and left. The problem is embarrassingly simple; Snap to guides is off. Just choose Snap to guides from the Options menu, and all the text and graphics will get right in line for you, like obedient little soldiers.

Columns Incorrect

Either you have the wrong number of columns, or you want to change the spacing between your columns. You might think that you have to start all over to get back to the Page Setup dialog box. Not to worry. Just choose Column guides from the Options menu and change the settings. Of course, changing the guides or spaces won't rearrange the text you have already placed. You have to do that yourself.

Can't Find a File You Want to Place

Don't feel bad. It happens to us all. You hit ⌘-D, the file box opens with a list of some obscure bunch of files somewhere in the bowels of your folder hierarchy, and you just stare at the screen, wondering where the heck you put that graphic you were ready to place. Click Cancel to get out of the dialog box, then use the Find command in the Finder to find your file.

PageMaker File Will Not Print

This can be due to many things. If the print job won't even start, there is probably something in the file that is not printable. The most likely candidate is a graphic that cannot be printed on your printer, such as an EPS (Encapsulated PostScript) file that you are trying to print to a non-PostScript printer, or a font that the printer can't handle.

If the file prints part way and then hangs up, you have a problem graphic in there, or the file is just too complex for the printer to take into its limited RAM all at once. Try compressing the whole file by using Save as to save it (click Yes when asked if you want to replace the existing item with the same name), then print it again. If that doesn't help, choose Proof print (print without graphics) in the Options dialog box (you get the Options dialog box by clicking the Options button in the Print dialog box). If the file prints without the graphics, then you can bet you have a graphic that is causing problems. If there are any uncompressed TIFF files in the document, replace them with compressed versions of the TIFF graphics. If there are some really complex TIFF, EPS, or PICT graphics, they can choke some laser printers. Print the document one page at a time to find out where the problem graphic is.

For some hints (sometimes very obscure, jargon-riddled hints) as to what is causing the problem, you can click the PostScript button in the Print dialog box, then click the check box for View last error message, and see the message generated by the mishap.

Twelve

Spreadsheets

• • • • • • • • • • • • • • • •

Featuring

- ◆ Choosing the best spreadsheet for you
- ◆ How to open an Excel spreadsheet
- ◆ How to enter data in an Excel spreadsheet
- ◆ How to change type style and format in Excel
- ◆ How to select a range of cells in Excel
- ◆ How to change number format in Excel
- ◆ How to enter and fill formulas in Excel
- ◆ How to use absolute cell references in Excel
- ◆ How to make a chart of data in an Excel spreadsheet
- ◆ Troubleshooting Problems with Spreadsheets

First Steps

To open a new document in Excel: 274
If you have not started Excel yet, double-click the icon for the application. If you have started Excel and are looking at an existing spreadsheet, choose New from the File menu, and when you see a small dialog box, click OK.

To enter data in a cell of an Excel spreadsheet: 276
Click in a cell and start entering either text, numbers, or an equals sign for a formula. To confirm the entry when you are done with it, click the enter button in the entry bar, or press Return or Enter on your keyboard.

To change the style or format of text in Excel: 277
Select the cell with the text first. Then you can use commands in the menu, or if a button exists in the toolbar, such as the Bold button or Italic button, you can simply click the button to change the text.

To select a range of cells in Excel: 279
You can either click in the first cell and Shift-click in the last one, or you can drag from the first cell to the last one, as long as you don't drag from the border of the first cell.

CHAPTER 12

To change the number format in Excel: 280

Select the cells with the numbers you want to format. Choose Number from the Format menu. In the dialog box that appears, choose the value type you want to format, then choose the code you want. You can see a sample of the format at the bottom of the dialog box.

To enter formulas in Excel: 281

Select the cell where you want the output of the formula to appear. Then you start the formula with the equals sign, enter the addresses of the cells, and put the operator signs between the addresses. You can also enter a range with a colon between the addresses of two cells, and use a function, such as SUM to complete the formula.

To make a chart for data in an Excel spreadsheet: 284

Select the range of the data you want to represent in your chart. Click the Chart Wizard button in the toolbar, and answer the questions the wizard asks you in the dialog boxes that come up. If you don't understand some of the settings, just leave them at the defaults; the wizard usually knows a good way to chart your data. When you click OK in the last of the dialog boxes, the wizard draws and labels your chart for you.

The spreadsheet is the computer version of the accountant's ledger. Many businesses use spreadsheets to keep track of transactions, budgets, receivables, payables, and the like. You can create spreadsheets that will help you balance your own budget and plan your finances.

The key difference between an accountant's ledger and a spreadsheet is that a spreadsheet does most of the accounting automatically. You enter each figure only once and the spreadsheet does all the calculating for you—no more punching long lists of numbers into a calculator. What's even better, a spreadsheet can easily accommodate changes in your figures. You can make corrections, or explore "what-if" scenarios, without endless erasing and scribbling.

But modern spreadsheets do more than just make calculations; they can create graphs of your data and work as database managers. They can, with the swoop of the mouse, sum up an entire column. They have special formulas built in, even nasty ones like finding percentages. They can even change the color of the type in your charts so they look more interesting.

Which Spreadsheet for You?

It used to be that spreadsheet applications didn't have many features. You could make a spreadsheet, do basic calculations of items in the cells, and print out your results. Today the choices are far more complex and as the Mac system software advances, spreadsheets such as Excel and Resolve expand to take advantage of the new versions. On the other hand, there are less expensive spreadsheet applications that may not have every feature in the world, but that can do what most people in business need: keep good records and help forecast financial developments.

High-Power Spreadsheet Applications

There are a number of powerful spreadsheet tools that are designed for the Mac, including Wingz, Resolve, Lotus 1-2-3 for Macintosh, and Excel, but the last two are the most prominent. If you want to create spreadsheets with color graphs for presentation purposes, Wingz shines, and if you like to use

HyperScript you can customize Wingz to a great degree. But Wingz can be slow to draw its spiffy graphs. If you want to get quick access to spreadsheet power, the best choices are Excel, Lotus 1-2-3, and Resolve.

Excel has long been a leader in the features department, but Lotus 1-2-3 has high-power features of its own, and both 1-2-3 and Resolve are relatively easy to learn. If you are an old hand at spreadsheets and macros, and you want raw power for customizing, calculating, or programming, Excel is probably the best choice. If you are looking for ease of learning, Resolve is best. For DOS compatibility and a good, intuitive interface that makes high-power spreadsheet work a breeze, try Lotus 1-2-3. If you have needs for specific features, such as a particular set of statistical functions or a certain type of graph, check out all three programs and see which is best for you. They all have lots of power.

Budget Spreadsheet Applications

If you just want to make a simple spreadsheet and don't need graphs, you can use a basic application like MacCalc. If you want to integrate a spreadsheet

---

Microsoft Excel 4.0

Product at a Glance

Publisher:
Microsoft Corporation
Upgrades from earlier versions are available, but not free

Requires:
Macintosh Plus or better
System 6.0.2 and Finder 6.1 or later; System 6.7 or later recommended
2MB of RAM for System 6.7; 4MB of RAM for System 7.0 or later
800K floppy disk drive for installation; 40MB hard drive with 8.6MB of free space
Any Mac-compatible printer

Description:
The leading spreadsheet software for the Mac, Excel is both easy to learn and powerful to use. You can set up and work with a simple spreadsheet without any fuss or muss, but you can also do all kinds of special calculations, graphs, automated entry and updating, and customizing to your heart's content. And if you ever have any questions or problems, there are always lots of other experienced users, books, and consultants you can turn to for help.

with another application such as a word processor or a database, you should look into Microsoft Works, BeagleWorks, or Claris Works. Of the three, Microsoft Works provides the most spreadsheet power, including fairly good graphing capability and most of the functions you need for business analysis. But it can't do anything with text in cells. Any low-cost spreadsheet will have limitations of this sort. So you might try one if you do only simple record-keeping and financial forecasting for a small business, but not if you need to develop complex, customized tables and sophisticated graphs. Low-budget spreadsheets also tend to lack programming tools, number-crunching power, and graphic finesse.

Using Excel

In the sections that follow, you can learn how to set up and use a simple spreadsheet (or worksheet) with Excel. The procedures guide you to understand the basic concepts of Mac spreadsheets in general, and some of the special powers you have when you use Excel. You can also use these steps to begin setting up your own spreadsheet, but for full use of the advanced features of Excel, see the *User's Guide* and *Functions Reference*.

The first step to take when you are making a new spreadsheet is to sketch out a rough plan. If you plot out the basic design and content of your spreadsheet, how many columns you'll need and how many rows, what kinds of titles will look best and what form of data will be presented, you can save yourself a lot of time and effort. However, not much planning is needed for the simple spreadsheet you'll create in this section. It will be very straightforward, and it will only take up about a half dozen rows and five columns.

Starting a New Document

Take one of the following actions to open a spreadsheet in Excel, depending on your situation.

- If you have not started Excel, double-click on the Excel icon, as shown in Figure 12.1, or double-click on an alias for it.
- To open a new spreadsheet if you have started Excel and are looking at an existing worksheet, choose New from the File menu, then click OK in the small dialog box.

Figure 12.1
The Microsoft Excel icon

You should now be looking at a blank page of a worksheet, like the one shown in Figure 12.2. It consists of small boxes, or *cells*, that are separated into rows and columns throughout the page. Each cell has a name; the cell in the upper left corner is in the A column and the 1 row, so it is called the A1 cell. The A1 cell should be highlighted when a fresh document is created.

At the top of the Excel window, there is a toolbar with lots of buttons in it. These are for graphics features and some commonly used commands. You'll learn how to use them as you work through the following sections.

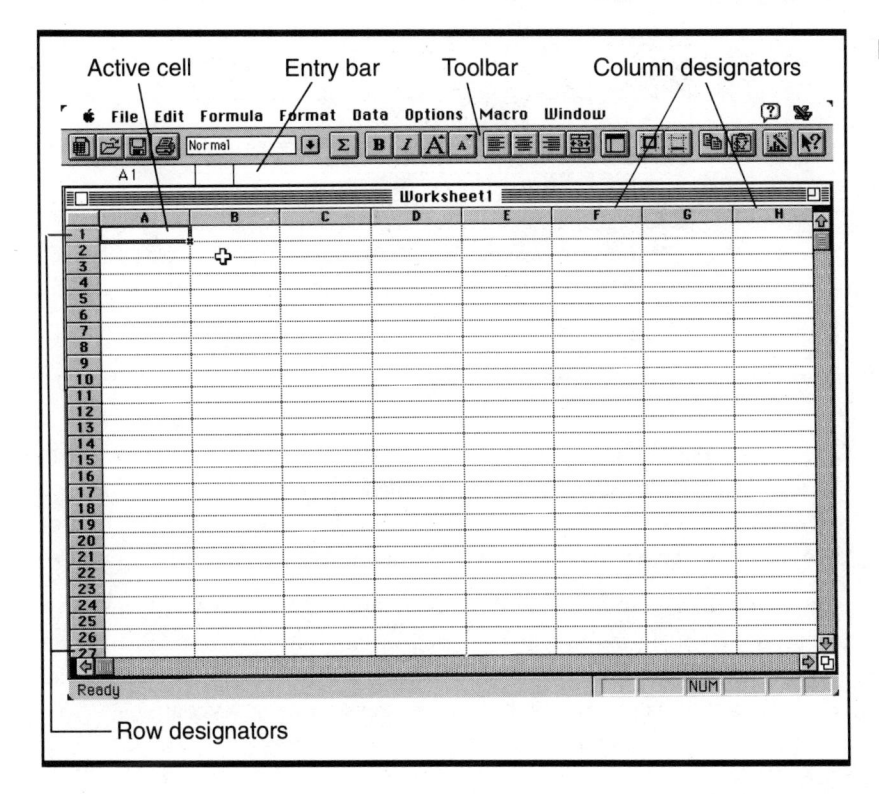

Figure 12.2
The Excel window

Using Excel **275**

You can highlight other cells by clicking on them with your pointer, which looks like a big plus sign now. Each cell can hold a single piece of information: either a number, a name, or a formula. The page of cells is expandable; you can scroll happily for quite some time either down or to the right. There is an end to the cells, but you probably won't fill them up for some time.

Entering Some Data

Start your worksheet by clicking in cell A3. Now type the word **Name**. Notice that the words appear in a bar near the top of the screen as in Figure 12.3. This bar is called the *entry bar*. If you make a mistake just use the Delete key to correct it or click on the X next to the entry bar near the top of the screen. This X is the *cancel button*.

Figure 12.3
Entering text in a cell

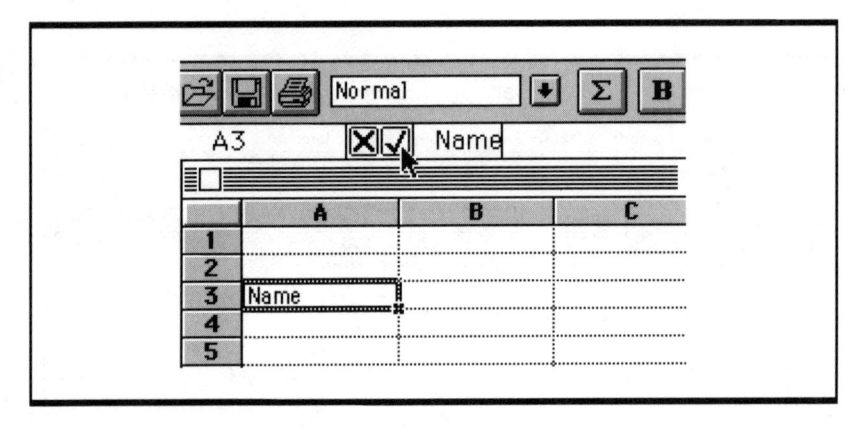

If you want to keep what you've typed, click on the check mark; this enters the word *Name*. Pressing the Enter key on your numeric keypad does the same thing. You can also press the Return key on your keyboard instead of the Enter key; this enters the word *Name* and selects the next cell down.

Tip
If you work down the columns you can use the Return key after each data entry and select the next cell.

Now that you can enter data into a cell, go ahead and enter the data shown in Figure 12.4. It forms a record of Mac sales in a shop back in 1991 (times and prices changed, as you can see). Move from cell to cell by clicking in the cell you want to use or by using the arrow keys on your keyboard.

	A	B	C	D	E
1					
2		First Sale	Second Sale	Third Sale	
3	Name	Classic	LC	IIsi	
4	Macintosh	1199	1729	2898	
5	Monitor	0	475	699	
6	Printer	465	999	1749	
7	Modem	139	139	465	
8					
9					
10					
11					
12					

Figure 12.4
Entering more text and numbers

Now look over your worksheet to make sure all the figures are right. If you made a mistake, just click on the cell with the incorrect data, select the incorrect part of the data in the entry bar (up at the top of the window), and edit it. The entry bar works just like a little word processor. You can select, delete, or change the text in the entry bar just as you would if you were using Microsoft Word.

When all the data looks right, choose Save from the File menu. Save often in Excel; it can be hard to reconstruct a spreadsheet if you lose it to a power surge or something.

Changing Type Style and Format

Now that you have some data, you'll want to make it look a little nicer. The following exercise shows how to make bold and italic text, and how to center whatever you have in a cell.

1. Click on *First Sale* in cell B2.
2. Click on the B button located above the entry bar. Now cell B2 should be bold. This is a simple way to make a title stand out more.
3. Repeat these steps for *Second Sale* and *Third Sale* so that all the column titles are bold.
4. Names like Classic and LC are not column titles, but they should also stand out, so let's make them italic. Click on *Classic* in cell B3.

Using Excel **277**

5. This time, we'll use a shortcut method to change all the names at once. Hold down the Shift key on the keyboard while clicking the mouse on cell D3. *Classic* should be highlighted normally, while *LC* and *IIsi* should now look highlighted in a new way. These cells are shown differently so that you know which one was clicked first.
6. Now click on the I button above the entry bar. All three cells should now be italic.
7. Finally, we'll create a title and anchor it. Click in the cell C1 so that it becomes selected.
8. Type **Macintosh Sales Price Comparison** and click the check mark. Don't worry if the text gets too long to fit inside the cell. Excel knows what to do in situations like this. When you click the check mark, the text appears on the spreadsheet.
9. Make sure that you have clicked the check mark, and that cell C1 is still selected. Then click the Center button (two buttons to the right of the Italic button). Your spreadsheet should now look like Figure 12.5.

Figure 12.5
Formatting the spreadsheet

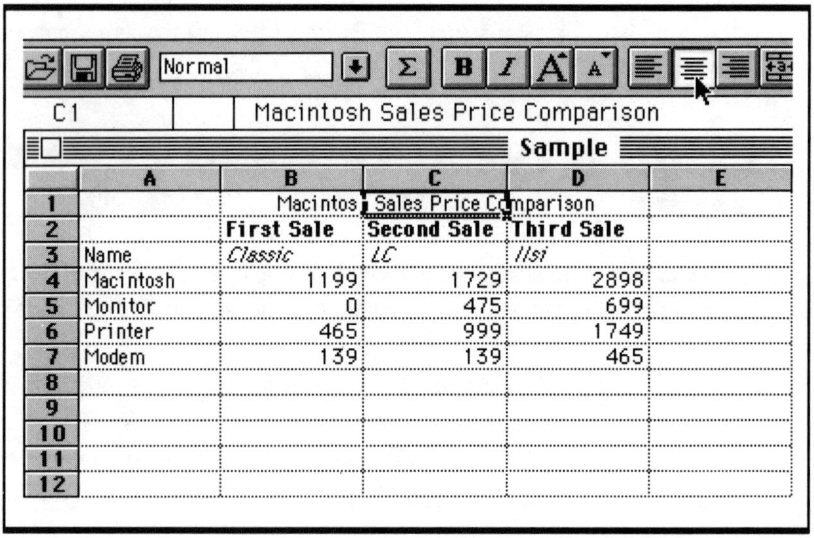

278 *Chapter 12: Spreadsheets*

Using Insert

No matter how much planning you do, you'll almost always run into something that needs to be changed. For example, even though you have a nice title, now things seem a little squished. It would be nice if there was a blank row between the title and the rest of the table. Luckily, Excel is flexible; you can easily insert a blank row where you want it.

1. Click on the number two row label. This selects the entire row.
2. Select Insert from the Edit menu.

You should now have a new blank row in your table. This time, the insertion was not entirely necessary. In many cases, though, it can mean much more than aesthetics. For example, it can separate ranges on which you use different functions.

Using the Font Dialog Box

The title over the table is nice, but to my eye, it's not quite impressive enough. Let's use a bigger font for the title.

1. Start by clicking on cell C1; this selects the heading.
2. Choose Font from the Format menu to bring up the Font dialog box.
3. Click 18 under Size and click in the Bold check box.
4. If you have a color monitor you might try selecting a color as well.
5. Click in the OK button to finish up.

You now have a spreadsheet title that stands out clearly.

Range Selection and Changing the Number Format

For a last change in format, you can select all of the cells that contain numbers and force these numbers to look more like dollar amounts.

1. Select all of the cells with numbers in them. Start by clicking on the upper leftmost number, in cell B5. Don't let your finger up from the mouse button, though; drag the mouse to the lower

rightmost number, in cell D8. Then release the mouse button. This highlights the entire *range*, or block, so you can work with it all at once.

2. Choose Number from the Format menu. This should bring up a dialog box with some very odd looking figures that may read like hieroglyphics if you've never seen them before. These lines of gibberish actually do have meaning. They are formatting characteristics that tell the computer how to display numbers. The default setting is General. This means that it displays numbers right-justified and without a decimal point in most cases.

3. Choose the third format down. This should be 0.00. This tells the computer you want all the numbers to look like dollars and cents with the decimal in the right spot.

4. Notice that the format you choose and an example of this format appear below. You might also note that this example is taken from the top leftmost cell that you choose. You should experiment with the other formats to try to get a feel for what they mean. When you've finished experimenting and you're back to 0.00, click in the OK button.

You now have a nice spreadsheet that shows how much each Mac, monitor, printer, and modem sold for.

Using Formulas

So far you've created the entire worksheet by typing the information in each cell. This is fine for making a short simple listing of prices, but if you want to show a value that's the sum of the sales figures, you should use a *formula*.

A formula is simply a mathematical equation relating the data in two or more cells of the spreadsheet. You can write formulas that perform a variety of mathematical operations, from addition and subtraction to finding percentages and averages.

The main reason you use formulas is because they'll change if you change the cells they refer to. This is because they use *variables* that refer to the cells containing your figures. For instance, the formula *=A1*A2* multiplies the figure in cell A1 by the figure in cell A2, regardless of what the actual figures in these cells are. This flexibility makes formulas the key time-saving feature of spreadsheets.

The following short procedure shows how to add up the amounts shown in a group of cells.

1. In cell A10, type **Subtotal** and click the check mark.
2. Click in cell B10 and type =. Typing = starts a formula.
3. Now type **B5+B6+B7+B8**, as in Figure 12.6 (look at the entry bar, not the cell), then click the check mark.

This formula tells Excel that the value to be put in this cell equals the sum of all the cells from B5 to B8. Another way to add up simple sums like this is to select the cell (B10), click the sum button (Σ) in the tool bar, then select the cells to be summed (B5 to B8). You can also write formulas that will subtract, multiply, or divide figures by using these mathematical operators: – for subtraction, * for multiplication, and / for division.

Whenever you type a formula, the entry bar displays what you typed, but as soon as you click the check mark, the cell will show the numerical value of the sum. The entry bar always shows the formula while the cell itself shows the value of the result of that formula.

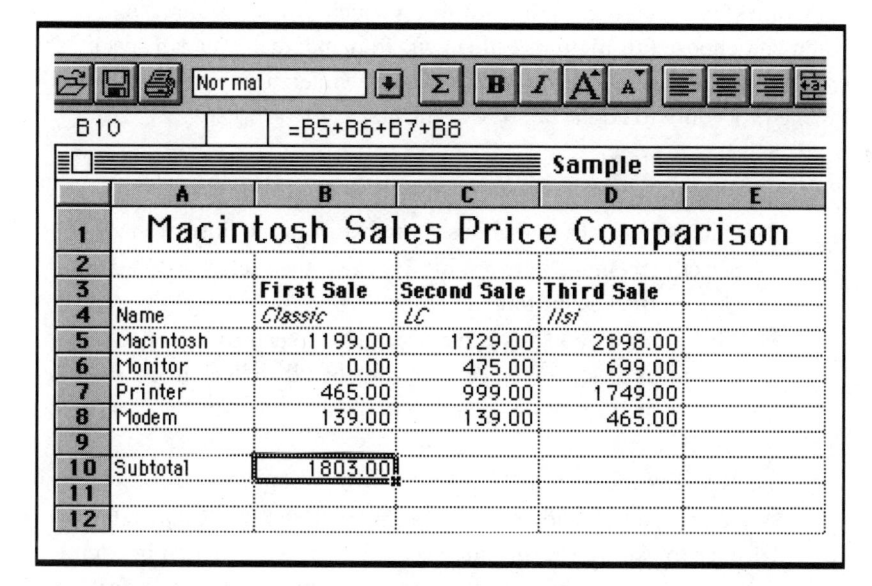

Figure 12.6
Using a formula to add up numbers

Using Excel **281**

Using the Fill Function

You can now add up the other two columns for Mac sales, but you can use a shortcut to do the task more quickly. You can tell Excel that you are going to do the same sort of calculation to get the results in cells C10 and D10, but you will be using the data in columns C and D to get the sums. Excel can fill in these similar formulas, basing them on the one you put in cell B10.

1. Click on cell B10 and drag to cell D10 so that all three are selected.
2. Under the Edit menu choose Fill Right.

Wow! If everything went well, you just got Excel to do a bunch of work for you. All three cells should now have the subtotals for their corresponding columns. Fill is one of the simplest, but most useful, functions of spreadsheets. You'll find that you can use it just about anywhere.

Absolute Cell Referencing

Sometimes Excel has a hard time knowing which cell you want it to refer to when you choose Fill Right or Fill Down. To help Excel, you can specify an *absolute cell reference*. To see how these absolute references work, use the following procedure to add a Tax row to the table.

1. To prepare for inevitable changes in the tax percentage, add a separate area for it. Select cell A15 and type **Tax %**.
2. Click in cell B15 and choose Number from the Format menu.
3. Select Percentage in the Value Type list, then select 0.00% and click in the OK button.
4. Now enter **0.065** (this is the tax rate) into cell B15. Notice that it displays as a percentage after you click the check mark. This is because you formatted cell B15 to display a percentage in steps 2 and 3.
5. Type **Tax** into cell A11.
6. Select cell B11 and enter the formula **=B10*B15**. The reference to cell B15 is absolute because it has a dollar sign in front of it. If you fill the formula to other cells, it will always refer back to cell B15 for the second multiplier. Click the check mark, and the tax for column B appears.

Chapter 12: Spreadsheets

7. By selecting cells B11 through D11 and choosing Fill Right from the Edit menu, you can extend the formula over all three cells.

The figures that appear in cells B11, C11, and D11 are the results of the formulas. They all refer to the tax number in cell B15, so if the tax rate changes, all you have to do is change the figure in B15 and all of the tax figures in cells B11, C11, and D11 will change automatically. This sort of setup (a bunch of formulas that have the same absolute cell reference) can save an awful lot of work if you have hundreds of figures that are dependent upon one variable like the tax rate.

Completing the Spreadsheet

You now have everything you need to make a Total row in the table. This will complete the table and review some of the steps you used previously.

1. Enter **Total** in cell A13.
2. In cell B13, type =SUM(B10:B11). This is a shorthand way of totaling a column of numbers. It finds the total of the Tax and Subtotal for the B column.
3. Complete the other formulas for this row by using Fill Right.
4. Make the row bold by using the Bold Button.

Note
A colon between two cell addresses indicates the range from the first cell to the second cell.

Great. You are all done with the table. It should look like Figure 12.7. After it's all set up, you might try experimenting by changing some of the price entries. Notice that the values for the totals and the taxes change when you change the prices. After you have completed the chart in the next section, you will notice that the chart changes to represent the new figures as well.

Using Charts

Charts are surprisingly easy to create in Excel and they can look quite impressive. All you need to know is what data you want to chart. After you select the data, Excel does the chart work for you.

You can make a meaningful chart for the sample table you've just completed, comparing how the price of each piece of each computer relates to the others. You shouldn't chart the totals, since they are so much larger they would throw off the scale. However, you will need to select the labels of the rows and columns since you have to tell Excel to put the names of each computer on the chart.

Using Excel **283**

Figure 12.7
The completed sample worksheet

	A	B	C	D	E
1	Macintosh Sales Price Comparison				
2					
3		First Sale	Second Sale	Third Sale	
4	Name	Classic	LC	IIsi	
5	Macintosh	1199.00	1729.00	2898.00	
6	Monitor	0.00	475.00	699.00	
7	Printer	465.00	999.00	1749.00	
8	Modem	139.00	139.00	465.00	
9					
10	Subtotal	1803	3342	5811	
11	Tax	117.195	217.23	377.715	
12					
13	Total	1920.20	3559.23	6188.72	
14					
15	Tax %	6.50%			
16					

Use the following procedure to get the idea of how Excel can make a chart out of your spreadsheet data. Save your spreadsheet before you graph it. For more information on saving, see "Saving and Printing an Excel Document" later in this chapter.

1. Drag the mouse from cell A4 to cell D8. This selects the range of data you want charted.
2. Now scroll the spreadsheet to the left until H is the leftmost column so the chart can have a page of its own.
3. Click on the Chart Wizard button in the toolbar (it's usually near the right end, with a little bar chart on it). Notice that the help bar at the bottom of the screen tells you what needs to be done to complete the chart.
4. Drag from cell H2 to cell M15 and release the mouse button. The chart wizard then shows you a bunch of dialog boxes; you just confirm things or make choices, and Excel draws the graph for you
5. In the first dialog box, check the range of your spreadsheet; if it is A4 to D8, click the Next button.
6. In the second dialog box, select the Area type chart, in the upper left corner, then click Next.

284 Chapter 12: Spreadsheets

7. In the Format box, click format number 4; it will show your data on a grid, for easy comparison. Then click Next.

8. Accept all the defaults in the next dialog box; they all have to do with formatting, and you don't need to fool with them, so just click Next.

9. In the last dialog box, enter a title, such as **Macintosh Sales**, then click OK.

The chart in Figure 12.8 appears, in all its clarity and style, right where you placed it. A fine thing, and so easy to do, too.

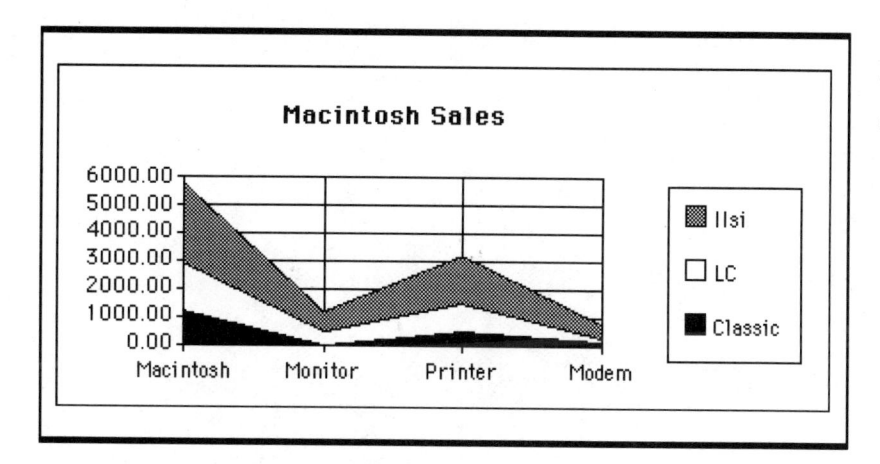

Figure 12.8
The chart for the sample spreadsheet

Saving and Printing an Excel Document

To protect your work in Excel, save it often, like every ten to fifteen minutes. All you have to do is choose Save from the File menu, or press ⌘-S. The first time you save a document, you must name it and choose where to place it in your folder hierarchy. There's also an Options button that allows you to password-protect your file and save in many different formats. For more information on this, see "Saving Your Work on a Document" in Chapter 4.

After creating your table and chart, you can print them out. Before you print, choose Print Preview from the File menu; you get a look at exactly what the printed pages are going to look like. It's always a good idea to preview before you print, because sometimes printing spreadsheets can take a while.

When you are sure your spreadsheet is ready to go, choose Print from the File menu and click in the OK button in the dialog box. The printer will chew on the spreadsheet and chart for a while, then give you a hard copy. Make sure you save before you print. Printing seems to be one of those times when programs lose data the most. When printing out the file you just created, the table and the chart should come out on different pages. You might try moving the chart under the table to get them on a single page. For more information on printing, see Chapter 3.

Troubleshooting Problems with Spreadsheet Applications

The following subsections cover the problems you are most likely to have while working with spreadsheet applications.

Not Enough Memory

This problem will occur when you're trying to open a spreadsheet. Spreadsheets have become huge in the past few years and now require a considerable portion of your RAM. The first thing to check when trying to cure this problem is any special utilities that you've loaded into the System Folder. These can be "turned off" by removing them from your System Folder and then rebooting your Macintosh. These programs are usually small utilities like virus checkers, screen savers, and print spoolers. They're usually not completely necessary and removing them temporarily won't hurt.

If things still don't seem to be working, you might try increasing the memory that's being allocated to your spreadsheet. See Chapter 7 for more information on memory allocation. Finally, if Excel still says you're out of memory, you'll need to increase the memory of your Macintosh by adding more RAM. This should only be done by a qualified technician.

Gridlines Don't Go Away When Printing

The rule is, if you can see them on the screen, then they are going to come out on the printer. To turn them off, choose Display from the Options menu. You will get a dialog box with some interesting options. Just click on the Gridlines check box and they'll go away. In Resolve, choose Show from the View and Cell Grid check box. You might also want to preview your printing before you actually print. This can tell you in a few seconds what your printer will tell you in a few minutes.

All a Cell Displays Is ###### or ******

This is caused by having your column width set too small. Widen you column manually with your mouse. Place the mouse pointer on the right border of the column you want to widen, and when your pointer turns into two arrows pointing left and right, just drag your mouse to the right to make it wider. When you release the mouse button your numbers will come back.

Formulas Don't Display the Correct Answer

First, check your formula for mistakes. If you are using a built-in formula, check to make sure the name is spelled correctly. If you made up the formula yourself, make sure the parentheses are all in the correct locations.

If your formulas are correct and the numbers displayed don't change even if you change the cells they relate to, then your spreadsheet has been set to manual calculation. To set it back to automatic calculation in Excel, choose Calculation from the Options menu and select Automatic under Calculation. Click in the OK button and everything should be fine. In Resolve, choose AutoCalc from the Calculate menu.

In Excel, You See the "Cannot Resolve Circular Reference" Error Message

This means that a formula is relating to a cell that relates back to the original formula. There is almost no way to fix this problem other than by changing your formula. Look at each cell that the formula in question is referencing. Do any of these cells reference the original cell? Maybe one of these cells relates to another cell that relates to the original cell. The problem can be tricky to track down. Once you do find it, see if you can find an error in the logic used to set up the formula.

The Microsoft Excel *User's Guide* also gives some hints on how to use manual calculation to make circular referencing actually work. Intentional circular referencing should not be taken lightly, though. In most cases, it won't correct the problem, and the only way is to try a totally different approach.

In Excel, Column Labels Don't Appear in Charts

Some types of charts don't have enough space to add the labels of the columns as well. This can usually be resolved by choosing Add Legend from the Chart menu in Excel's charting module. However, if you selected your data without selecting the labels, they will not appear. To remedy this situation, just start a new chart and make sure you select all the labels that you want to see on the chart.

Thirteen

Databases

Featuring

- Choosing the best database managing application for your needs
- Introduction to relational and flat-file databases
- How to design a database
- How to open a FileMaker Pro database
- How to enter data in records of a FileMaker Pro database
- How to use the FileMaker Pro toolbar to move around and change your view
- How to sort and find records in FileMaker Pro
- How to create and print envelopes from a FileMaker Pro address list
- How to save copies and print FileMaker Pro records
- Troubleshooting problems with FileMaker Pro

First Steps

To open a new document in FileMaker Pro: 300

If FileMaker Pro is not running yet, double-click the application icon first, then click the New button in the dialog box that appears. When the New File dialog box appears, click the New button, type in a name for the file, place it in your folder hierarchy by using the file list, then click New again. If a document is open, just choose New File from the File menu, name and place the file, and click New again.

To set up fields for records in FileMaker Pro: 301

Go to the Define Fields dialog box; if you have just opened a new document, you are there automatically. If not, choose Define Fields from the Select Menu. In the Define Fields dialog box, enter the name of each field, select a type if you want something other than the default text type, and click Create. You can start entering the name of the next field immediately. Use the Options button to set automatic entries in fields, and to verify fields.

To enter data in records in FileMaker Pro: 302

Choose Browse from the Select menu if you are not in Browse mode. Click in the blank space to the right of the first field, and begin entering data. You must press Tab to advance from field to field.

CHAPTER 13

To page or scroll through the records in Browse mode in FileMaker Pro: 303

Choose Browse from the Select menu if you aren't in Browse mode. Click on the pages of the rolodex icon in the toolbar on the left side of the screen to move from record to record; if you can see lines of text on a page, you can click the page to move to a new record. To scroll quickly through the records, drag the bookmark on the right side of the rolodex icon.

To sort records in FileMaker Pro: 304

Choose Sort from the Select menu. In the dialog box that appears, select the field that you want to sort by first, and click the Move button to put the field on the sort list. Then click the icon of the sorting order you want. You can select and move one or more fields and click a sorting order for each of them, too. When you have the setup you want, click the Sort button and the records are soon sorted.

To find a record or a group of records in FileMaker Pro: 305

Choose Find from the Select menu. In the blank record that appears, you can fill in data in one or more fields to limit what records are searched for. Make sure the toolbar is showing; click the toolbar icon at the bottom of the window if it isn't in view. Then click on the Find button to begin the search for records that have data matching what you entered.

Databases are tools that allow you to manage large amounts of information. A database is pretty much like a rolodex, one of those address-holders with all the cards attached to double rings. As each card in a rolodex holds one address, each *record* in a database contains a bunch of information on a single subject. The cards in a rolodex are all kept in order on the double rings; you can take out a card and change a person's address, then put it back. You can add cards or remove them. You can do the same things with records in a database, but you don't even have to take them out.

The big difference between a database and a rolodex is that with a database you can resort the records in lots of ways, and do it instantly, without winding up with a bunch of cards scattered all over your desk. You can ask the database to find a record or a bunch of records, and then tell it to display the data in any of a whole bunch of formats or *layouts*. You can also tell the database to pull certain bits of information off each record and make a neat report out of it. And a database can do all this easily, even if you put much, much more information in it than you can cram into a rolodex.

Databases are great for stores that need to have data on everything they carry at their disposal instantaneously. In fact, the machine that reads the bar code off your groceries at the supermarket is connected to a kind of database. You can make smaller databases to keep track of almost anything you are interested in. For example, if you are an audiophile, you can make a database to list your CDs, tapes, or records. If you love books, you can catalog your library. If you cook, make a personal cook book of favorite recipes, with your latest variation added to each one.

In terms of work, you can make a list of all the important business contacts you have, with their addresses and telephone numbers, and some important notes about your latest dealings with each of them. A rolodex would get real messy if you tried to put this much on it; a database can take it all in stride, and it doesn't mind if you change it every time you make a business contact. You can see an example of this type of database in "Using FileMaker Pro" later in this chapter.

Which Database Application for You?

Databases were the first applications that were developed for the consumer world, so there is a wide array of choices. There are complex databases that are designed to run large businesses and small ones that are made solely for the purpose of holding your address book. Most people will probably want something that's in between. Fortunately, this is the category that most databases fit into. You can choose between a simple flat-file database that puts all the information in one file, and a big, powerful relational database that keeps data in separate, connected files. The following sections cover each type of database, starting with the most expensive and working down.

Relational Databases

A relational database is a collection of related data that is stored in a structure made up of a number of files. Where a flat-file database stores all related information in one file, a relational one allows the sharing of information between many related files.

If you think of a flat-file database as a single rolodex with a bunch of phone numbers in it, you can think of a relational database as a magical rolodex that can call up some of the numbers listed in it and draw on other rolodexes at those numbers for information. But even that is too limited a view; it is as if each magical rolodex can contact not only other rolodexes, but all kinds of other data storage files—from price lists to personnel profiles, a single database file can make use of a tremendous scope of information. The key concept is that the database is not just the single file, it is the whole structure of related files.

There is one relational database, Helix Express, that has a Mac-oriented programming language based on icons. It is best suited to people who are new to the world of database programming. Experienced programmers may find it baffling or limited, however.

Large databases like 4th Dimension from Acius and Foxbase Pro from Fox seem difficult to manage at first, but they give you unmatched flexibility in the long run. You can collect many categories of information in different files, and have different people updating each file; the database automatically takes the updated stuff from one file and feeds it into the others so they all stay current. This is much nicer than a flat-file database, where you have to update changes in every record affected by any change in another record. But a relational database is much harder to set up. When a large business wants to have a database set up that requires the speed, size, and flexibility of a relational one, they often hire a consultant to do the designing for them. The database might track sales, customers, personnel, inventory, and overhead expenses, and relate all of these things to each other in a number of ways. Whew. Quite a feat of organization.

Not all uses of relational databases are so vast, though. Small businesses can use them to track sales and customers, for instance. And some are easier for nonexperts to set up. If you are interested in using a relational database with a relatively friendly Mac approach, 4th Dimension is definitely the prime candidate.

4th Dimension was designed by a couple of French Macintosh enthusiasts, specifically for the Mac. It makes excellent use of the Macintosh interface, so that you can quickly learn to design and implement a database that is made up of many indirectly related files storing different kinds of specific information. The whole structure is made up of simple connections that are represented graphically, so you know exactly what you are doing as you build the relationships between files.

For a commonly used example, if your business has one file called Invoices containing records of all the company's sales, and another file called Customers with information about each customer, you can set up a simple relation between the Invoices file and the Customers file, as shown in Figure 13.1. Now, if you want each customer's invoice to show the customer's name and address, you can use the Customer field in the Invoices file to access the Customers file; it finds the record for the customer and has access to his or her address.

The beauty of this setup is that it saves you from having to enter data in two places. You enter the customer address in the fields in the Customers file, and then, when you are making out an invoice, you just specify the customer, and your Mac fills in the address for you. Notice that the example in Figure 13.1 also has a subfile for Line items, so you automatically update your sales data for every transaction.

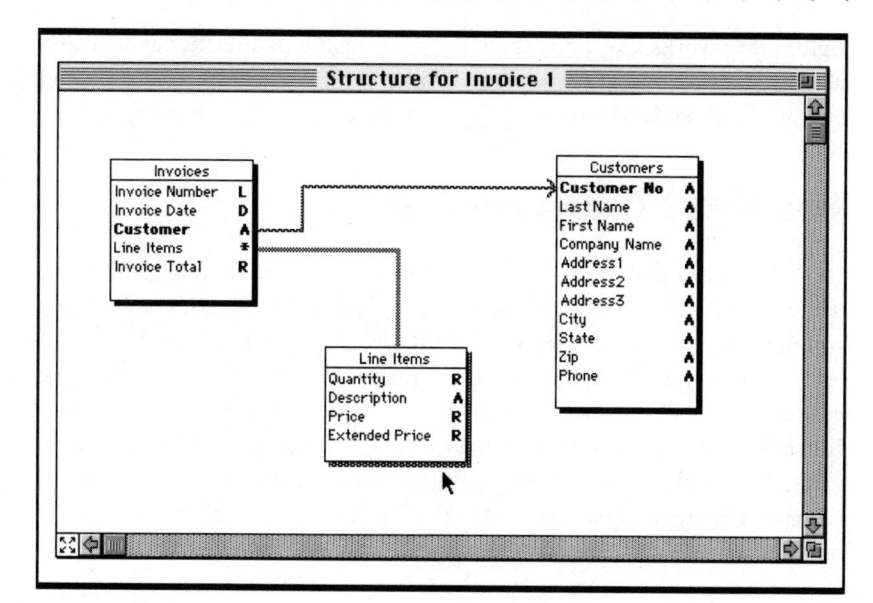

Figure 13.1
Graphic view of a 4th Dimension database structure

This simple use of a relational database can save huge amounts of time for a small business. If you are willing to pay the higher price for the application and take the time to set the database up properly, you won't regret it in the long run.

Flat-File Databases

Medium-scale, single-file databases may not have the features that the large databases have, but they are usually much easier to learn and much more affordable. A few, like FileMaker Pro from Claris or File Force from Acius, have some of the powers of relational databases. Others, like Panorama from ProVUE, are strictly flat-file databases. File Force is good for setting up a simple set of relationships between databases, and Panorama is a powerful flat-file tool that works well for users who are accustomed to spreadsheets.

The rest of this chapter focuses on FileMaker Pro, a leading Mac flat-file database application. It is a very straightforward database with a great deal of flexibility, and it's extremely easy to use. FileMaker Pro actually incorporates the rolodex concept into its graphic interface; you can flip through the records of your database just like you are flipping through the cards of a rolodex. But FileMaker Pro is no toy. It has a lot of power, including a lookup feature that works like a one-direction relationship in a relational database. As databases become more powerful and complex, it is a rare thing to find one such as FileMaker Pro with power that is easy to take advantage of.

Budget Databases

Small databases and address books are numerous and are more affordable than their heavy-duty cousins. They aren't relational and might not even give you the ability to create your own layout for your data. Don't let this lack of features scare you, though; they can be great for what they do. Many people like to keep an address book with a program like Touch Base by After Hours. Touch Base can print out your data on sheets that will fit in your daily scheduling book. For the technologically advanced, they can also upload information to other applications. Many business people find these to be essential for keeping track of all their contacts.

Product at a Glance

FileMaker Pro

Publisher:
Claris
Upgrades from FileMaker and File-Maker II are available, but not free

Requires:
Mac Plus or better, LC or better recommended
System 6.7 or later
2MB of RAM if running System 6; 4MB of RAM if running System 7
40MB hard drive with 3.5MB of free space; 80MB hard drive recommended
Any Mac-compatible printer with standard fonts

Description:
In the complex and confusing world of powerful databases, FileMaker Pro is a welcome exception. It provides the power that demanding database users want, but it is relatively easy to use and inexpensive, so novices can feel at home with it quickly. It offers great flexibility for different layouts and data types, and it has a scripting language that is relatively easy to program with. You can even set up ways for one file to look up data in another file, and update automatically if that file is changed. You can even incorporate photographs or QuickTime videos in records. And the interface is always straightforward and intuitive, so you can learn by experimenting.

Using FileMaker Pro

FileMaker Pro started as a simple database years ago and has become an easy-to-use, yet powerful application. Databases are difficult to learn at best, but Claris has done a good job at making FileMaker Pro the easiest to get started with. It has the same type of interface that you might remember from MacWrite II and MacDraw. In the following sections, you'll use FileMaker Pro to create a small, familiar address book type of file that tracks your business contacts.

Designing a Database

Before you plunge into the building of a database, you should plan out its design. You may even want to make a rough sketch with a pencil and paper, so you have an idea of how you are going to organize things. Even if you just scribble the thing out on a napkin, any design is better than no design. After all, a database is a just a way of organizing information. The better you organize it, the easier the information is to find and use.

The basic building blocks of database organization are *fields* and *records*. A field is an area that stores a single piece of information. It's like one line on a card of your rolodex. Each field of your address book will store a different type of information. You put together a bunch of fields to make a record.

A record is about the same as a single rolodex card. It contains all the information about a single item. You put the records into some kind of logical order, so you can zip through them and find things quickly. Alphabetical order works well for lists of names or objects.

If you are organizing a list of names and addresses, for example, you set up fields for the name, street number, city, state, and zip code for the records. Then you fill in the fields with data for each person, so each one has a separate record. Then you put the records in alphabetical order, so you can look up any person's information by going to their name. In the sample explained below, you'll see each step of the process in detail.

Opening a Document

You have to take different steps to open a new document in FileMaker Pro, depending on whether you have started the application or not. Use the following steps if you have not started FileMaker Pro:

1. To start the application, double-click on the FileMaker Pro icon, as shown in Figure 13.2, or double-click on an alias of it. A dialog box appears, asking you to open an existing document or create a new one.
2. Click on the New button. The New File dialog box appears.
3. Type in a name you like, such as **Business Contacts**.
4. If you want the file to be stored in a different folder from the one listed, use the menu under the folder title to move a new folder.
5. Click the New button again. The Define Fields dialog appears, with the cursor in the Name box.

Figure 13.2
The FileMaker Pro icon

To open a new document if you have already opened FileMaker Pro and are looking at an existing database file, use the following steps:

1. Choose New from the File menu. The New File dialog box appears.
2. Type in a name, such as **Business Contacts**.
3. If you want the file to be stored in a different folder from the one listed, use the menu under the folder title to move to a new folder.
4. Click the New button again. The Define Fields dialog box appears, with the cursor in the Name box.

Setting Up the Fields

You are now ready to set up the fields of your address book. Follow these steps to make them:

1. Start by typing **First Name** in the Name box (if you make a typing mistake, use the Delete key to fix it). The Create button comes to life.
2. Click the Create button, as shown in Figure 13.3. Notice that the field name is displayed in the text box.
3. Repeat steps 1 and 2 to create fields for the following information:

   Last Name

   Street Address

   City

   State

   Zip Code

   Phone Number
4. Now look over your field names in the list box at the top of the dialog. If you created a field name that has mistakes in it, select the field name. Then select the typo in the Name box, type in

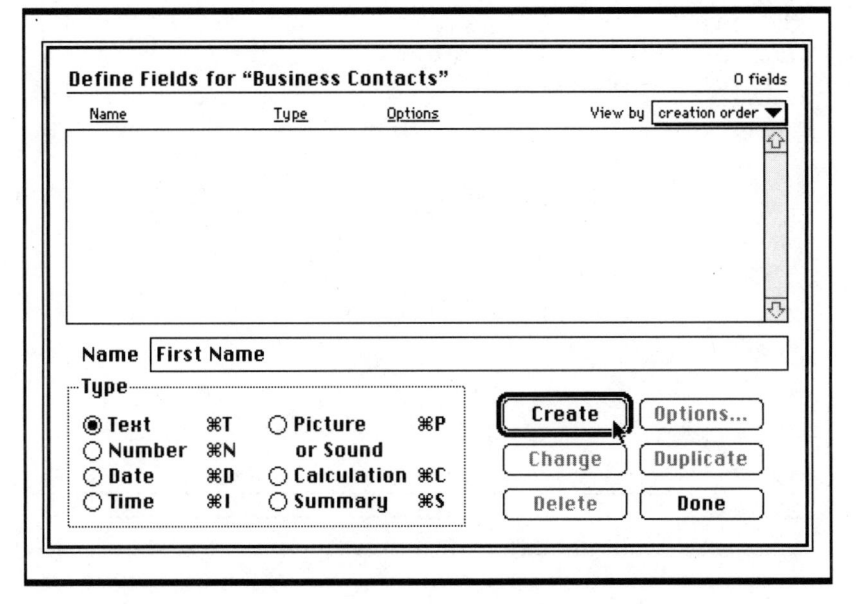

Figure 13.3
Defining fields for database records

the correction and click the Change button. This corrects the selected field name.

5. When the fields are all correct, click the Done button.

The Define Fields dialog box goes away and a blank record appears, with the fields you defined.

Entering Records

After you click the Done button, FileMaker moves into *Browse* mode. This is the place you go when you want to enter or edit a record. Use the following steps to create your first record, beginning with the First Name field.

1. Click in the blank space to the right of where it says First Name.
2. Type **Tracey**.
3. Press Tab to advance to the next field.
4. Type **Smith** and press Tab again to advance.
5. Fill in the remaining fields for Tracey, using the information in Figure 13.4.

Tip
To see what mode you are in, look at the indicator bar at the bottom of the window, near the left side.

Figure 13.4
Entering a record's data in the fields

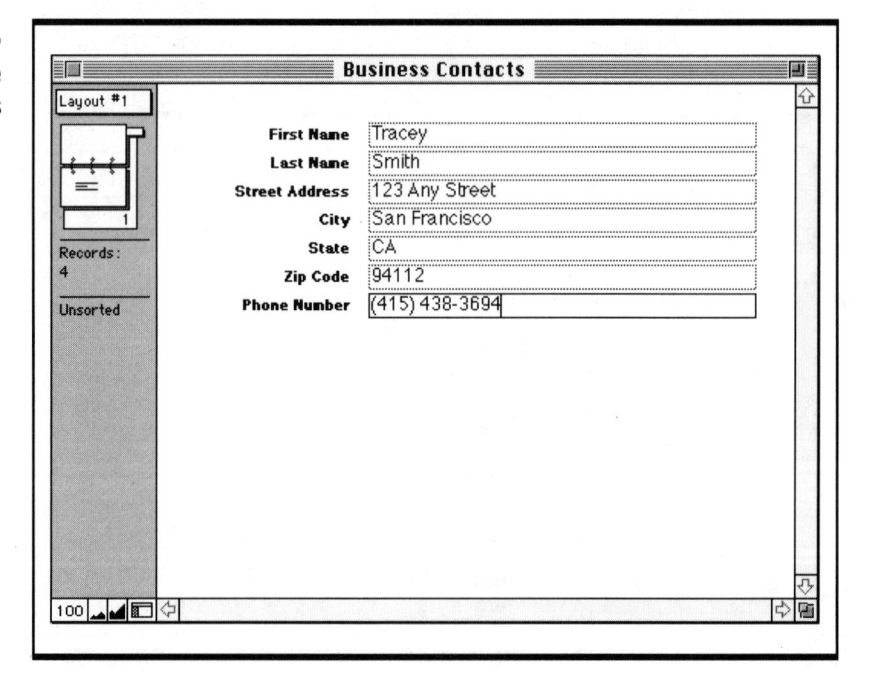

302 Chapter 13: Databases

6. Choose New Record from the Edit menu. You now have a blank record and the cursor is in the First Name field. You did not destroy the last record, you merely added another blank card to the rolodex-type stack.

7. Create the following records, using the same procedure you used for Tracey's:

Adam Adams
789 Some Blvd.
New York, NY 12345
(123) 555-0987

Mike Mandel
456 That Way
Chicago, IL 76543
(321) 555-4567

Mark Mandel
456 That Way
Chicago, IL 76543
(321) 555-4567

> **Note**
> If you press Tab when you have filled the last field of a record, the cursor advances to the first field in the record again.

In most applications, you'd want to save after doing all this, but you do not have to save your work in FileMaker Pro; the application saves your files to the FileMaker Pro folder. In fact, there is no Save command in FileMaker Pro's File menu.

Using the Toolbar

Now that you have a little database to work with, you can manipulate it with the tools FileMaker Pro offers. Some of the most accessible and useful of these tools are located on the toolbar in the area to the left of your record.

- The title "Layout #1" at the top of the bar means that this is your first layout. You will create another layout later on.
- Just below the layout marker is a picture of a rolodex. This rolodex is a representation of your database file. If you click the bottom card of the rolodex, you advance to the next record.

Clicking the top card moves you to the previous record. (If you are at the top card of the database, the previous card button will be blank; if you are at the bottom the next card button will be blank.) You can move quickly through the database by sliding the bookmark. Nifty, isn't it?

- The buttons at the bottom of the window let you change your view of the database. The number 100 tells you the magnification percentage that you are seeing. To magnify the card, click on the button showing a large mountain; to shrink the card, click on the button showing a distant mountain, and to get back to 100 percent, click on the current percentage number to the left of the mountains.

- The last button looks just like a little FileMaker Pro window with the toolbar highlighted. Clicking on this button makes the toolbar disappear. This can be great if you need a little more space to work with, especially if you are working on a small-screen Macintosh.

None of these lower buttons changes your database; they just change the way you see it, so you should try them all out. Experimentation is the best way to make yourself comfortable, and a good program like FileMaker Pro encourages you to experiment.

Sorting Records

OK, so you've got an address book and you can flip back and forth between the records. So far, so good, but you may be wondering how this is any better than the rolodex on your desk. Well, for starters, it's a lot more flexible. If you want your records to be in a particular order, you can have FileMaker Pro sort them in just about any order you can imagine. For example, you could have FileMaker Pro do what you'd normally do with a rolodex—sort alphabetically by last name. Or you could sort the addresses by state, or by first name, if you have trouble remembering last names. Sorting is one of the most often used features of a database. Follow the steps below to sort your database by last name.

1. Choose Sort from the Select menu. A large dialog box appears with many choices in it. You can ignore most of them for now. The important things are the two list boxes. The box on the left

represents each of your fields. The box on the right represents the sorting order.

2. Click on Last Name in the left list box.

3. Click on the Move button as in Figure 13.5.

4. Last Name appears in the sort order list. This means that the alphabetical (ascending from A to Z) sorting will start with the last name of each person, just like in a real address book. You still have a problem, though; the two brothers have the same last name.

5. To sort by first names too, click on First Name in the left list box, and then click the Move button again. Now when the computer gets to the brothers it will sort them by their first names.

6. Click the Sort button to put your address book in alphabetical order.

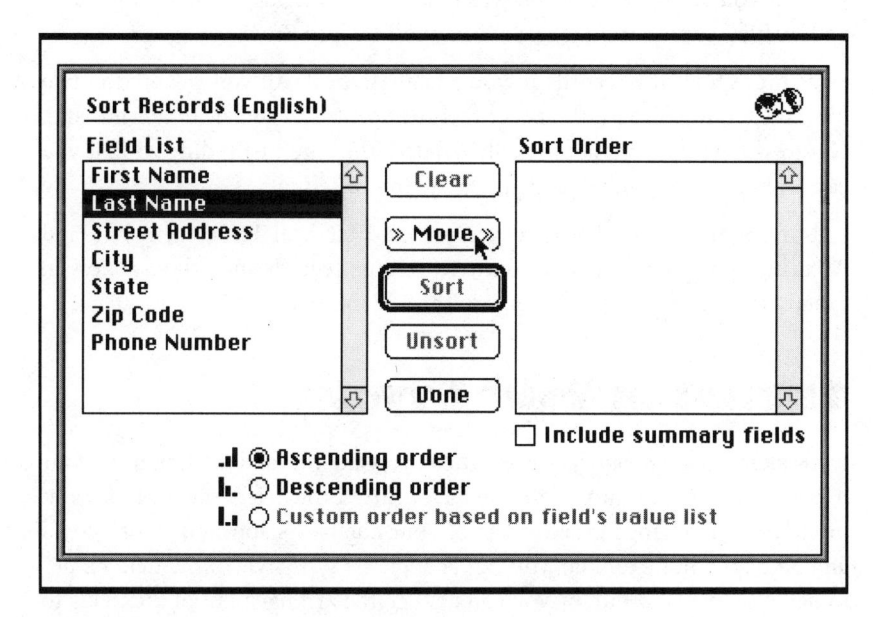

Figure 13.5
Setting up sorting order

Finding Records

You can also use FileMaker Pro to find records or particular groups of records. Suppose you need to contact everyone in Chicago for a business convention. If you were using a real address book, you'd have to leaf through the whole thing page by page, looking for contacts that live in Chicago. This would be tedious. Using *Find* mode, you can easily select all the people from Chicago and separate them out, even if you have hundreds of contacts.

1. Choose Find from the Select menu to enter Find mode. A panel appears with the field names and blank spaces, much like what you see when you enter data for a record.
2. Make sure that your toolbar is showing. Click the toolbar button at the bottom of the screen if the bar is not in view.
3. Tab down to the field labeled City and type **Chicago**.
4. Click on the Find button in the toolbar or press the Return key on your keyboard.

You're done! No leafing, no looking. You should now be back in the Browse mode with only the people from Chicago showing. You can double-check to see that you are truly in the Browse mode by pulling down the Select menu and making sure that there is a check mark next to Browse.

Run through all the records in your database now. All you see are the two brothers from Chicago; the other records you typed in earlier are missing. Not to worry; they are not actually deleted, they are just hiding so that you can look at the specific data that you are interested in.

To bring all the records back, just choose Find All from the Select menu. Find All brings you back to where you were. All the records should now show in exactly the way you typed them into the address book.

Changing Your Layout

FileMaker Pro's *Layout* mode is where you do the actual design of your database file. To get into it, choose Layout from the Select menu. In Layout mode you can change every aspect of your database's appearance on screen and on paper. For example, you can change the type style of the field names to make them stand out, or you can change the arrangement of the fields to give certain information priority. In fact, you can even have several layouts that you switch between. In this section, we'll spruce up your address book a bit and create a new layout for it.

1. After choosing Layout from the Select menu, select all of the field names. To do this, move the pointer to a position above and to the left of all the field names, then drag a selection rectangle down and to the right until it encloses all the field names

completely. Release the mouse button and check that all of the names have *handles* (small boxes on the corners).

2. Now that they're all selected, pull down the Format menu to Font.
3. Choose Times from the Font submenu. (If Times isn't installed choose another of your favorite fonts.)
4. Choosing Times makes the type look a bit small, so pull down the Format menu again. This time go into the Size submenu and choose 14 or 18.

Great! Those field names look much better. It would be nice, however, if they were arranged a bit better. This is easy; just click and drag the field where you want it to go. Using this method I moved the fields as in Figure 13.6. You can copy me or pick your own format. The style of your database file is entirely up to you, so be creative.

You can also change the size of your fields by dragging the handles. Make sure the tip of the pointer is on a handle, not on the whole field. To make a field larger or smaller just drag the handle until the field is the desired size, as shown in Figure 13.6.

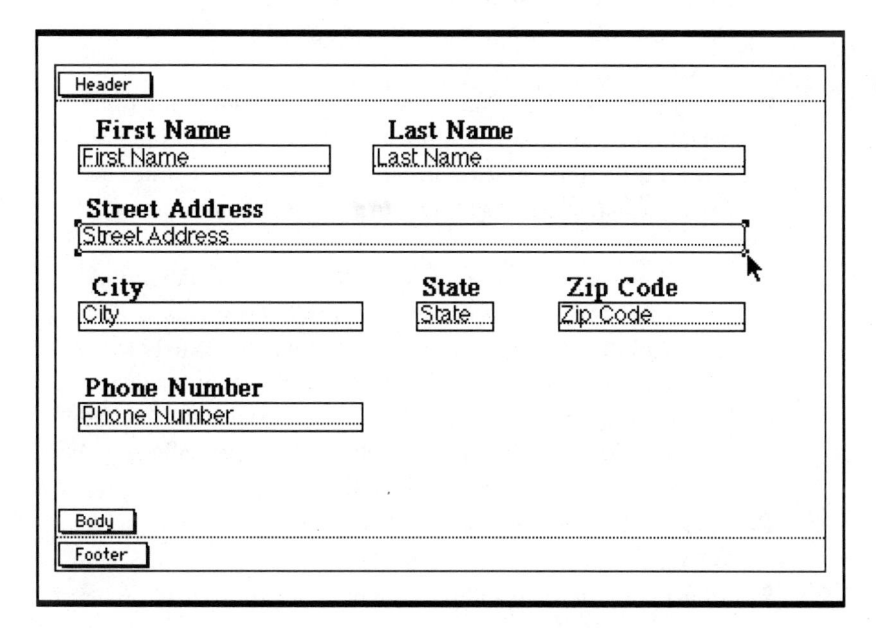

Figure 13.6
Reformatting the fields

Using FileMaker Pro **307**

Adding to the Database

Once you've set up the basic structure of your database, you're pretty much done. Oh, you'll add records, and delete them, and change them, but File-Maker Pro takes care of the real work—sorting records, finding them, keeping them safe.

There will be times, though, when you'll want to change your database's structure. Maybe your needs have changed, or maybe you have needs that you didn't anticipate when you planned your database. Then you'll want to add new fields. Let's add a Notes field and a Last Contact field to your address book, so you can keep track of your last contact with each person.

1. Pull down the Select menu and choose Layout. This takes you to Layout mode, where you can change the design of your database.
2. Choose Define Fields from the Select menu. You see the same dialog box that you began this chapter with.
3. Type **Notes** in the Name box and click on the Create button.
4. Type **Last Contact** in the Name box and click on the Create button.
5. Now you have two more fields to work with. Instead of clicking Done, this time click on the Options button to automate the Last Contact field.
6. Again you see a dialog box swarming with options. You don't need to learn them all now, but just think what you could do, given a little time and experience! For now, just click in The Creation Date check box under the heading "Auto-enter a value that is."
7. Place the pointer on the words *Creation Date*, pull down the menu, and select Modification Date. By choosing this setting, you've told FileMaker to automatically update this field to the current date every time something inside the record changes. Each time you talk to the person, you can make a note in the new Note field, and the date will change automatically, so you'll always know when you last talked to the person.
8. Click the OK button and then click the Done button to get back to your new layout.
9. Adjust the font, size, and position of the fields to match the rest, as in Figure 13.7.

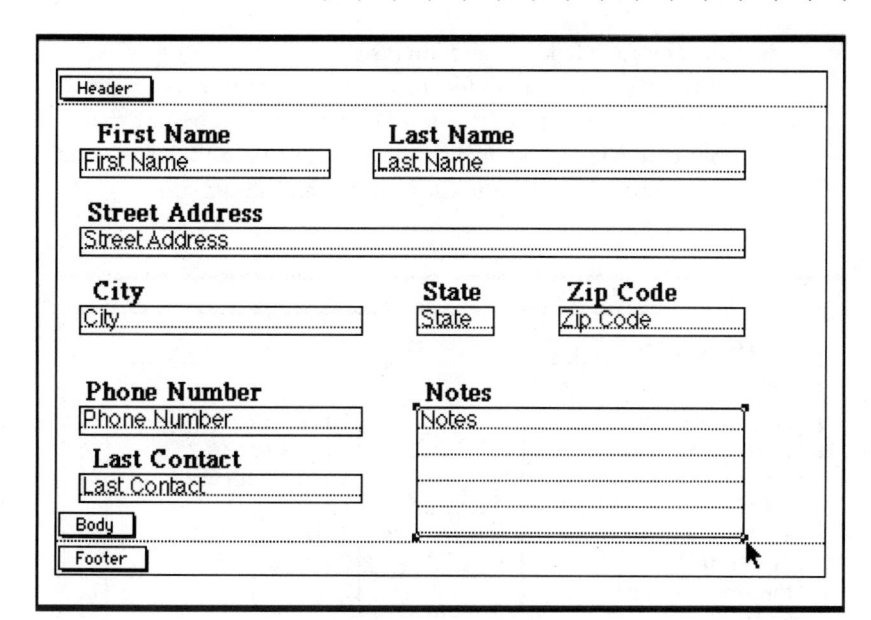

Figure 13.7
Formatting new fields to match a layout

Creating a Mailing

For the grand finale, we'll make your address book capable of producing envelopes. Creating mailings is one of the greatest features of databases. Once you set up FileMaker Pro to print out your envelopes, you can go have lunch. When you come back your printer will have produced a tremendous amount of work with only minimal effort on your part.

Before you envision a mass mailing to the world, create the new layout. Don't worry about the old layout; FileMaker Pro saves it and you can get back to it in the Layout menu at the top of your toolbar.

1. First, make sure you are still in the Layout mode. Choose Layout from the Select menu if you aren't.
2. To start a new layout, choose New Layout from the Edit menu. FileMaker Pro presents you with a dialog box to let you set the name and type of your new layout.
3. Type in **Envelope Layout** and click in the Envelope radio button.
4. Click the OK button. The dialog box that appears allows you to choose which fields you want to be printed on your envelope.

Using FileMaker Pro **309**

5. Click on each field you are interested in, then click the Move button. The field names for the envelope appear on the right side of the dialog box. The order is important, so be sure that your dialog looks like Figure 13.8 when you are all done. If you make a mistake, click the Clear button and start again.

Figure 13.8
Setting the field order

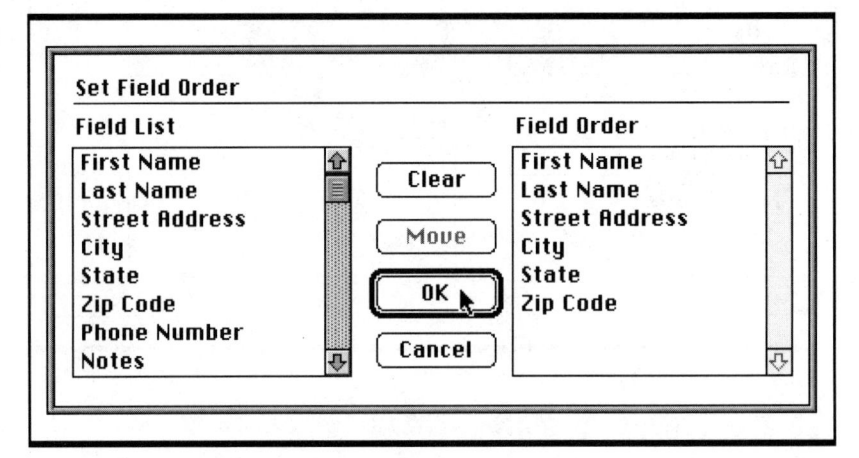

6. When you're done, click the OK button to get back to designing the layout of the envelope. The fields you selected are stacked up at the bottom of the window.

7. Orient the fields so that each is on its correct line, as shown in Figure 13.9. This can be a little tricky when working with small fields. Here are a couple of hints for moving fields around:

- Use the magnification buttons (below the toolbar) to magnify what you're working with.
- Fields can be moved by a single pixel by selecting the field and using the arrow keys. This is great for tiny adjustments.
- Drag a selection rectangle around all the fields if you want to move the whole batch to a better position on the envelope. To deselect the whole batch, click somewhere in blank space with the pointer.

When you get the layout looking something like Figure 13.9, pat yourself on the back. You have just created an envelope layout. You can switch back to the first layout by using the toolbar. Click on Envelope in the Layout box at

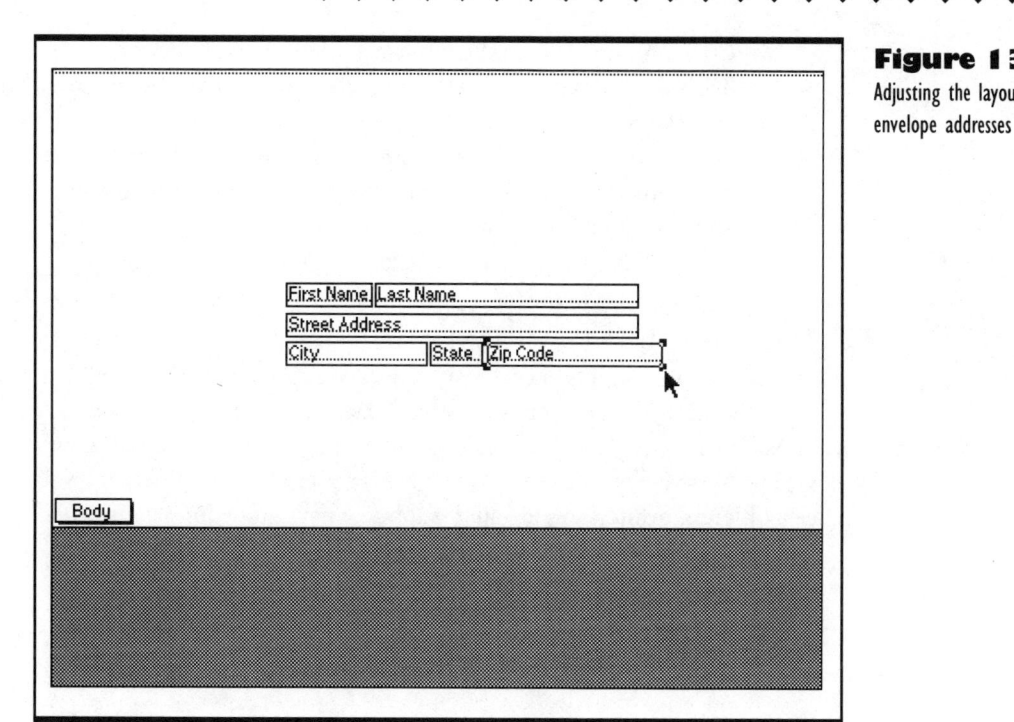

Figure 13.9
Adjusting the layout for envelope addresses

the top of the bar and a pop-up menu will appear with all your layouts in it. Look at the first layout if you want, but then switch back to Envelope layout and try looking at some of the data in it by choosing Browse from the Select menu. You may want to go back to Layout mode to resize and move the fields a bit to line up the parts of the address.

Once the address looks good, everything would be dandy if you had envelopes preprinted with your return address. But preprinted envelopes are expensive, and you have a Mac to work with. So why not have FileMaker Pro print your name and address in the correct position of each envelope?

All you have to do is add a *header* that will be the same on every envelope. The header is separate from the *body* of the layout, where the record fields appear.

1. Go back to Layout mode by choosing Layout from the Select menu.
2. Make sure that you're back in the Envelope layout by using the pop-up menu for layouts at the top of the toolbar. Click on it and select Envelope Layout.

3. Click on the A tool in the toolbar. This allows you to create fields of text that don't relate to the data that you've entered in the records.
4. Move your cursor to the header section of the layout and type in your return address. Don't worry, the field expands as you type, and you can press Return to start a new line.
5. Click the pointer tool, then click in the return address to select it and drag it to the left side of the header area, as shown in Figure 13.10.

This example, although it looks great on the screen, is somewhat simplified. To actually make the envelopes print you have to set the computer up for your exact envelopes and your exact printer. The following example shows how to print envelopes on a LaserWriter NT. The steps may be different if you have a different printer, so see your printer's owner's guide for details.

1. Choose Page Setup from the File menu.
2. Choose Envelope - Edge Fed from the pop-up menu for the Tabloid option, click the Landscape orientation option, and click OK.

Figure 13.10
The completed layout for an envelope

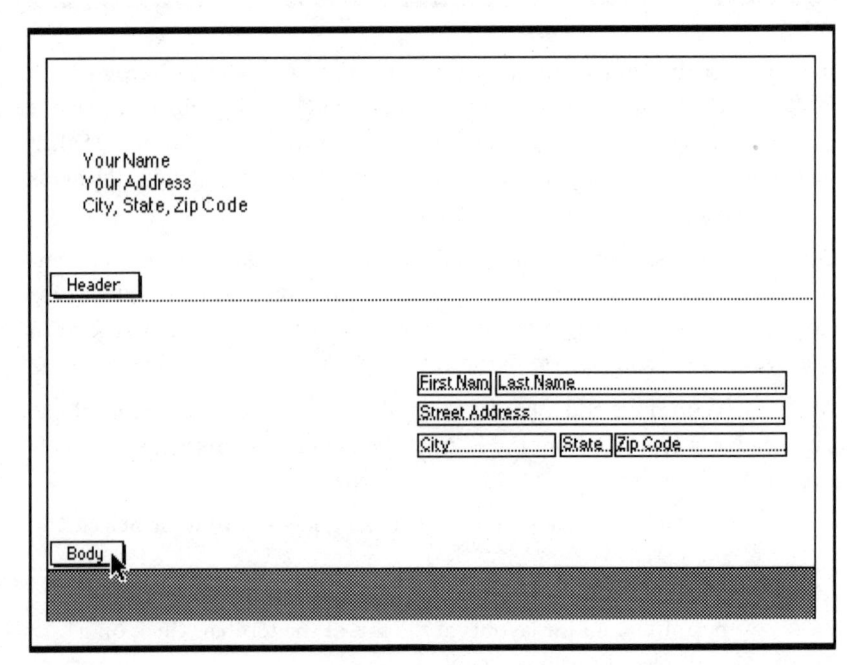

Chapter 13: Databases

3. In Layout mode, raise the address fields until they are in the center of the upper envelope, just under the header. Make sure your return address is still placed correctly in the header area.
4. If you see a slashed line under the address fields, raise the body marker in the bottom left corner of the envelope until the slashed line disappears, so your layout looks like Figure 13.10.
5. Choose Print from the File menu.
6. In the Print dialog box, click the radio buttons for Manual Feed Paper Source and the Current Record.
7. Open your LaserWriter NT multipurpose tray, as explained in "Manual Feed Printing" in the owner's guide. Place the envelopes face down in the feeder.
8. Click Print. Click OK in the two PrintMonitor dialog boxes.

Your envelopes print out!

Saving and Printing a FileMaker Pro Document

One of the best features of FileMaker Pro is that it saves your work automatically. You never have to choose Save while working with FileMaker Pro. In fact, it's not even an option. As soon as you enter data or change a layout it automatically saves everything for you in the FileMaker Pro folder. However, if you want, you can save a file to a different folder by choosing Save a Copy as from the File menu.

Printing in FileMaker Pro is not as cut-and-dried as saving, but there are quite a few added features to help you know when everything is going to print out well. To print the address book that was created in this chapter, simply choose Print from the File menu and then click the OK button in the Print dialog box.

For most cases this should be all you need to do to print out your file. However, there are a few exceptions. FileMaker likes to print out everything, and if you have hundreds of people in your address book this could be pretty inefficient. In these situations it would be better to print only a portion of the file. Near the bottom of the Print dialog box there are a few options that allow you to print different portions of your file, such as just the current record. Choose the one that you need and go on printing as usual. For more information on printing, see Chapter 3.

Troubleshooting Problems with FileMaker Pro

The following subsections cover the problems you are most likely to have while working with FileMaker Pro.

Not Enough Memory

This problem will only occur if you have just double-clicked on the FileMaker icon. Since FileMaker is an extremely complex program, it takes up a considerable amount of your Mac's RAM.

To solve this problem, you need to free up some memory to give to FileMaker. Start by turning off any system extensions you don't need. These devices can be "turned off" by removing them from the System Folder or by holding down the Shift key when your Mac is starting up.

If this doesn't work, you might try increasing the amount of memory allocated to FileMaker Pro. See Chapter 7 for more information on memory allocation. If you can't give FileMaker Pro enough memory to start it, you'll have to add some RAM to your Mac. See a qualified technician for help.

When You Press Tab, the Cursor Goes to the Wrong Fields

Unfortunately, the computer is not quite intelligent enough to decipher in exactly what order you would like the cursor to go. It moves the cursor to the next field in the order that the fields were created. This is fine for most purposes, but when fields get moved around, then FileMaker Pro gets confused.

To fix this, choose Layout from the Select menu. Then choose Tab Order from the Arrange menu. A small window will appear on the screen to help with the different options for setting the tab order. In your database file, your fields should be displayed with an arrow next to them. If the Tab Order window covers your fields, you can move it by dragging it from its title bar. Each arrow now displays its current order. Click in the Create New Tab Order radio button to clear the incorrect order. To set their new order, click on each field in the correct order. When you're finished, click in the OK button and your troubles should be solved.

Missing Records

You may have accidentally deleted a record, so before trying anything else, see if you can undo the deletion by choosing Undo from the Edit menu. If this doesn't help, you may be in the wrong mode for viewing your records. For example, if you're in Find mode, only a small portion of your records are available for viewing. Just choose Find All from the Select menu, and you'll be back in Browse mode, and back in business.

Fourteen

Managing Personal Finances

Featuring

- Choosing the right personal finance application for you
- Creating a new file for Quicken accounts
- Opening a Quicken account
- Recording a check in the Quicken register
- Entering deposits in the Quicken register
- Using the Quicken categories list and adding categories to it
- Writing checks in Quicken
- Using Quicken memorized transactions to save on check writing
- Printing Quicken checks and reports
- Troubleshooting problems with Quicken

First Steps

To open a new file for Quicken accounts: 322

If you have never opened Quicken before, you see a dialog box that asks if you are upgrading; click No in it to get into the dialog box for naming your new accounts file. If you have used Quicken before, it opens a window showing the last check register you had open. In this case, choose New from the File menu and click New File in the small dialog box that opens. The dialog box for naming opens, so you can name the file for your accounts. Once you have named your new file, click New. When the dialog box for setting up a new account opens, enter the name of the first account you want to open, enter the balance of your account and the date of your last bank statement, and add a note or the account number for reference. Click OK and Quicken sets up the account; the account register soon appears in a window.

To record a check in the Quicken check register: 326

The Quicken register works much like a standard paper check register. First you enter a date, then press Tab to move to the next field, where you enter the check number. You must press Tab after entering data for each of the following fields: the description or name of payee, the amount of payment, a memo (if you need to add one), and the category. When you have filled in all the data, click Save to complete the entry and lower your balance.

CHAPTER 14

To enter a deposit in the Quicken register: 327

You enter a deposit much as you enter a check, but you tab past the number field, enter a description of the source instead of a payee, and tab past the payment field so you can enter the amount of the deposit in the deposit field. You can use a category for a deposit if you get deposits regularly from the same source. When you click Save, your balance increases.

To write a check using Quicken: 330

If you don't have Quicken checks, you have to obtain them before you can start. Then choose Write Checks from the Account menu. When you see the check writing window, enter information in the date, payee, amount, address, memo, and category fields. Press Tab to move from field to field (if you press Return, Quicken thinks you are clicking the Save button). After filling all the fields, click the Save button to complete the transaction.

Do you need help with your financial affairs? You can't get cash advances from your Mac, but you can get help with the nitty-gritty chores of keeping your finances in order. Personal money managing applications make it simple to manage your checkbook and keep track of your financial situation. You can automate recurring transactions, print out checks, plan your budget, and check your net worth, all without having to scribble tiny ciphers in a giant double-entry ledger. And the Mac does all the calculating for you, so you can be sure your records are accurate when it comes time to prepare your tax returns.

The best personal finance applications make it easy to set up your check register and bookkeeping files. They automate repetitive tasks, but make it easy for you to enter the figures that vary month to month. You can keep simple records of where your money came from and how you spent it, or you can generate sophisticated reports to aid in financial planning.

Which Money Managing Application for You?

There is a wide range of applications that can help you with your personal finances. The simplest ones are just computerized checkbooks with the ability to print out checks and keep a tabulated register. The most advanced financial management applications can do specialized tasks for different types of financial management. Some can take care of small business needs like accounts payable and receivable, inventory control, and payroll. Other money managing applications can track investments and project their future values, based on detailed analysis of data you enter.

Bargain Budgeting Tools

Of the personal finance tools that cater to the penny-pincher, Quicken is the most popular, and for good reason. The interface and documentation are easy; anyone who can keep a check register and balance their checkbook can master the Quicken system. Checkbook II covers most of the same ground, and although the interface is not so intuitive, the program provides tools to design your own checks, and it has a database for addresses. But the basic jobs of recording cash flow and preparing records for tax purposes are much easier to handle in Quicken. Quicken can memorize your regular monthly payments and print out the checks for you, and it makes budgeting a clear and simple process, because the categories of transactions are so intuitive. For more information, see "Using Quicken" later in this chapter.

There are also special-purpose applications, such as MacIntax, that do a great job of preparing federal and some state tax forms. TurboTax is another tax-preparation application, but it is much less intuitive and direct; you have to be a spreadsheet whiz to get all your data entered. Both of these tax tools can accept input from Quicken and from the more sophisticated financial management applications.

High-Cost Financial Management Applications

The higher priced money managing applications aim at either the professionals who want investment portfolio management, or the small business people who want to take care of all their accounts, their payroll, and their

---

Product at a Glance

Quicken

Publisher:
Intuit, Inc.
Upgrades available

Requires:
Mac Plus or better
System 6.7 or later
2MB of RAM
1MB of free disk space required; 40MB hard drive recommended
Any Mac-compatible printer, although some print checks more easily than others

Description:
Quicken is the best personal accounting application for users who don't have a degree in bookkeeping, but who want to get better control of their finances. It can't do business tasks like payroll and invoicing, but for personal finances it is more than adequate. It is about as easy to use as a paper checkbook register, and it takes advantage of the Macintosh interface, so you don't have to learn any special skills to enter your checks and deposits, keep track of what you spend in different categories, and print out checks and reports. It can also memorize repeated transactions, so you don't have to enter data over and over each month. The documentation and support are also excellent.

inventory. Andrew Tobias's Managing Your Money (MYM) is the leader in the investment managing arena and the most expensive choice. Mind Your Own Business (MYOB) is a good example of the small business package. MacMoney is cheaper than either MYM or MYOB, and is somewhere between the two in features; it can be used as a personal finance tool like Quicken, but it has more power to calculate things like loan payments and the ability to generate color graphs. If you have a simple business, you may be able to get by with MacMoney. If you have a growing, varied business, MYOB would be a better choice. If you are developing an investment portfolio and are willing to do lots of data entry to make good projections and keep accurate records for taxes, get MYM and get busy.

Using Quicken

Quicken takes the pain out of writing checks and keeping financial records. You set up one or more accounts, then enter transactions, categorizing each deposit, check, and withdrawal so you can track it later. If you order personalized checks for your type of printer, you can print checks instead of writing them out. This saves a lot of time and effort, and keeps your records up-to-date automatically.

When your bank statement arrives, you just enter the information and Quicken reconciles the account for you. You can create a wide variety of both personal and business reports that display transactions by time period, category, class, payee, or account. At the end of the year, at tax time, you have the information you need at your fingertips.

Creating a File for Your Quicken Accounts

When you first open Quicken, you have to start an account. You can keep bank accounts, cash accounts, and credit card accounts with Quicken, but to start with, you open a standard bank account for checking.

This section and the ones that follow use a simple account as a model. You can create this test model to become familiar with how Quicken works before you start entering your real-life checkbook figures. Take the following steps to create a first account called Home Checking:

1. Double-click the Quicken icon, as shown in Figure 14.1, to start the application. What you see depends on whether the application has been used before.

   - If the application has never been opened on this disk, you see a message box asking if you're upgrading from an earlier version of Quicken. Click No. A dialog box for naming a new accounts file appears.
   - If the application has been opened before, you see the check register that was last open. For example, if you did the Quick Tour, you see one of the Sample Data accounts. Choose New from the File menu. In the small dialog box that opens, click New File. A dialog box for naming a new accounts file appears.

Figure 14.1
The Quicken icon

2. Enter a name for the file in the File for your accounts box. Click to put an X in the Home categories check box if there isn't one there already. Check the Business box too if you have both home and business accounts.

3. Click the New button. Quicken makes your file; a message box tells you how the category-copying is coming along. Then the Set Up New Account dialog box opens, as shown in Figure 14.2, but without the data filled in.

Using Quicken **323**

Figure 14.2
The Set Up New Account dialog box

```
Set Up New Account
Account Name: [C & T Checking]
Account Type:
   ● Bank Account      ○ Asset
   ○ Credit Card       ○ Liability
   ○ Cash
Opening Balance: [543.21]  as of: [11/22/93]
Note: Enter the ending balance from your last bank statement.

Description: [#0-314-04321]
(optional)
Credit Limit: [0.00]
(optional)

[ OK ]   [ Cancel ]   [ Notes ]
```

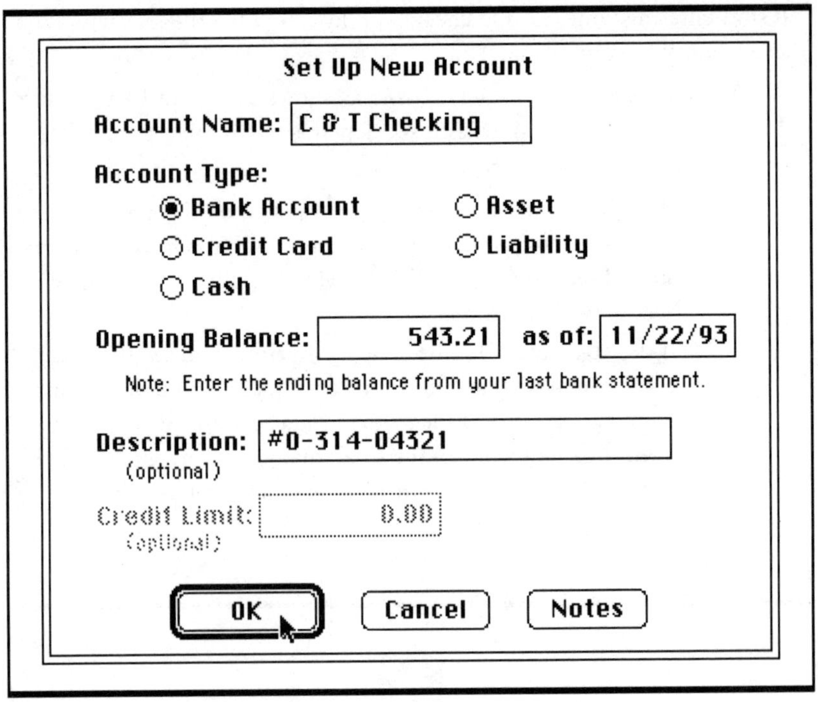

Opening a New Account

You are moving right along. You have created a file to keep all your accounts in, and now you are going right ahead and making your first account to put in that file.

1. Make sure you're looking at the Set Up New Account dialog box. Then enter an account name in the Account Name text box at the top. The name should tell what the account is for, or who uses it.
2. Leave the default Account Type selection at Bank Account. Press Tab to move to the next field.
3. Enter the opening balance of the account. This should be your ending balance from your last bank statement, and it should be reconciled.
4. Enter the date of the bank statement from which you took the ending balance.

5. Enter an account description, if you want; I put my account number here.
6. Click the Notes button at the bottom of the box if you want to add things like the bank's address and telephone number. Click OK in the Notes dialog box when you are finished.
7. Click OK in the Set Up New Account dialog box when you are satisfied with the entries. Quicken creates a new bank account and displays the account register as shown in Figure 14.3.

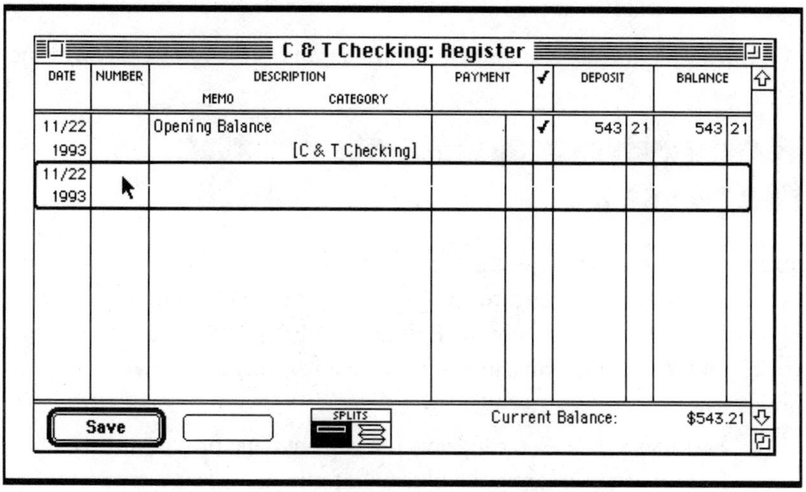

Figure 14.3
The Register window, showing a new checking account

DATE	NUMBER	DESCRIPTION MEMO CATEGORY	PAYMENT	✓	DEPOSIT	BALANCE
11/22 1993		Opening Balance [C & T Checking]		✓	543 21	543 21
11/22 1993						

Current Balance: $543.21

Using the Check Register

The register is a record of all the transactions that occur in an account. It looks like the paper check register you probably carry around attached to your checkbook, with entries for date and type of transaction, check number, description, amount, and account balance. There is also a column for a check mark to tell when a check or deposit has cleared.

Each account has a separate Quicken register. Although the register for different account types display different column headings, all registers work the same way.

The first empty transaction line in the register appears with a bold frame around it; this is the one you can fill in. You enter transactions in the register

Using Quicken **325**

by typing information in the fields; the fields are just like the spaces you see in your paper check register. Press Tab to move from field to field. When you write a check using Quicken rather than by hand, Quicken enters the check information in the register automatically. See "Writing Checks" later in this chapter for details.

Once you have entered some transactions as described in the section that follows, you can use the scroll bar to move through the register window. A date box appears next to the scroll bar when you drag the scroll box. The displayed date shows you the date of the transaction that will be selected if you release the scroll box at that point.

You can search for, change, or delete transactions in the register at any time.

Recording a Check in the Register

To enter a transaction in the register, you just fill in the fields. If a blank transaction is selected, as in Figure 14.3, just fill in the fields. If it's not selected, choose New Transaction from the Edit menu (⌘-N). Once you have selected the blank transaction, you can enter the data for a handwritten check to the grocery store.

1. Enter a date. You can leave the current date, or type any date you want. Pressing the plus (+) or minus (–) key increases or decreases the displayed date by one day. After entering the date, press Tab.

2. Enter a check number as shown in Figure 14.4. Press Tab to move on.

3. Enter the description. When recording a check, enter the name of the payee. Otherwise, enter a word or phrase that describes the transaction. Press Tab to continue.

4. Enter the amount of the payment. That's the amount of the check in this case. Use this field for bank fees and withdrawals, too. Press the period key or spacebar to move from the Dollars field to the Cents field. Press Tab to go to the Memo field.

5. Enter a memo if you need to. This field is optional. You can use it to indicate an account or invoice number. Press Tab to go on.

6. Enter a category. You can type it in, or choose Category & Transfer List from the Shortcuts menu, then find the category that fits and double-click it. See "Using Categories" later in this chapter for details.

7. Click Save to complete the entry, as in Figure 14.4. Quicken does the arithmetic for you, and selects the next transaction line.

Skip the little field with the check at the head of the column (the one to the right of the Payment field). It is for checking off cleared checks as you reconcile your account when you get your monthly statement from the bank.

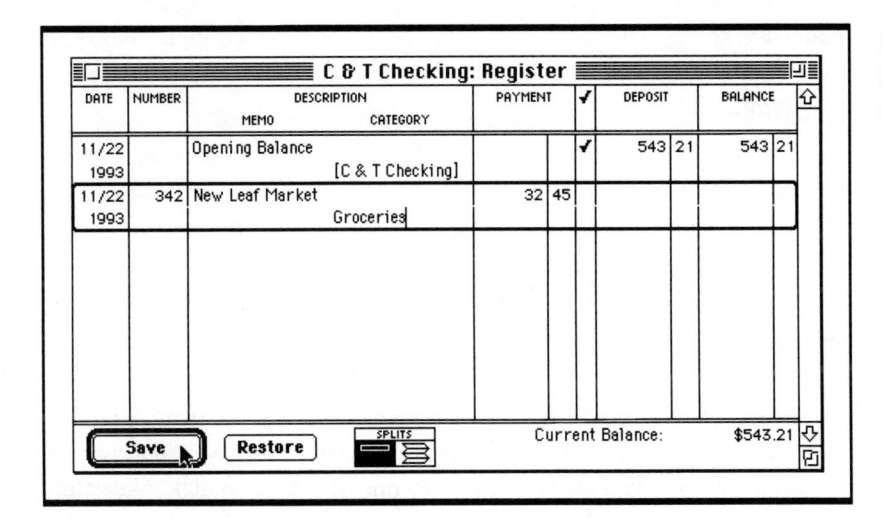

Figure 14.4
Recording a check in the register

Entering Deposits in the Register

To get a little more practice, enter a couple of deposits in the register. Tab past the number field and enter a description instead of a payee. Tab past the payment field and enter the amount of the deposit. If you need to specify where the deposit came from, and it is a regular source of income, you can make a category for it, as described in "Setting Up a Category" later in this chapter. Click Save when you are done entering each deposit. Quicken does the math, and your balance goes up. A nice thing, even though it never lasts.

Correcting Mistakes in the Register

If you make a little mistake of just a couple of characters in a field, press the Delete key to back up over them, then type in the correction. If you decide a whole field is wrong, choose Undo from the Edit menu, then start the field entry from scratch. If you decide a whole transaction is wrong and you haven't saved it yet, click the Restore button instead of Save. Quicken clears all the fields except the date, so you can start over.

If you decide a transaction is wrong after you have saved it, but before any money has changed hands, you can choose Delete Transaction from the Edit menu. Quicken puts up a little dialog box to make sure you want to do this risky thing. Click Delete if you do.

If you write a check and then void it after entering the transaction in the register, just select the transaction and choose Void Transaction from the Edit menu. Quicken undoes the change in your balance and puts the word *VOID* in front of the name of the payee.

Using Categories

The secret to controlling your finances is seeing the patterns that are hidden in all the detailed information in your accounts. The Category field is the tool that helps you see the patterns. Quicken uses the Category field to sort information into reports. You can create reports at any time to see how you are doing on the different categories of income and expenditure.

Categories let you track expenditures for specific items. For example, you might want to see how much money you have spent fixing up the old car you are driving. If you categorize these checks as car-repair transactions you can create a report showing all the money you have poured into that old heap. To limit yourself, you can create a budget and then compare budgeted items to actual amounts.

Your needs determine the categories you set up. Think carefully about the categories you want. If you want to compare what you budget with what you actually spend, you need a category for each comparison you want to make.

Quicken provides you with two lists of categories—one for home, and one for business. You can use these lists if you want, or you can create your own list of categories.

Choosing a Category or Transfer Account

When the cursor is in the Category field in the register, you can either type in the category if you know it, or you can choose it from a list. To get at the list, choose Category & Transfer List from the Shortcuts menu (⌘-L) or double-click on the Category field. Select a category from the list by double-clicking on the category name, as shown in Figure 14.5. Quicken copies the category name to the Category field.

If you can't find a category that the check fits into exactly, you can create your own category. See the section that follows for information on how to do this.

You can also specify transfers of money from one account to another by choosing the name of an account from the list. You must have several accounts set up to use this feature. See the chapter on transferring money between accounts in the Quicken *User Manual* for details.

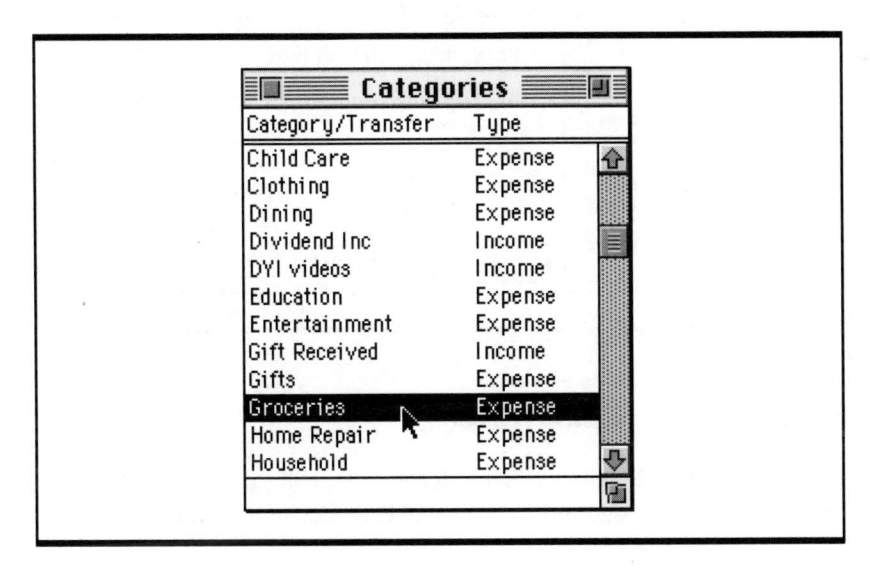

Figure 14.5
Choosing a category from the Category & Transfer list

Using Quicken

Setting Up a Category and Adding It to the List

Use the following steps to define a new category and add it to the list so you can choose it for future checks or deposits.

1. Choose Set Up Categories from the Shortcuts menu. The Set Up Categories dialog box appears.
2. Enter a category name, and if you want, enter a description.
3. Specify whether the category is an expense or income item and if you want it stored as a tax-related item (anything you have to report for taxes is tax-related).
4. Click Save to add the new category to the list, as shown in Figure 14.6. Click Restore to discard it if you change your mind, then click the close box to exit the dialog.

If you type a nonexistent category name in the Category field on the register, Quicken tells you the category cannot be found, and offers you three options: select another category from the list, set up this category, or cancel.

Figure 14.6
Setting up a new category

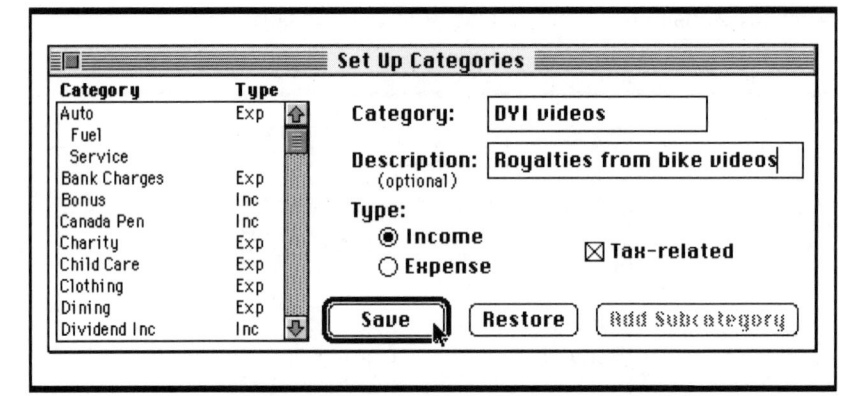

Writing Checks

If you have ordered Quicken checks for your type of printer, you can make out a check on your Mac and Quicken will enter the information in the check

330 *Chapter 14: Managing Personal Finances*

register and print the check for you. To do this, follow these steps:

1. Choose Write Checks from the Account menu (⌘-J). A blank check appears in a window.
2. Change the date if you need to. Press Tab to move to the next field.
3. Enter the payee name in the Pay to the Order of field and press Tab.
4. Enter the amount of the check in the $ field and press Tab. Quicken fills in the next field for you. The cursor goes on to the Address box.
5. Fill in the payee name and address if you intend to mail the check in a Quicken window envelope.
6. Press Tab to go on to the memo field where you can enter memo information if you want. You might want to give the payee additional information—memo information is printed on the check. Or, you might want the information for your own records. Press Tab to go on to the Category field.
7. Assign a category, in the same way you do for any other transaction.
8. Click Save when you are finished, as in Figure 14.7. If you click Restore, the transaction is deleted.
9. Click the close box when you are done. The register window returns.

Warning

After typing the name, press Tab to move down to the next line of the address. If you press the Return key, the check is saved and a new blank appears.

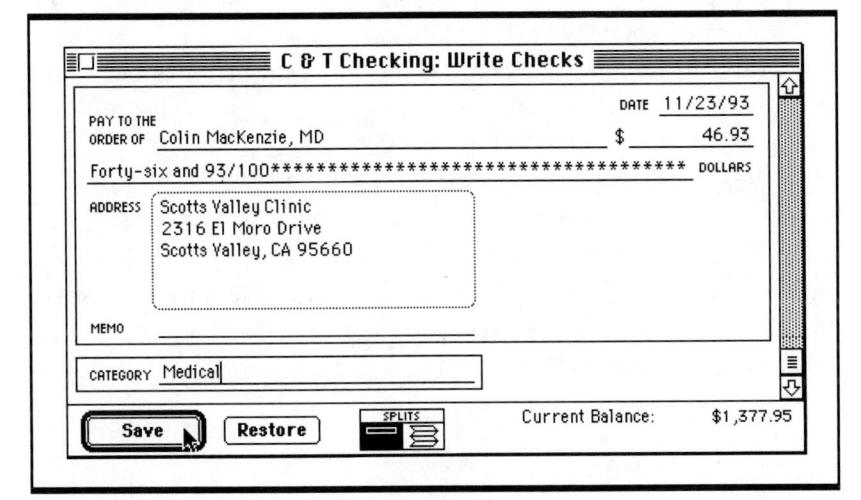

Figure 14.7
Writing a check

Using Quicken **331**

Your check is recorded in the register. You can make corrections in the register and they will appear on the check, if you haven't printed it yet. If you saved a check with mistakes on it, you can select it in the register and choose Delete Transaction from the Edit menu, then confirm the deletion in the dialog box.

Memorizing Transactions

If there are checks that you write every month, you can put them on a Memorized Transaction List. Then you don't have to reenter the information every month. If the amount of the check varies from month to month, you can leave the amount blank and fill that field in each time you make out a check.

To create a memorized transaction, use the following procedure:

1. Choose Write Checks from the Account menu.
2. In the Write Checks window, enter the check exactly as you want it to appear each month. For example, if the amount is likely to change every month, as it usually does with the telephone bill, leave the amount blank.
3. Choose Memorize Transaction from the Shortcuts menu (⌘-M). Quicken memorizes the transaction.
4. You can complete the check and save it as a specific transaction; for example, if you did not enter an amount, you can do so now.

Once you've created your memorized transactions, you can use them to write checks by following these steps:

1. Get ready to write a check. If you are already in the Write Checks window, you're set. If you're in the register, choose New Transaction from the Edit menu.
2. Choose Memorized Transaction List from the Shortcuts menu.
3. When the list displays, double-click on the item you want. Quicken creates the check for you.

If you decide the memorized transaction is not needed after all, you can select it in the register and choose Delete Transaction from the Edit menu, as long as you haven't printed out the check yet.

You can change information in a memorized transaction at any time by choosing Edit Transaction from the Edit menu (⌘-E). Just make your changes and click Replace in the dialog box.

To delete a memorized transaction, choose Memorized Transactions List from the Shortcuts menu. Then select the transaction you want to delete and choose Delete Memorized Transaction from the Edit menu (⌘-D). Click OK in the displayed dialog box to confirm.

Printing

You can use Quicken to print custom Quicken checks or checks made by other companies. You can also print reports that give an overall picture of your finances. How you do this depends on the kind of printer you have. The following sections tell you how to do some of the most common printing jobs in Quicken. Read your Quicken manual for more information on printer setup.

Printing Checks on a Page-Oriented Printer

Use the following procedure to prepare for printing and print checks by the page:

1. Load the checks in the paper tray. Make sure the checks are face up. The top of the checks should face into the printer. If you are printing to an Apple Personal LaserWriter or HP LaserJet IIP, load the checks face down. Since the printer pulls the top page off the pile, you have to reverse the order of the checks so the first sheet is on top when you're looking at the checks face down.
2. Choose Check Setup from the File menu. Make sure that the settings match the paper you have for checks and that the style suits you.
3. Choose Print Checks from the File menu and fill in the Print Checks dialog box.
4. Click OK, as shown in Figure 14.8.
5. Check the settings in the Print dialog box and click OK to begin printing.

Figure 14.8

Printing checks to a page printer

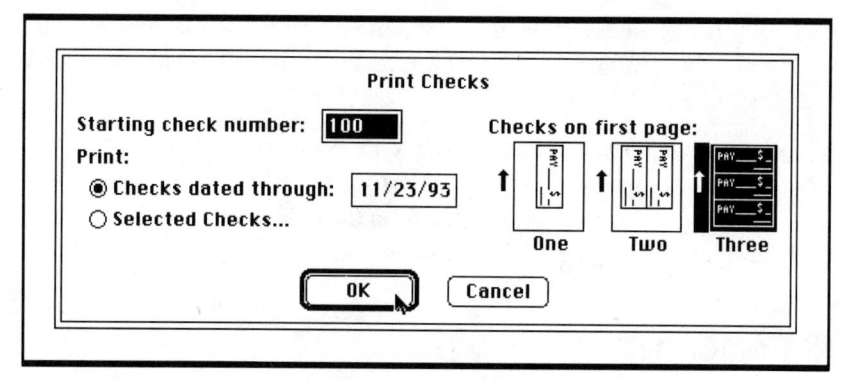

```
┌─────────────────────────────────────────────────────────┐
│                     Print Checks                         │
│                                                          │
│  Starting check number: [100]   Checks on first page:    │
│  Print:                                                  │
│  ⦿ Checks dated through: [11/23/93]  ↑  ↑               │
│  ○ Selected Checks...                                    │
│                                      One  Two  Three     │
│         ( OK )   ( Cancel )                              │
└─────────────────────────────────────────────────────────┘
```

6. After your checks print, Quicken asks if they printed correctly. If they did, click Yes. If they didn't, click No and start the procedure over.

Printing Checks on a Continuous-Feed Printer

It's probably a good idea to do a test run before actually printing the checks, to make sure everything is lined up correctly. Then follow these steps to print your checks.

1. Load the checks in your ImageWriter.

2. Choose Print Checks from the File menu and fill in the Print Checks dialog box. If you are printing a sample check, click the Check Alignment Test button.

3. Click OK.

4. Position the top check. If you're printing to an ImageWriter I, align the fifth line of the check with the top of the type head. Snap the roller into place to hold the checks in place. If you're printing to an ImageWriter II, align the top of the check with the top of the plastic guard in front of the print head. If you're printing to an ImageWriter LQ, align the top of the check with the top of the print head.

5. Click OK.

If the checks do not come out with the text aligned correctly, start the paper again, adjusting the alignment to correct the problem.

Creating Reports

You can also use Quicken to create reports based on your transactions. Entering transactions in the register, whether by hand or by writing checks, creates a database of all your transactions that you can sort and summarize in a report.

For example, to create a summary of your tax-related information, first make sure you've designated your tax-related items. Then open the Reports menu and highlight Home. Move into the Home reports submenu and select Tax Summary. A dialog box appears. Specify the information you want the report to contain by filling out the dialog box. Quicken searches the account(s) you specified, collects the information you requested and displays it, as shown in Figure 14.9.

You can print out a report by choosing Print Report from the File menu when the report is in view. Select any options you need in the Print dialog box, and click the Page Preview button to see how the report will look. Click Print in the Preview window to begin printing.

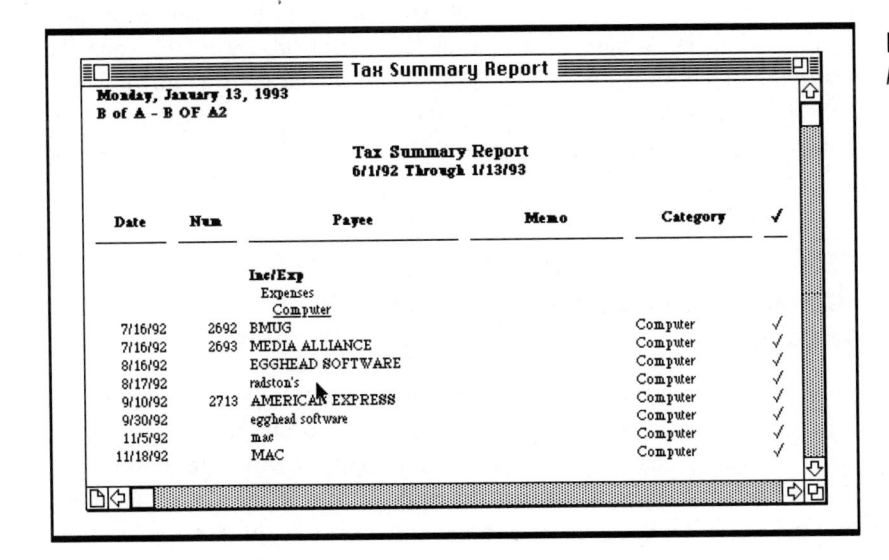

Figure 14.9
A tax summary report

Using Quicken **335**

Troubleshooting Problems with Quicken

The following subsections cover the types of problems you are most likely to encounter when using Quicken to keep your financial records.

Can't Enter a Transfer from One Account to Another without Entering the Data Twice

Quicken actually has a nifty way to transfer money and write both the withdrawal and the deposit for a transaction at the same time. You just write up the transaction for the withdrawal, then choose the name of the account you are depositing in the Category field of the transaction.

For example, to transfer money from your checking account to your savings account, first make sure you have created both accounts in the same file, then write out a check. When you get to the Category field, choose Category & Transfer List from the Shortcuts menu, then scroll all the way down to the bottom of the list and choose the name of your savings account. Bingo; two transactions appear in the registers: one for your check and one for the deposit.

Can't Change a Category or Account Name, or Can't Delete a Category or Account

You can't make big changes to categories or accounts while you are looking at transactions in the register. You have to list the accounts or categories first. For example, to change the name of an account or to delete it, you first choose Account List from the Account menu. When the list of your accounts appears, select the name of the account you want to edit, then choose Edit Account from the Edit menu. The Account Info dialog box opens. You can edit the name, the type, and the description of the account, then click OK. If you want to delete an account after closing it, just select the account name in the Account List, then choose Delete Account from the Edit menu.

I Keep Saving My Checks When All I Want to Do Is Move to the Next Field

You have to press the Tab key to move from field to field when entering data in the check-writing fields. If you press the Return key, Quicken thinks you are giving the keyboard shortcut for clicking the Save button. Most annoying. I really have a strong tendency to do it when I'm entering the address at the bottom of the check.

The answer is easy. Choose Other Settings from the Options menu, and when the dialog box opens, click in the check box next to the option that says "Pressing Return tabs to the next field." Click OK, and you can go ahead and enter data in checks without having to worry about those premature saves.

Can't Figure Out What to Do with Categories

If you aren't an accountant, you may wonder what all those categories are about. Why fill in a category for a check, if you have already written in what the money went to in the description field? Or why have a category for income, if you know where the money is coming from?

The answer is that the description field is for telling WHO the money went to or came from. A category is a way of recording WHAT you spend the money on, or what type of source it came from.

Categories are useful because you can tell Quicken what you are spending each check on, then make up a report at the end of a month and see how much you spent in each category. Usually, all you need to do is see how much money you have been spending on things, and then you'll learn to budget more wisely.

Fifteen

Integrating Your Work

Featuring

- How to cut, copy and paste via the Clipboard
- How to copy and paste things to and from the Scrapbook
- How to correct Clipboard mistakes
- How to update items with dynamic links
- How to publish editions and subscribe to them
- How to use frames in ClarisWorks
- Troubleshooting problems with data integration

First Steps

To copy or cut part of a document to a different place: 342

> Select the block of text, graphics, or other data, and choose Copy or Cut from the Edit menu. Scroll to the location where you want to place the data, or click in the window where you want to place it. Click with the I-beam or drag with the pointer to define where the data will be placed. Finally, choose Paste from the Edit menu to insert the copied or cut data.

To place an item in the Scrapbook: 348

> Select and copy the item to get it into the Clipboard. Choose Scrapbook from the Apple menu and choose Paste to add the item on the top page. You can cut and paste items from page to page in the Scrapbook to rearrange their order.

To paste an item from the Scrapbook into a document: 349

> Open the document you want to paste the item into, then open the Scrapbook by choosing Scrapbook from the Apple menu. Scroll through the Scrapbook to the item you want, and choose Copy from the Edit menu to copy the item into the Clipboard. Then click in the window of the target document, place the insertion point, and choose Paste from the Edit menu.

CHAPTER 15

To create a publisher item in an application that supports publish and subscribe: 353

Select the item first, then choose Create Publisher from the Edit menu. In the dialog box that appears, enter a name for the edition file that will contain the publisher item, then click the Publish button. The publisher item appears on the desktop with a gray textured border.

To subscribe to a published item in an application that supports publish and subscribe: 353

Open the document in which you want the published item to appear, and place the insertion point. Then choose Subscribe to from the Edit menu. In the dialog box that appears, find the edition file in the file list and select it. Click the Subscribe button and the data in the file appears in your document; if you select it, it displays a linked pattern border.

To use a frame in Claris Works: 357

Open a document for any of the environments. In the window of the open document, choose Show Tools from the View menu, then click on any of the top tools for drawing, text, spreadsheets, or painting. Drag the pointer for that tool to make a frame, and inside that frame you can use all of the functions of the environment. You can also click on the pointer tool and move the whole frame inside the document where you placed it.

Once you have had some experience creating documents in two or three different applications, you will begin to see opportunities to include data from one type of document inside other types of documents. For example, you might want to include a graph from your spreadsheet application inside a financial report you are creating with a word processor. Or you might want to put titles you create in your word processor under graphics you create in your drawing application. The Mac makes it as easy to move things from one application to another as it is to move parts of the same document around. Practically any kind of data you can see in one document, you can move to another document, as long as the two documents have compatible formats.

This chapter explains the different ways you can integrate data of different types within a single document and transfer data into documents created by other applications or even other users. The first section describes how to move and remove parts of documents by means of the Clipboard. The second section describes linking documents created by the same and different applications. The third section explains the Publish and Subscribe features found in many Mac applications running under System 7, which allow the exchange of information between documents belonging to different users and created by different applications. The fourth section describes integrated applications and how to use frames in Claris Works to combine both text and drawing elements in one document.

Cutting, Copying, and Pasting

This section describes how to move and remove parts of your documents. It explains the Clipboard and tells how to use it to cut, copy, and paste things, either inside a document, or between documents, or between documents created by compatible applications.

Introducing the Clipboard

Your Mac provides a special temporary storage place called the *Clipboard*. When you cut something out of a document, it is held in the Clipboard. You can undo the cut and bring the item back from the Clipboard, or you can paste the item in the Clipboard someplace else. You can also copy an item in a document, which leaves it where it is and places a duplicate in the Clipboard. This copy can be pasted into the same document or other documents.

The only odd thing about the Clipboard is that normally you don't ever see it. You can see what's in it in the Finder and in some applications (choose Show Clipboard in the Edit, Window, or View menu) but otherwise, the Clipboard does its work behind the scenes. You cut, copy, and paste without ever having direct contact with the Clipboard. If you are like me, and you are curious about where the heck the Clipboard actually is, just go to the Finder and open the System Folder. There it is. Double-click the icon, and you get a window showing what's in it.

Whenever you are cutting and copying things into the Clipboard or pasting things out of it, keep in mind that the Clipboard can only hold one item at a time. If you copy an item into the Clipboard so you can paste it somewhere else, but then cut something else before you get around to pasting, the copied item will be lost, and the cut item will be all that is left in the Clipboard. For a way to recover from this error, see the Troubleshooting section at the end of this chapter.

Although the Clipboard holds only one item at a time, you can paste that item as many times as you want. Pasting does not remove the item from the Clipboard. It will stay there until you either cut or copy something else, or shut down your Mac.

Cutting and Pasting to Move Parts of Documents

To move part of a document, you select it and cut it out of its original place, then move to the new place and paste it in. For example, if you want to move a sentence that seems out of place, use this procedure:

1. Select the sentence that's out of place by dragging the I-beam over it, as shown in Figure 15.1. (In graphics applications, drag a selection rectangle or lasso around the image, or click on it if it is a selectable object.)
2. Choose Cut from the Edit menu, or press ⌘-X.
3. Place the insertion point where you want to paste the text, as in Figure 15.2. (If you are placing something in a graphics application, scroll the window until you can see the spot where you want to paste the item.)

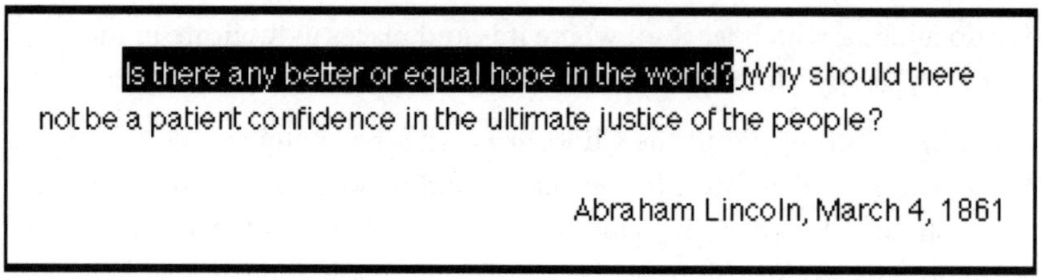

Figure 15.1
Selecting text to move

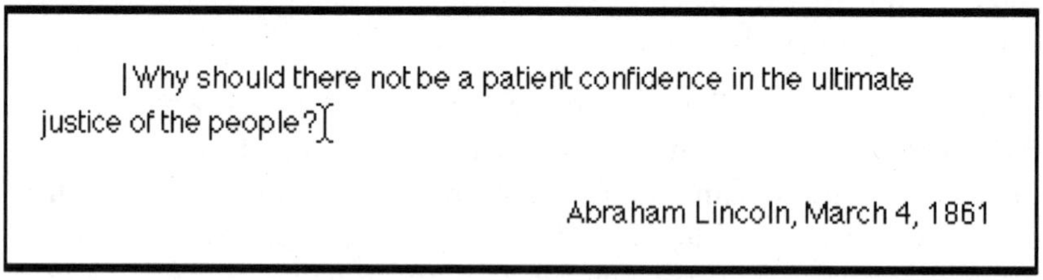

> Is there any better or equal hope in the world? Why should there not be a patient confidence in the ultimate justice of the people?
>
> Abraham Lincoln, March 4, 1861

Figure 15.2
Placing the insertion point for a paste

> |Why should there not be a patient confidence in the ultimate justice of the people?
>
> Abraham Lincoln, March 4, 1861

4. Choose Paste from the Edit menu, or press ⌘-V. The new text appears, as in Figure 15.3.

5. In a bitmapped graphics application, drag the pasted item to the place where you want it. In a text or object-oriented application, adjust the pasted text style, or the surrounding text and images, so the old blends well with the new.

This procedure works for cutting items out of one document and pasting them into another one, too. If you have two or more documents open when using an application, make your cut in one window, then click in the second window, or choose the second window from the Windows menu. Find the place where you want to paste the item in the second window and paste it as described above.

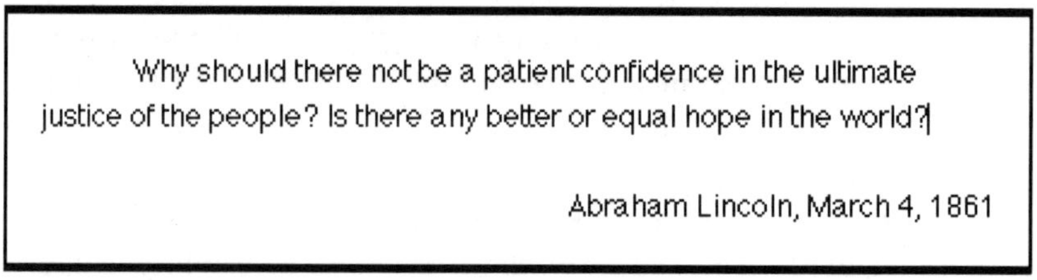

Figure 15.3
The text moved to the right place

> Why should there not be a patient confidence in the ultimate justice of the people? Is there any better or equal hope in the world?|
>
> Abraham Lincoln, March 4, 1861

344 *Chapter 15: Integrating Your Work*

One minor problem with cutting and pasting from one document to another: The style of the cut and pasted text usually stays the same, so the newly pasted stuff, like text, for example, may look different from the stuff all around it. To fix this, select the pasted text, then apply the style of the surrounding text to it. If you have styles like those in Word, you can just choose Style from the Format menu, choose the surrounding text's style from the list, then click OK. Otherwise you have to match the surrounding text by choosing each attribute from the Font and Format menus. PageMaker is an exception to this rule. If you use the pointer tool to place a text block, it keeps its size, shape, and style. If you use the text tool, the pasted text block assumes the size, shape, and style of the stuff that's surrounding it. A fine thing, PageMaker.

Copying and Pasting

The procedure for copying and pasting items in a document or from one document to another in the same application is just the same as that for cutting and pasting. The only difference is that the original item stays in place when you choose Copy from the Edit menu or press ⌘-C.

Copying Parts of Documents between Applications

To move items from a document created by one application to a document created by a different application requires a little more preparation and care than moving things around in the same application. It is better to do the moving process by copying items rather than cutting them, since a moved item may not come out exactly the same if you try to move it back to the application that created it. Take these steps to move items between different applications:

1. Make sure the applications have compatible formats. If you are copying items from one bitmapped graphic application to another, you will not have much trouble. But if you are trying to move an item from an object-oriented graphics application to a text processing application, you may need to take special preparatory steps. See Appendix A and see your applications' documentation for more information.

2. Open both applications, then open the origin document, which has the item you want to move, and the destination document, where you want to paste the item. For example, I might open SuperPaint and Word, as in Figure 15.4.
3. Select the item in the origin document, as the graphic border pattern is selected in the SuperPaint window in Figure 15.4.
4. Choose Copy from the Edit menu or press ⌘-C. Since Super-Paint is just working with a bitmap, all I have to do is choose Copy from the File menu in the sample shown. But you may have to enter a special command to copy the format in a certain way; for instance, in order to copy something from a PostScript graphics application to a word processing application, you must press the Option key when you choose Copy from the Edit menu.
5. Switch to the destination application and document. You can choose the destination application's icon in the Applications menu, or you can click in the window of the destination document. Window clicking sometimes confuses the application, so I normally go via the Applications menu.

Figure 15.4
Selecting a graphic to copy

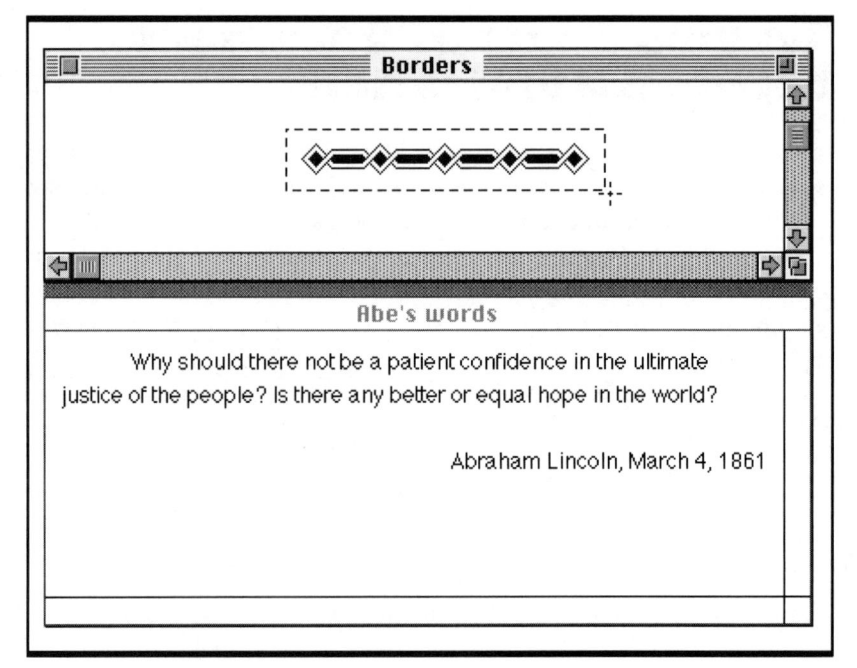

6. Place the insertion point or position the window where you want to place the item. In Figure 15.5 I placed the I-beam where I want the border to show up.

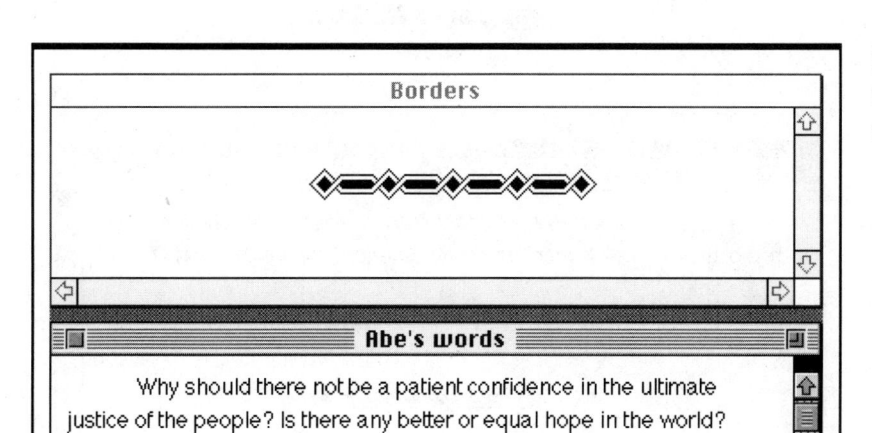

Figure 15.5
Placing the insertion point for a graphic

7. Choose Paste from the Edit menu or press ⌘-V. Your copied item appears, as shown in Figure 15.6.

If the item isn't quite in the right place, you can often move it with tabs. In Microsoft Word you can change the size and shape of placed graphics by selecting them and moving the corner handles in and out.

If the item does not appear, or if a blank space the size of the item appears in the destination document, see the Troubleshooting section at the end of this chapter.

Cutting, Copying, and Pasting **347**

Figure 15.6
The placed graphic

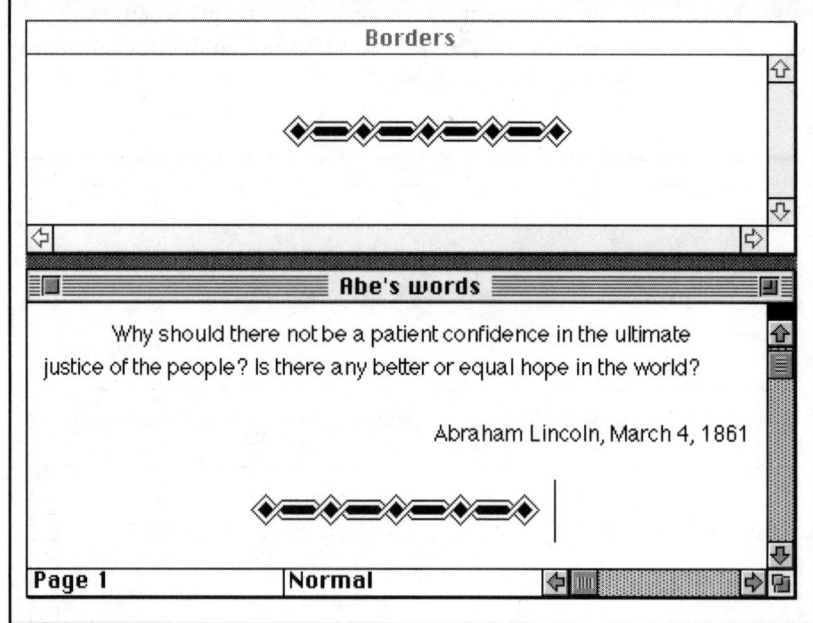

Using the Scrapbook

The Scrapbook is an Apple menu item you can use to store things you want to have on hand to paste into documents over and over. It is a permanent storage place, unlike the temporary Clipboard. Use these steps to put an item into the Scrapbook:

1. Copy the item from a document into the Clipboard.
2. Choose Scrapbook from the Apple menu. The Scrapbook opens, with the item on the current page showing. You can scroll to a different page if you want. It's best to leave your most-copied item on the front page.
3. Paste the new item onto a page; it takes over that page and moves the other items in the Scrapbook back a page. You can cut and paste items from page to page in the Scrapbook if you want to rearrange their order.

You can leave the Scrapbook window open and switch to other applications, then choose Scrapbook from the Applications menu to get back to the Scrapbook when you need it.

To paste an item from the Scrapbook into a document, follow these steps:

1. Open the document you want to paste the item into, then open the Scrapbook.
2. Scroll through the Scrapbook to the item you want to paste.
3. Copy the item from the Scrapbook to the Clipboard; you do not need to select it to do this.
4. Click in the document window, or choose the application for the document in the Applications menu to make it active.
5. Paste the item into the document and adjust the surrounding text or images to blend well with the pasted item.

Figure 15.7 shows the path an item can take from an origin document to a destination document, by way of the Clipboard and the Scrapbook.

If you do a lot of cutting and pasting, especially if you are designing page layouts, you may find the Scrapbook cumbersome. You can purchase other desk accessories, such as SmartScrap or ClickPaste, that serve the same purpose and provide sizing and hierarchical storage functions.

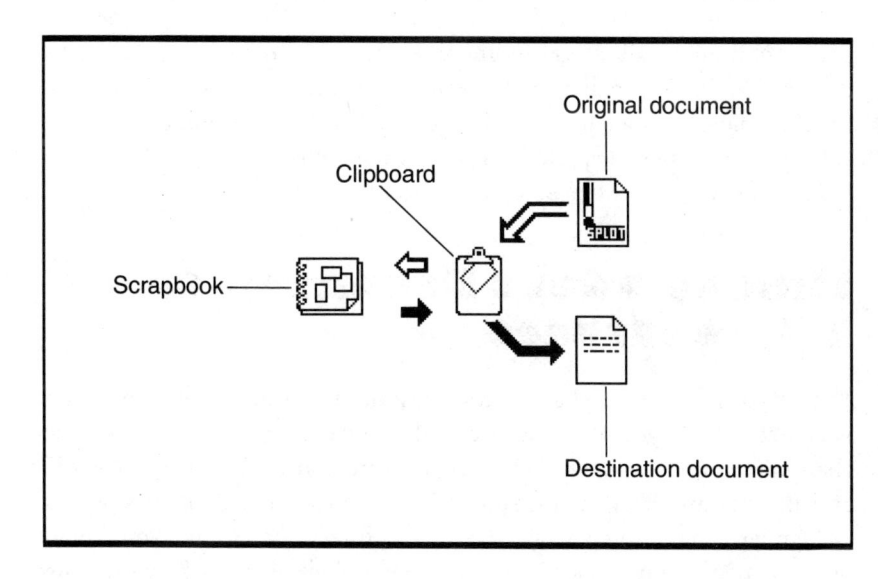

Figure 15.7
A way to cut and paste through the Clipboard and the Scrapbook

Cutting, Copying, and Pasting

Undoing Clipboard Mistakes

If you ever cut an item from a document and realize it was a mistake, you can put the item back by choosing Undo Cut from the Edit menu or pressing ⌘-Z. If you do something else after the mistaken cut, you can still go back to the place where you made the mistake and paste the item off the Clipboard. As long as you haven't cut or copied anything else into the Clipboard, the item you cut by mistake will still be there.

> **Note**
> Items that are replaced in the Clipboard memory of the Mac are held in a secret storage spot called the Undo buffer.

You can even recover something you cut just *after* copying or cutting another item into the Clipboard. Choose Undo from the Edit menu or press ⌘-Z to undo the last cut or copy; the Clipboard is restored to the previous item, the one you want to recover. Go back to the place where you mistakenly cut the item and paste it back into your document.

Dynamic Updating with Links

Some applications allow you to link one document to another, so that the data in a *dependent* document will update automatically when corresponding data in a *supporting* document is changed. Similar forms of linking are available in several different application groups, but in this section, I will describe linking as it works in Microsoft products such as Excel and Word.

Linking a Text Document to a Spreadsheet

You can copy and paste a chart from a spreadsheet into many word processing documents, but if you are using Microsoft Word and Excel, you can link the chart in your text document to the original spreadsheet document, so whenever there is any change in the spreadsheet, such as a bunch of sales figures changing when the company has a good month, the chart in the Word document is updated automatically. The following procedure tells how to create the link so the word processing document is dependent on the spreadsheet document.

1. Open Excel and open the supporting document, then display the chart you want to copy into the Word document.
2. Select the whole chart; first double-click in the middle of it to go into chart mode, then choose Select Chart from the Chart menu (is that redundant, or what?). Things should look something like Figure 15.8.

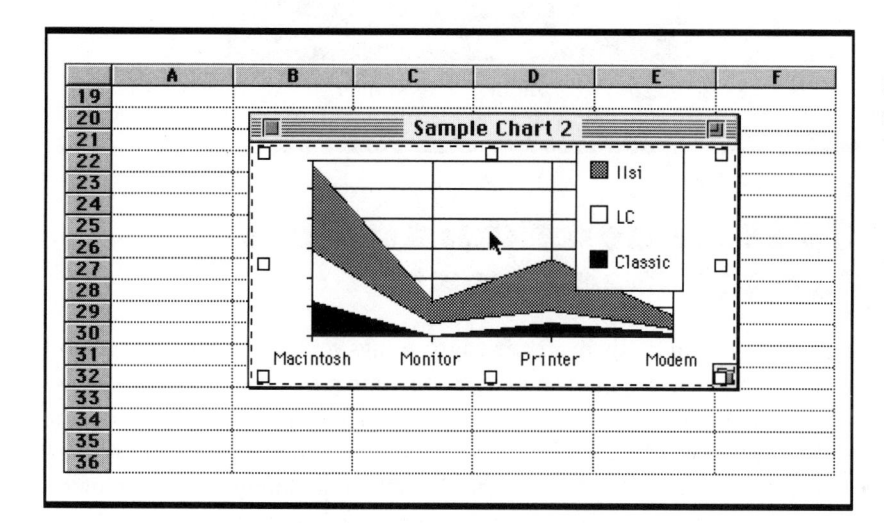

Figure 15.8
Selecting a chart in a supporting document

3. Choose Copy from the Edit menu.
4. Switch over into your Word document and place the I-beam where you want to place the chart.
5. Choose Paste Special from the Edit menu. When the dialog box opens, click the Paste Link button. The chart appears in your Word document, as shown in Figure 15.9.
6. Now, if you want to see magic, go back to Excel, update a number somewhere deep in the spreadsheet, then check out the chart both in Excel and in your Word document. Yow.

Figure 15.9
A linked chart in a dependent Word document

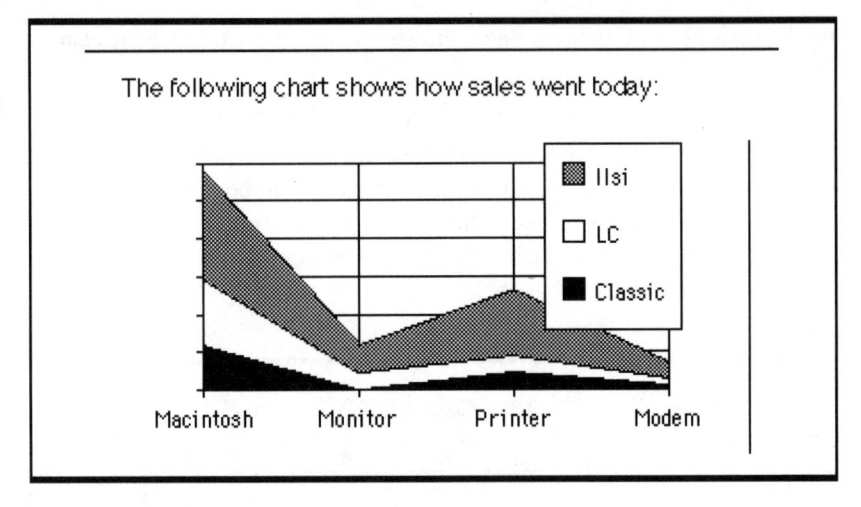

Special Considerations for Linked Documents

As you might expect, there are a few little things you have to take care of with this automatic updating business. For one thing, the whole scenario works best if both the supporting document and the dependent document are in the same folder. So if you are working on a project and you have the supporting document (like, the Excel spreadsheet in my sample) in that project's folder, just put the dependent document (the Word one, in my sample) in that same folder. And if you ever update the supporting document when both it and the dependent document are open, save the supporting document first, then save the dependent document. If you save the dependent document first, the references can get mixed up.

Publishing and Subscribing to Parts of Documents

Some applications allow you to create items that automatically update after being copied to other documents. It is as if these applications can cut and paste new information into your documents all by themselves. Applications with this automatic updating feature will have commands such as Create Publisher and Subscribe to in the Edit menu.

When you make a change in a document with a *publisher* item, the change will also occur in any *subscriber* items that have been placed in other documents. This automatic updating is especially useful if there are several users on a network relying on the same information in different documents. Each user can work on a part of a project and publish the parts of their documents that need to be put into the final document for the whole group. Other users can see the updated version of the final document as work by each member progresses. They can also subscribe to specific parts of each other's work in order to keep abreast of day-to-day developments without having to exchange barrages of memos or phone calls.

For example, if a construction team is working on a bid for a big job, one of the people would make a spreadsheet of estimates, in Excel perhaps, and another might write up a proposal in Word. Both of these people could publish and subscribe to each other's work. The manager might subscribe to both the spreadsheet and the text proposal, to see how things are going without having to pester the team workers.

To create a publisher item and an *edition* file that contains the updatable information, follow these steps:

1. Select the item you want to make into a publisher. For example, you might have a table of time and cost estimates for making a construction bid.
2. Choose Create Publisher from the Edit menu. The Publisher dialog box opens.
3. Enter a name for the edition file that will contain the Publisher item. For example, the edition file could be called Estimates.
4. Click the Publish button.

The edition file appears on the desktop, with a gray textured border, as shown in Figure 15.10.

To tap into the updatable information in the edition file, follow these steps:

1. Open a document in which you want the information from the edition to appear, and place the insertion point.

Figure 15.10
An Estimates edition file, with its publisher and subscribers

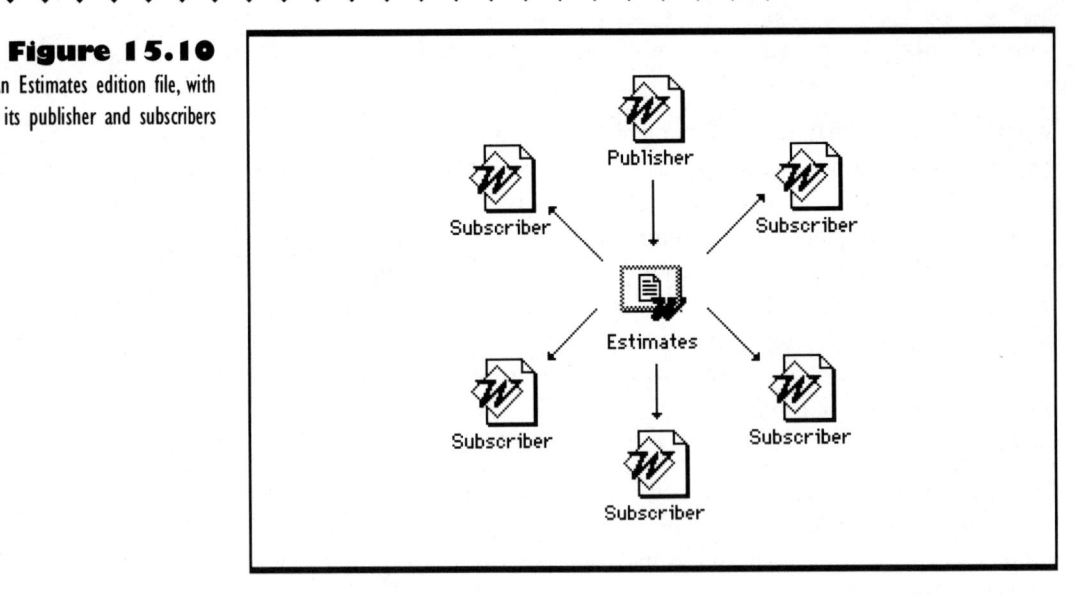

2. Choose Subscribe to from the Edit menu. A dialog box opens, with a list of files; the edition files have a gray rectangle icon. For example, the Estimates edition file would have a gray rectangle icon next to it in the file list box.
3. Find the edition file you want and select it.
4. Click the Subscribe button. The item in the edition file appears in your document; if you select this item, it displays a linked pattern border. The linked pattern border does not show if the item already has a border, so if you subscribe to a table like the estimates one, you will not see the tell-tale border.

Use the Publisher options and Subscriber options commands in the Edit menu to update editions automatically or manually, to see when the edition was updated last, to cancel updating, or to locate and open the publisher document. For more information on using published information, see the *Macintosh Networking Reference*.

Using Integrated Applications

Some applications allow you to work with different tool elements, such as word processing or drawing tools, without having to start different programs and switch between them. These are often called *integrated* applications because they put all the tools for different types of work in one program.

Typical integrated applications have a word processor, a draw program, a spreadsheet, and/or a database. If you're just starting with the Mac and want to work with several types of applications, an integrated package can seem like a great bargain when you compare its cost of the integrated application with the prices of all the separate applications. And it can be a good deal, as long as you don't have the specific and complex requirements in any one area. On the other hand, the tools available in integrated applications are adequate, but fairly simple; if you do work that requires lots of powerful special features from an application, you may find that the part of the integrated application that you need most is too limited. This can get frustrating, especially if you know that there is a stand-alone application that offers all the features you need.

Integrated applications are best for mixing different kinds of documents. In most integrated applications, you can work with one tool or part, such as the drawing part, then copy stuff into a document created by another tool or part, such as the word processing part. This is how Microsoft Works and Word-Perfect Works (formerly BeagleWorks) are set up. The only problem with such integrated applications is that once you have placed an item, you can't edit it without going back into the tool or part that created it. You have to edit the original document, then do a second copy-and-paste procedure to put the edited data in place. For example, if you want to change a detail in the drawing you placed in your word processing document, you have to go find the drawing document, edit it with the drawing tools, then select the edited drawing, copy it to the Clipboard, go back into your word processing document, and finally paste the edited drawing over the original version there. Not too tidy a procedure.

In some of the integrated applications you can use publish and subscribe to keep your pasted items up to date, but you still have to go find the original to edit it, and then you have all those editions files floating around and making life in the Finder more complicated.

But there is one integrated application, Claris Works, that lets you work with different tools all in one document. Claris Works does the best job of putting all the tools at your fingertips without making things seem too complicated or clumsy. Claris Works is also handy because it does not use much RAM or hard disk space; this makes it ideal for PowerBook users and people with compact Macs that don't have lots of memory or storage.

Claris Works 2.0

Product at a Glance

Publisher:
Claris
Upgrades from Claris Works 1.0 available, but not free

Requires:
Mac Plus or better
System 6.7 or later
2MB of RAM with System 6.7; 4MB of RAM with System 7
1.5MB of free disk space required; 40MB hard drive recommended
Any Mac-compatible printer with standard fonts

Description:
There are many integrated applications with the word *Works* in the title, but Claris Works is the only one that really works well. It has a very straightforward interface, and the different modules or environments work much like other great Claris applications such as MacDraw Pro, MacWrite Pro, and FileMaker Pro. You can jump effortlessly from working on a word processing document to a drawing, a painting, a spreadsheet, or a database. And you can send your work over modems or network by using the communications tool. The powers of each environment are limited, however. You cannot do such things as style sheet changes or high-power macros in spreadsheets. But if your needs are met by the basic tools of each environment, Claris Works can solve all your application needs in one small, easy-to-learn, inexpensive bundle.

Opening a ClarisWorks Document

When you want to begin work in Claris Works, you can start with any kind of document, created in any of the different environments. To open a new document in the environment you want, take one of the following actions, depending on your situation.

- To open a new document if you have not started Claris Works, double-click the Claris Works application icon in the Finder. When the dialog box opens with all of the environments listed, click the radio button by the name of the environment you want to work in, then click OK.
- If Claris Works is already open, choose New from the file menu to open a new document. Then click the radio button of the environment you want to work in and click OK in the dialog box.

A window opens with the appropriate tool palette for the environment you chose. To find out what each of the tools does in each of the environments, see your *Claris Works Handbook*, or use the nifty Help window, which you can get to by choosing Claris Works Help from the Help menu (the one with the question mark in a balloon).

For the sake of simplicity in the following procedure, I tell how to open an already existing Claris Works document in the drawing environment.

Using ClarisWorks Frames

This section describes how to use one integrated application, Claris Works, to combine data of two types. In general, this involves opening a document in one environment or another (using one tool or another), then creating or editing in that environment, and using a different tool to make a frame for a different environment, right inside the original document. Working within the frame you can do all the things you expect to in the environment of the tool that made the frame.

For example, if you open a drawing document in Claris Works, such as the Sample Objects document in the Tutorial Folder that comes with Claris

Works, you can use the following simple procedure to make a text frame and edit text in that frame. Before you can follow this procedure, you must have the complete Claris Works installed on your hard disk, including the Tutorial folder. Depending on which version of Claris Works you have, you may find different sample documents, but the procedure will work on whatever draw document you have.

1. In the Finder, find the Claris Works folder, open it, and open the Tutorial Folder.
2. Double-click the Sample Objects document in the Tutorial folder inside the Claris Works folder.
3. When the window opens, note that it says DR after the title; you are in a drawing document in the Claris Works drawing environment, with grids and graphics objects that you can select and do things to, much as if you were in MacDraw Pro.
4. Scroll down to the stars in the document, so you have a bunch of open space to work in.
5. Choose Show Tools from the View menu, then click on the text tool in the toolbar; it's the A by the pointer tool in the upper left corner of the window. The pointer becomes an I-beam when you move into the document window.
6. Drag the I-beam to make a rectangle. An insertion point appears in a frame with gray borders. This is a text frame, as shown in Figure 15.11.
7. Enter text in the frame. You can edit, add to, or delete text in this frame, much as if you were working in MacWrite Pro. If you add text until it fills the frame, it extends down the page automatically, just as if you were adding text to a newspaper column.
8. You can click on the pointer tool in the toolbar and move the text frame to a different position. Note that if you select something else in the window, the gray frame around the text disappears.

There are almost endless combinations of different frames that you can use to create different types of documents. You can put a spreadsheet inside a word processing report, for example. You can create columns for text and add illustrations if you want to make a newsletter or advertising brochure. Or you can make a database of products and add illustrations for clarity. For more information on frames and how you can use them to create all kinds of documents, see the Claris Works documentation.

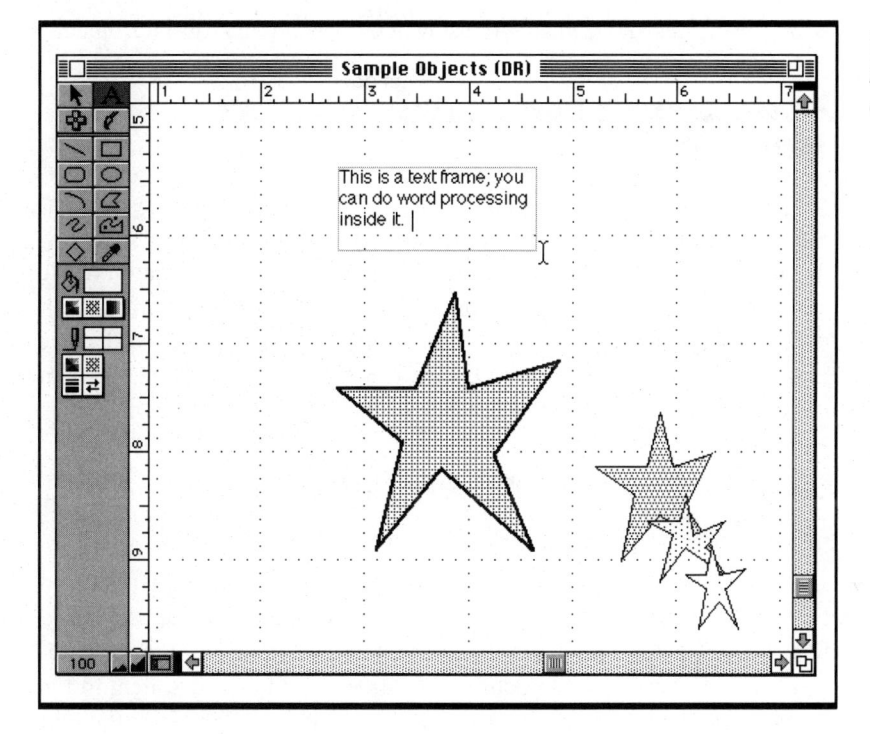

Figure 15.11
A text frame in a Claris Works drawing window

Troubleshooting Problems with Data Integration

The following sections cover the problems you can have when cutting and pasting, using linked documents, or using publisher and subscriber documents.

Pasted Graphic Doesn't Appear in Text Document

You paste a graphic into a document created by a word processing application, and the graphic doesn't appear, or just an empty frame appears. Try displaying the item by choosing Show Clipboard in the origin application (if the application has that menu option) or choosing Show Clipboard from the Edit menu in the Finder. When you have seen the graphic in the Clipboard, paste it into the destination document. If that does not work, try pasting the item into the Scrapbook, as described in "Using the Scrapbook" in this chapter.

Can't Find an Item Quickly in the Scrapbook

You want to copy something out of the Scrapbook often, but you get sick and tired of scrolling through all the other stuff in there to get at your often-used item. The answer is simple. Scroll to the often-used item, cut it to the Clipboard (choose Cut from the Edit menu), then scroll to the first item in the Scrapbook and paste the often-used item over it (choose Paste from the Edit menu). Now that item you want will be right up front every time you open the Scrapbook.

Can't Save a Dependent Linked Document

You created a link to a brand new document by placing an item that was copied out of it, but when you try to save your dependent document, you get an error message about saving to an untitled file. The problem is that you haven't saved the supporting document yet; switch over to that supporting document, save it and give it a name, then switch back to the dependent document and you can save it just fine. By the way, if you ever rename a supporting document that is not in the same folder as its dependent document, or if you ever move supporting and dependent documents to different folders, you may have to redirect the links so the dependent documents can find their supporters. For more information on this, see the Microsoft application's *User's Guide*.

Can't Subscribe to an Edition You Can See in the File List

If you are working on a network and you can see an edition file listed on your network, but it does not have the correct border, or if you cannot see it at all, then the file may not have the right permissions, or you may not have access rights on that server. See your network administrator, or see Chapter 6, "Linking Programs Over the Network," in the *Macintosh Networking Reference*.

Only Part of an Excel Edition Appears When You Subscribe to It

If an Excel edition has both data and a graph in it, you can only subscribe to the data. To see the graph and the data, you have to subscribe to it all as a picture; just hold down the Shift key when you click the Subscribe button in the Subscribe To dialog box. The data and the graph both appear.

Can't Tell If an Edition You Subscribed to Is Updated or Not

To make sure you are looking at an updated version of the edition you have subscribed to, select the subscriber item, then choose Subscriber Options from the Edit menu. When the dialog box opens, check the date in the lower left corner to see when the edition was last updated by the publisher. If you think that was after you got your last update, click the Get Edition Now button and your subscriber item will be updated immediately.

Can't Tell What Items in a Document Are Subscribers

If you are wondering what parts of your document are subscribers, you may be able to find out by one of a couple means. Some applications, such as

Excel, have a Links command in the File menu. If you choose that command, you can choose Subscribers in the Link Type box and see a list off all the subscribers in your document. In other applications, the subscribers have patterned borders or double brackets around them. For example, In Microsoft Word you can choose Show ¶ from the View menu, and gray double brackets appear at the beginning and end of each subscriber.

Appendix A

Graphic File Formats

Table A.1 below summarizes the compatibility of the most common graphic file formats with the major graphics applications described in this book. The formats, starting with the lowest resolution and working up, are defined as follows:

- MacP (MacPaint): The original Macintosh paint format; 72-dpi resolution, black-and-white images. Widely supported, even by DOS graphics and publishing applications. Prints on many printers, but jagged.
- PICT (Picture): Format for many object-oriented draw-type graphics. PICT 2 can be high resolution and color, but the format does not do well in publishing applications or on non-PostScript printers.
- EPS (Encapsulated PostScript): Format for high-end drawing and illustrating applications. Each image has low-resolution screen version and high-resolution PostScript code. Widely supported by desktop publishing for PostScript printers; not good for scanned images or color bit maps, and non-PostScript printers can only print low-resolution version.
- TIFF (Tagged Image File Format): Bit-mapped format that can be any size and resolution. The higher the resolution and the more color/grayscale involved, the more gigantic the files. Widely

used, in compressed forms, by publishing applications in both Mac and DOS worlds. Most high-resolution printers do well with TIFF.

Table A.2 Compatibility of Major Graphics File Formats

Application	Import/Open	Edit/Create	Export
Adobe Illustrator	EPS	EPS	EPS, PICT
Aldus Freehand	MacP, PICT	EPS, PICT	EPS, PICT
Aldus PageMaker	Place: MacP, EPS, PICT, TIFF	Resize: MacP, some PICT, EPS, TIFF	PICT via Clipboard
Aldus SuperPaint	MacP, EPS, PICT, TIFF	EPS, PICT, TIFF	EPS, PICT, TIFF
Claris MacDraw Pro	MacP, PICT, EPS, TIFF	MacP, EPS, PICT	EPS, PICT

Appendix B

Installing the System Software on a Customized Mac

If you have done a lot of work to customize your System Folder, adding special fonts and sounds, adding special customizing extensions and control panels, and setting up your Apple menu and lots of application preferences, you don't want to lose all these specifications and customizing files when you install new system software. If you just run the Installer program that comes with the new system software, you can bet it is going to clobber some of your customizing work.

To avoid this catastrophe, do not install the system software as instructed by Apple in their installation procedure, and do not install by simply starting up the Mac with the Install 1 disk and clicking OK and Install. Instead, use the following procedure, which saves all your custom files and preferences, and puts them back into the new System Folder after you have installed Apple's system software. Keep in mind as you do this procedure, though, that the goal is to put as much of Apple's new software in the System Folder as possible, and to merely add your customizing stuff on top of that base. Also, to avoid compatibility problems of old applications and new system software, make sure you run the Compatibility checker on the "Before You Install" floppy disk that came with your system software disks.

> **⚠ Warning**
>
> You should either be very sure of what you're doing or get help from an experienced Mac user or a qualified technician to do this custom system software installation. It is not a simple process, and mistakes can cause serious problems.

To install new system software and preserve your customizing, follow these steps:

1. Check out your hard disk. Start up your Mac using the Disk Tools disk that you get with the system software set. Double-click the Disk First Aid icon (the little ambulance) and click the OK and Start buttons to run a check on your hard disk. If you have a third-party hard disk (not an Apple one), run a disk checker such as Norton Disk Doctor or Silverlining to check the hard disk driver. Also make sure the driver is compatible with the system software you want to install; you may have to call the manufacturer or dealer to make sure you have a compatible disk driver, but DON'T overlook this critical step. If your disk driver is sick or incompatible, or your hard drive is "hosed," as they say, the new system software will go crazy on it. Also, if your hard drive has partitions, I recommend you reformat it without partitions. Apple system software doesn't always work with partitions.

2. Open the System Folder on your hard disk. If you have lots of special fonts (or only a few fonts because you use Suitcase) in the System file (this means you have a pre-7.1 version of the system software), drag that file out of the system folder into a folder that you name something like "Sys file in Here."

3. Drag the Finder from your hard disk's System Folder to another folder and call it "Finder in here."

4. Change the name of your System Folder to something like "Old system folder."

5. Get out all your system software disks and restart your Mac, inserting Install 1 at the startup beep or chime.

6. Click OK in the Installer's welcome screen. When the Easy Install dialog box appears, you can do a full, easy install, or a custom install, depending on your situation:

   - If you have enough disk space or aren't sure which drivers you're going to need for printers and/or networking, click Install in the Easy Install dialog box.
   - If you want to save space on your hard disk and you know what printer and/or network drivers you need, click Customize, Shift- click the things you need to install, then click Install button.

7. Feed the Mac the disks it asks for, until you see the message box telling you that installation was successful.
8. Click the Quit button and restart your Mac on the new system software.
9. Open the new System Folder and your old System Folder; place and size the windows so you can see both at once.
10. Choose by Name from the View menu when each window is active, so you can compare the contents.
11. Drag your custom files from the old System Folder to the new one, but do so carefully. Close the new System Folder each time you want to add a new file, and drag the file to the System Folder icon, so the file gets put in the right place inside the System Folder. Add your special custom extensions and control panels, and all the preference files for your applications and utilities, but do NOT copy over any files that Apple has just installed. For example, don't copy old extensions like your printer drivers and the PrintMonitor over the new ones. Leave the new Apple control panels and Apple Menu items in place, too. If you are reinstalling because you were having system crashes, and you think an extension or control panel was causing the crashes, add the suspicious item first, from the original floppy you got it on, not the old system folder. Then try out the system before adding other stuff. If you still have problems, contact the manufacturer and see if you can get a more compatible version of the extension or control panel.
12. Close the old System Folder and open the old System file and the new System file (if they're pre-System 7.1), so you can see what's in both windows. If you are installing System 7.1 or later, open the Fonts folder instead.
13. Close the new System file and System Folder and drag your special custom fonts and sounds (if you have any in the old System file) to the new System Folder icon. If you are installing System 7.0 or earlier, most fonts and sounds go into the System file (in System 7.0, non-TrueType outline fonts, like PostScript ones, go in the Extensions folder); for 7.1 and later, all fonts go in the Fonts folder. Do not copy over any of the newly installed Chicago, Geneva, and Monaco font resource files that have size

367

numbers after the titles. Leave the Indigo sound, too. If you are using Suitcase and PostScript fonts, you don't have to do this step: just drag all the TrueType fonts in the new System file (or in the Fonts folder) to the Trash.

14. Restart your Mac.

You now have all new versions of the Apple system software, including fonts, extensions, control panels, and Apple menu items. To this base you have added your fonts, your custom files, and the preferences for your applications and utilities.

If you have problems with some of your custom files or applications not working, try reinstalling fresh copies of the latest versions from the floppies to make sure your old version wasn't corrupted. Also, make sure you have the version that is the most likely to work with the new system software.

If you have lots of problems running the new system software, you may have a hardware problem; the most common ones are not enough RAM in your Mac, an accelerator card that is not compatible with the new system software, and a video card that needs a ROM update to work with the new system software. If you fix all those things and still have problems, see a qualified technician or call Apple Support.

INDEX

Page numbers in **bold** refer to primary discussions of topic; page numbers in *italic* refer to "First Steps."

SYMBOLS

#####, in spreadsheet cell, **288**
*****, in spreadsheet cell, **288**
% key, *30*
    for command shortcuts, 37
+ (plus sign), in windowshade handles, 255
· (accent mark), in file name and file order, 118
^ (caret), in file name and file order, 118
! (exclamation point), in file name and file order, 118
(sum) button, in Excel, 281
ä

A

About This Macintosh (Apple menu), 39, *154*, 157
absolute cell references, in Excel, **282–283**
accent mark (·), in file name and file order, 118
accented characters, 77
Account menu, Write Checks, 331, 332
accounts file, creating in Quicken, *318*, **322–324**
accounts in Quicken
    changing name, 336
    transfers between, 329, 336
active window, 40
Actual size (Page menu), 254
acute accent, 77
ADB (Apple Desktop Bus) icon, 14
adding text, in MacWrite Pro, 206
Adobe Illustrator, 218, 220, 221
    file formats for, 364
Adobe Type Manager, 74, 79

alert boxes, 45
    Application Not Available, 107
    bomb, **49–51**
    for emptying trash, 42
alias
    in Apple menu, 99
    for application icon, 93
    for files, 152
America Online, 171
anchoring title, in Excel, 278
Apple Desktop Bus (ADB) icon, 14
Apple HD SC Setup program, 131–132
Apple LaserWriter, 58
Apple menu
    About This Macintosh, 39, *154*, 157
    Chooser, 59
    Control Panels, 22, *155*, 160, *167*, 172
    Key Caps, 76, 79
    opening applications from, **99**
    Scrapbook, *340*
    vs. Applications menu, 99
Apple Menu Items folder, 168–169
AppleTalk networks, 11, 15
    radio button for, 60
application disks, **140–141**
application files, backup copies of, **141–142**
Application has unexpectedly quit message, **163–164**
Application is Busy or Missing message, 136
    given in error, 148
Application Not Available alert box, 107
applications, **90–91**
    backup copies of, 134
    copying document portions between, 345–347
    folders for, 92

installing, *88*, **91–93**
integrated, **355–359**
managing, **98–100**
memory allocation for, *155*, **158–159**
opening, *88*, **93**
opening automatically at startup, *166*, **170**
opening from Apple menu, **99**
quitting, 50, **107**
switching between, **100**
troubleshooting problems, **106–108**
Applications menu
    Finder, 101
    Hide Others, 113, 120
    vs. Apple menu, 99
Arrange menu, Tab Order, 314
At Ease, 34, 90
Autoflow (Utilities menu), *239*, 251
automatic calculation, in Excel, 288
automatic updating, with publish and subscribe, *341*, **352–354**

B

background printing, **68–69**
    in MacWrite Pro, 211
    in Microsoft Word, 203
backup copies, 96, 134
    on floppy disks, *124*
    of system and application files, **141–142**
backup utilities, 134
bad media, disk errors from, 149
batteries, 13
BeagleWorks, 274, 355
Best Quality (Print dialog box), 79
bitmapped fonts, 73
    icon for, 73
    printer variation, 74
    problems printing, 79
bitmapped graphics
    jagged text in, **234**
    vs. graphic objects, 226
black and white, setting, 175
block of text
    locating lost in PageMaker, 266
    selecting, 197
bold type, in Excel, 277
bombs
    alert box, **49–51**
    from memory shortage, 162
    at startup, **164**
Bootman, 164
brightness control, 22, **174**
Browse mode, in FileMaker Pro, *293*, 302
budgeting, 328
bulletin boards, 171
bytes, 128

C

cable, for printer, 59
Calculate folder sizes check box, 183
cancel button, 276
"Cannot Resolve Circular Reference" message, **288**
Canvas, 218, **219–220**
carbon copies, printing, 58
caret (^), in file name and file order, 118
cassette, 63
categories in Quicken, 327, **328–329**
    choosing, 329
    creating, **330**
    uses for, **337**
Caution icon, in alert box, 45
cdevs, crash from, 164
cedilla, 77
cells in Excel, 275
    absolute references to, **282–283**
    moving between, 276
    selecting range, *270*, **279–280**
Center button (Excel), 278
center tabs, 200, 208
Central Processing Unit (CPU), **6–7**
characters
    accented, **77**
    overlapping, 79
Chart Wizard button (Excel toolbar), 271, 284
charts
    column labels in, 289
    from Excel data, *271*, **283–285**
check register (Quicken), **325–326**
    correcting mistakes in, 328
    recording check in, **326–327**
    recording deposit in, **327**
Checkbook II, 320
checks
    printing, **333–334**
    recording in Quicken, *318*, **326–327**
    voiding, 328
    writing in Quicken, *319*, **330–332**
Chooser
    missing printer icon, 78
    printing setup on, *54*, **59–60**
circle-shaped tool, in PageMaker, 248
circular references, in Excel, 288
circumflex (^), 77
Claris Works, 274, **356**
    frames in, *341*, **357–359**
    opening document, 357
Classic, 22
Classic II, 8
Clean Up Window, 51
cleaning
    hard disk filter screen, 133

keyboard, 49
mouse, 48
Cleaning Page document, 64
Clear (Edit menu), 198
clearing, Clipboard, 162–163
clicking, 35
   troubleshooting problems, 46
ClickPaste, 349
clip art, 218
Clipboard, 170, **342–347**
   clearing, 162–163
   and MacWrite Pro, 207
   moving, copying and replacing text
      with, **198**, **343–347**
   undoing mistakes, **350**
clock, 174
closing
   all windows, 51
   control panels, 180
   windows, 41
color, 8
   setting display, 175–176
Color Classic, **10**
color control, **174–177**
Color palette, in PageMaker, 248
color wheel, 176
Column guides (Layout menu), 249
column guides in PageMaker
   lining up items, 267
   problems moving, **266**
columns
   adjusting in PageMaker, 257, 267
   creating in PageMaker, 249
   hiding in List view, 104
   missing from List view window, **106**
columns in Excel
   adjusting width, 288
   labels in charts, **289**
commands, choosing from menus, 36
Commands (Tools menu), in Microsoft
      Word, 203
communications, with PowerBook, 13
compact Macs, **9**
Compatibility Checker, 171
compressed files, 138
   copying, 141
   utilities for, 133
CompuServe, 171
Conflict Catcher, 183
continuous-feed printer, printing checks on,
      334
Control palette, in PageMaker, 248
control panels, 168, 171, **172–180**
   closing, 180
   installing, *166*
   missing, **182**
   opening, *167*

problems from, **183**
Control Panels (Apple menu), 22, *155*, 160,
      167, 172
Control Panels folder, 169
   INITs in, 171
cool documents, 180
copies, printing multiple, 67
Copy (Edit menu), 198, *340*, **345**
copying
   document segments between applica-
      tions, **345–347**
   entire floppy disk, *125*, **142–143**
   to floppy disks, 138
copying text
   with Clipboard, **198**, *340*
   in MacWrite Pro, *189*
   in Microsoft Word, *189*, 197
Courier font, 72
cover page, printing, 67
CPU (Central Processing Unit), 6–7
crash
   of hard drives, **147–148**
   of system, 367
Create Publisher (Edit menu), 353
cropping tool, in PageMaker, 248
cursor, 6. *See also* insertion point; pointer
   movement in FileMaker Pro, 314
curved line tool, in MacDraw Pro, 228
custom color, 177
customized Macintosh, **166–183**
   installing system software on, **365–368**
customizing
   extensions. *See* INITs
   files, discarding, 172
   icons, **180–181**
   troubleshooting problems, **182–183**
Cut (Edit menu), 198, *340*, 343

D

data, 6
   in RAM, shutdown and, 7
   subscribing to Excel edition, 361
data disks, **141**
data entry
   in Excel, 270, **276–277**
   in FileMaker Pro, *292*, **302–302**
data integration, **340–341**, **342–362**
   Clipboard, **342–347**
   dynamic links, **350–352**
   publish and subscribe, **352–354**
   Scrapbook, 107, 170, *340*, **348–349**
   troubleshooting problems, **360–362**
data storage. *See also* disks; floppy disks;
      hard disks
   in Scrapbook, 348
databases, **291–315**, 294. *See also* fields in
      database; FileMaker Pro

design, **299**
  moving through, 303–304
  selecting, **295–298**
Date
  for desktop view, 103
  organizing files by, 116
  setting, 174
decimal point tabs, 200, 208
default settings, for printing, 67
defragmenting
  disks with bad media error, 149
  hard disks, *124*, **135–137**
Delete Account (Edit menu), 336
Delete Transaction (Edit menu), 328
deleted text, restoring, 213
deleting, *31. See also* erasing
  memorized transactions, 333
  text, 38
  text in MacWrite Pro, 206
  text in Microsoft Word, 196
dependent documents, automatic update with dynamic link, 350
deposit entered in Quicken register, 319, 327
desk accessories, and memory use, 163
desktop, **32–34**
  adjusting, *167*
  changing pattern, 173–174
  changing view of documents and folders, 102–103
  color of, 176–177
  floppy disk icon absence from, **151**
  folders on, 90
  rearranging icons on, 51
  rebuilding, 133, 146, 147
  saving document on, 98
  troubleshooting change in, **182**
  troubleshooting problems, **46–51**
desktop publishing. *See also* page layout applications; PageMaker
  growth of, 240
DeskWriter (Hewlett-Packard), 57
  care of, 62
  cartridge problems, 82
destination document, for copy and paste, 346
diagonal-line tool, in PageMaker, 247
dialog boxes, **43–44**
dimmed commands, 36
  File menu, Open command, 102
disappearing text, in word processors, 213
Disinfectant, 171
disk cache
  adjusting, *155*, **159–161**, 180
  and backup process, 135
disk drives, floppy disk stuck in, **151–152**
disk errors, from bad media, 149
Disk First Aid, 148, 149, 366

Disk Tools disk, 24, 366
DiskDoubler, 133, 138
disks, 126
  checking capacity, **145**
  determining for current folder, 147
documents, 90
  automatic update with dynamic link, 350
  changing view on desktop, **102–103**
  cutting and pasting, 343–345
  finding, *89*, **101**
  folders for linked, 352
  keeping original and edited version, 98
  managing, **100–105**
  opening, *88*, **94–95**
  printing, *55*, **66–70**
  problems saving linked, 352, **360–361**
  saving, 89
  saving for first time, **96–97**
  specifying for startup, **170**
  switching between, **101–102**
  troubleshooting problems, **106–108**
  word processor for short, 192
  word processors for long, **191**
Domestic (U.S.) keyboard, 178
dot-matrix printers, **58–59**
double-clicking, 36, 46
  to open applications, 93
double-sided pages, in PageMaker, 246
dragging
  documents to open applications, 94
  icons, **35–36**
  icons to install applications, 92
  items to Trash, **42**
drawing, in Claris Works, 358
drawing applications, **219–221**
driver software, troubleshooting, 26
dynamic links, **350–352**

E

Edit menu
  Clear, 198
  Copy, 198, *340*, **345**
  Create Publisher, 353
  Cut, 198, *340*, 343
  Delete Account, 336
  Delete Transaction, 328
  Edit story, 267
  Edit Transaction, 333
  Fill Right, 282
  Paste, 198, *340*, 344
  Paste Special, 351
  Subscribe, 354
  Undo, 197, 213
  Undo Cut, 350
Edit Story window, 267
Edit Transaction (Edit menu), 333
editing, *31*

in MacWrite Pro, *188*, **206–207**
in Microsoft Word, *188*, **196**
edition file
    creating, 353
    determining version of, **361**
    problems subscribing to, **361**
Eject Disk (Special menu), *125*
ejecting floppy disks, 26, 93, 98, *125*, 127, 137
    when icon is hidden, 150
electrical surges, 134
    and hard disk crash, 147
electronic bulletin boards, 171
Element menu
    Line, 259, 260
    Text wrap, 261
Empty Trash (Special menu), *31*, 42
emptying Trash, *31*, 42
    problems with, 47
end of list, moving file to, 118
entry bar, in Excel, 276
envelopes
    FileMaker Pro to print, 309–311
    return address on, 311–312
EPS (encapsulated PostScript) format, 220, 363
equations. *See* formulas
Erase Disk (Special menu), 139, 145
erasing
    during initialization process, 139
    floppy disks, **145**
    mistakes in Kid Pix, **223–224**
error messages, 50. *See also* messages
Ethernet network, 10
Ethernet/AppleTalk networks, 11
Excel, 272, **274–286**
    absolute cell references, **282–283**
    charts from, *271*, **283–285**
    completing spreadsheet, **283**
    data entry in, 270, **276–277**
    dynamic links for, 350
    fill function in, **282**
    Font dialog box, 279
    formatting numbers in, *271*
    formulas in, *271*, **280–281**, 288
    inserting in, 279
    opening document, 270, **274–276**
    saving and printing in, **285–286**
    selecting cell range in, 270, **279–280**
    type style and formatting, 270, **277–278**
exclamation point (!), in file name and file order, 118
expansion cards, 10, 12
    inserting, 14
    NuBus, 26
extensions
    disabling during startup, 172

problems from, **183**
Extensions folder, 169
    INITs in, 171
Extensions Manager, 183
external drives, 7
    connecting, **16–17**
    ID number for, 16
    problems from, 50
    turning off or on, 18, 132
    vs. internal, **129–130**

F

Facing pages, in PageMaker setup, 246
fan, 21
Farallon PhoneNET, 15
FastBack utility, 134
fax modem, 13
fields in database, 299
    adding new, **308**
    moving between in FileMaker Pro, **314–315**
    moving in layout, 310
    setup in FileMaker Pro, *292*, **301–302**
File Force, 297
file formats, for graphics, **363–364**
File menu
    dimmed Open command, 102
    Find, 89
    Get Info, 47, 121, *155*, 159
    Make Alias, 93
    New, 194
    New Folder, 36, 113
    Open, *88*
    Page Setup, 69
    Place, 251
    Print, 55, 66, 203, 211
    Print Preview, 285
    Put Away, 42, *125*, 137, 150, 151
    Save, 89, 96, 203
    Undo, 207
file names
    and placement in list, 118
    problems trying to change, 121
File Sharing, 163
FileMaker Pro, 297, 298, **299–315**
    adding to database, **308**
    Browse mode, *293*
    creating mailing, **309–313**
    data entry in, *292*, **302–302**
    database design, 299
    field setup, *292*, **301–302**
    finding records in, *293*, **305–306**
    Layout mode, **306–307**
    moving through database, 303–304
    opening document, *292*, **300**
    saving and printing in, 313
    sorting records, *293*, **304–305**

toolbar, 303–304
troubleshooting problems, 314–315
files, 90
    changing listed order, *111*
    collecting for PageMaker, 243–244
    compressed, 138
    decrease in loading speed, **148**
    finding, **119–129**
    locating, 94
    locating on forgotten floppy, **152**
    locating in PageMaker, 268
    lost while moving, **108**
    organizing schemes for, 116
    placing in folders, 114
    printing to, 67
    troubleshooting problems with, **119–121**
fill function, in Excel, **282**
fills
    graphics without, 232
    in MacDraw Pro, **230**
    problems spilling, 234
financial management software, 321–322
Find (File menu), *89*
Find (Select menu), 293, 306
Find All (Select menu), 306
Find dialog box, 44
    More Chances button, 120
Finder, 32, 33, 101, 106, 168
    performance of, 134
    printing window in, 70
    System Folder, Clipboard, 343
finding
    buried window folder, 120
    documents, *89*, **101**
    files, **119–129**
    folders, **119–129**
    records in FileMaker Pro, *293*, **305–306**
first-line indent, 199, 207, 213
Fit in window (Page menu), 254, 257
flashing PrintMonitor icon, 69
flat-file databases, 295, **297–298**
floating palette, 247
floppy disks, 7, **127**
    800K vs. 1.8Mb, 128–129
    backup copies on, *124*
    care of, **137–139**
    copying entire, *125*, **142–143**
    copying to, 138
    ejecting, 26, 93, 98, *125*, 127, 137
    ejecting when icon is hidden, 150
    erasing, **145**
    formatting, **139–140**
    ghost icon, *125*, 151
    icon absent from desktop, **151**
    information bar for, 145
    inserting, *124*, 137
    locating files on, **152**

    locking and unlocking, 121, **144**
    names for, 138
    preparing, *125*, **139–140**
    storage capacity, 128
    stuck in disk drives, **151–152**
    System Startup disk, 19
    troubleshooting problems, **146–152**
    uses for, **140–141**
    vs. hard disks, 129
folder size calculation, 179
folders, **109–121**, 112
    for applications, 92
    changing listed order, *111*
    changing view on desktop, **102–103**
    creating, *110*, **113**
    on desktop, 90
    determining disk for current, 147
    determining parent, 119
    displaying contents, 104
    finding, **119–129**
    finding buried window, 120
    hiding contents, 104
    for linked documents, 352
    List views to work with, **117–118**
    looking inside nested, *111*
    moving icons to, 104
    naming and nesting, **113–116**
    placing file in, 114
    saving document in new, 98
    troubleshooting problems with, **119–121**
Font dialog box, in Excel, 279
Font Smoothing, 79
Font Substitution, 79
fonts, **71–77**
    changing in Microsoft Word, 202
    installing, *55*, 75, 367–368
    Key Caps to compare, **76–77**
    kinds of, **72–74**
    for PageMaker, 260, **266**
    removing, 75
    for text in graphics, 231
    text switching to Geneva, 80
    for views, 179
Fonts folder, 73, 169
Format menu, 202
    Font, 279
    Number, 280
formatting
    characters, displaying in Microsoft Word, 201
    correcting for paragraphs, 213
    floppy disks, **139–140**
    numbers in Excel, *271*
    text in Excel, *270*, **277–278**
    text in Microsoft Word with ruler, **198–201**
formulas in Excel, *271*, **280–281**

accuracy, 288
4th Dimension, 295–296
Foxbase Pro, 295–296
fractional-width spacing, 79
fragmented memory, 162
fragmenting, 136
FrameMaker, 243
frames, in Claris Works, *341*, 357–359
frames for graphics, in MacDraw Pro, 231–232
Freehand, 218, 220
    file formats for, 364
freeze-ups, from memory shortage, 162
front of list, moving file to, 118
frozen screen display, troubleshooting, 49–51
Full Disk error message, **147**

G

General Controls window, 173–174
Geneva font, 71
    troubleshooting text switching to, 80
Get Info (File menu), 47, 121, *155*, 159
ghost icon, 36
    of disk, *125*, 151
glare on screen, **22–23**
Goodies menu, Small Kids Mode, 222
graphic objects, vs. bitmaps, 226
graphics, **218–235**. *See also* Kid Pix; MacDraw Pro
    adding text to, **230–231**
    adding to PageMaker, **261–263**
    creating with MacDraw Pro, *217*
    file formats, **363–364**
    frames in MacDraw Pro, **231–232**
    placement in PageMaker, *239*, **252–253**
    poor printed appearance, **235**
    and printing problems in PageMaker, 268
    problems with pasted not appearing in document, **360**
    problems placing object in, 234
    selecting application, **218–221**
    troubleshooting problems, **234–235**
    without fill, 232
graphs, subscribing to Excel edition, 361
grave accent (`), 77
gray shades
    displaying, 175
    filling graphic object with, 230
grayed commands, 36
grayed ruler, 201
grayscale, 8
    printing, 235
    printing on ink-jet printer, 57
grid alignment, 234
grid for icons, 179

gridlines, preventing print in spreadsheets, 287

H

handles
    for objects in MacDraw Pro, 228
    for selected database field names, 307
Happy Mac icon, 17, 23
hard copies, 56
hard disk icon, absence of, 26, **146–147**
hard disk window, 113
hard disks, **7–8**, 11, **126–127**
    care of, **131–137**
    check before new system install, 366
    checking available space, 133
    connecting external, **16–17**
    connecting and initializing, **131–132**
    crash, **147–148**
    damage from moving, 14
    defragmenting, *124*, **135–137**
    head parking, 130
    installing system software on, 20
    names for, 138
    startup, 5, **19–20**, 24, 127
    storage capacity, 128
    system software on, 133
    troubleshooting problems, **146–152**
    vs. floppy disks, 129
hardware, 8. *See also* floppy disks; hard disks; memory; mouse; printers
    LocalTalk, 15
    troubleshooting problems, **21–27**
head crash, 132
head parking, 130
headers, for envelope return address, 311–312
headings, text style in PageMaker, **260–261**
HeapFixer, 164
Helix Express, 295
help balloons, showing and hiding, **39**
Help menu, Show Balloons, 39, *154*
Helvetica font, 71, 72
Hewlett-Packard, DeskWriter, 57
hidden files, 145
hidden formatting characters
    displaying, 201
    viewing in MacWrite Pro, 209
hidden windows, 100
Hide Others (Applications menu), 113, 120
hiding
    folder contents, 104
    help balloons, **39**
hierarchy of folders, 94–95, *110*, 112
    and List views, 103–104
    recommendations, 116
hierarchy menu, displaying, 106
highlighting, 35, 36

horizontal printing, 70
hot documents, 180
hot spot
    for Kid Pix paint can, 225
    of mouse pointer, 35, 46
HyperCard folder, 114, 115

I

I-beam, 37–38, 194, 196
icon view, 102
    for font files, 73
    settings for, 179
icons, 33, 91
    customizing, **180–181**
    moving, *30*
    moving to folder, 104
    rearranging on desktop, 51
    selecting multiple, 41
    selecting or opening, *30*, **35–36**, 104
ID number, for external drive, 16, 131
Illustrator, 218, 220, 221
    file formats for, 364
images. *See* graphics
ImageWriter, 60
    care of, **65–66**
    fonts for, 73
    magnets in, 139
    overlapping characters, 79
    page break problems, 83
    printing checks on, 334
    Select button, 78
ImageWriter II, 58
"in use" items, and emptying trash, 47
inactive windows, 40
indent markers, 200
indenting
    first line, 199
    problems with, 213
index, from PageMaker, 242
initializing process
    for floppy disks, *125*, **139–140**
    for hard disks, **131–132**
INITPicker, 183
INITs, 163, **171–172**
    crash from, 164
    installing, *166*
ink, problems from, 82
ink cartridge
    in DeskWriter, 62
    in StyleWriter, 61–62
ink-jet printers, **56–57**
ink smudges, from LaserWriter, 82
input, 6
inserting
    in Excel, 279
    floppy disks, *124*, 137
insertion point, 37, 38, 194, 205

placement for PageMaker text insertion, 266
setting blinking rate, 174
installer, starting, 20
installing, 5
    applications, *88*, **91–93**
    fonts, *55*, 75, 367–368
    INITs or control panels, *166*
    sounds, 367–368
    system software on customized Mac, 365–368
    troubleshooting problems, **21–27**
integrated applications, **355–359**
interface, 8
internal drives, 7
    vs. external, 129–130
International keyboard, 178
italic text, 202, 210
    in Excel, 277–278

J

jagged text
    in bitmapped graphics, 234
    troubleshooting, **78–79**, 80

K

Key Caps (Apple menu), 79
    to compare fonts, **76–77**
keyboard, **6**, 32
    cleaning, 49
    control setting, **177–178**
    plugging in, 14
    on PowerBook, 12
    troubleshooting problems, 48, 49
    to work with text, **37–38**
keyboard shortcuts, in Microsoft Word, 203
Kid Pix, 218–219, **221–226**
    correcting mistakes, **223–224**
    creating picture, *216*
    drawing lines in, 223
    opening documents, *216*, **222**
    paint can in, **225**
    saving and printing in, **226**
    stamps in, **224**
    wacky brush painting, **225**
kilobytes, 128
Kind, for desktop view, 102–103

L

La Cie drives, 130
Label, for desktop view, 103
Largest Unused Block amount (About This Macintosh), 158
laser printers, **58**
    network cable for, 15
LaserJet IVM, 58

LaserWriter
    and background printing, 68
    care of, **63–65**
    cartridge problems, 82
    check printing on, **333–334**
    ink smudges from, 82
    Page Setup dialog box for, 69–70
    preventing start pages from, *54*
    printing envelopes, 312–313
LaserWriter Font Utility, 65
layers, in MacDraw Pro, 227
layout
    adjusting in PageMaker, **256–259**
    for database, 294
    indicator in FileMaker Pro toolbar, 303
Layout (Select menu), 306, 308, 314
Layout menu
    Column guides, 249
    Turn Autogrid Off, 234
    View, 254
Layout mode (FileMaker Pro), **306–307**
LC III, **12**
left aligned tabs, 200, 208
letter size, selecting in PageMaker, 246
letters, word processor for, 192
Library palette, in PageMaker, 248
lights, and screen glare, 22
Line (Element menu), 259, 260
line spacing
    in MacWrite Pro, 209
    in Microsoft Word, 201
lines
    adding thick in PageMaker, 258
    drawing in Kid Pix, **223**
    in PageMaker, 260
linked documents, folder for, 352
List views, **103–105**
    column missing from window, **106**, **183**
    determining type, 106
    settings for, 179
    to work with folders, **117–118**
loaded text icon, 251
loaded windowshade handle, 257
LocalTalk hardware, 15
Lock Guides (Options menu), 266
locked files, and name changes, 121
locked floppy disks, 121, **144**
locked items, and emptying trash, 47
logo for newsletter, 252–253
long documents, word processors for, **191**
Lotus 1-2-3 for Macintosh, 272–273

M

Mac II, 26
Mac Plus, 21
MacCalc, 273
MacDraw Pro, 218, 220, 221, **226–233**
    creating graphic images in, *217*
    creating shapes, **228–229**
    file formats for, 364
    fills in, **230**
    frames around graphics, **231–232**
    grid alignment in, 234
    layers in, 227
    magnifying view of, *217*
    moving and editing objects, *217*
    opening document in, *216*, **227–228**
    saving and printing in, **232–233**
MacIntax, 321
Macintosh
    parts, **6–8**
    selecting model, **8–13**
    setup, *4*, **13–17**
    setup to run from hard disk, 5
    shutdown, **18–19**
    turning on, *4*, 17
Macintosh Basics icon, 32
MacMoney, 322
MacP (MacPaint) format, 363
MacPaint, 218
MacUser, 171
Macworld, 171
MacWrite Pro, 192, **204–211**
    editing in, *188*, **206–207**
    hidden formatting characters in, 209
    moving or copying text in, *189*
    opening new document in, *188*, **204–205**
    ruler in, **207–209**
    saving and printing in, **210–211**
    style of text in, **210**
    text entry in, *188*, **205–206**
    undoing mistakes, *189*
magnets, and floppy disks, 139
magnified views
    for database, 304
    in MacDraw Pro, *217*
    in PageMaker, 254
mailing, creating with FileMaker Pro, **309–313**
Make Alias (File menu), 93
Managing Your Money, 322
Manual Feed button, 64, 67
margins, 82
    lining up items in PageMaker, 267
    marker in MacWrite Pro, 207–208
    in Microsoft Word, 201
    in PageMaker, 246, 248
    text alignment in MacWrite Pro, 208–209
master pages, in PageMaker, *239*, **249–250**
MasterJuggler, 74
mathematical equations. *See* formulas
megabytes (MB), 8, 128
Memorize Transaction (Shortcuts menu), 332

Memorized Transaction List (Shortcuts menu), 332
memorizing transactions, in Quicken, 332–333
memory, 7, **153–164**
    allocation for applications, *155*, **158–159**
    allocation for word processors, 212
    on Compact Macs, 9
    control settings, **180**
    for FileMaker Pro, 314
    monitoring use, *154*, **157–158**
    and multiple open applications, 100
    and screen font, 80
    for spreadsheets, **287**
    troubleshooting problems with, **162–164**
memory bars, full, **162–163**
menu bar, 33
    in PageMaker, 248
menu commands
    number of blinks, 174
    selecting, *30*
menus
    choosing commands from, **36**
    tear-off, 232
messages
    Application has unexpectedly quit, **163–164**
    Application is busy or missing, 136, 148
    "Cannot Resolve Circular Reference," **288**
    Disk Full, **147**
    "Not enough memory to open the application," 212
    Out of Memory, **162–163**
    Out of Space, 134
microphone, 14, 178
Microsoft Excel. *See* Excel
Microsoft Word, **191**, **193–203**
    changing style of text, **202–203**
    dynamic links for, 350
    editing in, *188*, **196**
    graphics in, 347
    moving or copying text in, *189*
    opening new document, *188*, **193–195**
    saving and printing in, **203**
    shortcuts, **203**
    subscriber in, 362
    text entry in, *188*, **195**
    undoing mistakes, *189*
Microsoft Works, 274, 355
Mind Your Own Business, 322
mistakes, *189*. *See also* undoing mistakes
modal dialog box, 44
modeless dialog boxes, 44
modem port, printer connection to, 60
modems, 15

Modular Macs, **10–11**
    setup, 14
    startup sound on, 26
money managing applications, selecting, 320–322
monitor, 10, 21
mouse, **6**, 32, **34–35**
    cleaning, 48
    control settings, **178**
    plugging in, 14
    troubleshooting problems, **46–51**
    to work with text, **37–38**
mouse pad, 35, 48
mouse pointer, hot spot on, 35, 46
moving
    icons, *30*
    losing files while, **108**
    windows, 41
moving hard disk, damage from, 14
moving text
    with Clipboard, **198**, **343–345**
    in MacWrite Pro, *189*
    in Microsoft Word, *189*, **196–197**
multiple icons, selecting, 41

N

Name, for desktop view, 102
names
    for files, 97
    for floppy disks, 138
    for folders, *110*, **113–116**
    for hard disks, 138
nested folders, **113–116**
    looking inside, *111*
networks
    connecting to, **15–16**
    printers on, 59
    servers, 11
New (File menu), 194
New Folder (File menu), 36, 113
Norton Backup, folder backup with, 135
Norton Utilities, 137
    Disk Doctor, 148, 149, 366
    KeyFinder, 76
Not enough memory to open the application message, 212
Note icon, in alert box, 45
NuBus expansion cards, 26
numbers, formatting in Excel, *271*

O

objects
    moving and editing in MacDraw Pro, *217*
    problems placing in graphic, **234–235**
Open (File menu), *88*

opening
    control panels, *167*
    icons, *30*, **35–36**
    new accounts file in Quicken, *318*
    windows, 36
opening applications, *88*, *93*
    from Apple menu, *99*
    automatically at startup, *166*
opening document, *88*, **94–95**
    in Claris Works, 357
    in Excel, *270*, **274–276**
    in FileMaker Pro, *292*, *300*
    in Kid Pix, *216*, *222*
    in MacDraw Pro, *216*, **227–228**
    in MacWrite Pro, *188*, **204–205**
    in Microsoft Word, *188*, **193–195**
    in PageMaker, *238*, **245**
optimum window size, 41
Options dialog box, Proof print, 268
Options menu
    Calculation, 288
    Display, for Excel gridlines, 287
    Lock Guides, 266
organizing schemes, for files, 116
orientation of page
    in PageMaker, 246
    for printing, 70
origin document, for copy and paste, 346
Out of Memory message, **162–163**
Out of Space messages, 134
outline fonts, 73, 74
    icon for, 73
output, 6

P

page breaks, problems in ImageWriter, **83**
page icons, in PageMaker, 248
page layout applications, **238–268**. *See also* PageMaker
    selecting, **241–243**
Page menu
    Actual size, 254
    Fit in window, 254, 257
page numbers, in PageMaker document, 249
page setup
    in PageMaker, *238*, **246**
    for special printing, **69–70**
Page Setup (File menu), 69
Page Setup dialog box, in PageMaker, 245, 246
PageMaker, *107*, *240*, **242–268**
    adjusting text blocks, **254–256**
    changing page view, **254**
    column creation, 249
    document window, **247–249**
    file formats for, 364
    graphics in, *239*, **252–253**, **261–263**

heading text style, **260–261**
layout adjustment, **256–259**
lines in, 260
magnified views, 254
master pages in, *239*, **249–250**
opening document, *238*, **245**
page setup in, *238*
pasteboard in, 249, 266
preliminary page setup, **246**
problems printing in, **268**
rough sketches and file collection, **243–244**
saving and printing in, **263–264**
text placement, *239*, **251**
text style after cut and paste, 345
troubleshooting problems, **265–268**
Tutorial folder, 244
vs. QuarkXPress, **241–242**
page-oriented printer, check printing on, **333–334**
pages
    printing range, 67
    view in PageMaker, 254
paint, problems spilling, 234
paint applications, **219–220**
painting, with wacky brush, **225**
Panorama, 297
paper
    adding to DeskWriter, 62
    adding to ImageWriter, 66
    adding to LaserWriter, **63–64**
    adding to StyleWriter, 61
    jam in printers, **81**
paper source, for printing, 67
paragraphs, correcting formatting, 213
parent folder, determining, 119
partitions, 136
password protection, in Excel, 285
Paste (Edit menu), *198*, **340**, 344
Paste Special (Edit menu), 351
pasteboard, in PageMaker, 249, 266
pasting
    problems with graphic not appearing in document after, **360**
    from Scrapbook, 348, 349
path, in drawing, 220
patterns, in Kid Pix, **225**
Pen menu, in MacDraw Pro, 229
Performa 200, 8
performance, disk cache and, **159–160**
perpendicular-line tool, in PageMaker, 247, 258, 260
personal finances, **318–337**. *See also* Quicken
Personal Press, 241
phono-plug adapter, 14
photocopying, vs. printing, 67

379

Photoshop, 107
PICT format, 363
    for screen image, 55, 70
pictures. *See also* graphics
    creating in Kid Pix, *216*
Place (File menu), 251
Place command (PageMaker), 261
Plain Text (Style menu), 202, 210
plus sign, in windowshade handles, 255
point, 71
pointer, 6, 33. *See also* I-beam; insertion point
    in Excel, 276
pointer tool, in PageMaker, 247
port, for printer, 59–60
portable Mac, turning off, 18
PostScript fonts, 73, 74
PostScript laser printer, 58
power
    to external disk drives, 132
    troubleshooting problems, 21
power cord, 14
power outage, and work loss, 96
PowerBook Macs, **11–13**
    half-off state, 18
    startup sound on, 26
    turning on, 15
PRAM (memory), 26
    zapping, 148
Preferences, 169
Preferences files, *124*
Prime button, on DeskWriter, 62
Print (File menu), 55, 66
    in MacWrite Pro, 211
    in Microsoft Word, 203
Print dialog box, 43, 67
Print Preview (File menu), 285
printer drivers, 78
printer port, 59–60
printers
    care of, **61–66**
    connecting, 15
    dot-matrix, **58–59**
    envelope printing on, 312
    icon missing from Chooser, 78
    ink-jet, **56–57**
    laser, 58
    paper jam in, **81**
    preparing, *54*
    problems from, 50
    selecting, **56–59**
    setting resolution in PageMaker, 246
    status lights on, **81–82**
    turning off, 18
printing, **53–83**, *54–55*. *See also* fonts
    background, **68–69**
    checks in Quicken, 331

    current document, *55*
    in Excel, **285–286**
    FileMaker Pro, **313**
    to files, 67
    off-center, **82**
    screen snapshot, *55*, **70–71**
    documents in Microsoft Word, **203**
    in Kid Pix, **226**
    in MacDraw Pro, **232–233**
    in MacWrite Pro, **210–211**
    in PageMaker, **263–264**
    problems in PageMaker, **268**
    in Quicken, **333–335**
    setup on Chooser, *54*, **59–60**
    single sheet on LaserWriter, 66
    special page setup, **69–70**
    troubleshooting, **78–83**
    window in Finder, 70
PrintMonitor, **68–69**
    MacWrite Pro and, 211
    Microsoft Word and, 203
    quitting window, 80–81
PrintMonitor Documents folder, 170
program disk, 91
projects, organizing files by, 116
Proof print (Options dialog box), 268
publish and subscribe, *341*, **352–354**
publisher item, creating, *341*, 353
purchasing, *4*
    selecting model, **8–13**
Put Away (File menu), 42, *125*, 137, 150, 151

Q

QuarkXPress, **241–242**
question mark disk icon, 17, 23, 24
Quicken, **320–321**, **321**, **322–337**. *See also* categories in Quicken
    account file creation, *318*, **322–324**
    check register, **325–326**
    check writing, *319*, **330–332**
    deposit entered in register, *319*, 327
    memorizing transactions, **332–333**
    printing checks in, 331
    printing in, **333–335**
    recording check, *318*, **326–327**
    reports in, 335
    saving in, 337
    transfers between accounts, 329, 336
    troubleshooting problems, **336–337**
quitting
    applications, 50
    PrintMonitor window, 80–81
    problems with applications, 107
Quote INIT, 171

R

RAM (random access memory), 7, 126, 156–157
RAM cache. *See* disk cache
random access memory (RAM), 7, 126, 156–157
reading files, problems with, **148–149**
records in databases, 294, 299
    entering, **302–303**
    finding in FileMaker Pro, **305–306**
    missing in FileMaker Pro, **315**
    restoring complete list after find process, 306
    sorting, *293*, **304–305**
recovering
    deleted text, 213
    Trash, 42
rectangle shape tool, 231
recycling, cartridges, 64
Redux, 134
relational databases, **295–297**
removing
    fonts, 75
    System Folder, 182
repeat rate, for keyboard, 177
replacing text, 38
    with Clipboard, **198**
    in MacWrite Pro, 206
    in Microsoft Word, 196
reports, in Quicken, **335**
Reset button, 50
Resolve, 272, 273
Restart (Special menu), 19, 50
ribbon
    in ImageWriter, 66
    in Microsoft Word, 202
right aligned tabs, 200, 208
rotating tool, in PageMaker, 248
rows, inserting blank in Excel, 279
ruler
    displaying, 199
    formatting text with, **198–201**
    in MacWrite Pro, **207–209**
    in PageMaker, 248, 250
    problems moving in PageMaker, **266**
Ruler (View menu), 199
ruler guides
    lining up items in PageMaker, 267
    in PageMaker, 254

S

Sad Mac icon, 24, 25
sans serif font, 72
Save (File menu), *89*, 96
    in Microsoft Word, 203
saving, *89*, **96–98**, **134**

before shut down, 18
document for first time, **96–97**
during edit process, 97
in Excel, 277, **285–286**
in FileMaker Pro, 303, **313**
in Kid Pix, **226**
linked documents, 352, **360–361**
in MacDraw Pro, **232–233**
in MacWrite Pro, **210–211**
in Microsoft Word, 203
multiple documents and, 102
in PageMaker, 250, **263–264**
in Quicken, 337
scientific notation, 72
Scrapbook, 107, 170, *340*, **348–349**
    locating item in, 360
screen
    gray waves across, 23
    troubleshooting dark display, 21–22
screen dump, 70
screen glare, **22–23**
screen savers, 22, 182
    and bombs, **164**
screen snapshot, printing, *55*, **70–71**
scroll bars, 41
    in PageMaker, 248
scrolling, *31*, 41
    records in FileMaker Pro, *293*
SCSI (Small Computer System Interface)
    for external disk drive, 131
    ID number, 146
    ports, 11
SCSI hard drive
    connecting, 16
    troubleshooting, 26
Select menu
    Find, 293, 306
    Find All, 306
    Layout, 306, 308, 314
    Sort, *293*, 304
selected block of text, 197
    for editing, 206
selecting
    cell range in Excel, *270*, **279–280**
    icons, *30*, **35–36**, 104
    menu commands, *30*
    multiple icons, 41
    printers, **56–59**
selection rectangle, 41
    for icons in folder, 105
serif font, 72
Set Up Categories (Shortcuts menu), 330
Set Up New Account dialog box (Quicken), 324
setup, to start from hard disk, 5
setup disk, 91

381

shades of gray, filling graphic object with, 230
shapes, creating in MacDraw Pro, **228–229**
Shift-clicking, 41
    to extend selected text, 197
short documents, word processor for, 192
Shortcuts menu
    Memorize Transaction, 332
    Memorized Transaction List, 332
    Set Up Categories, 330
Show Balloons (Help menu), 39, *154*
Show Gridlines (View menu), 229
Show Invisibles (View menu), 209, 212
Show @ (View menu), 201, 212
Show Ruler (View menu), 207
showing, help balloons, 39
shut down, 5, **18–19**
    and RAM contents, 7
Silverlining, 136, 366
SIMMs (Single In-line Memory Modules), 157
Size, for desktop view, 102
size box, to expand window, 104
size of graphic, in PageMaker, 252–253
size of text, changing in Microsoft Word, 202
size of window, 41
Sleep (Special menu), 18
Small Icon, for desktop view, 102
Small Kids Mode (Goodies menu), 222
SmartScrap, 349
Snap to guides, in PageMaker, 267
snap-to-grid, for icons, 179
software. *See also* applications; system software
    for external drives, 16
Sort (Select menu), *293*, 304
sorting records, in FileMaker Pro, *293*, 304–305
sound
    input, 14
    installing, **367–368**
    at startup, **26**
source disk, for copy process, 142
space, in file name and file order, 118
spacing
    fonts and, 74
    fractional-width, 79
Speaker Volume slider, 178
special characters, determining keystroke for, 79–80
Special menu
    Eject Disk, *125*
    Empty Trash, *31*, 42
    Erase Disk, 139, 145
    Restart, 19, 50
    Shut Down, 18
    Sleep, 18

Speed Disk, 136, 137
spelling mistakes, undoing, 207
spreadsheets, **269–289**. *See also* Excel
    linking to text documents, **350–351**
    selecting, **272–274**
    troubleshooting problems, **287–289**
    uses for, 272
square-corner tool, in PageMaker, 248
stamps, in Kid Pix, **224**
start pages, 63
    preventing from LaserWriter, *54*
    turning off, **65**
starting installer, 20
startup
    bomb at, **164**
    disabling extensions during, 172
    opening application automatically at, *166*, **170**
    sound at, **26**
    system software location for, 25
startup drive, 17, 24
    hard disk setup for, **19–20**, 127
    System folder on, 16–17
Startup floppy disk, **140**
Startup Items folder, *166*, 169, 170
static electricity, and floppy disks, 139
status lights, on printers, **81–82**
Stop icon, in alert box, 45
StuffIt, 133, 138
style, for PageMaker heading text, **260–261**
style bar, adding patterns in MacDraw Pro, 232
style indicator, in Microsoft Word ruler, 201
Style menu, Plain Text, 202, 210
Style palette (Windows menu), 248
style of text
    after cut and paste, 345
    in Excel, *270*, **277–278**
    in MacWrite Pro, **210**
    in Microsoft Word, **202–203**
    problems with, **212–213**
    in word processor, *189*
StyleWriter, 60
    cartridge problems, 82
    paper feeder, 81
    Ready light, 78
StyleWriter II, 56–57
    and background printing, 68
    care of, **61–62**
    cartridge problems, 82
stylus pointers, 15
subscribe. *See* publish and subscribe
Subscribe (Edit menu), 354
subscribers, determining parts of document as, **361–362**
subscribing to published item, *341*
    problems with, **361**

Suitcase, 74
sum button (à), in Excel, 281
SuperDrives, 128
SuperPaint, 218, 219–220
    file formats for, 364
support department of software manufacturer, 51
surge-protected outlet, 14
switching
    between applications, **100**
    between documents, **101–102**
switching floppy disks, problem from computer requiring, **152**
Symbol font, 72
system disks, **140–141**
System files, 168
    backup copies of, **141–142**
    Fonts folder, 74
    size of, 163
System Folder, 24, 114, **168–170**
    Clipboard, 343
    customized and installing new system software, 365
    on hard drive, 16, 20
    PrintMonitor, 68–69
    removing, 182
    on startup disk, 140
    Startup Items folder, *166*, 169, 170
system heap, 164
system software, **8**
    customizing file compatibility, 171
    on hard disk, 19, 133
    installing on customized Mac, **365–368**
    location for, 25
    shut down, 18
    troubleshooting, 24
    version of, 34
system software extensions, 171

T

tab markers, 200–201
    in MacWrite Pro, 208
Tab Order (Arrange menu), 314
table of contents, from PageMaker, 242
tabs, indents with, 213
target disk, for copy process, 142
tax preparation software, 321
tax-related information, report summary of, 335
TeachText, 193
TeachText folder, 115
tear-off menu, 232
temperature
    and floppy disks, 139
    and hard drive, 132
terminator, for SCSI hardware, 16, 131
test pages, from printer, 63

text
    adding to graphics, **230–231**
    deleting, 38
    disappearance in word processors, **213**
    in PageMaker, *239*, **251**, **254–256**
    replacing, 38
    selecting, 197, 208
    threading to next block in PageMaker, 266
text documents, linking to spreadsheet, 350–351
text entry, *31*
    in MacWrite Pro, *188*, **205–206**
    in Microsoft Word, *188*, **195**
text tool, in PageMaker, 248
Text wrap (Element menu), 261–262
thick lines, adding in PageMaker, 258
Tidbits disks, LaserWriter Font Utility, 65
TIFF (Tagged Image File Format), 268, 363–364
tilde (»), 77
time, setting, 174
Times font, 72
title bar, of active window, 40
toner cartridge
    for LaserWriter, 64–65
    problems from, 82
toolbar, 203
    in Excel, 275
    in FileMaker Pro, 303–304
Toolbox, in PageMaker, 247
Tools menu, Commands, 203
Touch Base, 298
trackballs, 12, 15
transactions, memorizing in Quicken, 332–333
transfers, between Quicken accounts, 329, 336
Trash, *31*
    copying font to, 75
    dragging items to, **42**
    emptying, *31*, 42
    problem dragging to, 47
    recovering item from, 42
triangle, in windowshade handles, 255–256
troubleshooting problems
    applications and documents, **106–108**
    customizing, **182–183**
    dark screens, 21–22
    data integration, **360–362**
    in FileMaker Pro, 314–315
    floppy disks and hard disks, **146–152**
    with folders or files, **119–121**
    frozen screen display, **49–51**
    with graphics, **234–235**
    hard disk icon absence, 26–27
    hardware and installation, **21–27**

locating system software, 25
   with memory, **162–164**
   mouse and desktop, **46–51**
   in PageMaker, **265–268**
   printing, **78–83**
   Quicken, **336–337**
   screen glare, **22–23**
   with spreadsheets, **287–289**
   startup sound and, **26**
   system software, 24
   with word processors, **212–213**
TrueType fonts, 72
   icon for, 73
TurboTax, 321
Turn Autogrid Off (Layout menu), 234
turning off Mac, 5
typeface, 71
typing
   troubleshooting problems, 48
   undoing, 207

U

umlaut, 77
Undo (Edit menu), 197, 213
Undo (File menu), 207
Undo Cut (Edit menu), 350
undoing, typing, 207
undoing mistakes
   in Clipboard, **350**
   in Kid Pix, **223–224**
   in MacWrite Pro, *189*
   in Microsoft Word, *189*
unlocking, floppy disks, **144**
users, organizing files by, 116
utilities, to manage extensions and control panels, **183**
Utilities menu
   Autoflow, 239, 251
   Start Pages, 65

V

variables, in Excel formulas, 280
version, of system software, 34
View (Layout menu), 254
View menu, 102, 117
   Ruler, 199
   Show Gridlines, 229
   Show Invisibles, 209, 212
   Show @, 201, 212
   Show Ruler, 207
views
   control settings, **178–180**
   of database, 304
Views control panel, 104, 183
voiding checks, 328

W

windows, **40–41**
   closing, 41
   closing all, 51
   closing PrintMonitor, 80–81
   Edit Story, 267
   locating open, 51
   moving, 41
   opening, 36
   for PageMaker, **247–249**
   printing in Finder, 70
   size box to expand, 104
Windows menu, Style palette, 248
windowshade handles, 255
   dragging, 267
   loaded, 257
Wingz, **272–273**
Word. *See* Microsoft Word
word processors, **187–213**, *188–189*. *See also* MacWrite Pro; Microsoft Word
   bargain, **193**
   features, 190
   selecting, **191–193**
   troubleshooting problems with, **212–213**
word wrap, 195, 205
   around graphic, **261–263**
   preventing split phrase from, **213**
WordPerfect, 191
WordPerfect Works, 355
worksheet, in Excel, 275
WriteNow, 193
write-protection of floppies, 144
writing files, problems with, **148–149**

X

X icon, 23

Z

zoom box, 41

SYBEX

FREE BROCHURE!

Complete this form today, and we'll send you a full-color brochure of Sybex bestsellers.

Please supply the name of the Sybex book purchased.

_____

How would you rate it?

____ Excellent   ____ Very Good   ____ Average   ____ Poor

Why did you select this particular book?

____ Recommended to me by a friend
____ Recommended to me by store personnel
____ Saw an advertisement in _____
____ Author's reputation
____ Saw in Sybex catalog
____ Required textbook
____ Sybex reputation
____ Read book review in _____
____ In-store display
____ Other _____

Where did you buy it?

____ Bookstore
____ Computer Store or Software Store
____ Catalog (name: _____)
____ Direct from Sybex
____ Other: _____

Did you buy this book with your personal funds?

____ Yes   ____ No

About how many computer books do you buy each year?

____ 1-3   ____ 3-5   ____ 5-7   ____ 7-9   ____ 10+

About how many Sybex books do you own?

____ 1-3   ____ 3-5   ____ 5-7   ____ 7-9   ____ 10+

Please indicate your level of experience with the software covered in this book:

____ Beginner   ____ Intermediate   ____ Advanced

Which types of software packages do you use regularly?

____ Accounting   ____ Databases   ____ Networks
____ Amiga   ____ Desktop Publishing   ____ Operating Systems
____ Apple/Mac   ____ File Utilities   ____ Spreadsheets
____ CAD   ____ Money Management   ____ Word Processing
____ Communications   ____ Languages   ____ Other _____
                                                           (please specify)

Which of the following best describes your job title?

_____ Administrative/Secretarial   _____ President/CEO

_____ Director   _____ Manager/Supervisor

_____ Engineer/Technician   _____ Other _____
                                                        (please specify)

Comments on the weaknesses/strengths of this book: _____

_____

_____

_____

_____

Name _____
Street _____
City/State/Zip _____
Phone _____

PLEASE FOLD, SEAL, AND MAIL TO SYBEX

SYBEX, INC.
Department M
2021 CHALLENGER DR.
ALAMEDA, CALIFORNIA USA
94501

SYBEX

SEAL

Keyboard Shortcuts on the Mac

Finder Shortcuts

Copy (not move) icon to another window	Option-drag icon
Select icon by name	Begin typing name (without pauses between characters)
Select multiple icons	Shift-click, or drag selection rectangle
Select name of selected icon for editing	Return or Enter
Eject a floppy disk	⌘-Y (leaves no ghost)
Temporarily eject floppy disk	⌘-E (leaves a ghost icon)
Take a picture of the current screen	⌘-Shift-3
Stop a switch-disk nightmare	⌘-. (period)
Rebuild the desktop file	⌘-Option + start up Macintosh Classic
Disable all extensions at startup	Shift + start up Macintosh Classic

Window Shortcuts

Open window that encloses active window	⌘-↑
Open window of application or Finder and close current window	Option + choose application or Finder from Applications menu
Zoom a window to largest size possible without hiding desktop icons	Option + click zoom box
Move a window without making it active	⌘ + drag the window
Close all Finder windows	Option + click a close box
Escape from application window to Finder	⌘-Option-Esc